For Alison with much love
from

D1461900

1 my. 1984

Elizabeth Balneaves -

The Windswept Isles

SHETLAND AND ITS PEOPLE

1 Lerwick.

The Windswept Isles

Shetland and its People

ELIZABETH BALNEAVES

John Gifford
London

ISBN 0 7071 0565 X

© Elizabeth Balneaves 1977

First published in Great Britain 1977 by
John Gifford Ltd
125 Charing Cross Road
London WC2H 0EB

DEDICATION

For my husband, whose Shetland ancestry
became mine, by adoption and choice.

Also by Elizabeth Balneaves:

The Waterless Moon
Peacocks and Pipelines
Elephant Valley
Mountains of the Murgha Zerin

Printed in Great Britain
by Butler & Tanner Ltd
Frome and London

Contents

Acknowledgements

A list of acknowledgements invariably appears to be a cold substitute for an author's boundless gratitude to those who have helped create a book. Personally, without my long association with the islands, due entirely to my husband's Shetland ancestry, I might well have been a stranger in a strange land. As it was, it took years to work out the complicated genealogy of even the one small village in which we live, where only first names or nicknames are used. Eventually, beginning as "the Manse wife", although my connections with the Church are entirely fortuitous, living as we do in what used to be the minister's house, I too came to be addressed by my first name. When a half-dead lamb was brought to my doorstep at 5 o'clock in the morning, I was more deeply touched by the gesture than by the trust placed in my scanty veterinary knowledge. The lamb survived and another bond was forged.

Now looking back over nearly forty years since first I saw the Shetlands, so much has yet to be learned and should the reader glean something from the succeeding pages of the unique atmosphere of the islands, then I can only express my humble thanks to all those friends and strangers who have contributed family histories, anecdotes, information, and who have gently but firmly tried to correct my mistakes, offering their time and experience unstintingly on my behalf.

I am deeply indebted to Mr. Tom Henderson, friend of many years, past County Convener and now Curator of Shetland's County Museum, for firstly consenting to read the manuscript and giving so freely much needed advice and criticism. In spite of many commitments he spared no effort to find and print all the photographs of earlier days which I requested. I myself was kindly allowed to photograph several of the most precious finds in the Museum.

To Mr. Longmuir and the staff of the County Library, I would like to say "thank you" for innumerable books on loan, often long overdue, for their patience in seeking out ones which I wished to consult and for allowing me access to valuable and rare volumes from an unparalleled collection of Shetlandic literature.

It would be an impossible task to include all those who have willingly answered my questions and done their best to explain all manner of Shetland customs. To rank them in any kind of order would be invidious. To Robert Leask I would like to extend my special thanks for trusting me with his map of the south Mainland *meithes* and providing me with so many personal notes on Shetland's past. To Jimmie and Anna Gray of Geosetter I owe my introduction to Foula. The kindness and hospitality of their relatives Bobbie, Eric and Aggie Isbister and Edith Gray doubled the delights of that most fascinating of islands. My warmest thanks to Anna for handing over to me all her notes; to Jimmie for acting as "guide" without whose help I should never have found or drunk of "The Waters of the Sneug". To both of them for lending me a positive library of books, two rare photographs, reading the manuscript and adding their own helpful suggestions, my grateful appreciation.

Throughout the islands I met with the utmost kindness and hospitality. Mr. Peter Moar with his long archaeological experience and interest in Unst, generously introduced me to Mr. Andy Irvine without whose untiring and enthusiastic help I might never have discovered the Scalloped Stone of Gunnister. My warm esteem and affection goes to Lizzie Priest and Jackie Mouat and the Petersons in Unst: to Mrs. Anderson of Newhouse on Skerries and Mr. Robert Johnson on Fetlar. Among so many on Whalsay I should like to thank Jeannette Williamson for giving up so much of her time; Dr. Mack and Irene Anderson: Mrs. Arthur Williamson: Sandy Sandison, Willie Anderson, Andrew Moar and Robbie Irvine of Linthouse, an expert at "reddin kin", who traced my husband's family from the Skerries.

For much valuable information on Papa Stour I am indebted to Mr. Alex Johnson and my old friend George Peterson whose family entertained me so royally on Papa, also for his permission to quote his poem "Papa" from his book *Hairst Blinks Ower Papa*. For the hospitality extended to me by Stella and Norman Shepherd, with whom I stayed on at least two occasions; to Henry and Joy Anderton of Vaila for a special celebration and information on the island, and to J. Laughton Johnston, and Captain Alan Whitfield of Loganair for my visit to Fair Isle my sincere thanks.

To my dear friend and collaborator in films and "foys", Jenny Gilbertson, film-maker and producer, now in Hudson Bay, my gratitude for leaving me the manuscript of her radio play (broadcast in 1955), "Busta House", and allowing me to use it for help with the story. To my son, J. Laughton Johnston, the most objective of critics, my warmest thanks for reading the manuscript, and as Conservation Officer for Orkney and Shetland, guiding me through the labyrinth of Shetland's flora and fauna and general ecology. I am glad to have his permission to quote his poem "Willie's Shetland Boat", published in *AKROS*. My fond thanks also to my daughter-in-law Margaret Johnston (Maggie Riegler: Head of Department, Weaving, Gray's College of Art, Aberdeen) for allowing me access to her researches on the Fair Isle Patterns.

My thanks are also due to Mr. John Manson and Mr. Fenwick in connection with the chapter on oil: to Mr. Jack Keddie for photographs and plates and to Roy Gruneberg and Roy Pederson for permission to reproduce their map of the Norn names of Shetland.

Around "the South end" as we call it, I am indebted for all manner of details and impressions to Mrs. E. Laurenson of Brake, Laurie Leask of Bigton, Willie Leask of Ireland and Bobbie Smith of Longhill and last but not least the 1973 crew of the Burra boat *The Bairns's Pride* for an unforgettable night's fishing off the Foula Banks and, incidentally, my passage from Foula to Scalloway.

If there are any omissions, the fault is mine and I realise that the list should be twice as long. Lastly I would like to thank my long-suffering family for enduring uncomplainingly many hours of neglect: my husband Jim, for continual encouragement, and work on the glossary and bibliography: my daughter-in-law Patricia for her generous help with part of the typescript; my friend and agent Hope Leresche for her unfailing co-operation and advice and my publishers for their remarkable patience.

The author is grateful to those people whose photographs have been reproduced in this book and whose names are acknowledged in the captions. All pictures which appear without an acknowledgement were taken by the author.

1. *A Network of Islands*

REACHING OUT NORTHWARDS towards the Arctic Circle and the land of the midnight sun, the islands sprawl in a long ragged archipelago, ice-hewn, sea-torn, flung like the pieces of a giant jig-saw between the North Sea and the Atlantic; treeless, peat-patterned, ringed with white sand or rising up swiftly into rocky headlands, their grassy platforms shaved by sheep, headlands with seabirds forever circling their shoulders. In the narrow funnels fulmars plane to and fro on the air currents, while far below the broad shiny seals play in the long rollers, their bodies encased and held for a moment in a wall of green like flies in amber, and above them the terns scream, curved like crescent moons in flight before the arctic skua.

From Sumburgh Head to Muckle Flugga pinnacles of knife-edged stacks spring fearsomely out of the open sea, great free-standing arches and dark wicked skerries meeting the swell conceived in some far-off Atlantic gale in a pounding fury of white water. Three thousand miles of tattered coast fringed with countless beaches; scooped into concentric circles of pale emerald and purple where the kelp fringe clings; beaches pebble-packed, pencilled with a scrawl of brown dried tangles; shallow shelves heaped with boulders, smoothed and moulded into spheres of elephant grey like outsize cannon balls, and tiny coves gouged out of the black pitted outcrops of igneous rocks, red granite, Old Red Sandstone, or serpentine, green like watered silk, echoing endlessly to the crash and drag of waves on shingle.

Hialtland, Yealteland, Schotlande, Hitland, named in turn by Icelandic skalds, Norse colonists, Hansa merchants and Schveningen herring fishers, Shetland's arbitrary position on the average map might even yet justify her claim to being the *terrae incognitae* of the ancients. Inevitably the march of progress has caught up with her anonymity, but with a cataclysmic suddenness for which no one was prepared. Too soon, from Texan millionaires to Middle East sheikhdoms, Shetland will represent only one thing—oil. Invaded yet again, not for the first time, but now to be raped by twentieth-century industrialists, as fiercely competitive and demanding as their Viking predecessors of A.D. 800.

1

Still wearing like a garment the spell of places accessible only by sea or air, she is the most distant of the northern isles, on the same latitude as South Greenland, the Gulf of Alaska, Leningrad and Oslo. No statistics can evoke the fascination that Shetland has exerted over travellers, writers, ornithologists, geographers and archaeologists.

Known to have been first settled nearly 5000 years ago and sharing with Orkney the distinction of having more ancient monuments to the square mile than any other part of Britain, its past emerges in a closely-woven tapestry of divergent cultures and peoples, overlapping and integrating one with the other, each leaving behind, for those who seek it, some tangible evidence of their presence.

Strung with lochs like fishes' scales, threaded with voes, over a hundred islands lie like so many sand castles infiltrated by the incoming tide. Journeys by road are long, angled by fingers of water running deep into the land, and scarcely anywhere is one more than two and a half miles from sight or sound of the sea. Crofts huddle in scattered hamlets, a mosaic of dry stane dykes coiled round between them and the scattald where new stiff lines of wire and fence creep ever further outwards, demarcating the extent of ownership. *Planti crubs* that once sheltered the green and purple cabbages from the salt winds and the hungry sheep lie empty, the squares and circles of carefully-built stone walls slowly gathered back into the encroaching turf, or in some rare angle of the setting sun looking like tilted saucers in the olive parks.

Here and there the landscape comes alive with ponies, a frieze of miniature war-chargers, velvet black, bright chestnut, piebald, skew-bald dappled like autumn leaves, with flowing wind-tangled manes and tails. A stallion, neck curved low, outstretched, nostrils flaring, corrals his mares in a frenzy of possessiveness. Around them foals, flung flat on the heather like rag puppets, limp, asleep, suddenly scramble to their feet and prance bewildered, stiff like rocking horses, or, straddling unsteady legs, worry their dams for milk. Small sheep crop the bright green holms, in unconscious isolation, their *crö* a precipice of rock with sea pinks lighting up its crevices, below them the clawing, hungry waves. On the steep hillsides their cousins range, with long experience avoiding the patches of bog in an endless, circumscribed pattern of narrow sheep *gaets*.

Beyond the cultivated areas, in the interior of all the larger islands, remain the sombre miles of lonely dales, a tundra-like perspective of lichen green and brown, splattered with a mirror-work of amber pools and runnels where peat diggings like black wounds have scored the moorland. Bog cotton flutters like spent spume, and snipe dart from the flags of wild iris beside the burns flanked with rushes, the *floss* once

2   Tractors trailing a flurry of gulls up and down the steep slopes near Bigton.

harvested for *simments*, twisted into ropes in the winter evenings to make the peat basket and the *kishie*.

In the voar, later even than the Scottish spring, tractors tilt against the steep rigs, trailing a string of gulls like paper kites. Near the crofts dark figures bent by wind and work plod back and forth, tethering the sheep, the cross-breds that have needed winter fodder, waiting for the lambing in late April or May. In the fresh winds of the Beltin Ree the cows are put out to the sweet grass and boats are tarred and painted ready for the summer fishing. On a hillside a man is casting peat, flaying the banks, laying back the slabs of turf so that the *tushkar* can cut cleanly, setting the long rectangles of coal-blue and chocolate-brown, soft as butter, above the bank in crenellated tiers to let the wind blow through and dry them ready for the "raisin".

Then comes the time of the long days, the Simmer Dim, when the brief twilight of the northern night sees some of the local men at "*da eela*" and bed is like sleeping in daylight, a grudging necessity after long hours of work. Out to sea the herring shoals, silver and blue, have added their lure to the boats for a short season of brimming boxes or empty

3

baskets. Even then a golden day of sun and glittering seas dies overnight, forgotten in wind and rain or days of fog, a milk-white blankness of land and sea and eyeless windows assailed by the monotonous endless bleating of the foghorn on Sumburgh Light.

Comes the caa'in of the sheep and the low hills are crawling with long lines of men. The shout of "mind that yowe!" and the line wavers, breaks and scatters, men whistling wildly for dogs with lolling tongues, panting, quivering, crouching, belly to the ground, but never wholly masters as sheep as swift as themselves dive between a pair of legs, plunge through the heather, the ragtag of winter fleeces flying from their scrawny necks to outwit the men and dogs and send them cursing in pursuit.

The crops are gathered in now to the whirr of gleaming harvesters, the hay sometimes still cut with a scythe in long swathes of slow, rhythmic labour, with pauses to sharpen the blade, and a soft swish as the gathered heaps are drawn across the ditches between the rigs on an old wooden door. Strip cultivation is yet a feature of the landscape, fanning down a steep hillside in bright bands of ochre and cinnabar where the bere ripples and neat lines of tufted colls point seaward.

The sun moves from St. Ninian's Isle by the back of Foula. The *skroos* are built in snug lines, netted and secure. The peats are home and at the back o' Hallamass the cattle are taken in to shelter again, to spend the dark winter in byres. And now the winds that blow even on the finest days, draining the warmth from the sun, sweep the islands in sudden gales that blacken the potato shaws and every green thing they touch, clawing and roaring at stout walls, the voes and bays shelter a huddle of fishing boats; days when the sea rises up in a spouting wall of water between and around the islands.

Whooper swans on the loch cluster like spindrift by the reedy banks and boats are drawn high in their winter noosts. Lights spring up like candles in the early dark and the mail boat batters her way north from Aberdeen long overdue, the airport packed with impatient grounded oilmen, and ominous piles of sand line the roadside.

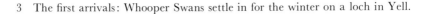

3   The first arrivals: Whooper Swans settle in for the winter on a loch in Yell.

2. *The Land and the People*

ALL ISLANDS IMPOSE upon their people a kind of tyranny, a love-hate relationship that controls the pattern of living, restricting the individual man in his most ordinary daily life to a parlous intimacy, a continual compromise with the elemental sea, at once the bringer and destroyer. For Shetland, geographically, historically and economically, her entire history is indivisible from the moon-drawn tides that saw her beginning, two or three billion years ago when the "Old Rock" was born.

The most inaccessible of all the northern isles, battered by conflicting currents, lying in the path of cyclonic storms that sweep eastwards between Iceland and the British Isles, even in summer freakish day-to-day fluctuations of wind and weather intensify Shetland's island image. Her approaches are formidable from any angle, from the out-flung spit of rock that is Muckle Flugga, cleaving the north-west tide wave, south to the headland of the dinning *röst*, *dyn rastr ness*, Dunross-ness, the roaring ripway that guards Sumburgh Head.

Both the North Sea and the Atlantic are forces to be respected, but the grey North Sea knows every trick a body of water can provide. Fifty-foot waves, pits and depressions and strange upward domings produce unparalleled conditions, and all through recorded history the seaward journey is littered with tales of wreck and storm. Olaus Magnus called it "The Devouring Whirlpool" and in the context of the twentieth century the Geographical Journal reports with rigid economy of phrase that "No type of drilling vessel has been trouble-free in the very severe conditions of the North Sea.... With increasing experience the problems of severe weather and extreme wave heights are being overcome, but the North Sea represents a much greater challenge and hazard than any tropical waters."

The *North Sea Pilot*, that most conservative seaman's guide, described conditions in 1875 in vivid and telling prose, repeated verbatim today: "In the terrific gales which occur usually four or five times in every year, all distinction between air and water is lost, the nearest objects are obscured by spray and everything seems enveloped by thick smoke

4 Muckle Flugga and the Out Stack (Ouesta), lying out on a spit of rock at the most northerly tip of Unst. Built in 1854 and completed in 26 days, the third of Shetland's lights to be exhibited—Sumburgh Head was the first in 1821. It was only in 1939 that a radio transmitter receiver was installed in the light so that the Keeper could communicate with the shore station at Fiska Wick. Before that a daily trip had to be made by one of the shore crew to this point, the cliff edge on Hermaness, a tough climb of nearly 3 miles, 657 feet up the rough track from Fiska Wick in order to receive signals from the light confirming the state of the currents or occasionally asking for a doctor. Although the light appears close to the shore, it is one of the most difficult and dangerous of access, with fierce tides and currents swirling round the narrow entry, between high walls of rock on the seaward side. Designed by Thomas Stevenson, father of Robert Louis, his signature was found in the old visitors' book.

... in this confused and tumbling, bursting sea, vessels often become entirely unmanageable and sometimes founder while others have been tossed about for days together. . . ."

It is scarcely surprising to read that King Haakon "lost a long keel" in Sumburgh Röst. When the wind blows nor'-westerly the *röst* is quiet as a mill pond, crossed almost unnoticed, but when the windborne waves roll in from any other quarter they meet the tidal currents either streaming shoreward or on the ebb. Only those who have experienced its full fury can appreciate the demonaic power of this maelstrom of water, of waves and tides battling over perhaps a three-mile area.

None knew these wild seas better than the long-line fishermen of the late eighteenth century, their fishing *meithes* pinpointed with neither sextant nor compass but by the height of the water up a headland as seen from an open boat, a precision point where they could take a cross bearing, out at the Bools, 12 miles off with "Water i' da Burgidale", at da Broons for halibut, or Hallilee at Head . . . "The fishers who with small Norrwey yoals adventure far into the Sea and oft times endure hard weather . . . so far as to almost sink the land . . . and often they lie some nights and days at Sea and not come ashore . . ."

It was Thomas Stevenson, father of Robert Louis, who first measured the force of an ocean wave. With his newly-developed wave dynometer he studied the waves that assailed his native Scotland and found that in winter gales "the force of a wave might be as great as 6000 lb. to the square foot". He it was who designed Sumburgh Light and Muckle Flugga but even his calculations could not predict the wave that broke open a door in the lighthouse at Muckle Flugga 195 feet above the sea. In the Out Skerries, 6- to 13-ton blocks have been prised out of their places 70 to 75 feet above the sea. At the Isle of Stenness, the Grind of the Navir and Haaf Gruney, great boulders are lifted up like pebbles and scattered inland. And every year on small beaches where the sea's force strikes, young grey seal pups born to storm and tempest in the late autumn gales lie stranded, exhausted or dead, waiting for the Black Backs to finish them off.

These were the seas upon which tossed the frail craft of Neolithic man; seas challenged by the early Vikings who bequeathed the proto-type of the Shetland boat; waters which carried the squat Dutch her-ring busses, the cumbersome galleons of the remnants of the Spanish Armada, Van Tromp's unfortunate fleet and Dutch East Indiamen tak-ing the northabout passage, and Shetland sixareens out at the "haaf" fighting out the gales when a morning's swell might turn to storm-force winds with blizzards so fierce that at their height it was impossible to see the man on the next *taft*.

It was not only in winter that gales descended with a suddenness for which no one could have been prepared. In 1832 105 men were lost from Unst, Fetlar, Mid and South Yell and Nesting. In the volume dealing with relief measures for the Highland and Islands of Scotland it was reported that of the families left that day "four were much in debt. Thirty left dependents destitute or very poor or aged in poverty. Five were in tolerable circumstances and forty of the lost men were unmarried." In July, 1881 a gale from the north caught the fishing fleet on the edge of soundings some 40 miles north-west of Shetland. Ten boats and 58 men perished. Similar tragedies run like a dirge through the whole era of Shetland's fishing saga. Entire districts lost their breadwinners to the sea upon which they were forced to depend.

Shetland has an average of 236 hours per year of gales with wind gusts exceeding 90 m.p.h. a common occurrence. In 1963, 177 knots were recorded at Saxavord in Unst before the anemometer blew away. In a single month a larger collection of salt was measured in Lerwick than in the most exposed situation on the Norwegian coast over the whole year. Perhaps one might say of Shetlanders above all peoples that the sea is in their blood, that the salty stream coursing through their veins, chemically in the same proportion as in sea water, has produced a rare outcome, a predominating essence that exists in crofter and fisherman alike.

Of necessity much has changed in the Shetlander's outlook, his priorities throughout the years; the original image still extant at the beginning of the present century has become blurred, like a faded photograph, but none the less real to those of us who knew him well. After the udaller's pride in croft and land of the Viking period came the long bitter years of the truck system when he and his family were held in thrall to despotic landlords. Few openly rebelled. His sensibilities blunted by a life lived at starvation level, he never knew when at any moment he might be summarily ejected to make room for the more profitable sheep. If he improved his land the rent was raised accordingly.

In times of war he was pressganged out of his islands. During the Napoleonic Wars a poverty-stricken woman could be persuaded to pledge her boy child to the navy for an annual retainer until he reached the age of 12, occasionally without her husband's knowledge with disastrous results. Even in the 1830's and 40's, although more than 9000 men were engaged in the fishing, there still seemed no respite from hardship and privation.

The Reverend George Clarke writing from Lerwick in March, 1837 to the Reverend James Everett says: "I find it difficult to give you anything like a description of the deplorable state of things in these

8

islands. A number of persons have within the last two months left our shores. Every vessel has taken less or more and some of them have been crowded, men, women and children flying from starvation, some emigrating to America, others to places of which they know nothing."

In a report from the Synod of Lerwick in the same year we learn that "in 1835 the crops in Shetland were deficient, the ling fishing failed; the herring fishing along the whole east coast of Scotland was unproductive; the whale fishing was worse than unproductive; and during the succeeding winter an unprecedented mortality among the sheep, horses and cattle swept off nearly the whole of their stocks. In 1836 the ling fishing was again unproductive; the herring and whale fishing were total failures, and thus all who engaged in these pursuits, that is nearly the whole male population of the islands, were involved in still greater difficulties."

As though that were not enough, the potato crops failed for years in succession until in 1846 the islanders were on the brink of starvation. These were the days of what are still known as "the meal roads", when under the auspices of the Board for the Relief of Destitution in the Highlands and Islands of Scotland and with the co-operation of various landed proprietors "voluntary" labour was provided by the near-starving population and every able-bodied man and child, the youngest nine years old, the sole support of his widowed mother, carried the gravel in *kishies*, barrowed earth and stones, to receive at the end of the day his peck of meal.

Shetland's fortunes ebbed and flowed as the tides' harvests fluctuated. With the Crofters' Commission of 1885 at least security of tenure was assured and fair rents established. The herring fishing soared to unheard of catches and as rapidly declined. The 1914 War left Shetland with 600 dead, the heaviest loss in population in proportion to any county in Britain. The Russian and German markets for herring were lost. Even the returning crofters, assisted by loans, allotted new crofts, found that the freight to markets in Aberdeen offset any benefits that might have accrued. In the late 1920's many ponies were shot by their owners as the price commanded by them could not cover their transport to Scotland while lambs brought a return of a mere few shillings each.

Gradually, almost imperceptibly, things began to improve. There was a revival of the white fishing using modern methods, an increasing demand for Shetland wool and hosiery, and the old people's pension—five shillings a week in 1909—had substantially increased. There was electricity in Lerwick; a regular steamer service south; the first aeroplane landed in 1933 and by 1937 there was an air service to complement the twice-weekly boats. The Second World War turned Shetland

5 After a night's fishing off the Foula Banks the crew of the Burra boat, *The Bairn's Pride*, land their catch at Scalloway.

into one of the most important bases in the British Isles and few are unemployed. Just over 200 years ago a labourer received a shilling a day; male servants 15 shillings a quarter in addition to food and washing, and female servants 5 shillings a quarter with food. Today, £30 to £40 is not an unusual pay packet for semi-skilled workers hastening to cash in on the oil industry.

Materially the changes over the past century are virtually unbelievable but the origins remain the same and it is important to set them down, to remember the lost identity quickly before it passes into myth and legend. While progress is to the young, experience is still with the old, a way of life which in spite of the many scathing comments to the contrary, although far from being a paradise, did embody some elusive quality of "being" as opposed to mere existence—a way of life which strangely has been newly "discovered", mainly by reporters, outsiders and opponents of the coming invasion of the islands by yet another set of immigrants.

Its essence lay not merely in a mute acceptance of subsistence living but in small delights equally as valuable as a television set today and largely enjoyed with a childlike innocence requiring neither drink nor drug for "kicks". Of course there were sheep-stealers, fornicators and adulterers: you can find them all being dealt summary justice by Court and Kirk, the records of which naturally record the evil that men did and not the good, which irrationally enough is invariably forgotten. And yet, in spite of the regular import of Hollands gin and Faroe brandy, its consumption was a mere fraction of that disposed of by the islanders today and in the Statistical Accounts of the Shetland Islands of 1793 and 1841 the balance of criticism compiled by the clergy of every district comes out heavily on the side of sobriety and industry.

In describing a typical Shetlander one must tread a tight-rope between the wishful thinking of the idealist and the historical background. He is a man of slow, deliberate words and long silences born of ancestral voyages in southern seas, of white nights on look-out in the Greenland or Antarctic whaling; of transmuted personal struggle with oar and rope and net, palms grown hard and rough as dogfish skin when sail meant hauling endlessly on frozen sheet—something still remains in his make-up from the days at the Old Fram Haaf when no landfall was his by choice, only the nearest the sea would let him run to; when a skipper with some sixth sense, of which echo-sounder and radar have robbed him, could bring in his torn and battered craft by the *moder-dai* and having won the battle might rest a hand on the still quivering stern and say: "Du did weel. A'm ower weel plaesed wi' dee."

At home the women watched the seas with bitter hatred, struggling with croft and bairns, joining the *delling* teams when the Shetland spade was the only instrument used to break open the unwilling soil. In Whalsay and the Skerries the women had to get up at three o'clock in the morning to bait the lines while every child had to *redd* his line on getting home from school and then might have to *shill yoags* for bait before going to bed. And every spare minute was spent knitting, endlessly, to add to the two or three pounds their men might bring home from a season's fishing.

Now they can sit at home in comfort, watching the clock nevertheless, to listen on the trawler wave-band to their men who arrange to call in at stated times. In spite of all the modern aids to navigation the sea does not change and any night you can find the descendants of the men of the old sixareens standing straddle-legged aft the wheelhouse on slippery decks awash with salt, a mere foot of gunwale between them and the great heaving swell off the Foula Banks, mending torn nets with the flick of a knife, cutting away the frayed ends, patiently weaving the rents into new orange squares as though secure in the shelter of their own firesides.

A casual meeting reveals nothing, a long acquaintance little, for the Shetlander is a modest man reluctant to spin a yarn of his own experiences. He might have been first mate on a freighter running through Cristobal and the Panama Canal; a purser on a ferry plying between the Gulf Islands; bo'sun on a merchantman on the Far East run or skipper on a timber ship trading with the Baltic, bringing home tall stone bottles of vodka from Riga, Japanese tea-sets or abalone-shell pin trays.

Gifted with a rare natural intelligence, an ability to construct, to mend, to take to pieces anything from a clock to a fiddle and put them together again, there was little he could not set his hand to with a stubborn patience born of necessity. Round the four corners of the globe Shetlanders meet, for they have some of the nomadic instinct of the Scot but are always ready and eager for a "*hamefarin*". Capable of working from dawn to dusk when spirit and weather coincide, there is nothing the Shetlander dislikes more than being pinned down to a specific time schedule. Woe betide the impatient and hustling southerner who confidently expects a job of work begun on Monday to be completed by Tuesday. The work will eventually be finished with an expert care and craftsmanship now rarely to be found, but between the beginning and the end a fine day will see his workman casting peats, caa'in sheep, planting tatties. The materials themselves expected on the boat will either sit for weeks in Aberdeen or lie cunningly concealed for days in some obscure corner of the steamer stores.

Conservative to the point of obstinacy, which time and again has hampered progress, once committed to some innovation his enthusiasm is real and practical. The first experiment in breaking in hill grazing with the War Department's emergency equipment from Sumburgh was begun in Quendale in 1946. In twelve years the total ground reseeded in Dunrossness alone exceeded 1700 acres and today reseeding continues throughout all the crofting areas of Shetland at the average rate of 1000 acres per annum.

In the old folk, tradition manifests itself in a strange nostalgia for

12

the remembered past, of crofts, *kirn* milk and *blaand*; of legs of *grice* salted and kept for high days and holidays; of crops that failed and the infinite inventiveness that made variety out of dishes whose ingredients were basically the same. The hot water bannocks, the braandiron bannocks, the pan bannock and the fat bannock; *brünies* and scones with oatmeal and *burstin* brünies, for nothing was wasted and shop bread was seldom bought except maybe on a Saturday. Of *stap* and *crappen*, liver *muggies*, stuffed cods' heads and tatties with turnips; of the old saying:

6   Robert Laurence Goudie, still able to wield a hay rake at the age of eighty.

Let other lands ower Shetland craa'
She doesna' care a rap!
We hae a dish that dings them aa'
Fresh liver, heeds and stap!

You will still find among the old an almost youthful emphasis on small joys that had nothing to do with money, in days of hardship by any standards ..." Oh ... but we aye hed enough!" The fiddlers and the dancing after a day at the herring gutting that had lasted from six in the morning till sometimes midnight, when the lasses tramped maybe three miles back from their place of work to their common lodging in Bressay and, changing out of their skin jackets and aprons, Baltic boots and Shetland stockings that came right up over the thigh, fingers bandaged against the salt that bit into cold hands, gaily tramped back another three miles to dance until the small hours and still murmered wistfully: "Oh, but it was jolly!"

For the young in Shetland today it is a very different world. Perhaps because of their greater isolation the impact of twentieth-century ideology has hit them harder and more suddenly, so that for the moment they exist in a kind of limbo, grasping with fierce determination all the new things that are there for the taking with a ruthless disregard for everything that is old, outmoded and unrealistic in a society that holds out opportunities their parents never dreamed of.

In spite of this, Shetland students in the south tend to drop out so frequently that a survey was undertaken to find out why, after a year or so at college, often within reach of their intended goal, they gave it all up to return to what they would be the last to describe as "The Old Rock" almost unaware, certainly unable to explain why, to find less academic jobs back in the islands.

Relationships are involved, naturally, in a small community and family ties are strong, stronger than they themselves would admit. They complain openly of the lack of entertainment, such as discothèques, cafés, cinemas; hopefully imagine that "oil" may bring with it the swinging life they crave, and yet at the same time admit that Shetland will never be the same again. No doubt like everything else a solution will eventually be reached, but meanwhile with young men of under 20 earning salaries to which even University graduates cannot aspire, and much more yet to come, one wonders just what will be the outcome?

Although Shetland's affiliations are basically as Norse as the roots of the tongue her people speak, a language that is now a cross-bred Norse and Scots, the true Shetlander has an ancestry as polyglot as any in the world if you care to look back far enough. Within its inhabi-

14

7 Ready to cast off—aboard *The Bain's Pride* leaving Ham Voe, Foula.

tants runs a distillation of many races and who can possibly deny the
long lines of genes and chromosomes that laid down a Shetlander's phy-
siognomy? Interwoven with that of the long-headed Megalith builders
from Gozo and Malta; the round-headed Beaker Folk thrusting up the
North Sea coastline; Celt, Pict, Scandinavian, Scot, Dutch, German,
and aeons before that, although no trace remains, perhaps his first pro-
genitors were the reindeer hunters of the Circumpolar Stone Age, the
nomads of the European and Asiatic tundra; the Eskimoes moving east-
wards across the ice along the northern shores of Alaska and Canada
to Greenland or the remnants of the Maglemose culture escaping from
the drowned lands of the North Sea.

From the moment one sets foot on the islands, be it by sea or air,
slipping in to Bressay Sound, one of the finest natural harbours in the
world, which saw the longships of Haakon of Norway, the blazing
Dutch fishing fleet trapped by French gunboats; the warships of two
World Wars; or stepping off a plane with Jarlshof crouched below the
heights of Sumburgh Head, one is standing on the topmost layer of
highly individual and unique cultures and the stones at your feet might
equally well have been handled by Iberian, Pict or Viking.

The islands are littered with the remains of Neolithic settlements.
The walls of some crofts and houses occupied today are built from stones

15

salvaged from nearby sites; from the *rönis*, neatly piled stones cleared from a nearby field, you can still pick up the artefacts of Shetland's first inhabitants. There are beaches where Norse sinkers tumble back and forth among the seaweed and the driftwood; the finest standing broch in Scotland where through the centuries that followed its building, Norse lovers and their ladies were storm-bound in flight.

To stroll through the capital of Lerwick with its narrow lanes and water-lapped piers, its lodberris and fine mansions, is to remember the ramshackle collection of booths that marked its beginning when women bartered their home-knitted stockings for Hollanders gin, tobacco and brandy. To stand beneath the ancient castle of Scalloway, seat of the Stewart earls, is also to recall the Scandinavian "Thing" or parliament the Scottish rule replaced.

8   Aboard the *Grima* tickets are issued by the Purser for the 20 minute journey to Ulsta in Yell. Shetland's first roll-on, roll-off ferry, along with her sister ship the *Fivla* which plies between Yell and the most northerly island of Unst, a matter of 10 minutes; passengers complete with car can travel from Mainland to Unst and back in a day.

16

There is yet a sense of timelessness, of small villages and peat smoke curling from the crofts and long empty distances where a man can think and be alone. But the tide is coming in and like the first beachcombers it is somehow vital to snatch all that is left before its incoming wave. Much has already vanished, discarded relics of another age. Above the stony *ayres* once-flourishing fishing stations lie empty as a dream, the old drying sheds quietly crumbling away. In the booths where the Hansa merchants traded, sheep shelter, fulmars nest in the broken lodges of the *haaf* fishermen and docks and sea grass cover the skeletons of sixareens.

The Shetland spade, the *bismer* (scales) and the *kolli* lamp are museum pieces preserved for tourists in a reconstructed croft house of 100 years ago. Few would know how to use them now. There are no longer old men sitting in the sun making wicker baskets or rush *büdie's* for the line-caught fish: *kishies* that used to be carried on the backs of women, knitting as they brought home the peats, are exported as waste-paper baskets. You won't find a *meshie* for a pony anywhere but in the museum. You can still buy *reistit* mutton but only in a few houses will you find it hanging from the ceiling together with a string of *piltaks*.

Spinning wheels are snapped up by buyers from the south at fantastic prices, for wool is sent away to be spun in factories in Scotland. Even the sheep are grudgingly attended to, for the crofter is now neither farmer nor fisherman. He has become a man of property, a builder, he works on the roads or drives sand lorries, services helicopters or supply vessels for the oil rigs and in the evenings the clack of the knitting machine has replaced the gentle whirr of the spinney. Silos stand along-side disused corn-drying kilns and the once busy water mills spanning the burns are a mere trickle of stones, a couple or so preserved as curiosities from the 500 that were active in 1816.

Already the fishing *meithes* are quite forgotten and no one but the old could take you to them now. Where whaling and herring stations hummed with life, aluminium storehouses, water and oil storage tanks, overshadow the stone breakwaters growing daily to accommodate supply boats for the oil rigs. Dredgers loom ominously off-shore and out to sea where Foula once rose alone on the horizon an exploration ship stands out nor'east. Where crofts once flourished land is churned up and drains, mains and cables score the green; black wounds of ditches open up the heather as cement mixers, earth-moving equipment, ditchers, grabs and bulldozers nose around some mush-room growth of dreary pre-fabricated houses so closely packed that one could barely string a washing line from door to door.

Shetland has known no greater upheaval since the clearances and it looks ominously as though this is the second time round.

3. *The Old Rock*

THE EXILED SHETLANDER, possibly even more deeply committed to his land of origin than the notoriously sentimental Scot, half-serious, half in jest, may sometimes refer to his homeland as "The Old Rock", surely the unconscious understatement of all time. How old *is* this rock? What ancient thrusting and compressing, volcanic eruption and glacial action, went into the eventual emergence of the islands as we know them today? The perspective is infinite, a looking back as through some vast geologic telescope to a young earth, still enveloped in perpetual night, waterless, like a giant time-bomb of molten rocks, gases and lavas, waiting for the cooling of its rocky shell so that the cloud cover can fall in centuries of rain, filling the depressions of ocean basins, spilling out like a blanket.

Geologists tell us that Shetland can lay claim to some of the most ancient rocks in the world, laid down at the same time as the Laurentians of Canada, the earliest-known sedimentary rocks. They already existed before the first spawning of microscopic life. They saw the slow emergence of the invertebrates; drowned repeatedly in the advance and retreat of the seas that now cover 70 per cent of the earth's surface, gathering to themselves newer and more diverse variations. Weathering, over-ridden by their own sediments as volcanic action thrust and contorted, they emerged finally after four long periods of glaciation still with a variety of rocks so well exposed and in such bewildering complexity as to rival any other county in the British Isles.

The Geological Survey map of Shetland, patterned like an abstract painting in a brilliant patchwork of flamboyant colour, is symbolic of a geological evolution in miniature. From the most northerly island of Unst, with its intricate fusion of gneiss, serpentine, gabbro and metamorphosed sediments, down through the central backbone of Mainland, streaked in long parallel lines of north–south graining, of schist and gneiss and blue-grey limestone, to the outlying islands of Foula and Fair Isle, its composition is startling in its diversity. Within an area of a few miles in Hillswick Ness alone, even the most ordinary check list will include kyanite, garnet, precious serpentine, actinolite and talc,

18

while the black igneous rocks of Eshaness are studded with agate and occasionally amethyst.

Two thousand million years ago, in North Roe, in the extreme northwest of Mainland, outcrops of gneiss covering a rough triangle formed by the island of Uyea and the tip of Uyea, laid down part of the basement on which the Caledonian Mountains were formed, a mere two to four thousand million years after the earth itself. It cannot have been long after this beginning that the first known soft-bodied animals appeared, their impressions left in mud and sand both in England and South Australia. The warm seas of the Cambrian period that followed were now alive with life and all ancestors of animals known today, except perhaps the chordates, lived in these waters.

The great continents still lay naked, devoid of life, without green,

9 Kittiwakes' Haa', between Easter Hoevdi and Selchie Geo Foula.

without soil. The first link in the long experimental chain of life, however, had been forged and more than 420 million years ago, coinciding with the green serpentine of Unst and Fetlar, the first land plant appeared on the coastal shallows. Related to the seaweeds that had learned to resist the pull and drag of the tides, perhaps not unlike the tangles torn up by winter gales around our coasts, they made the transition from sea to land.

Fossils of these primitive land plants have been found in the sandstone of Walls and Fair Isle and in the museum at Lerwick a piece of Old Red Sandstone from Fair Isle still holds the imprint of Dawsonites *sp. nov.* The simplest land plant known, belonging to the Psilopsida, it was rootless, without leaves, but sprouted a hanging sac in which spores were produced. There are only four living species left, growing in tropical and sub-tropical swamps.

In a glass case nearby in the same museum lies a lump of stone, a Breccia from Fladdabister, formed about 470 million years ago as a scree on a mountainside; a slab of pegmatite buckled into a white serpent shape by compression deep below the earth's surface and recovered at Aith Voe, while beside them, from the Cletts at Exnaboe in the most southerly tip of Mainland, rests a piece of Old Red Sandstone bearing, like a stilled sea seen from a great height, ripple marks on its surface.

It took millions of years for the blue-grey limestone, the schist and gneiss of the Caledonian mountains, to emerge out of the ancient seas. Gradually weathering over aeons of time into a semblance of their present shape and height, after a long period of erosion, the area was overlaid by the Old Red Sandstone about 400 million years ago, still visible in strips of sandstone and flags occurring mainly along the east coast of Mainland, in Eshaness, Aithsting, Sandsting, Lerwick, Dunrossness and the islands of Papa Stour, Foula, Bressay, Noss, Mousa and Fair Isle. Indeed, the Old Red Sandstone may well have extended as a uniform area from the Moray Firth to Sogne Fjord and Dals Fjord in Norway. At the same time a small sea scorpion ventured out of the seas, the first amphibian to leave its print on the Devonian rock.

Throughout the earth's changing eras the land has constantly been invaded by the seas in response to movements in the earth's crust and every so often profound volcanic activity raised mountain systems, only to crumble, disintegrate, ground down by erosion, their skeletons swallowed particle by particle by the hungry seas. At one such period about 350 million years ago the solidified roots of a volcano are believed to have been responsible for the red granite of Ronas Hill and Muckle Roe, while in Papa Stour and Eshaness lavas and ashes cascaded on to the land surface.

Another couple of hundred million years passed by in the warm and humid climate of the Carboniferous Age during which half the world's workable deposits of coal were laid down; amphibians were developing rapidly and in the swamp forests gigantic insects appeared. The seas swarmed with fishes, leaving remains of their fossilised bodies exposed in the old Brindister Flagstone Group from Ness of Sound near Lerwick to Shingly Geo near Exnaboe and Sumburgh Head. Fish remains have also been discovered in similar groups of flagstones at the Voe of Cullingsburgh in the north of Bressay, and near Melby in the north-west.

Unless one is a dedicated and extremely knowledgeable geologist it may be difficult to become wildly enthusiastic over a lump of rock however ancient its origin, but when captured forever within this rock one can actually see and touch the imprint of a creature once as alive as a Spiggie trout and not very much larger, the relic or trace of a former living fish preserved over millions of years, one cannot but be strangely moved.

We have become such practical people, so blinded by the cold-blooded logic of science, that there is little room left for the delights of surmise, the poetry of myth and legend. Mere earthly things become commonplace, forgotten and lost in the glitter and showmanship of the exploration of outer space. Consider for a moment the almost immaculate reproduction of extinct mammals, fish and insects that lived here long before man himself evolved. Three hundred million years ago in Shetland seas a mid-Devonian lung fish left the delicate imprint of its being, a milestone in the long struggle for perfection. It was by no means the ideal, merely a prototype, but by a strange alchemy preserved for comparison with later models.

And here, from Shingly Geo in Exnaboe, Dunrossness, are *Pentlandia macroptera*, etched like a drypoint of scale and fin, along with scattered fragments of *Pterichthys, Dipterus, Coccosteus, Homosteus, Glyptolepis* and *Diplopterus* from Melby, a shoal of silver flirting tails and shining scales, whose descendants millions of years later help to fill the bulging, weighted trawl.

Within the coal forests the sun shone over a luxuriant vegetation while the warm rain and seasonal floods brought new fertility to the accumulating layers of peat that one day would cover the greater part of our islands, peat that was recovered from the sea bed at Lerwick, Scalloway, Whalsay and Stenness. It was not until the age of early reptiles that the forests of the North Sea gave way to arid desert conditions and the sands in due course became the sandstone of the so-called Permian stratum in which North Sea gas became trapped. Subsidence of the general basinal area began about 200 million years ago, but it was

10 *Pentlandia macroptera:* from Shingly Geo in Dunrossness (now in the County Museum in Lerwick) where "three hundred million years ago in Shetland seas, a mid-Devonian lung fish left the delicate imprint of its being ... etched like a drypoint of scale and fin. ..."

another 100 million years before the great continental beds averaging about 10,000 feet in thickness were laid down.

Shetland's rocks were already old before the Rocky Mountains, the Andes and the Panama Ridge were formed, the result of the latter being the Gulf Stream Drift which has had such an influence on our climate. At the height of the Cretaceous flood, seas covered most of the British Isles, "except for scattered outcroppings of ancient rocks", which would mean that parts of Shetland were still above water. Then, one thousand million years ago, at the beginning of the Pleistocene, the dawn of our own geological age, the first of four successive glaciations spread across the planet and at the same time man entered the scene.

At the height of the last Ice Age much of the world's water was locked up in the ice cap. A vast plain emerged and the Dogger Bank became land. First it was a low, wet land covered with peat bogs, but by about 10000 B.C. forests of birch and pine spread in from the neighbouring high lands. Animals moved down from the mainland and became established. Bears, wolves and hyenas, wild ox, bison, the woolly rhinoceros

22

and the mammoth roamed the new territory, and hard on their heels came man with his crude stone implements.

As the glaciers began to retreat the melting waters of the ice cap that covered the whole of Scandinavia surged into the land-locked Baltic. About 7000 years ago the Baltic Lake burst its banks and poured out into the North Sea. The new land became an island. Probably man escaped to the mainland before the intervening channel became too wide, but most of the animals perforce remained and little by little their island shrank like a prehistoric Kariba; food became scarce and finally the sea covered the island claiming the land and all its life.

It was not until trawlers began fouling their nets on an extraneous collection of objects that the story emerged. They hauled in loose masses of peat which they called moorlog; the bones of large land mammals, stone implements, in fact the entire flora and fauna of Stone Age man. In 1934, it is remembered in Shetland today, a Strath boat fishing about 30 miles north-east of Shetland brought up in its trawl two mammoth tusks later to be displayed in the Aberdeen Regional Museum. From the drowned lands of the North Sea? At one time, ice moving westwards from Scandinavia had flowed right across Shetland and at Dunrossness there yet remains a large boulder of laurvekite chipped from a parent rock near Oslo, which had been carried by the mile-deep sheet of frozen sea in the same way as similar rocks found at North Haven in Fair Isle. All over the islands erratics and striae bear witness to the second phase when the ice retreated, rough hilltops were smoothed and valleys and voes gouged out by the grinding mass.

How often glaciers re-formed or retreated in Shetland we do not know, for at the end of the last Ice Age Shetland had its own ice cap, erasing most of the signs of earlier events. The ice acted on the land like a giant bulldozer, scooping out the softer valley soil and leaving the hard hilltop rocks behind. The retreat of the ice through the entire four glaciations was long, often interrupted when the edges of the ice sheet halted, shelving like the great Columbian icefields in sharp, blue-green declivities, only to re-advance and spread further down the valleys. These halts are marked everywhere by terminal moraines, the heaps of boulders picked up like pebbles by the great weight of the frozen mass, acting on the ground like an abrasive, and eventually extruded beneath it or dropped over its edge. An example is easily seen near Cunningsburgh, a short way off the road at the burn of Mail.

In cross-section, a valley cut by a river has gently sloping sides but an ice-cut valley or loch has a completely different contour. The Loch of Cliff in Unst and the Loch of Girlsta in Mainland are splendid models of such U-shaped valleys flooded to form long, narrow lochs. One authority has suggested that the higher areas of Foula may never have suffered an extreme glaciation and that the contours and corries of its swooping depths show that they were only collecting areas for ice.

While on the Continent oakwoods replaced conifers, wind and rain began Scotland's deforestation, and pine woods and hazel groves gave way to peat moors. At the same time Britain sank to between 20 and 40 feet below her present level. This depression has been succeeded by a slow re-elevation so that the sinking is marked by a raised beach, the so-called 25-foot beach conspicuous around all the mainland coasts.

In Shetland, however, the raised beach is missing and there has been a gradual sinking with no re-elevation. In fact the islands may well be a partially drowned range of hills with the sounds, like Bluemull Sound between Mainland and Yell, the remains of great rivers. The practical result of this phenomena is that ships of some considerable tonnage can approach relatively close to Shetland's shores in a number of places. Off the west coast of Foula, near the Kaime, the declivity is so steep that on a calm day one could take a liner alongside, close enough to be able to stretch out and touch the cliffs with one's hand.

Indeed, streams, sea and ice have so worn down the Shetland islands that were the sea to rise 100 feet only a few of its higher points would survive, so that one day, long after the lifetime of even our great great great grandchildren, the sea might eventually reclaim its own.

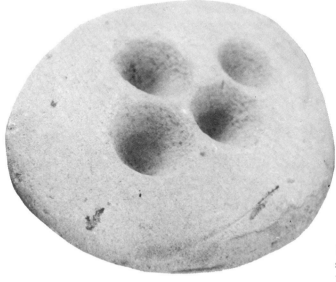

11   Cup-marked stone (sand-stone) found in Swinister, Sand-wick.

4. *Circumpolar Adventurers*

A SILVER LINE like a knife streaked the horizon, above it a faint purple outline like a cloud. A man pointed, excited. The child at the woman's breast whimpered and fought weakly for the milk that had almost dried up. In the thwarts the animals lay now quiet, waiting the release from the sea, the hunger. In a little while the purple cloud became land, olive brown, a glimmer of sand spun between the skerries. Then came the birds. Quite near the shore puffins scuttered across the choppy water and the spaniel heads of seals rose up and eyed them curiously but without fear. Above them an arctic skua pursued a shearwater in mid-air until he dropped his catch. Near the shore the bonxies, the great brown skuas, came out, heavy as bombers to attack the gannets and from cracks in the dark rock tysties watched the intruders anxiously.

As the boats grated on the wide arc of a sandy beach the men clambered out with some last new strength to pull it up out of the surf. Anxiously they would scan the landscape. At least there were no woods or forests against which their primitive tools were less than useless. They looked around and viewed the open country with some satisfaction.

On the limestone belts and porous sandstone they could foresee the possibility of growing crops. Around the coast and on the offshore holms green pasture offered feeding for their stock. The sea could supply food to keep them from going hungry in these hard early days. And then there were the birds, whose eggs can be gathered on the cliffs and whose fat young will make good eating. There was peat and turf with which to build the first temporary shelters and driftwood and kelp on the beaches.

Over the years archaeologists have been able to piece together the lives of these first farmer colonists who in time built snug dwelling places, tilled the earth with stone harrows to grow grain, raised cattle and built with incredible ingenuity about 200 cairns including both chamber and cist burials, in addition to the temples of Staneydale, Yoxie and the Benie Hoose. The circumstantial evidence from around 2000 to 1500 B.C. is indisputable. Although the Shetland Islands are already richer than any other county in archaeological finds, revealing

25

some of the most exciting discoveries of the century, from the heel-shaped cairns of the Megalith builders to the Viking longhouse, they are there in such profusion that half are yet unknown. In part this is due to Shetland's isolation, contributing to the expense and difficulties involved in finding sufficient numbers of skilled and willing archaeologists with time and money to probe further, and partly to the inevitable fact that each new culture or civilisation will inevitably build upon the previous one, often burying or destroying forever the one vital link that is required to complete the perspective.

For the armchair anthropologist however, small clues are scattered, diffusely, dimly understood, but at least suggesting that these small boatloads of Neolithic farmers from the coasts of south-west Europe and the Mediterranean may not have been the first to beach their craft in some sheltered voe.

Through the island of Mousa in Shetland, runs the north 60th parallel, continuing on by Cape Farewell in Greenland, the Gulf of Alaska, Yakutsk, Leningrad and Oslo in a long curve round the North Pole. Twelve thousand years ago in the earliest post-glacial period, in Scandinavia men were moving wherever land was habitable, foraging, fishing and fowling. Anthropologists have found flints and other signs of habitation more than 10,000 years old on "permanently" frozen shores of the Arctic in northern Canada, which must then have been an open sea. It is not at all beyond the bounds of possibility that the Shetlands, the Orkneys and perhaps the Faroes were reached and settled by a seagoing race coming from west to east long years before the agricultural colonisation by other settlers from the Mediterranean, by men and women of the Komsa culture, already well established by 5000 B.C., travelling by the eastern route round the ice.

Some 25,000 years ago a great ice sheet covered northern Europe down to the centre of England, northern Germany and Poland and stretched far across northern Siberia. The vast plain of present-day Europe was covered with willow herb, dwarf birch and Alpine poppy, latticed with game trails and the migration routes of the mammoth herds of the tundra, which were pursued by hunters whose lives depended on the great animals they trapped. In a slow process over thousands of years the ice retreated, the climate grew warmer and pine forests forced the mammoth ever further north until man had to turn to other game, the reindeer. In time the reindeer too moved on, ahead of the encroaching forest that took over from the tundra, and on his heels was the primitive hunter.

As the ice retreated the hunters spread out over the tundra and at Meindorf the artefacts of Stone-Age man were dated at about 15000 B.C., found in a camp occupied for about four months when the Arctic summer burgeoned into life. By 7000 B.C. there were settlers all along the central fjords of Norway. Two thousand years later man was moving through southern Scandinavia, across the land bridge which then connected Sweden with the Continent and there he met the sea. The reindeer on which his life depended, hemmed in between the Atlantic on the west and the dwindling ice cap on the east, struck off north along the Norwegian coast, swimming the wide, deep fjords and leaving their pursuers stranded on the shore.

The skin boats that the Stone-Age hunters had cobbled together to ferry them over lakes and valleys filling up with the waters of melted ice were useless against the stormy conditions of the open seas and some drastic alterations had to take place. Like every innovation there must have been a long period of trial and error before a suitable craft was devised. Eventually the *umiak* type of craft developed, the framework stitched and lashed together, then covered with stretched skins, which gave it all the elasticity and seaworthy properties of a Dunrossness yoal. Once familiar with this novel adjunct to living, the reindeer hunters found other unexpected game in waters teeming with great fish, with seals and whales, and the harpoons originally devised for reindeer-hunting suddenly came into their own as the ideal weapons for use in the open sea.

Long voyages were common in these days and Neolithic people could and did cross and re-cross the North Sea. Shetland itself need not have been so far off course for these circumpolar adventurers. Scandinavia, Greenland, Iceland and the Faroes were all well within the compass of such Stone-Age explorers and the tools that were theirs recur time and time again from Norway to New England. The list is impressive in any context.

Harpoons, first invented for seal hunting among all Arctic communities as far as Greenland, are still almost indistinguishable from those belonging to the reindeer-hunters of Hamburg. The skinning knives excavated at Meindorf, a sharply-curved piece of antler with a flint moulded at the curve, had developed in northern Norway into an L-shaped knife of slate, and identical knives of bone are used today in Greenland.

There were other items brought to the Arctic Ocean by woodland hunters, material manifestations of a culture that ranged further and wider than man could have dreamed possible. Hollow ground adzes of stone, found commonly over northern Europe, have also been discovered in New England and occasionally in the States bordering the Great Lakes. Here, in the northern isles, in the Rinyo culture of Orkney, ground stone celts were used, sometimes mounted as adzes in perforated antler sleeves, in addition to flint or chert scrapers, rough stone knives

27

12　All the way up the burn of Catpund, near Cunningsburgh are the remains of steatite workings, left by both Neolithic man and Viking, the marks of rough scrapers still
visible.

and bone implements including shovels. In Shetland, at Jarlshof, perforated adze-socketed chisels from the metacarpals of oxen were found, a type of tool current in the Maglemose culture, when the bone was provided by elks.

Carved stone balls about the size of carpet bowls, also typify the Orcadian Rinyo culture and stray examples of these have turned up in places as far apart as Ulster and north-west Norway. Nobody has yet been able to explain their use, nor the purpose of still more curious spiked objects which once again have close analogies in the taiga zone of Northern Eurasia.

In addition to similarities to specific Rinyo types in Sweden, Esthonia and Finland, many rough tools of slate or schist, particularly those of Shetland origin, are decidedly reminiscent of those described by Gjessing and are to be found all round the Atlantic Ocean from Norway to Siberia and even to North America. It may well be that these carved stone balls were an inspiration peculiar to Orkney; bolster shaped and cushioned mace heads are certainly more numerous in Orkney than any other county in the British Isles, but again, they occur in Stonehenge, whereas specimens of cushioned mace heads found in Fife and the Hebrides prove to have been constructed from porphyritic rhyolite from Northmaven in Shetland.

Most of the ground stone celts found in Shetland could only have been used as adze blades and such specialised adzes are rare in the rest of Britain and western Europe generally. They were, however, the "favourite tool of woodworkers throughout the taiga zone of northern Eurasia and America" constituting yet another link between Shetland and the circumpolar Stone Age. A last charming and wholly feminine bond with that distant past is the bone girdle clasp found at Jarlshof which bears such a close resemblance to specimens from the Middle Neolithic cemetery of Vesterbjers in Götland. Vesterbjers belongs, not as one might expect, to the Neolithic farmers of southern Sweden and Denmark, but curiously enough to the Swedish branch of the circumpolar hunter-fisher population of the northern Eurasiatic taiga zone.

The final interpretation of a circumpolar hypothesis in relation to Shetland must be left to further and more scholarly deductions, but the late Stone Age farmer-colonists owed much to a strangely unified culture that had its roots not solely in the legendary south. Over thousands of years, small tangible objects connect us and invaded, intermarried, conquered, thrall or freeman, their blood is our blood and the sleep that overtook them in cairn or cist or brown peat bank is no different from our own from the Polar Seas to the Aegean.

5. *The First Farmer Colonists*

About 14 miles north-east of Lerwick, separated from Lunnasting by a scatter of grassy holms and the little island of Linga, lies Whalsay. A fishing community, its area covers a mere eight square miles, but historically it can lay claim to two of Shetland's most ancient sites, dating from at least 2000 B.C. and the arrival of our first clearly documented inhabitants. One will probably never know why such an island was chosen for the important temple of Yoxie and the adjacent house of its officiating priesthood, except that islands have always held some compelling attraction for religious sects. Perhaps it merely offered a safe refuge and being small and insignificant was unlikely to be of interest to settlers or invaders. Much later, Celtic missionaries or Papae elected to establish themselves on other islands like Papa Stour, Papa Little and Burra, their self-imposed celibacy made easier because the sea was a natural barrier between the flesh and the devil. St. Ninian's chapel itself was raised on the isle of that name joined to the land by a slender sandy ayre.

If you leave the north road on Whalsay about Challister and walk out east, skirting the eminence of Gamla Vord, almost on the edge of the low broken coastline of rock and skerry, between Yoxie Geo and Whelsie Geo, you can look down on what local folk call Pettigirth's Field. From the height above, like an aerial photograph, the dim outline of squares of fields develops slowly, bounded by the ridges of long-forgotten dykes and the two excavated ruins of Yoxie and the Benie Hoose. "Benie Hoose", a corruption of the Norse *Bonhoos* or "prayer house", was still in use in the present century as a sea name for the church, just as the minister was never referred to at sea by any other name than "the upstander" or "beniman".

At first sight there seems nothing particularly impressive about the stones of these odd-shaped roofless remains and little to indicate their origin or antiquity save a curious and unusual formation. And yet, in spite of the ravages of wind and weather, the foraging sheep and the turf and lichens that obscure so much, over an area of 64 feet in length and 36 feet in breadth lies a replica of a late Stone-Age temple at Hal

13 The Benie Hoose, Whalsay. Lying within 100 yards of the temple of Yoxie, the Benie Hoose (Bonhoos ON=prayer house) is easily the most outstanding of its kind yet discovered in Shetland. The forecourt (in the foreground) led back to the inner chamber (in the background with figure) which was equipped with drains and is believed by Wainwright to find its precedent in the record of priests' houses near some of the temples in Malta.

Tarxien in Malta.

Suddenly one is trying to read into these weathered rocks some human element, willing to life the men who shaped and carried and built, who chose with such care a special situation and succeeded in producing the once elegant clover leaf pattern of its interior. The Benie Hoose, a still larger monument lying within 100 yards of Yoxie, must have been the living quarters of its acolytes, tending the crops, the sheep, and participating in some strange and pagan rites. As such it is outstanding in its construction and vastly superior to all other dwel-

31

ling houses of that era found in the islands. Here, too, was a forecourt like that of Yoxie, inner chambers and even drains. The proximity of the Benie Hoose to Yoxie, its entire layout and design, approximate almost identically to similar records of temples in Malta. Both buildings have the distinction of being the first and only known examples of their kind in the British Isles and could have been intended for the pursuit of religious and ritualistic ceremonies.

In addition to the temples of Yoxie, the Benie Hoose and a third at Staneydale, a whole series of heel-shaped cairns were uncovered scattered from Tingwall to Unst, the best preserved on Vementry off the west of Mainland. The discovery of the origins of the beliefs which inspired the buildings, their design running in an orbital pattern from one civilisation to another, was momentous. No one had hitherto imagined that these curious erections, exclusive in Britain to the Shetlands, could have had even the remotest connection with the passage graves of a Mediterranean civilisation; that the burial customs in 1500 B.C., the temples of Staneydale in Sandsting and Yoxie in Whalsay, have their counterparts in Gozo and Malta; or that the tenuous threads stretch back through the centuries to the great days of Mycenae, to the Minoan culture of Crete, where "the dead were carried to decent family tombs, usually like round houses built above the ground, and were laid to rest in their finery . . ."

This custom of burying the dead by inhumation collectively in chambered tombs was in existence in the third millenium B.C. in the eastern Mediterranean. The standard Minoan practice for burial at all periods was interment in a communal or family vault used for many generations. Sometimes these chamber tombs were cut in the ground but elsewhere were built up above ground with dry-walled masonry and roofs of stone corbelling or wood.

Emanating from Sardinia, the Iberian peninsula, Malta and even farther east, they came, farmer colonists, small groups of well-organised adventurers from that great nursery of trading and seafaring peoples, the Mediterranean. And when these first inhabitants to leave behind them some palpable image of their presence set foot on Shetland soil, they brought with them just this one common denominator, the cult of the dead. It may have been a reverent belief, or maybe a forlorn hope that when the heart had ceased to beat and the pulse fluttered to its infinite stillness the spirit of the hunter, the woman, the child, must live on. Simply they set about safeguarding the comrade, the help-mate, from the desecration of wild animals, protecting him from wind and weather and perhaps just from morbid sightseers.

Some of them worked their way through France and spread east-wards over northern Germany and into Spain. Another group crossed from the Mediterranean to the Atlantic, trekking along the Pyrenees and on by way of Brittany to England and Ireland. Yet a third and even more enterprising stream chose the long sea route by way of Spain and Portugal, crossing the Bay of Biscay and sailing round the north of Scotland, some to press on via Orkney and Denmark to Sweden and others, by-passing Orkney altogether, settled in Shetland.

In a deep belt along the Atlantic coasts of Europe, from Norway, Denmark and southern Sweden, Germany, Holland, from the Shetlands and the Orkneys through Ireland, Wales and western England to the peninsula of Brittany and all along the coasts of Spain and Portugal, are strewn thousands of monuments of roughly dressed stone, often in conjunction with barrow-like mounds. There were stone circles, like the Ring of Brodgar in Orkney, single standing *menhirs* thrust out of the bare ground like gigantic phallic symbols, and now and again a turf-covered barrow where a man could squeeze in between the stone uprights of the entrance and crawl along a passageway ending in a cruciform chamber.

A stone-chambered tomb in Arran seems to have been first used in or around 3160 B.C. and a timber mortuary house within a round barrow at Pitnacree near Aberfeldy about 2860 B.C. Although related to and serving the same purpose as the Shetland heel-shaped cairn, the latter was a variety of chamber tomb developed in Shetland by people with traditions of their own, who perhaps reached the islands not by way of the north of Scotland but directly from south and west.

In the Middle Ages these monuments were all regarded with suspicion, their origins undoubtedly satanic and referred to as "The Devil's Den", "The Devil's Ring", "The Giant's Chamber" and so forth. The Shetlander ascribed them to the Picts, dark small folk who were supposed to work all night and retreat to underground chambers by day when they were said to have lost their strength.

The great henge monuments, the Stones of Stenness, the Ring of Brodgar and the Ring of Bookan in Orkney, may have been inspired by a later wave of incomers, the Beaker Folk who practised individual burial in short cists. Shetland has no such spectacular stone circles but scattered throughout the islands a series of standing stones rise stark from field and moor, two in Unst being particularly impressive—the one near Uyeasound on the road to Muness and the other near the old House of Lund in Westing.

In addition to the heel-shaped cairns and temples, more than 60 houses of these earliest inhabitants have been identified. Most of the sites are separate one from the other and occupy almost the same position as do the present crofts along the seashore. In fact their whole existence, the layout of the fields, the crops, animals and way of life differed

33

scarcely at all from the Shetlander of only a generation or so ago. They grew barley and milled it in trough querns, a find of carbonised seed recognisable as such surviving for over 3500 years, the most northerly grain find in Europe and the first example of its kind in Britain.

They owned domesticated animals, horse, ox, sheep, pig and dog. They cleared their fields of stones, gathering them together in *rönis*, a system still practised today. Drystane dykes were attached to the houses either to enclose animals or keep them from eating the crops. The crofters fished and supplied themselves with fresh fish; bones of ling and cod were found at Jarlshof, shellfish and probably seals. They had enough mutton, cheese and butter most likely churned in a bag of animal skin. The houses would have their closest counterpart in the black houses of the Western Isles but even in early times the Shetland croft was far advanced in comfort and amenity.

The beginning of human life in Shetland is much earlier than was first suspected. Radiocarbon dating has already revolutionised archaeological timings and now gives a minimum time span from before 4000 B.C. to 3500 and probably 3000 B.C. for sites found in Scotland from the Tweed Valley to the Forth. There was definite coastal activity especially on the Scottish west coast, where fish that could only have been caught by offshore fishing, such as wrasse, sea-bream, conger and ray, were part of the diet of island fishermen. These communities may well have been derived from similar peoples in western France; the type of mattock with a shaft hole used by them and by the whale-eaters of the Forth is in common with those of the contemporary hunter-fisher groups of Denmark and North Germany.

14 Standing stone on the road to Muness, Unst, like a petrified tree trunk, erected, who knows, as a boundary post, a landmark for shipping, or for some ancient religious practice.

6. *Beakers and Cup Marks*

THE SHETLAND COLONIST farmer of about 1000 B.C. knew nothing of the contemporary metal-using cultures of the Mediterranean. It would have been almost as difficult to describe a railway train or an aeroplane as to tell the men and women gathering limpets on the beaches of Channerwick or Gulberwick, tilling their small fields with stone ploughs near Scatness or tending their flocks around the dunes at Jarlshof, of the glories that then were Crete and the lands of their fathers. Of the palaces of Knossos, the wealth of the Mediterranean carried by sail and oar to deck the women of Phaistos, of cedar from Lebanon, copper from Cyprus, wine, olive oil and ivory. Hands blistered as he sweated with his neighbours over yet another house or cairn, or combed the beaches for timber precious as gold, the Bronze-Age people of Alaca Huyuk were burying their royal dead in tombs filled with offerings that included bronze standards inlaid with silver, necklaces of gold and precious stones of the most sophisticated and advanced artistry, while their humble counterparts in the temples of Yoxie or Staneydale were grateful for the thick wool fleece that helped to keep out the salt sea spray, their dead surrounded by rough steatite vessels, quartz scrapers and axe heads.

Of the warm shores of that ancient past scarcely a racial memory would remain, only perhaps in legend and story handed down by word of mouth and told by grandfathers who had been told by their grandfathers. In the small glow of a peat fire, children's eyes might gleam as the old man wrought with horny hands on toy querns and stone axe heads, or, no longer strong enough for the ploughshare, turned to making quartz scrapers, smoothing arrow shafts or bodkins on pieces of pumice stone, labouring with loving care over the typical thin Shetland knives of porphyry, painstakingly polished and finely sharpened. As he worked he might tell them how once there had been a great mother goddess who had been all-powerful and who blessed the grain that waved in the fields outside, the same grain, he would nod wisely, that their ancestors had brought in ships from a far-off land.

For centuries right into the late Bronze Age men in the Northern

35

Isles enjoyed a peaceful and comparatively comfortable existence. They were frequently employed in reconstructing their houses, constantly, as at Jarlshof in the southernmost tip of Shetland, forced to move away from the wind-blown sand that built up great dunes around their dwellings. The houses were oval in shape with a stoutly-built wall enclosing side cubicles and a large rear chamber facing into a central hearth or "courtyard" area. Timber gathered from the shoreline after a storm, then probably overlaid with turf, provided a roof with a vent to allow smoke to escape and admit a little light.

At the rear of the house cattle were stalled in the winter months, for a ring tether was found made from a whale's vertebra. The paved floor in the building in which they were kept was slightly dished in shape so that dung could be collected for manuring the fields, together with a strategically-placed sump into which the urine could be drained. The striking example of this method at Jarlshof is the first recorded instance of the use of fertilisers in Britain. The primitive pointed bars of stone used as ploughshares were to be eventually regarded with respect as demonstrating the earliest evidence of cultivation in the whole of Scotland.

In addition to cattle, these dune dwellers on the coastal strips around Shetland owned flocks of sheep, including some resembling the large-horned Soay breed, the Copper Age sheep of the Continent and others of the older "Turbary" stock whose descendants may well survive in the pure modern Shetland breed.

15   A *muldie küss* near the lochs of Hedlicliv, Foula. The fine scalped peat put up in heaps (küsses): muld—earth and covered with turf or stones then used to line the floor of the byre where its deodorant and absorbent properties are far greater than the normal straw; the final muld mixed with urine is used as a fertiliser.

Unfortunately, pottery recovered from this period is relatively scarce, most of the heel-shaped cairns having been rifled of their contents long before expert assessment could be made. Vessels of steatite, however, continued to be produced, and exported to Orkney, right up to the Middle Ages, and a hundred yards or so up the burn at Catpund near Cunningsburgh is one of the best known workings from whence it came.

Every so often all the way up the burn, one can find the odd discarded sherd tossed aside in the amber hollows, and note the gouge marks of stone implements still visible as though it were only yesterday that a man crouched, a thousand years before Christ, fashioning these simple shallow vessels from the pinkish-brown, malleable rock. Perhaps now and again he straightened his aching back and paused to look out to sea, to the island of Mousa, then without its famous broch, or sat and watched the play of wind on water or the cloud shadows racing across the green promontory of Helliness, climbing the rolling hills above Mail, the Ward of Bressay and the Noup of Noss, purple in the far distance.

Lacking flint, any material that could be worked was used. A handled club was found in a burnt mound in Bressay, almost certainly of the Bronze Age period. From a broch at Eshaness came a large whetstone possibly used in the making of polished axes. Indeed there had been at one time a flourishing "factory" in North Roe making axe heads from Rickiebite Felsite which have turned up sporadically all over the islands, even as far as Fair Isle. Most of the arrowheads were made of siliceous epi-schists but in the County Museum in Lerwick are one or two delicate barbed and tanged examples from Bressay and Eshaness made from crystalline quartz, incredible examples of skill and artistry in working this difficult material.

The islanders continued the megalith culture of burying the dead in chambered tombs, generation after generation, until in some overlap between the Stone and the Bronze Ages a new wave of immigrants arrived who practised individual interment. They had been the first people to reach the east coast of Scotland, as opposed to the settlers arriving by the Atlantic routes, to bury their dead in single graves. These new peoples consisted of two main groups of round-headed bowmen, collectively known as the Beaker Folk. Whether the burials were in stone cists or in cremation cists, beakers accompanied the skeleton or ashes, although no whole beaker has yet been found in Shetland.

It was obvious that racially they differed from the Neolithic megalith-builder. They were physically taller and more heavily built than the men who raised the chamber cairns, an average male standing about 5 ft 9 inches as against 5 ft 6 inches for Scotland. They were also broad of face and markedly round-headed as opposed to the long-headed Atlantic colonists.

The beakers were also divided into two categories, bell beakers, associated with archers, and necked beakers with the battle-axe folk. Again it was from the grave goods that such deductions were able to be made. A few Beaker Folk did reach Orkney and Shetland, their individual burials in short cists scattered over a wide area. A single, small sherd from Scatness was found in such a cist and a kist grave lies above Housabrek's Wick in the island of Foula, while a cremation cist was discovered inside the kirkyard of Norderhoos, uncovered when the kirkyard dyke was being re-built and a new foundation for the dyke being made.

In four Scottish beaker graves were stone bracers or archers' wrist guards along with the distinctive type of arrowheads, finely chipped flint points with barb and tang. Eventually this new way of burial appeared to be accepted both in Orkney and Shetland, sometimes a crouched skeleton in a cist and sometimes cremated bones either in a stone cist or in round or square-sided bowls of steatite.

Although most finds of this period have been made in Orkney, now and again we get tantalising glimpses of the possibilities of similar finds yet to be made in Shetland.

So far we have only been able to turn up from Underhoull in the island of Unst, from a site embracing early Iron Age, Broch period and Viking period, one tiny pale yellow glass bead together with toy mill stones and querns, but it is in these small glimpses of intimate human factors that history or pre-history comes alive. They can all be seen in the County Museum in Lerwick, poignant reminders of womanly vanity and childish delight in mimicking the daily tasks of the grown-ups.

It was only at the very end of the Bronze Age that an Irish smith came to Shetland, setting up his workshop in part of an abandoned dwelling-house at Jarlshof. In the mining districts of the Iberian peninsula itinerant bronze traders and smiths had been making regular journeys all along the coasts of Europe, bartering their bronze ware for jadeite from Brittany, jet from England and Baltic amber. They travelled in caravans, guarded by archers for whom, no doubt, they made the bronze rivets that held the polished stone wrist guards and the bronze buckle with which the strap was fastened to the wrist. The traders themselves were peaceable folk, philosophically accepting the megalithic customs of burial in communal or family vaults or occasionally introducing the new custom of single inhumation.

Before the arrival of Jarlshof's bronze-smith, metal had not even

16 Man-made circular basin carved out of a slab of rock not far below the waters of the Sneug on Foula. On the steep, sloping hillside Jimmie Gray suddenly noticed water shining at his feet. Pulling back the overgrown grasses this strange basin was revealed, about 1 ft. across and 6 inches deep.

begun to replace bone and stone for working implements. The Beaker Folk who had already arrived integrated well with the local inhabitants and although connections were kept up intermittently with Orkney no effective market for metal appears in either island group. The only bronze objects that survive are of Britannico-Hibernian type and had obviously been imported from Great Britain or Ireland. The Early Bronze Age is represented at present by one flat axe, the Middle Bronze by a dirk and two knife daggers, and the Late Bronze Age by two razors, two socketed knives and a socketed spearhead with loops on the socket.

Why this enterprising bronze-smith settled in Shetland we may never know, but one can imagine the curiosity and amazement with which the local people watched this expert at work. Dr. Curle found his casting pit, filled with clean sand in which clay moulds were placed while the molten metal was poured in, and it is from the broken moulds that we can tell what he manufactured. He produced socketed axes, socketed knives, slashing swords and sun-flower pins, all of Irish type and proper to the last phase of the Bronze Age.

Almost before the wonder of his artistry died away, further new-comers introduced the islanders to iron. Three miles north of Sum-burgh, near Wiltrow, were found the remains of an iron smeltery, a dwelling-house and three furnaces. At the same time there appeared at Jarlshof large circular stone-built houses with radial partitions springing from a central hearth. Attached to these dwellings was a new kind of underground chamber, an earth-house or souterrain, which may have been the invention of an intelligent crofter anxious to preserve stocks of perishable foodstuffs for winter feeding although souterrain builders are known as such in Britain.

Following upon this great age of discovery of the manufacture and use of metal began the real seafaring routes across the world in search of raw materials and exotic objects to satisfy the now sophisticated tastes of the European world. There were seagoing ships in the North Sea, a regular Spain–Brittany–Cornwall–Ireland convoy and the not-un-likely chartering of merchant ships on a commercial basis. It has been suggested that because the Bronze Age in Norway is much more strongly associated with sea traffic than agriculture, the "Norwegian Line" even then may have offered reliable vessels, dauntless courage and a readiness to venture anywhere.

Before we move on to the next great epoch in the history of Shetland, the brochs and the broch-builders, the Bronze-Age period in Shetland holds one more mystery which so far remains unsolved. At a place called Gunnister in the island of Unst lies a remarkable and unusual stone. Six feet by about three, roughly oval in shape with a flat surface, evenly spaced around its outer edge, are a series of man-made depressions, rather as though a giant thumb had been at work on a huge pie crust. Its nearest replica lies in the south-west corner of the palace of Mallia in Crete. There the stone is round, an offering table serving the same purpose as the *kernos*, used in the cult of the goddess from Mycenean to Classical times, ringed with the same type of cup mark gouged out along its rim.

17   The Scalloped Stone of Gunnister in Unst.

From this exotic setting one is led to Denmark and northern Germany where on small boulders left by the retreating ice appear the favourite motifs of Bronze-Age Scandinavian carvings, their dominant feature, the cup mark.

No one knows how the great stone of Gunnister came to lie just where it does, to what people or creed it owes its patently human connections. Sheep have sheltered in the shallow oval hollow that surrounds it, turf has grown and obscured much of its base and wind and weather patterned it with a mantle of yellow lichen. Perhaps one day it stood higher than now and on the outcrops of stone on nearby hillsides the remains of houses of some priestly cult, and in the voar when planting time came near, the people walked out across the springy turf to offer sacrifices to the sun or to whichever beneficent spirit might bless their crops.

41

7. The Broch-Builders

"Bjorn was a great man in sea-faring; was a-whiles viking and whiles in cheaping voyages. Bjorn was the ablest of men. One summer he saw a fair maid and great joy he took to gaze upon her. He asked after her of what kindred she was. She was sister to Thorir the Hersir, Hroald's son, and was named Thora Jewlhand. Bjorn set forth his wooing and bade Thora in marriage but Thorir denied him his suit and they parted with things in such case.

"But that same autumn Bjorn gathered him folk and fared with a cutter all manned north into the Firths and came to Thorir's at such time that he was not at home. Bjorn took Thora away and had her at home with him to Aurland. They were there winter long and Bjorn would fain make his wedding with her.

"Bjorn's father Bryniolf liked ill of that and said that Bjorn should not marry Thora without leave of Thorir her brother.

"Finally Bryniolf made ready a good cheaping ship and found men thereto so that Bjorn could fare out of the land. When Bjorn was all ready and a fair breeze set in then stepped he aboard of a boat with twelve men and rowed in to Aurland and there was Thora with his mother who warned him of his peril if he took her away.

"But Thora's clothes and precious things were there all laid ready to hand . . . Fared they now by night out to their ship, hoisted sail forthwith and sailed down the Sogn sea and thereafter into the main.

"They had an ill wind and big seas and wallowed long in the main because they were fast set on this to get them the firthest they might from Norway. . . . They sailed from the east towards Shetland in wild weather and struck their ship coming a-land on Mosey. There they bare off their cargo and fared to the burg that was there and bare thither all their wares and laid up the ship and mended that which was broke.

"A little while before winter came a ship to Shetland out of the Orkneys. They said there were these tidings that a long ship had come in the autumn to the isles . . . that the King would let slay Bjorn Bryniolfson whereso he might be laid hands on, and the like word-sendings made

42

he to the South Isles and all as far as Dublin.

"Bjorn heard these tidings and this withal that he was made outlaw in Norway. But straightaway when he was come to Shetland he had made his wedding with Thora. Sat they that winter at Moseyburgh ..."

And so Bjorn Bryniolfson took to wife Thora Jewlhand in the year A.D. 900 in the Broch of Mousa on the low green island off Sandwick, its great dry-built walls still standing after being built nearly 10 centuries before his arrival, and even today the most perfect in preservation and architectural ingenuity of all the known brochs.

Perhaps they were lucky, but more likely it was Bjorn's brilliant seamanship that brought them to the shelving south coast of the island, where somehow they managed to scramble ashore, make fast their ship and offload her cargo, stumbling through the threshing surf over the slippery Mousa flags. Thora would have her wedding kist full of dresses and capes and fine pleated chemises; her "precious things" gold and silver rings, bracelets of twisted silver and brooches ornamented in chip carving, penannular brooches and domed oval brooches from which her container for needles, scissors, knife and keys hung on fine chains. There would be other bronze-bound chests with eiderdown quilts and pillows, Thora's tapestry, her looms for weaving and making lace and braidwork; wooden troughs and butter kirns, iron cauldrons, kitchen utensils and drinking vessels for the home-brewed beer and mead, and elaborately carved bed-heads.

Under the loose pine decking they must have brought away stores of food, of butter, dried fish and possibly meat, also dried, honey, oats and barley, onions and cheeses, along with swords, battle-axes, shields and spears for the men, great cloaks, warm furs and long-sleeved woollen jackets. They may even have taken with them a couple of rough-coated hunting dogs with iron collars and almost certainly there would have been room for their gaming boards to help pass the black cold nights so far from home. All this would have to be carried by one man at a time through the tiny opening at the base of the broch, along a paved passage four feet wide and sixteen long with a door halfway which could be barred against the bitter winds or the untimely arrival of an enemy.

Somewhere below the broch, where one can still see the remains of broch-period buildings, they managed to haul up their vessel into a kind of winter *noost* and mend her rents. When the spring came and the seas began to abate, Bjorn launched his ship and made her ready "and having wind at will he sailed her into the main". They found a strong wind to fill the bellying sail and were but a little while out when they came from the south to Iceland.

Scarce 250 years later another Norseman took refuge in the same broch. They called him Erlend and he had become enamoured of the comely Margaret, mother of Earl Harald Madaddson of Orkney. Earl Harald had just succeeded in banishing another of his widowed mother's lovers, together with the unfortunate offspring they had conceived, and was in no mood to countenance a second *affaire du coeur*. Erlend, however, was made of sterner stuff than the previous suitor and calmly abducted the lady from under Harald's very nose, bearing her off to Moseyjarborg.

The furious Harald gave immediate chase and with many men besieged the broch but found it still "an unhandy place to get at". Harald, unable to storm the tower, was left kicking his heels outside knowing full well that his political and warfaring commitments elsewhere would suffer badly from a prolonged siege. Eventually a reconciliation was effected with a promise of support in battle from Erlend, the urgency of the matter no doubt spurred on by the restless and miserable followers of Earl Harald, forced to camp out cold and hungry on the windswept isle while Margaret, Erlend and their men caroused in comparative comfort within the stout walls.

It was more than seven centuries before another great ship came to Mousa and the broch saw the last of its dramas. The North of Scotland steamer, the *St. Sunniva I*, sailing north from Aberdeen to Lerwick in dense fog on the morning of April 10th, 1930, like Bjorn Bryniolfson went aground on the island of Mousa. Unlike Bjorn's "good cheaping ship", however, after a couple of weeks the seas had battered the *St. Sunniva* to a total wreck.

The broch of Mousa still stands alone on this tiny uninhabited island and of all the brochs dotted around the coasts of Shetland like so many beehives, it is the only one that rises to anything approximating its original height. The most perfectly built and best preserved, it was probably the last broch tower ever constructed. The outcome of two centuries of broch building, it has been recognised as a miracle of engineering skill and one of the wonders of prehistoric Europe.

Peculiar to Scotland, the broch structures are found with very few exceptions in the Shetlands, Orkneys, Hebrides and on the mainland north of the Great Glen. Over the first millenium B.C. the climate had changed considerably. In Shetland the crofters of the day were forced down from higher inland sites, now gradually being encroached upon by peat and exposed to increasing rain and wind, to arable strips around the coast. Both in the British Isles and in Europe, Bronze- and Iron-Age peoples were in a constant state of strife.

The broch type of tower or fort was perfectly adapted to these unsettled conditions and as an example of strategic military architecture

44

it has rarely been surpassed. As a refuge it was ideal. Often guarded by a secondary line of defence in the form of ramparts and ditches, this kind of building presented the enemy with a literally impregnable fortress. In the typical broch the stair circled upwards from the foundations within two concentric hollow shells. The inside face of the wall was vertical but the outside, gracefully waisted about three-quarters of the way up, could rise safely to well over 40 feet. From the gallery running round the high wall head its occupants would have a point of vantage either as look-out or as a means of taking practical retaliation from high above their attackers.

The immense thickness of its base was impossible to undermine. No fire could drive out the defenders of this dry stone tower and the sole access lay in the one tiny passage, long and narrow, with a heavily-barred door or stone slab halfway along its length, a guard chamber on one or both sides giving additional protection beyond. A battering ram could scarcely have been used in this low confined tunnel and scaling ladders were useless against the curving sides.

By the second century B.C. stone-walled forts had been built in the

18   The broch of Mousa, still standing, the most perfect example of its kind, where 900 years after its building Bjorn Bryniolfson and Thora Jewlhand were married and spent the winter: 250 years later Erlend and Margaret, mother of Earl Harald Madadd-son, withstood a siege by Harald who found it "still an unhandy place to get at".

Western Isles and in the far north of Scotland, possibly the successors to the larger type of hill fort of the late Bronze Age and early Iron Age times. A wholly northern invention, true broch buildings must have resulted from the sudden vision of an inspired designer, realising the infinite possibilities embodied in a completely circular tower and gifted with the practical ability to put his invention into practice.

The broch of Mousa is 51 feet in diameter and still stands at its highest point at 40 feet. The staircase enters from an opening off the central court at scarcement level, where the narrow ledge is formed by stepping back the wall seven feet above the ground and it appears likely that the scarcements once supported a floor at this level. The three-feet-wide staircase climbs clockwise until it reaches the present wall height. Four feet six inches above the upper scarcement there is a landing from which entrance is provided into the court by an opening corresponding to the size of a normal doorway, which could only mean that there was at one time a second floor or gallery at this level.

At the existing wall top the inner wall inclines slowly inwards by means of corbelling which suggests the springing of a dome. It is most noticeable at the highest northern arc of the circumference, but as the wall top is now incomplete it is not possible to say how the broch was roofed. Outside the broch can still be seen the remains of a surrounding wall. Beehive huts once existed within this outer enclosure but all that can be traced today are a few fragments of a chamber near the broch entrance.

However temporary may have been the refuge, if such indeed was the main purpose of its erection, it seems incredible that a building of such ingenuity and engineering skill was not roofed in some manner nor had at least one upper floor. Considering the brilliance of design, theoretically and physically, it is highly improbable that the people who lived or congregated within its walls simple gathered together in a vacuum, milling around a central fire, while look-outs ran up and down the stairs of a hollow shaft ready to call the defenders to action on the parapet.

Bjorn Bryniolfson and his wife Thora, some 900 years after its building, could scarcely have spent the entire winter within a mere shell, not even huddled into the small chambers at ground level. They may have come ashore on Mousa by mishap, or Bjorn may have intended all along to occupy the broch knowing its defensive properties, but certainly 250 years later when Erlend carried off Margaret, mother of Earl Harald, he knew exactly where he was going and what he would find there. He expected to be pursued and chose the broch of Mousa deliberately, knowing it to be a safe stronghold even at that late date after its building.

The Norse by that time, through trade and travel, were fairly sophisticated in their way of life and it is inconceivable that a lover and his mistress would be prepared to "rough it" under conditions that did not allow them at least a modicum of comfort. Earl Harald Madaddson, who may have hoped to find the structure not as stout as it once was, noted the fact that it was "still an unhandy place to get at" and fared no better than the hundreds of others who had stood helpless in the face of this great stone monster that for centuries had continued to frustrate all attempts to penetrate the double thickness of its shell.

It is perhaps significant that in Shetland brochs surrounded its coastline and that this unique disposition led to the finding of the remains of a broch at Jarlshof, the entire site one of the most remarkable ever excavated in the British Isles, a site occupied by man over a span of 3000 years. Given the name Jarlshof by Sir Walter Scott in his novel *The Pirate*, the Old Haa' of Sumburgh surmounts a green mound at the very edge of the sea overlooking the West Voe, the archaeological site covering some two to three acres. The stormy seas that have continuously eaten away at Shetland's coastline had already swallowed up the southern part of the mound when at the end of last century a series of violent gales and mountainous waves tore out a further piece of bank revealing a section of a massive stone wall, part of an Iron-Age settlement, including a broch tower, adjacent wheelhouses and passage dwellings.

Here in this remote corner of Britain's most northerly islands small family groups had been living since the Stone Age, for the remains now visible cover three prehistoric and proto-historic village settlements. During the earliest period the islanders lived a simple Stone-Age existence although bronze was known in other parts of Britain; the second saw the building of the broch during its Iron Age occupation; the site remained inhabited all through the Roman rule in the British Isles with secondary buildings continuously added, down to the main Viking settlement around A.D. 800 which also expanded from time to time until its decline in the twelfth and thirteenth centuries. Replaced by a medieval farmstead it too was eventually abandoned to be succeeded in the late sixteenth century by the laird's house now known as Jarlshof.

The site must have seemed almost perfect in every sense to its first small bands of dune dwellers. Below the rampart of Sumburgh Head and opposite the Ness of Burgi on which stands a small blockhouse type of broch, these two most southerly promontories of Shetland thrust out into the sea like a giant lobster-claw enclosing the bight of the West Voe. From either point Fair Isle is visible and from Fair Isle, the Orkneys. As landmarks or look-outs they must have been invaluable. There

47

was an ample supply of fresh spring water and beaches for sea food, building stones and driftwood.

Since that first day of discovery in 1897 by Mr. John Bruce, owner of the estate, the area has been systematically explored by such leading archaeologists as Dr. A. O. Curle, Professor V. G. Childe and Miss B. Laidler and later by Dr. J. S. Richardson. Beautifully constructed paths of beach stones laid on edge lead up to the site and other walks thread their way on different levels around and above the ancient settlements. A mantle of springy grass sheared like velvet tops the edges of the roofless wheelhouses and from the slender iron staircase in a corner of the Old Haa' one looks down on a maze of excavations, on forecourt and roundhouse and kitchen midden, on all the small intimate details of family life from Stone Age to Viking. There are stone boxes for refuse; cleverly-built wall cupboards, central hearths where peat fires burned 3000 years ago; and sleeping quarters, saddle-shaped querns for grinding corn, the site of a quartz knapper's workshop and the stone slab used by a potter to wedge the raw clay.

By the late Iron Age the eastern flank of the mound had been inundated by wind-blown sand in great dune-like drifts and it was on top of these that new immigrants to the site erected the broch tower, using local labour for its construction, probably in the first century A.D. to be followed by large oval houses built in the courtyard. The people kept cattle, sheep, pigs and a few ponies. Fish and wild fowl were caught for the cooking pot.

Only two-thirds of the broch tower at Jarlshof have survived. Like all true brochs the original building was circular with a diameter of 29 feet 6 inches, a 17-foot wall at its base. There is the usual scarcement 7 feet 6 inches from the floor and although the entrance had been swept away by the sea a small cell built into the thickness of the wall at the west side probably served as a guard chamber. Six stone steps give access to the well, over 13 feet deep, the shaft proper being cut through the solid rock. Although the original structure has suffered both from the elements and man himself the broch at Jarlshof approximates in all respects to the traditional Shetland broch tower.

At the broch of Clickhimin, however, lies the ultimate solution to the enigma of the Shetland brochs. Referred to as the possible Mycenae of northern barbarian Europe, the excavations were undertaken by Mr. J. R. C. Hamilton, Inspector of Ancient Monuments for the Ministry of Public Building and Works. At some time before the arrival of the broch-builders, a large force of immigrants arrived in Shetland and took possession of what was then a small islet in the freshwater loch of Clickhimin, three-quarters of a mile south of Lerwick. About the fourth to the second century B.C. they erected a wall round its shores,

19   Remains of the ancient ring fort of Clickhimin type on an islet in the loch of Huxter, Whalsay. The blockhouse with central passage and side chambers faced a narrow causeway to the island on which it stood. Over the centuries the building has crumbled away and stones taken from it have been used to build the planti-crubs on the nearby hillside.

12 feet thick and 15 feet high enclosing a roughly oval space of 125 feet by 120 feet. Eight feet inside the entrance they first constructed a huge blockhouse and for the first time, writes Mr. Hamilton, "the domestic arrangements inside such an early Celtic fortress were completely revealed".

This ring fort was in fact a tenemented half-timbered building with the first and second floors reached by ladders, the living quarters of a close-knit community as well as its stronghold. Reading the official guide book to Clickhimin in the light of the astounding possibility that multi-storied buildings in Shetland had actually been developed two or three hundred years before Christ, is like finding the key to a cipher. "The tier of three recesses separated one from the other by lintels ... the openings on to the courtyard five feet above ground level...entrances none of which is provided with door checks or bar holes ... their elevated position 'abnormal'...."

49

Now Clickhimin and hundreds of other similar forts suddenly take on a new dimension, fulfilling the double purpose of shelter from wind and weather and safety from attack. The Celtic clan, socially and domestically closely integrated, was able to live in comfort and yet ready at a moment's notice to rush through the doors of the living quarters on to the parapet in defence of the stronghold. In the same manner as that of the wheelhouse era, a single-storey adaptation of the radial "high rise" of the blockhouse and broch period, daily life at Clickhimin must have been very similar to that lived in Ireland. There, on the level of the upper floor, was some kind of room or protected balcony projected outwards known as the *grianon*—literally "sun-room".

In the great Irish legend of the Ulster cycle, its cultural roots in the Gaul of the third century B.C., the size of houses is given by one dimension only, now clearly seen as the diameter of the round clan forts; palaces are described with many doors with beds between the doors opening on to the rampart. Evidence is found also in the detailed description given in the tale of Briciu's feast. Briciu of the Poison Tongue, the mischief-maker, built a new palace in which to entertain King Conchobar and the warriors of Ulster. There were nine compartments from wall to wall and a royal compartment for Conchobar in the fore-part of the palace, "higher than all the compartments of the house, the twelve compartments of the twelve chariot warriors of Ulster constructed round it". Doors gave access through a stone casement to the rampart walk and the floors were of spruce supported on stone ledges. Similar peripheral arrangements occurred inside Iron Age or Hallstatt forts about 700 to 500 B.C. in the Alpine area.

Tales of the Irish hero Cuchulain and the tribal chiefs identical with the chariot riding head-hunting Celts were portrayed by classical authors in the last centuries before Christ, while in Irish epics one of the romantic tales of Diarmuid and Grainne tells how the couple escape through one of these exits. Diarmuid protests that they cannot leave "for Finn is in Teamhir and it is he himself is the keeper of the gates, and as that is so we cannot leave ..." Grainne, however, shows herself either to be more determined or more skilful in devising their escape for she points out that "there is a side door of escape from my *grianon* we will go out by it ..."

All the Irish epics lay stress on the throngs of people in palaces, kings, warriors and womenfolk with their attendants who sat in their raised *imdai* like boxes in a theatre; below them the fire where the beast was cooking for what was called the "Champion's Portion", the first and finest cut; watching the boasting of famous heroes and cheering on their favourite as the men drew their swords for combat at the fire. Shadowy

50

figures, half-obscured by peat smoke, now and then the gold hilt of a sword or an armlet glinting like jewels dancing this way and that until the final bloody thrust. Like the Vikings to come, their feasts lasted for days and no one was forced to leave the gathering to sleep in a miserable hovel outside the main building; they slept where they were, in the nine, in the twelve compartments, wall to wall, one above the other. The continued pattern of circular dwelling sites may well have run from Neolithic to Iron Age, the broch tower the ultimate in upward building determined by the increasingly unsettled times and carried out by professional builders.

Implements and pottery belonging to the broch men at Clickhimin show a greater use of deer antler and whalebone in the making of large perforated pegs, antler plates, a weaving comb, an antler knife, a dice and a whalebone cup. The stone implements were similar to those of other brochs including pebble pounders, hones, steatite discs, steatite beads and spindle whorls. Painted pebbles with dot and line motifs were found both at Clickhimin and Jarlshof and according to one archaeologist may have been used as a sling shot. Few metal objects have been found but these include the head of a ring pin and a spiral finger ring. The people used pottery with carinated shoulders and articles of steatite, quite probably made at Cunningsburgh, showed that local labour had again been employed as at Jarlshof in the building of the tower. Native islanders would have been recruited who brought with them their own cooking pots and utensils, much as labourers today might come to work on a site bringing lunch box, Thermos flask and mug.

Flanking the inner face of the ring wall at Clickhimin had stood byres and outhouses with rough cobbled floors overlaid by a thick deposit of black peat scalped from the moor and spread as bedding for the cattle in winter in place of straw too valuable to use for the byre. This age-old practice survived in Shetland, especially in the island of Foula, up to very recent times, almost denuding the rare flat areas of soil. The fine peat, called "muld" (*myldekause* from the Old Norn) is not only very absorbent but acts as a natural deodorant and together with the dung can be used as manure. Near the abandoned crofts still lie stone covered mounds of scalped earth, where peat was taken. By this time the trough quern had been replaced by the sadle type and all over the islands examples of these can be seen in ruined crofts or near ancient places of habitation, the basic necessity of any farmer from Neolithic man up to the last century.

Most important of the finds made in broch sites in Shetland has been the textile equipment of a specialised nature known to the Glastonbury Lake villagers of Somerset. This included femur-headed spindle whorls, bone bobbins, weaving combs and slotted lengths of bone. The broch people, too, had their own indoor amusements and played a kind of backgammon with small parallelepiped dice. Bone dice of the type known from the British Iron Age were also found in Ireland at Ballinderry and in another crannog at Lagore were dice like those of the Roman period. The discs which turn up so often may also have been used with gaming boards. Beautifully incised sandstone discs have come from Jarlshof, one with a Celtic running spiral design and one bearing a roughly carved ship.

In Irish literature *Fidchell* a kind of battle game played by boys and men, is often mentioned, appearing rather like the Roman board game *ludus latrunculorum* and again at Ballinderry a gaming board of carved yew was found with a grid of small holes to take the pegs of wooden playing pieces. It is fascinating to speculate on man's earliest invented games and to relate the finds of Roman games in Ireland and in Shetland broch remains with fragments of Roman pottery and other goods both in Orkney and Shetland, showing that these objects had been acquired by some means or other during the broch period.

Also in the Roman context, during its later period, the people of Traprain Law were using Roman currency and obtained Roman wares from as far afield as southern Britain and the Rhineland and from there traded with the northern settlements in exchange for native products. One of the most common articles of barter from the north was leather, pelts from the Highlands and sealskins from the coastal settlements around Scotland. At Jarlshof, in the post-broch levels, seal bones were numerous and stone discs found on broch and post-broch sites may have been used in stripping and curing the skins for export. The polishers could have been useful for softening pelts, the whalebone pegs from Shetland sites used in stretching the skins to dry upon a wooden ground frame in almost the same way as is done today.

Clickhimin was by no means the only example of its kind in Shetland and other groups of settlers of the same origin and probably coming into Shetland at the same time spread out in various directions, building three approximately similar blockhouse-type fort dwellings. On the island of Whalsay, on the opposite side of the Loch of Huxter to the road, it is possible to distinguish the remains of what had once been a smaller replica of Clickhimin. Thrusting out into the loch had been a central passage and side chambers facing the narrow causeway on which it stands. Originally the fort had been enclosed by a ring wall but it is obvious from the almost total collapse of the fort into the waters of the loch that more than nature has been at work upon it. Nearby on the gentle slope of the hillside four or five circular *planti-crubs*, long since abandoned, are slowly disintegrating, their stone walls most likely pillaged from a site of no interest or usefulness, except for the already

52

20 Stone circles of planti-crubs on the island of Whalsay beside the loch of Huxter, the stones obviously taken from the remains of the ring fort standing on the small islet on the loch.

half-dressed stone, to the crofters of the eighteenth century. The causeway itself is lapped by the waters of the loch, emerging now only as stepping stones where once a small community trod back and forth tending their cattle and their crops, and gulls nest on the few low walls once so carefully and determinedly constructed on this lonely and desolate spot.

The third fort of this type is easily the most dramatic in situation and could have acted as a look-out for the whole of the south mainland, perched as it is on the heights of the Ness of Burgi opposite Sumburgh Head and Jarlshof. Clinging to the tip of this tiny promontory, joined to Scatness by a high narrow neck of jagged rocks, its approach even today is awkward and as Earl Harald would have said "an unhandy place to get at". There is indeed no indication that the site exists until the visitor has negotiated the slippery slabs of tilted blue-black spurs like a nightmare bridge, the lashing waves on either side below adding to the importance of keeping one's footing.

The Ministry of the Environment, however, daunted not at all by

53

this formidable approach, has made an excellent job of the restorations, but not until one is standing on the beautiful grassy platform of the headland itself does the neat green and gold of an Ancient Monument plaque appear, oddly anachronistic in this wild and wind-torn setting, giving details of the site. Lateral chambers and a central lintelled doorway dominate the inner end of a causeway leading through a double ditch and rampart system of defence. Far below the black spaniel heads of seals bobbing like corks in the swell or swimming delightfully on their backs in a kind of nonchalant butterfly stroke; the shags on the black rocks drying their bat-like wings, above them the arrowed wing-tips of fulmars coming in to nest on the crevices of the steep rock face: such an exposed situation betokens a site chosen specifically for its strategic purpose.

That the brochs had military connotations is obvious and these unique towers could well have been the result of a composite blend of native and south-western elements drawing upon their united experiences in fort building to produce the highly-specialised defensive broch. The occupants did not fear for their cattle or crops so that it would seem that they feared only for themselves, being taken as prisoners, hostages or slaves. The expanding Roman Empire depended enormously on the acquirement of slaves: Tacitus mentioned slaves as one of the prizes of the Roman conquest of Britain.

The argument against slave trading in the Northern Isles is obvious—surely there were enough well-set-up, healthy and vigorous men and women in Britain itself? If indeed agreements had been reached between the Romans and the Orcadian chieftains then some form of taxation would have been decided upon, a tribute that would scarcely include slaves. It seems much more likely that marauding bands of piratical unscrupulous warrior tribesmen, owing allegiance to no man, but taking advantage of a hundred years of feuding and pillaging, turned their hands to any trade that could bring in quick returns. In addition, the hill fort tribes, the string of vitrified forts facing the broch province over the entire frontier belt, took toll wherever it was possible. The early Irish legendary hero, Labraid Loingseach boasts that "he smote eight towers in Tiree ... eight strongholds of the men of Skye ... he ventured upon many of the islands of Orkney". Both sides took hostages and slave trading could well have played as sinister a part as it was to do later in the raids of Niall of the Nine Hostages, the first High King of Ireland, and whose mother Caireann is said to have been a British captive.

The hill fort tribesmen, who left relics of their exotic personal adornment at the Braes of Gight in Aberdeenshire, were every bit as ruthlessly warlike as the Vikings still to come. In a broch midden at

Gurness in Orkney were found two hands severed at the wrist, still bearing rings of La Tène metalworkers in Europe, three on the finger of one hand and two on the finger of the other, and the hands in all probability belonged to a warrior caught in a punitive or pillaging raid upon the islands.

Whatever the history of its occupants, Celtic war lord or Pictish farmer, householders or refugees, like all the other brochs in varying stages of decay but still proudly the best preserved, Mousa stands empty as a long-abandoned house with scarcely a shred of evidence to betray its past. For those who climb its staircase the wind tumbles and whirls sighing like voices clamouring to be set free. There remains a strange eeriness about the place filled with so much of Shetland's past. The baying of hounds, the clash of swords, rough words of men quietening the frightened women as a slave ship was sighted off shore; whimpering children aroused from sleep to be borne swiftly for safety within its dark galleries; Norse lovers murmuring above the sleeping warriors are now forever stilled, their only echoes the soft whirr of the storm petrels nesting in the crevices, their lives lived out at the *far haaf*, to return every few days to relieve the nesting mate.

Ponies of the famous Mousa stud range below the elegant cooling tower profile of the broch, galloping down the hillside like small horses of the Steppes to greet with equal zest their owners or the visiting stallion. Like the sheep, every so often one of their number is lost over the banks, but like them survival is to the fittest. When July comes the common seals haul out to pup on the flat Mousa flags that built the broch and paved the streets of Lerwick. The cry of a raingoose plucks at the singing wind. Fulmars nest beneath the broch and every summer dedicated bird watchers spend nights in comfortless expectancy within its walls waiting for the "Ala moutie" to return from the open sea.

8. *"The People of the Designs"*

By the second century A.D. the age of broch-building had ended. The communities that once filled them with such boundless activity were either broken up, disbanded or even, like more modern families, may have wished for a house of their own. There seemed no question either of maintaining the brochs in repair in case of further need, at least not in Shetland. Orkney, which had been the centre of political power in the North, cautiously made a few additions to its broch defences, building a bastion at Gurness round the broch platform and reinforcing the stone rampart at Midhowe, but within these works a whole series of inter-related huts were built, gradually encroaching on the original.

At Jarlshof the men who had helped to build the broch moved in and had no compunction in tearing down part of the courtyard wall to construct a large roundhouse, copying certain features of the brochs such as a timber-frame gallery round the central hearth. With the insertion of radial stone piers, however, the dwelling was more or less the same as the traditional roundhouse of pre-broch days, and later a whole series of large wheelhouses were constructed both within the courtyard and the abandoned broch itself, by the direct descendants of the original broch builders, the wheelhouse culture a phenomenon of Shetland and the Hebrides. The same practice was followed at Clickhimin, Mousa, Levenwick, Clumlie and Burland and for several centuries the basic material culture remained the same until the arrival of the first Viking colonists.

The wheelhouse, as its name suggests, still kept to the circular structural design with piers arranged like the spokes of a wheel dividing it into compartments in the age-old manner, except that now it was all on ground level. Tradition dies hard, especially in Shetland, the very isolation of which tends to perpetuate customs and crafts which survived in a relatively pure form from very early times. Many crofts of the nineteenth century were still constructed in the same way as their ancestral Viking farmsteads of a thousand years before.

The number of compartments within the wheelhouse would depend

56

The author on Ronas Hill, at 1468 ft, Shetland's highest. Composed almost entirely of red granite, 350 million years old, it supports 15 of Shetland's 25 arctic-alpine flowering plants.

The *Good Shepherd* at North Haven, Fair Isle, the boat which plies between the island and Mainland. (Photo by J. Laughton Johnston.)

Brindister Loch at midnight in summer — the nights of the Simmer Dim. (Photo by J. Laughton Johnston.)

Lerwick from the clock tower looking towards Bressay.

not only on the status of the owner but on the size of the family unit, usually about eight to ten individuals. Inside each cubicle or *immda* there was a stone bed with its head to the wall, the foot being made use of as a bench on which to sit facing the fire. In winter they wrapped their feet in sheepskins piled up on the bench behind and kept specially for this purpose. Mattresses made from hides were stuffed with straw with coverlets of both warm sheepskin and leather. The main wall at the back of each *immda* was hung with matting, probably made from the *floss* gathered by the burns. For greater privacy they could be closed off with screens of leather or rush matting.

Many of the small family possessions would be made of perishable materials disintegrating over the centuries, but we do know that each household already owned barrels and vats made of staves and held together by hoops in the orthodox fashion. At Jarlshof even the circular stone settings were found which had been designed to hold these large containers upright and broken barrel staves were recovered at Clickhimin.

The circle of paved compartments were separated from the central hearth area by upright kerb stones and the floor must have been kept constantly swept, probably with heather brooms, for accumulations of rubbish were slow, mainly remaining in layers of peat ash which were then covered with new paving. Built-in cupboards, *aumbries*, were incorporated in the construction and in Jarlshof there is a passage roofed with large lintel stones above which a space was left to form a kind of loft. Wooden doors in the building were secured by bars which slipped into holes left for them in the stone walls.

Again we have to depend on Irish sources for any kind of description of the laws or social life of the time, for it is believed that although the Shetlander, whatever his origin, would have been poorer, in essentials he bore a close resemblance to the Irish *Oc Aire*: "It is from a grandsire he has inherited property ... He has properties sevenfold: seven cows and a bull: seven pigs and a *Muc Forais* ... (a house-fed pig, a custom still extant in the nineteenth century), seven sheep ... He has land sufficient to maintain three times seven *cumals* ..." In Ireland the basic units of value and exchange were the cow and the *cumal*, literally "bondswoman" and worth four cows. "Then on the pasture land of the tribe he supports seven cows for a whole year"... he leaves the seventh cow at the end of the year to pay for the land (grass for feeding to develop centuries later into *hoga-leave*—permission to graze animals or cut peats in another scattald entailing payment for the liberty). "He has a share in a kiln, in a mill, a barn and in a *scaball cocuis*" (a cooking pot).

Methods of cooking in these early times have actually been tested out today. Mounds of burnt stones have been found, usually near a convenient source of water. The heated stones boiled a trough full of water in about half an hour and a few hot stones added from time to time would keep it on the boil. A joint was also cooked by roasting in a stone-lined pit previously heated by building a fire within it; the meat was cooked mainly by the residual heat from the stone lining, with the addition again of an occasional heated stone.

At Clickhimin the large wheelhouse inside the tower remained the principal dwelling throughout the entire post-broch period and within easy reach of its door inside the ring wall huge middens gradually accumulated over the pre-broch byre and hut foundations. Their position seems scarcely to have changed up to the eighteenth century for many were the visitors to Shetland who remarked upon this insanitary custom! At Clickhimin just below a layer of builders' rubble associated with the construction of the wheelhouse was found a fragment of a Roman glass vessel of the late 1st or early 2nd century. Another fragment of Rhenish polychrome ware datable to the mid-3rd century appeared in an established wheelhouse context.

At the same site an unusual but not unique feature in Shetland is a stone showing two depressions shaped like footmarks side by side. The stone lies on the threshold of the gateway in what was probably its outermost defensive wall. Similar footmark sculptures have been found in Scotland and in many parts of the world and there is a tradition that such carved footprints had a symbolical use in early ceremonies of inauguration. A seventeenth-century account of installing the Lords of the Isles describes the chief elect standing in such a footprint indicating that he should walk henceforth in the steps of his ancestors. No relics of Viking age were found at Clickhimin and it is assumed that the site was abandoned prior to their arrival.

Until the coming of the Norsemen peace reigned in Shetland. Men tilled their fields and grazed their flocks and with a steady rise in population, no longer decimated by war or slavery, further settlements arose, usually on the older and outmoded buildings, using stones from the abandoned brochs. It was during this period and well into the time of the first Norse settlers that a new kind of incised art on stone began to appear all over the islands. On free-standing boulders repeated from the Shetlands to Pabbay in the west, Aberdeen and Deeside to the Forth–Clyde in the south, flowered an entirely unknown series of spectacular designs cut into the flat surfaces and known collectively as Pictish symbol stones.

Their distribution delineates the boundaries of what eventually came to be called Pictland and of which undoubtedly Orkney and Shetland became part, and were inhabited by "so-called" Picts, up to the time of the coming of the Norsemen. Symbol stones appear in the districts where there were brochs, in the Northern Isles the north of Scotland and the Hebrides. Dating to some period after the 5th century, the early examples with their beautifully controlled forms in a free-running linear design represent both abstract and animal, fish and bird in some long-forgotten hieroglyphic. The symbolic crescents, V rods, Z rods, highly stylised cats, fish and domestic fowls bear a striking resemblance to the marginal drawings in the illuminated Celtic manuscripts such as The Book of Deer, now in Cambridge University Library, but it is a delicate question as to which came first.

When considering the Pictish element in Shetland it is impossible to separate the two major sites of Papil in Burra and St. Ninian's Isle in Dunrossness, nor yet to ignore their previous and subsequent history. Both could equally well be discussed in Stone Age, Iron Age, Bronze Age or Viking contexts, but although it may appear to involve a kind of chronological leap-frog, it is best to introduce them now, along with "The People of the Designs" whose imprint is easily the strongest and most impressive in both these unique and exciting sites.

The two sites of Papil and St. Ninian's Isle are literally inseparable and in the light of recent interpretations, in order to understand fully their relationship, one must return to the excavation of the site on St. Ninian's Isle begun in 1955. The end product, if one might call it that, of this remarkable dig was the revelation of the St. Ninian's Isle Treasure as it came to be known, and for those of us who were fortunate enough to have been in Shetland at that time and occasionally taking part, it was as exciting as though we had discovered it ourselves. It revealed, in retrospect, a cross-section of life from the late Bronze Age, through the Iron Age, the period of the Brochs, into the Wheelhouse phase and on into Viking and medieval times.

The excavation, begun at the suggestion of Dr. W. Douglas Simpson then Librarian of the University of Aberdeen, by a party of students under the guiding hand of the late Professor Andrew C. O'Dell, continued over five summers. The density of burials confirmed local tradition that the church had served not only the island but the neighbouring part of Mainland. Indications of pre-Christian occupation came in the third season when a small area in the centre of the nave revealed at a lower level a mass of domestic and funeral debris. By 1959 an extensive complex of prehistoric walls, pavements and graves was discovered extending well beyond the limits of the excavated area. Most of the structural evidence had been completely destroyed by the intrusion of later pre-Christian and Christian burials and also re-building. Short cists were unearthed containing fragments of urns. One grave contained many small well-rounded quartz pebbles apparently set in a clay floor

21 St. Ninian's Isle, famous as the site of one of the most important archaeological finds of the century: Foula on the horizon and the village of Bigton in the middle distance.

and both cists held burnt and calcined bones suggesting cremation burials. Rim fragments of urns found parallels in Jarlshof, Clickhimin and Underhoull and appeared to fit in to a Broch-period context. The most important find at that level was a necklace of 17 bone-and-antler beads. It was now obvious that beneath the church existed a multi-phased Iron-Age complex of both domestic and sepulchral remains.

From the excavations have come no less than 22 worked stones. The cross-incised or cross-marked stones, all of which are grave markers of one kind or another, fall within the pre-Norse cemetery, or as late as the supposed Norse re-building era when steatite was used. It has been suggested that the ascription to St. Ninian cannot be older than the twelfth century, that neither Ninian nor his pre-Northumbrian successors had anything to do with the north of Scotland, let alone Shetland, but it is admitted that most of the pre-Norse dedications were lost in the divisions that cleft the Christian church life following on the Norse invasions.

The stones found in Papil and in St. Ninian's Isle can now no longer be seen as unrelated fragments but are proved beyond doubt to have been corner and medial posts, once part of shrines related to the early Christian sarcophagi of western Europe and the Mediterranean. The cult of the preservation of the bones of saints in Britain began in the 5th century A.D. Disinterred after a number of years, the remains were then enclosed in some form of box in such a way that either by removing the lid or by way of some aperture the holy, but visible relics could be seen and touched.

Then came the transition in ecclesiastical architecture from wood to masonry, the first perhaps St. Boisil of Old Melrose around 700 A.D. and "solid" shrines standing above opened tombs replaced the wooden "lych-gate" type of structure. The multi-piece stone shrine to which belong both the Papil and the St. Ninian's Isle fragments, and the dedications composed in Pictish Ogam although still mainly untranslatable, suddenly become understandable. Characterised by possessing separate corner stones, side and end panels, the lids were probably flat like the early Christian sarcophagi of western Europe and the Mediterranean. Of the two types of "corner-post" shrine, as they are called, the normal "single" shrine consists of four corner posts each with two grooved and adjacent faces, the grooves taking the lateral edge of the two shorter ends and the two longer sides. The flat slabs of the end and side panels were prepared with "tongues" to engage in the grooves of the corner posts and once fitted together were held rigid by the fixed corner posts, in a "dry-stane" type of structure without mortar. Excluding the lid, the *single* shrine is made up of eight parts, four posts and four panels. A *double* "corner-post" shrine is divided on its shorter axis into two equal compartments with 13 parts, and these *double* stone shrines are so far unique to Shetland. The clue to a double "corner-post" shrine lies in the three-grooved medial post of which no less than three separate posts have been found on St. Ninian's Isle, proving the existence of two of these double shrines, two three-grooved median posts to each shrine. The well-known pictorial side-panel represented in the famous Papil Stone is the decorative long side belonging to a single "corner-post" shrine and the numbers recovered from both sites represents a collection of ecclesiastical stone monuments unparalleled in either Britain or Ireland.

The decorated faces of many of the corner posts are undoubtedly of Pictish design. On one post stylised beasts stand on their tails forming out-turned spirals with two similar spirals repeated below. On another they stand above a triquetra knot their tails curving in in-turning spirals. Other corner posts depict both horizontal and vertical S-scrolls and one a series of cup-marks arranged in diamond form. Although Wilson describes the beasts as "S-dragons", creatures representing the ram-headed serpent, the averter of evil and the guardian of treasure, surviving the transition between paganism and Christianity, it is difficult to regard them as any other than the well-known Pictish "hippo-camp" symbol.

The Monks' Stone which can be seen in Shetland's County Museum in Lerwick, described and figured by Moar and Stewart, represents one of the many narrative Pictish stones designed after the introduction of Christianity to these northern isles. In solemn procession walk four stout monks or holy men in cowled cloaks each bearing a staff or crozier and one distinctly carrying either a holy book or a portable altar slung round his neck. Along with them rides either an elderly man or possibly a bishop, astride a smart-stepping pony, ears pricked forward and complete with bridle and reins. There is a delightful sense of purpose about the little group, headed towards a Cross, symbolising the message they are bringing or the place whereon they intend setting up the Cross itself. Beneath their feet a continuous frieze of double spirals possibly represent the waves of the sea on which so many of them risked their lives.

The Papil Stone (in the Museum of Antiquities in Edinburgh) is a thin, reddish sandstone slab, standing upright, which may well have marked the grave of some notable around A.D. 750. Two-thirds of the stone are taken up with a well-integrated composition headed by a decorative cross, on either side of its shaft a panel with similar monks to those of the Monks' Stone, two on each side facing each other while below an animal in linear design with lolling tongue and upcurved tail is posed realistically, solidly standing on four clawed feet. Although reminiscent of the Pictish wolf, it is apparently a dog similar to that incised on the wall of Johnathan's cave in Fife. On the lower third of the stone and obviously a later addition almost in the form of graffiti, two strangely unbalanced figures with knobbly knees and crane-like

62

bills peck vigorously at a human head, tilted over their shoulders what are described as Germanic axes.

A strong argument for the re-building of local chapelries by Christian Norsemen can be put forward by the presence of five stones from St. Ninian's Isle all made of steatite. There is no steatite on the island but the working of this stone was a favourite Norse activity and the material for the St. Ninian's collection may well have come from the quarry at Catpund near Cunningsburgh. There are cross-marked slabs and cross-shaped slabs and a steatite hog-back grave cover, unornamented but so far without parallel in Shetland.

The only slab which can be called medieval (twelfth century or later) was found face downwards within the nave and is believed to have been a burial within the new enlarged church. A large, flat slab with the incised outline of a cross is now in Bigton Church and a small medieval cresset, the shallow hollow at one end designed to receive oil from a floating lamp wick can be seen in the County Museum.

From the stones alone, found not only in Papil and St. Ninian's Isle, it can be determined how strong the Pictish element was in Shetland of the 8th century. The discoveries at both these places underline the importance of recovering a complete composite shrine, parts of which may easily have been discarded as worthless. Their significance unnoticed, they could be lying among the heaps of rubble still unexplored in Papil or buried in the midst of some röni merely awaiting enlightened recognition. The St. Ninian's Isle Treasure itself strengthens the Pictish position, the first important evidence of non-symbolic Pictish art in metal work.

The hoard, found on July 4th, 1958, close to the centre of the east end of the nave and covered by an irregular sandstone slab with the fragment of an inscribed cross, consisted of 28 pieces of ornamented silver and the jawbone of a porpoise. Enclosed in a box of larchwood, of which only a few fragments survived, it was believed at first to have been part of the church plate hidden at the time of a Viking raid on the monasteries of the Celtic church. There were many similar such incidents especially in Ireland where in 825 St. Blathmac and the monks of Iona took the shrine of St. Columba and buried it in the earth covered with a thick layer of turf. St. Blathmac himself was murdered because he refused to disclose its hiding place but part of the Iona community escaped and later recovered the shrine.

Certainly the hoard on St. Ninian's Isle had been hastily buried, the objects tumbled together, the bowls inverted, all suggesting a moment of panic. Its owners never returned to retrieve it and many burials throughout the centuries must have missed it by inches. It seems highly improbable that Vikings, always eager for rich prizes, would plan a deliberate raid on such a tiny and insignificant church, but one can imagine the situation should Viking ships be sighted, perhaps off Channerwick, one of the earliest settlements, the news spreading throughout the district. A local Pictish chief, realising that though he might not save his cattle, he could at least try to dispose of the family treasures, may have bundled them up together, roughly, demanding even the brooches that the men and women of the tribe were wearing and tumbling them into a box probably put together from driftwood, hurried off to the only safe place he could think of, the church on St. Ninian's Isle. We do not know whether he would have to stumble across a narrow ayre, his feet slipping in the deep sand or launch his primitive boat and row with a desperation born of necessity. Time must have been short and one wonders whether the monks who perhaps helped him conceal it then left with him to take to the hills or fall victim as he obviously must have done, to a roving band of piratical Vikings. No one can have been left who remembered the event for through all the years of future building and re-building the hoard remained where he had placed it.

Owing largely to the fact that the treasure was found in sacred ground the theory that it was composed of church plate was immediately accepted, and cannot yet be ignored. The six drinking bowls of silver, carefully wrapped in a cloth, were regarded as the chalices; the hemispherical bowl as being used in the washing of hands and the hanging bowl, the first complete one to be found in Scotland was regarded as a votive chalice. The many brooches were ascribed to liturgical vestments, the largest like that of Columcille, part of his official insignia along with the chapes as stole-ends, the inscription on one side of one of them even reading *In Nomine Dei Summa*. The spoon and pronged instrument were identified as a communion spoon for the administration of the Eucharist and as a fork or knife for use in the breaking of bread and the silver pommel and other silver fittings were believed to belong to a eucharistic flabellum.

The definitive account of the treasure published in 1973 for the University of Aberdeen and compiled by Alan Small, Charles Thomas, David Wilson and others, is designed to prove beyond doubt that the hoard was a secular one. Each object has been scrutinised, photographed and elaborated upon, the reasoning behind their deductions seemingly irrefutable. Within the compass of the 28 silver objects are elements from all the major areas of insular art relating in style to Ireland, Pictland, Northumbria, Mercia, southern England and a strong Celtic style not produced in Ireland.

The brooches are certainly of Pictish origin made in the late 8th century and influenced by the true pennanular type as distinct from the

64

Irish ring-headed pin. Developed in Britain during the La Tène period, the earliest examples date from the third century B.C. and the distribution of these objects coincides remarkably with the areas of Pictish symbol stones. All are made from rather debased silver, cast and finished by hand tooling and were apparently worn by both men and women. A series of clay moulds for brooches of true pennanular form and found at the Brough of Birsay in Orkney are similar in every respect to the examples found on St. Ninian's Isle save that they are smaller.

The seven bowls are unique in Scotland and are regarded as tableware, most likely drinking bowls. Shallow drinking bowls were known and used throughout Europe and there are 8th- and 9th-century examples from Denmark. In the great burial of Sutton Hoo were ten bowls of Mediterranean origin and in another 7th-century find from Kuczurmare in the U.S.S.R. seven shallow bowls with rounded bases, a beaker-shaped bowl and a straight-sided silver vessel bearing the control-stamp of the Emperor Heraklios (610–41) were all secular objects. Two of the St. Ninian's Isle bowls however bear friezes of punched animal ornament and no other such animal friezes are known from Celtic vessels in Scotland. From all these examples the most important point which emerges is the striking similarity to the stone sculptures of Pictland where there is an almost complete absence of metalwork, and to the indisputable fact that Pictish stone art remains a vital, eclectic style standing in its own right and reflected irrefutably in the silverwork from St Ninian's Isle.

The hanging bowl, one of only three examples fashioned in silver known out of 150 specimens, is believed to be the ancient equivalent of the modern finger bowl, its richly decorated interior scarcely likely to be darkened by oil, and most likely in these days of sparse household furnishings without cupboards and shelves, hung up when not in use as a form of decoration.

The spoon is without parallel but with the loop for suspension at its tip we can only surmise that it was hung, along with the claw-like object from the girdle like the pierced spoons of the pagan Anglo-Saxon period, as much an adjunct to dress as the varied objects suspended from the waist-chain of a contemporary Norsewoman. The pommels and chapes are identified in Wilson's book as sword fittings, the inscription *In Nomine Dei Summa*—"In the name of God the Highest" on one side, a known and much used Latin formula. On the other side *Resadfilispusscio* can be translated only as "this is the property of Resad, son of Spusscio". From many other Pictish inscriptions it will be seen that, as with their incredible symbol stones, of which the hieroglyphics are undecipherable, the names are also in a language as yet unintelligible.

The suggestion that the silver pommel and the three other silver

22   The Little Kame, Foula.

fitting belonged to a eucharistic flabellum appears to be almost untenable when one reads that a flabella was used to keep flies away from consecrated wine and that the first recorded usage of such an object in western Europe came 50 years later than the date of the object in question from St. Ninian's Isle. The cones are considered in Wilson's book as more elaborate versions of the bone discs from other parts of Scotland, in effect as belt buttons for sword belts fastened with thongs, and the fact that all are heavily worn at the top gives credence to the supposition.

The tragedy for Shetland lies in the fact that only replicas of the treasure have been allowed to remain in the Museum in Lerwick. Had the finds been displayed in the county of their origin they might have remained not only as an inspiration to future archaeologists but an attraction, unique not only to Shetland, but to the whole of Britain and obviously a rarity for the entire archaeological world.

Long before the Scandinavians arrived, from the Gaelic west, from Scotland and Ireland came the first of a long line of missionaries of the Celtic church, possibly around the sixth century A.D. The first individual Christians in Scotland could have been legionaries, auxiliaries or camp followers from the eastern provinces of the Roman Empire as early as the second century A.D. It is around the close of the fourth century, however, that we hear of Scotland's first saint, Ninian of Whithorn. Bede says that Nynia was a Briton, a bishop who had been regularly instructed in the faith "at Rome." As one writer put it, "Where Rome had failed with the Sword, she returned to conquer by the Cross" and the Apostle of the Picts, a Romano-British provincial, a Roman citizen who had travelled widely in the western empire and established his monastery at Candida Casa, now Whithorn, in 397 among a partly-Romanised community.

St. Ninian's mission to the Britons and the Picts, whether deliberately or coincidentally, follows almost in the exact footsteps of the Roman legions. From Candida Casa the mission flowed north to the Clyde basin at Glasgow, by St. Ninian's at Stirling and up Strathmore by Arbirlot and Dunnottar; establishing an important station at Andet of Methlick, reaching the Great Glen at St. Ninian's Cell and penetrating as far north as Navidale in Sutherland. In the Celtic church the monastic centres and the outlying cells maintained by them were consistently named after the founder of the parent monastery, so that although in Shetland we have St. Ninian's Isle, this bears no more proof that he himself was ever on the spot than St. Ronans which simply shows the influence of Kingarth. Archaeologically, however, the presence of the ogham stone at the site of the chapel on this tiny island provides a genuine relic of the Celtic church on St. Ninian's Isle, an extension in fact of the traditional line of penetration from Strathclyde. Moreover, we can trace a series of equal-armed and often wheeled crosses carved on slabs, inspired by the early *Chi-Rho* stones at Whithorn, as far as Bressay in Shetland and beyond the Scottish area on to the Faroe Islands.

Now the Picts of the eastern coast preferred the slab cross rather than the cross free-standing and they adhered to the ancient equal-armed pattern. On the Bressay Stone both on the front and on the back of the slab we have an equal-armed cross within a circle, the arms expanded and the spaces in between filled with interlacing. On the Papil Stone the same form of cross appears but this time set upon a pedestal. Celtic slab crosses, some of of equal-armed and wheeled designs, are also found in the Faroes which goes far to substantiate the statement that St. Kentigern sent out missionaries "towards Iceland" and it was concluded that the cross slabs on the east coast were earlier and conceived under a different influence from that which gave form to the Irish crosses.

There is no doubt, however, that the Ninianic school was not the only influence brought to bear on the Northern Isles although it may well have been the first. Around the end of the 5th century in Ireland arose a different kind of Christian outlook born in the desert lands around the eastern Mediterranean and transmitted to the British Isles. Monks (*monachi*—solitaries) who had taken personal vows of poverty, chastity or solitude, formed an early feature of Christian life, a reaction against the temptation and delights of pagan Rome.

As far as Shetland is concerned St. Columba's missionaries are believed to be attested in the place name of Clumlie with its ancient *kurkifield (kirkfield)* and the exploratory zeal of the monks of Iona could well be perpetuated in Shetland as well as Orkney where Cormac had to obtain a safe conduct to visit that stronghold of the Picts.

Just as the Picts themselves were recognised by the Norse so were the Christian missionaries known as Papae, from whichever church they originated, the name surviving in the island of Papa Stour, *Papa ey Storr* (the big island of the priests) in Papa Little, Papa Geo and Papilwater. Sadly for the historian the Pictish language and the obvious meaningfulness of its art forms will probably never be translated. The classical education maintained by the Irish priests would gradually override Pictish, just as the Scottish tongue was to almost obliterate the ancient Norn 800 years later when Orkney and Shetland were pledged to the Scottish Crown and the Pictish church devastated by the Norse invasions of the 8th and 9th centuries, leaving the way open for the infiltration of Scotic Romanised clerks after the union of Pictland and Dalriada in 843.

23 Boats laid up inland from Ham Voe Foula, the steep shoulder of Hamnafjeld rising behind.

Nothing even faintly resembling the artistic code of symbolism of the Picts is known anywhere else in the world, and between the 5th and 10th centuries there developed this elaborate rigidly conventional sculptured language to which no solution has been found. From Shetland to Aberdeenshire and Mortlach to the Outer Isles this ideographic art was once understood, as articulate as the spoken word. Like the Picts themselves, it arose "like Pallas from the head of Zeus" apparently fully developed, only to end completely like other relics peculiar to the Pictish area; the massive double silver chains, the embossed armlets, the carved stone balls and even the brochs, almost the sole proof of the existence of the Picts as a people.

Missionary activity continued from Ireland as well as Iona from the time of Columba onwards and Gaelic-speaking missionaries did come to the Northern Isles at an early period. To a Gaelic speaker even Dunrossness, hitherto accepted by Shetlanders as meaning "the headland of the dinning röst" from the Old Norn, would be "Dun-ros" "promontory of the fortified settlement" which it would certainly appear to be at that time even although the broch had been partly destroyed. In fact *ros* in Gaelic and *ness* in Norse mean virtually the same thing and the duplication is quite in order as eventually Norse replaced the language of the country, whatever it may have been.

Many names in Shetland, including those listed as definitely Celtic in origin, are known to have been accepted into Scandinavian speech at an early date. Words like *airigh*, meaning hill pasture; *cnoc*—hillock and *coirce*—oats, are found in places such as Lancashire, Cheshire, Cumberland and Galloway, areas which never had a Pictish population but were early subjected in the tenth century to an immigratory

69

movement of Scandinavian settlers coming immediately from Ireland, Man and the Western Isles, who had been Gaelicised to the extent that they had adopted certain Gaelic words and habits of place-naming.

Fair Isle, halfway between North Ronaldsay or North Ringansay, North Ninian's Isle and Dunrossness in Shetland, which also has its St. Ninian's Isle, has a place in the north of the island facing Dunrossness called Roskilie, pronounced almost exactly like the Gaelic Roscille. Girvan McKay, who made a study of Gaelic names in Shetland visited the place Roskilie, being certain that it must have been an early missionary settlement. On the exact spot marked on the map he found a circle of embedded stones and an old stone dyke. On the south side of the road appeared groups of circular remains not unlike the crumbled stones of roundhouses or brochs.

The earliest known Christian place of worship on Fair Isle is said to have been the Church of the Holy Rood on a site now called Kirkless. Not far from Roskilie are the Geo (Geodha) and Heids of Peitron. This could be a corruption of Priton, i.e. Briton or Pict. So Roskilie may have been the site of a Gaelic-speaking mission to the Pictish inhabitants in the north of Fair Isle. There, Gaels may have given the name Burrian (Irish, Boireann) to a rock in the south-east of the island. In the south is a site known as Sallik Hoose, a corruption of the word meaning a lazar house or leper asylum. A further place of interest in Fair Isle place names is Malcolm's Heid, a high promontory on the west side. Old maps show the name as Mekum's Heid, which according to Fair Islanders is simply the local pronunciation of Malcolm which in Gaelic is *Maolcholluim*, "the tonsured one of St. Colum", perhaps the name of the monk who built the cell at Roskilie or named after the monastery of his origin—Iona.

So on another lonely island a man lived out his self-imposed banishment. Did his disciples reward him with the visible signs of their new-found faith? Or did he like so many others comfort himself with composing poems of exile, like one written so long ago in the early years of missionary endeavour, dreaming perhaps guiltily of home:

> My tidings for you: the stag bells,
> Winter snows, summer is gone.
> Wind high and cold, low the sun,
> Short his course, sea running high.
> Deep red the bracken, its shape all gone,
> The wild geese has raised his wonted cry.
> Cold has caught the wings of the birds;
> Season of ice—these are my tidings.

9. *West over Sea*

"'FIRST IS THE Air o'Grottin (Wick of Gruting). It was where the first Norse ship that came to the West landed. The date is said to have been A.D. 664 ... and from there they peopled Grottin and Finne (Funzie) and Strande. So Grottin claims to be the earliest Norse colony in the West ... To return to Fetlar, there were graves of men slain in battle and they were of the kind belonging to the Viking time. So it is probable that the former people left Fetlar ...

"There were many udal families and an old tradition said that all the patronymic families in Fetlar belonged to one family...it was to this family...that our folk belonged. The udaller at North Dale in 1600 was Olaf Nicholson...." These words were written by that remarkable man, Laurence Williamson of Mid Yell in 1922 and I have deliberately set them down thus for they could well be spoken by any born and bred Shetlander today. Even taking into account Scots immigration figures since the sixteenth century, it has been calculated that on the island of Whalsay alone, with a population of nearly 1000, the admixture of Scots and English blood is only about eight per cent—the number of immigrants at the present time is not quite five per cent. Fetlar, Yell, Northmavine and Delting, all even further off the beaten track, are probably of purer blood. Except for Lerwick there has never been any Scots invasion sufficient to alter radically the Norse blood of the Shetlanders. That is what everyone would like to believe but incredible though it may sound there is a great deal of truth in it and no people then or since have made such an impact racially and otherwise upon these islands as the Norse.

There is no reason either to dispute Williamson's assumption of such an early date. The old Norse name for the Picts, Shetland's earlier inhabitants, whom they called *Petta*, must have arrived before A.D. 700. Already by A.D. 500 Scandinavia had begun the long series of eruptions culminating in "the Viking Age" which was to last from the 8th to the 11th centuries, when the men of Norway, Sweden and Denmark became the most influential ethnic group in western Europe.

The Kvalsund ship, built and used during the 6th to the 8th centuries, was most probably the first to voyage across the North Sea, its replica incised on slate and found at Jarlshof.

Other groups, either as families moving out from the wild and rocky coast of Bergen, from Sognefjord, More and Trondelag, desperately seeking a decent area of arable land which they could call their own, or unscrupulous adventurers out to prey on the sea traffic in hides, furs and sea-ivory, could eventually have come ashore in Shetland, in Fetlar as easily as Unst, these tentative launchings the precursors of the later massive outpourings of the Scandinavian peoples to be feared collectively as Vikings, Rus, Danes or Norromen from the North Cape to the Pillars of Hercules, from Newfoundland to Byzantium.

Everything must have a beginning. Skilled shipbuilders and incomparable sailors from the earliest days, at some point a landless younger son, an exiled Norseman or an explorer well in advance of his time, but in whom the sap of future warlike aristocrats was already rising, set out from Hjeltefjorden, where he would have the most favourable crossing of the North Sea, to become the first Viking in Shetland.

Positive evidence from archaeological finds, substantiated in many cases by linguistic affinities, point with absolute certainty to the districts in Norway from whence came both Shetland and Orkney's ancestry. From modern Kristiansand, the coastal areas of south-west Agder, all up the rugged fjords of western Norway as far as north Trondelag bordering the great cleft of Trondheimsfjord, they set out in search of new lands in which to settle.

When the Vikings made their first appearance on the world's stage they were pagans and as such abhorrent to the Church, which naturally recorded fire, murder, pillage (*herja*) and little else. As explorers looking for new lands to settle or conquer, the Vikings behaved much as they would do at home—they practised *strand-hogg*, a recognised method of providing themselves with fresh meat at sea. When the need arose they simply sailed into the nearest fjord and killed someone else's cattle. If there was loot there for the taking so much the better, and loot there was in plenty overseas, where the Church had already built up a veritable treasure house of gold and silver plate, rich vestments and reliquaries. The sacking of monasteries was deliberate, sought out as offering no resistance, the booty spiritually meaningless but of considerable earthly value, and the monks, like sickly women in their long robes, brought upon themselves insult added to injury by being unarmed instead of standing on their feet and defending themselves like men.

The raids that inspired the prayer in the churches of England and Northern France: "From the wrath of the Northmen, O Lord deliver us!" stemmed virtually from an admixture of land hunger, piracy and

72

24   Vaila Sound with Foula on the horizon.

trade. It is the latter however, that is so often ignored, and between
the 8th and 11th centuries the Scandinavian peoples made their impact
felt in markets from the Baltic to Russia in Novgorod and Kiev; down
the Volga and the Dneiper to the Caspian Sea, the Black Sea and Constantinople; west and south to England, France, the Netherlands, Germany, Spain, Portugal; through the Straits of Gibraltar to Italy and
the Mediterranean; west and north to Scotland, Ireland and the
Hebrides, Orkney and Shetland, the Faroes, Iceland, Greenland and
even North America.

"The Norwegians supplied timber to Iceland, Icelanders supplied
Eirik the Red in Greenland with meal and corn, and Greenlanders
supplied coloured cloth to the broad-cheeked inhabitants of America.
From America come unblemished pelts and timber to Greenland and
Iceland and from these countries woollens, seal oil, sea ivory, fats, fal-
cons, back to the marts of Scandinavia whence they were dispersed
southwards through Europe." Across the Irish Sea Norse merchants

73

maintained a brisk trade in Welsh slaves, horses, honey, malt and wheat and Irish or Irish-imported wine. In A.D. 991 a treaty was signed between Olaf Tryggvason and King Ethelred in an endeavour to guarantee the safety of foreign merchant ships, their crews and cargoes, in English estuaries, together with full respect for English ships encountered abroad by the Vikings.

Through all this complex labyrinth of trade and conquest the Scandinavians required safe bases and sound havens from which to set off and return, accessibility for the merchants who used them and protection from the pirates who from the Baltic ravaged the coasts of southern Norway. Norse farmers dared not move far from their weapons when out in the fields and the crew of a merchantman regarded every sail as an enemy until proved otherwise. It was from the Baltic that Olaf Tryggvason prepared his raid on Flanders and England with an army of Norse, Danes, Goths and Slavs, the subsequent outcome of which was the conquest of England by the Danish kings Svein and Knut in 1013.

Although Orkney and Shetland would have little to offer in the way of trade goods and were scarcely worth ravaging they provided a remarkably convenient stepping stone. Already largely Norse, the islands became a home from home, invaluable as a midway point between Norway, the Western Isles and Ireland. Not the least of Shetland's attractions was the magnificent natural harbour of Bressay Sound where in 1263 King Haakon's war galleys were to assemble on their way to the Battle of Largs, an indecisive engagement against King Alexander III of Scotland.

The enigma of the Viking is made even more complex when trying to unravel the characteristics that laid down the roots of the people of the northern isles, by his consciousness of beauty, his love of personal adornment and his outstanding ability in fields far removed from warlike pursuits. "I am a keen player at *tafl* ('tables', a hunt-game sometimes confused with chess);" said Rognvald Kali, jarl of Orkney, "nine skills I know; hardly will I make a mistake with runes, I have books and crafts constantly in hand; I can glide on skis, shoot and row, to meet any occasion; I am master of the two arts of harping and poetry."

Then abruptly we are plunged into the absolute antithesis of these idyllic cultural pursuits in Egill Skallagrimsson's praise of Eirik Bloodaxe in his "Head-ransom":

> Swordmetal pealed
> on rim of shield;
> Strife round him reeled

Who ranged that field.
Heard was the yell
Of bladefury fell,
Ironstorm's knell
Past far sea's swell.

King reddened sword,
Came ravens a horde.
Bright lifeblood outpoured
As shafts flew abroad.
Scot's scourge bade feed
Trollwife's wolfsteed,
Hel trod with her feet
The eagles' nightmeat.

Bright fame he gat,
Eirik from that.
Eirik o'er sea
Paid the wolves' fee.

Yet these were the people who left a whole iconography, a unique art-style which made its influence felt on stone sculptures, ivory carvings and even the illuminated manuscripts of Christian Britain. Few everyday objects escaped ornamentation. Elaborate interlaced patterns of gripping beasts, animal heads, the eight-legged horse, Sleipnir; sensitive naturalistic ornament and strikingly original abstract-covered gilt bridle mounts, silver cups, rectangular brooches, sword hilts, leather belts ends, helmets and amulets. Delicate and intricate wood carvings, yet vivid and robust, climb up the swan-necked prows of ships like the ceremonial Oseberg ship and its votive wagon. This art form persisted until the end of the Viking age and examples found well within the interior of so many of the countries associated with their passage reveal, as little else can do, a long and often peaceful contact.

Outstanding in everything they did, the Vikings were immortalised in innumerable sagas, brilliant, bloodthirsty, heady stuff, but compiled by twelfth- and thirteenth-century Icelandic historians, intended to glorify, absolve and perpetuate deeds of valour, individual earls, king and warriors and as such factually suspect. Shetland never attained even the importance of Orkney in the stories, being occasionally and almost casually mentioned and yet it was Shetland that remained longest under Norse influence. Shetland has no St. Magnus Cathedral but it has its Jarlshof. There are many more Norse relics in Orkney but recent discoveries in Shetland suggest that skilled excavation could reveal infinitely more, and over the entire sphere of almost world-wide

Scandinavian connection nowhere is her influence more obvious than in the Shetland Islands.

Overshadowing anything that had gone before, it is the one great culture, that, surviving up to the present day, is in most danger of being lost forever. On Shetland the Norsemen left a remarkable impression, one that outlasted all others, that was to prove the most formative period in the history of the Northern Isles. They brought to Shetland the udal system, a structure of society that even outlived for a time the transfer of the islands to the Scottish crown. Above all they implanted their language so strongly that it speedily usurped whatever tongue had preceded it, absorbing only a few words mainly of Gaelic-Celtic origin and carrying these southwards as far as northern England.

In Orkney today 99 per cent of the farm names are of Norse origin; Foula place names are predominantly Norse with about 80 Scots words or hybrids to 800 Norse, while the Shetland vocabulary deriving from Old Norn covers everything from place names, sea names, animals, household objects and descriptions of people. Although much has been lost and Norn as a language now forgotten, enough remains in a wealth of imagery, place names and expressions to make an immediate and startling impact on even the most casual visitor, while at least 1000 years after the landing of the first Norseman on Shetland the Scandinavian can feel completely at home.

This word colonisation, if one might describe it thus, is not only widespread in place names in a general sense, in villages, voes and districts, but bound up in the most tender and intimate way with terms of endearment, nicknames, expressions of anger or even humorous behaviour. Each tiny hill, rock, brook, piece of field or meadow, every holm, skerry and corn rig bears still its old Scandinavian name handed down in the Norn tongue. Like clues in a crossword, these names can be traced to certain districts in Norway, and centuries later, although overlaid and distorted by Scottish spelling and interpretation, or in many cases obsolete, there are thousands of words still extant or in the memory of the old, quite intelligible to any Norse-speaker.

The wind, the weather, the sea names and the parts of boats, the colour of cows and sheep, the croft and its construction, farm implements, are so immutably Scandinavian, a Shetlander's speech so impregnated with Norn roots, that the scale and intensity of the Norse settlements can almost be summarised as a mass migration. Pure Norn survived in a fragmentary state in the memories of older inhabitants up to the very end of the nineteenth century and Dr. Jakobsen who made a classic study of Shetlandic Norn, was able to list more than 50,000 words, many of them no longer in daily use, and according to

76

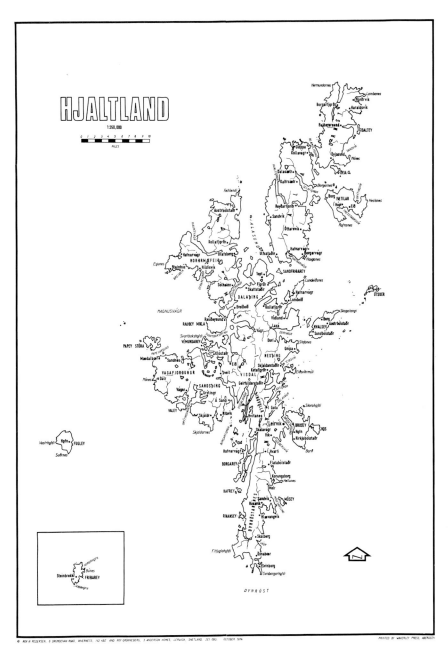

Shetland: the old Norn place names (reproduced by kind permission of Mr. Roy
Gruneberg and Mr. Roy N. Pederson). For a map of the modern place names, see
page 98.

most estimates a conservative one, while Dr. Marwick traced a similar list for Orkney, discovering that the speech of the Northern Isles was closer even than Faroese or Icelandic to modern Norwegian.

The subjugation was complete in every aspect and the sheer poetry and evocative imagery of the ensuing Norn is a continuing delight to trace, to study and sometimes still to hear in everyday speech like some faint echo of a livelier and infinitely more expressive past. Even customs have survived to a large extent unchanged, from the Shetland boat, clinker-built, its earliest prototype exported from Norway and assembled locally. A glance at Dunrossness yoals in the scattered boat *noosts* reveals at once the high tapered prow and stern. The proportions remain the same but where the Norwegian boat had five strakes from keel to gunwale the Shetland-built yoal has six.

The Shetland croft house has derived directly from the Norse long-house, remains of which can be seen in the Viking-Age settlement at Jarlshof dating from the beginning of the 9th century. It was the first viking house to be recognised in the British Isles and revealed a complex of buildings without parallel in Britain, the whole extending well into the fourteenth century. The original dwelling, a two-roomed house, measured some 70 feet by 20 feet with its longitudinal walls curving slightly inwards at the ends exactly like some of the small outbuildings seen today roofed by tarred, upturned boats. One end served as a kitchen or *eldhus* with oven and fireplace. The living room, *stofa*, lay east of the main doorway and on the north side of the floor can be seen the dais or *pallr* on which tables and beds were placed. Originally the long rectangular stone-lined hearth or *langeldr* occupied the centre of the floor.

Its builders probably came from the More, Trondelag, districts of Norway, for an incised slate found on the floor bore the outline of a ship like the Kvalsund boat of these coastal districts in use between the 7th and 8th centuries. Beside the house were four outbuildings, including a byre, a smithy and one which could either have served as a temple or bath-house. Baths and bath-houses are frequently mentioned in the old Icelandic sagas. *Baostofa* in ON (Old Norse) means a bathroom or bath-house and there is a patch of ground in Fetlar called "*de Bastivvategs*", literally "the bath-house rigs", proof that such places quite commonly existed.

The *Havamal* tells of guests being met at the table by their hosts, "with water, a towel and a hearty welcome". Certainly they were expected to appear at the *Thing*, or Parliament, "freshly washed" and Saturday was apparently relegated to bath night, all of which is in direct contrast to the description of the *Rus* or Vikings by the Arabs, who, having very recently received detailed instructions on personal hygiene from the

Prophet himself, through the writings in the Holy Quran (commands still carried out with fanatical zeal), were wholly disgusted at the personal habits of the *Rus*. The Danes in England however "combed their hair, had a bath on Saturdays and changed their linen frequently, in order to the more easily overcome the chastity of women and procure the daughters of noblemen as their mistresses", which makes rather a nonsense of the old maxim that cleanliness is next to godliness!

The survival of the customs of the Norse farmer settlers at Jarlshof in even the most homely details up to at least the beginning of the present century is remarkable. Small bone bits found in the Viking settlement had been tied into the lambs' mouths to prevent them sucking the milk from the ewes. This custom was used in times of hardship in Foula and other districts when the lambs which had reached a certain stage of growth were "*Kavilled*". A wooden stick was tied in their mouths and overnight they were separated from the ewes or *yogurts* which were then milked in the morning and the milk given to the children. The word *Kavill* comes from either ON *kefli* a wooden stick, or *kavlin-tree*, applied to a stick with a notch in the end for taking the hook out of a fish's mouth or stomach. In Foula too survived the old custom of lambo-tiende and the great-grandfather of a Foula man with several daughters left each of them a mare and a foal and 15 yowes. Today, children of Foula folk are still given a lamb when they are "named" or when they cut their first tooth.

The hand quern was still used at the beginning of the present century and only in the mid-nineteenth century was the old Norse type of scythe and single stilted plough replaced. The Shetland water mill, unique in Britain, with a horizontal wheel, straddled every burn capable of turning it, often several in a row down its course, a Norse design unchanged over hundreds of years. *Rivlins*, soft home-made shoes of cowhide with the hair still on, shaped rather like moccasins were still made and worn all over Shetland between the Wars and two Norse implements are still with us, the Shetland spade and the *tushkar*. The Shetland spade is only very occasionally used in small areas too restricted for a tractor but the *tushkar* comes out every spring when the peat "casting" begins. A long narrow-bladed instrument, its name is again Norse—*torfskerri*. A certain amount of skill and experience is required in handling it correctly.

More than half a score of words occur in place names which signify to some extent "enclosure" or "a piece of enclosed land". The fascination lies in the colourful use of the names to denote the different purposes for which the enclosures were originally built, usually for animals, and frequently one can still trace the remains of a dyke although here again the islander's propensity for using whatever material lies nearest

25 The three Setters or "saetr" (ᴏɴ mountain pasture—often in Shetland getting their names from the animals pastured there). In the foreground is Williamsetter: in the centre distance Ellister, and just visible in the distance is the little loch of Vatster (vatn = a lake, the corresponding place name in Norway being Vatstadr).

at hand for new buildings, or even using old stone foundations over again, tends to obliterate much that might be archaeologically valuable.

The name Garth or Gord (Goard) often occurs in the names of old towns, farms or crofts, coming from the ON *garo-r*, dyke or yard, a piece of ground with a house on it "The beautiful yard" in Aithsting is Fogrigarth; Efstegarth, meaning the uppermost yard or farm, is found in the Norse udal law defined in old Shetland property deeds dated 1554 as being "*fra da effste stein i field till den neste i fjoren*" ("from the highest stone in the hill to the lowest on the beach" thus defining the extent of property, again remaining in its original form after the Scottish "take-over" of the islands. The old Norse name for Constantinople was *Mykligaror*, in Shetland *Mukligarth*, meaning the big yard or enclosure. In south Yell we find a house called Galtigarth, once an enclosure for pigs or *gauts* and in the south of Foula there is Grisigarth, from *grice* or pigs, meaning the pigs' yard; Hestingarth, the horse enclosure and all over Shetland Lammigarth, the lamb enclosure.

One of the most familiar of Shetland place names, many of which are common to both Orkney and Shetland, is *bolstaor*, from ON "farm", and accounting for Fladdabister, Isbister and Symbister, which together with such descriptive terms as *slakki* (hollow, shallow valley); *bakki* (bank) and the common *brekka* (slope, hill) all point to certain well-defined areas of Norway. Other tests of specifically Norse influence are the many inversion compounds, place names in which the second element defines the first in the Celtic manner, such as Quoybernardis as against Angusquoy, adopted by the Norse from the Gaelic before the end of the 9th century and carried with them into north-west England and south-west Scotland.

A third word denoting an enclosure is *toon*, from ON *tun*, a piece of cultivated ground such as *de Hametoun* in Foula, just as in the south of Mainland, Bigton would be "an inhabited place" from *bygo, bygga*, to build but locally it is Bighton—the Tun at the Bight and not far away in Dunrossness is a township called *Bo*, or *Exnaboe*, originally a grazing place for oxen. When the Scots arrived they put their own interpretation on many Norn words. The district of Walls is an outstanding example. They heard the Shetlanders calling it *Waas*—Scots for walls—whereas it was indeed *Vaas*, the place of voes! Even Bigton was often written Bigtown.

All over the islands you will find "seters" (summer pastures), appearing as plain Setter, Williamsetter, Ellister, Vatster, Aithsetter, Voxter, Geosetter, pronounced Geoster. The derivation comes from ON *saetr* the mountain pasture, still commonly used in Norway where the cattle are taken into the mountains to upland pastures when the snow has gone, the herdsmen staying in huts on the lower slopes until they are brought down again in the autumn, a common practice in mountainous regions from the Alps to the Hindu Khush. Many of the Shetland *saetrs* get their names from the animals pastured there such as Colvister in Yell, (calf-seter); Marrister in Whalsay, (the mare-seter) and in Walls we find Swinister, quite obviously the swine-seter.

Hoga, (ON *haga*) can mean a piece of hill or uncultivated land enclosed for pasture, called until very recently the *scattald*, with the scat or land tax payable on it in the fifteenth century. In Whiteness there is Hogan, in Fetlar, Lambhoga. The word also occurs in some interesting conversational phrases such as *hoga-leave* (ON hogaloyfi) meaning the liberty to cut peats or graze animals on another scattald for a certain payment. To ride the *hagri* was a custom when neighbouring proprietors would ride in company round their scattald properties to inspect the marches or dykes. Every year they took a different boy with them, the son of a crofter living in one or other of the districts concerned. At every march stone the boy got a flogging, a rather hard way of making sure that he remembered the boundaries, so that when all these boys grew up, even should one of them have died, there would always be someone to refer to in case of dispute. This practice is described in the Statistical Account of the Shetland Islands by the minister for Tingwall, Whiteness and Weisdale who notes that the unfortunate boys "received some little award" for their floggings.

26 Building *dusses*, Williamsetter: Mr. and Mrs. Duncan are gathering up all the loose strands of hay and later the *dusses* will be taken home and built into *skroos* to stand, netted for winter feeding for the animals. Some of these, already built, can be seen on the right—in the background are peat stacks.

If each hillock, burn and holm had its name there were also countless names describing the colours of animals, all of which had an important part to play in the life of the community. In spring time the cattle were driven to the hills to pasture there until the harvest was over so that they might be kept out of the growing crops. After the crops were in, the gates were opened, a practice known as "slipping" the *okrigarth* (from *okri* ON *akr* meaning corn field) and *garth*, enclosure. The word "slipping" is still in use, signifying "to let out". "Slipping" a yowe could mean unfastening its tether or letting it out of the field. When on the hills, the cattle, sheep, swine and geese would wander at will. Cows still had to be milked and ponies and sheep were then almost as important to the crofter as fishing, so that no one thought anything of walking several miles, but unless every spot on the hill had its own distinctive name, to say nothing of an unmistakable description of the animals in question, probably each one different from the other, then the search might take hours.

A girl could ask someone coming from the hill: "Did du see my mooret hog ony wye?" "Did du see my blaiget yowe yestreen?" "Did du licht in wi my katmoget gimmer?" The person in question could immediately give the specific point at which the animal had been seen and from its description would know exactly which one was missing. *Moget, katmoget*, refers according to Jakobsen to a separate colour of the belly but in Dunrossness it is determinedly asserted as meaning a separate colour of the face. It is a small point but fascinating in derivation for *magi* is ON for belly—and *muggie* in Shetland is undoubtedly the stomach (of a fish). *Sholmet* is applied to a cow whose face is a different colour from its body with delightful Norse connotation of *hjalmr-* meaning helmet. A *sponget* coo is a cow covered with patches of colour different to that of its body. *Shaila* is a grey shade through black, applied generally to a sheep, really meaning hoar-frost, which gives the earth a delicate light colour, an expressive way of describing the grey on a darker body ground.

Expressions denoting the most subtle gradations of sulkiness, for instance, are endless, full of quaint symbolism and frequently humorous. Talking about an awkward character one will say, "He kyust him up intill a dulheit", or "he kjust a dulheit ower him" meaning that he threw a hiding hat over him, from ON *dyl-hottre* or *hattr*, and usually applied to someone who under some feigned pretence or other refuses to do what he had promised or been bidden. In the same way, degrees vary from a person being "*trumsket*"; *snusket, trullyet* or *trulshket*, all words defining sulkiness or obduracy. The two latter mean "trowie-like", from ON *troll* the supernatural beings known as *trows* in Shetland, who can be both awkward, obstinate and "ill-fashioned" as we might say in Scotland. Places inhabited by trows are quite common. There is Troyhoolen in Sandness meaning "the trows' knoll"; Trolliwater and Trolli Geo, the latter in Foula, Trolli Geo in Fair Isle, the loch of the trows and the trows or trolls' geo.

It was only natural that the sea should have provided an enormous number of words in Norn, most of which survive today, for sea traditions die hard and many of the names collected by Jakobsen are still vividly alive and understood. We still speak of the men who once went to the *haav* or the *far haaf*, from the Norn words *hav* meaning ocean. In pagan times people believed in the sea-god Aegir, who with his attendant minor spirits watched intruders in his element. The greatest care therefore was taken not to offend him and a number of mystic words were used by those who ventured out on the haaf, to a great extent agreed amongst themselves, although the main derivation was Norn.

Norn survived in nautical language due mainly to the reluctance of seagoing folk not only in Shetland but in Norway and the Faroes to use certain words at sea. A large number of names were *tabu*, so a special language which differed from ordinary speech was used exclusively when in a boat. This Shetland tradition is unique and in few places was this linguistic peculiarity so richly and consistently developed.

All fishermen have distrusted the presence of a minister on board. In early times the minister and the church represented the new faith which condemned the old gods, thus challenging the domination of the sea-god and were given names of their own. The church would be referred to as *de beni-hoose* (from ON bon-hoos) in Foula the minister was always called *de upstander*, in other districts *de beniman* (the prayer man) or the *predikanter*. All these words were poetic, mostly figurative in that they symbolised the characteristics of the person or animal to which they referred.

The cat had a great variety of sea-names, graphic, evocative and intensely realistic, such as *de foodin*, or *footer*, the lightfooted animal—*fittin* in Foula; *de rammi* derived from *raam*, *krammock*, paw, especially a cat's paw, from ON *hrammr*, meaning a paw of a beast of prey. Different districts in Shetland use their own derivations which also complicates ordinary speech, for even a few miles apart there appear diverse turns of phrase and even words. In Unst the cat's sea name is *de spjaaler*, meaning "the player" from *spela*, to play; in Sandwick the cat is called *de skaaver* or *skavnashi*, another delightful flight of fancy, for it means "the shaver" or "nose shaver" from the cat's habit of washing itself round its ears and down over the nose, while again *de voaler* could be nothing else but a cat describing as it does the cat's wailing cry, from ON *vala*, to wail or cry. It will now be obvious to the reader that Shetland has retained the old forms of address of "thee" and "thou" used largely

84

in family circles describing things or animals but rarely to outsiders.

The amazing thing is that any of these words could have survived at all, apart from the fact that many of them are still known. Nowhere else than in Orkney has the Norse imprintation been so strong, clearly indicating a very long period of peaceful settlement and also giving some insight into the characteristics of the old Norn tongue and its endless variations. If one of the fishermen wanted to talk at sea about his cow he would have to use the word *boorik*. *De boorik* means "the bellowing one", and the bellowing animal; in Foula a man mentioning his wife would refer to her as *de haimelt*, indicating that she was the one who sat at home while her husband was at the *haaf*—in fact all the Foula names were repeated to me this year.

The sea name for a limpet in Foula was *fjora* and the limpet bait used for fishing for sillocks, *de fjora* which properly means "the ebb" (ON *fjara*) where the limpets would be found. The *huggistaff* with which the fisherman strikes into the fish, usually a large skate or halibut to bring it aboard, or equally well catches the edge of the breakwater to draw the boat in, was called at the *haaf*, *de hodik*, from *hoder* meaning "threatening" (ON *huggva*—to strike).

The boat itself was *de faar* (ON *far* meaning conveyance) and the mast *de stong* or *steng*; the sail *de stegga* (ON skeki, a patch or rag). The baler still known as the *ouskerry* was called by the Unst fishermen *de switick* or *swattyek*, to pour out water in a splashing way. Kettles were *honger* and the fishing lodge *de hoyd*. In addition to these and many more too numerous to include, there were lucky words, retained from ordinary Norse words obsolete in daily conversation, such as *rakki*, the dog and *russi*, the horse, again both known yet in Foula along with such words as *edlar*, the eagle; *klingra*, the wild rose, *fjan* the devil and a host of others. The word for sea in Norn was *sjor* which survives today in *shoormil*, the foreshore, literally "the sea mark" (ON *mil*).

Two charming rhymes survived from Foula and Unst respectively up to Jakobsen's day in the original Norn, both oddly enough used to frighten naughty children:

> *Skela komina reena toona*
> *swarta hesta bletta broona*
> *fomtina haala and fomtina*
> *bjadnis a kwaara haala*

A *skekkel*, meaning a bogie or fabulous animal, not unlike the water horse of Shetland legend, comes riding into town on a black horse with a white spot on his brow. It had 15 tails and 15 children on each tail.

In Unst they appear to have invented a more drastic cure:

85

Buyn vil ikka teea
tak an leggen
slogan veggen
buyn vil ikka teea

"If the child will not be quiet", goes the translation, "take him by the leg and strike him against the wall."

Lastly there is one specimen of an old Norn proverb, one of the few perfectly preserved: "Gott (guyt) a taka gamla manna ro"—"It is good to take the old men's advice."

The similarity of Shetlandic words derived from Old Norn to modern Norwegian is startling, especially in words one can hear today from some of the older people, the place names and the sea names. There is a word quite frequently used when one is perhaps frantically searching through one's pocket for a key or small object, *trivvlin* or to *trivvle*. The Modern Norwegian is *trivle*, meaning to catch up or grab. A rag is still called a *cloot* as it is in Scots but it comes from the Norwegian *klut* and was one of the sea names for the sail; likewise "to play" is still *spille*—the sea name for the cat, *de spjaaler*, and *skave* is used today in the sense of chipping or shaving.

The old place name of Hestingarth would be perfectly understood today in Norway where a horse is still *hest* and the pig still *gris* and *vik* a creek, occurring again and again in Shetland names like Channerwick, Gulberwick and so forth. The first poem quoted here is almost translatable word for word; *aswarta* meaning black has only changed over the years to *sverte*; *broona*, "brown" likewise to *brun*; the tail, *haala* is now *hale* and *bjadnis* the plural of *barn*, child.

The word to burn is still *brenne* and peat, *torv* is commemorated forever in jarl Torf Einar great-grandfather of Sigurd the Stout, who ruled Orkney for many years, and is reputed to have cut the first turf to burn in the fire at Torfness in Scotland "for timber was scarce in the isles". Einar in any event claimed the discovery of the method of cutting peat and was nicknamed "Torf" ever after.

There are many personal names in Norse scattered throughout the islands in place names which are fascinating to track down. In Haakon Haakenson's saga we are told that Balti was the name of a man in Shetland surviving in Balta and Baltasound, in Unst. The island of Samphray was named after the woman who no doubt owned it, for women as well as men not only held land but laid claim to it in Norse times and Sandfrithr must have owned Samphray, the old form Sandfrithroy. One called Atli gave his name to Atlaness in Burra and Frakkister in Fetlar probably belonged to a Viking Frakki.

The slow process of change and disappearance of the spoken Norn probably began seriously after 1379. During the fifteenth century, when the islands passed to the Scottish Crown, Scots came to replace a language that was already being regarded as not only archaic but was rather despised as the language of the common "natives". Most Orcadians perforce were bi-lingual in the seventeenth century but by 1750 it was in the last stages of dissolution and by 1773 it was recorded "that there is scarce a single man in the country who can express himself on the most ordinary occasion in this language". In Shetland, Norn was to last a little longer, especially in the island of Foula, no doubt because of its remoteness, and there even within living memory people can recall their great-grandparents using words and expressions that were certainly Norn.

As to the chronological sequence of Norse names in the islands, there again has been much controversy and the actual interpretation of the historical significance of Scandinavian place names often conflicts with archaeological evidence, which in turn conflicts with the saga dating. Taking all the evidence into account one can assume that although the main Norse settlement took place around A.D. 800, small bands of pagan Scandinavians arrived in Shetland between A.D. 750 and 800 or even earlier, as Williamson believed. It is also certain that the first Norse were indeed settlers (although they would undoubtedly have carried arms), both from the archaeological evidence and the additional substantiation by place names. Among the earliest pagan burials of Norsemen in the Northern Isles those of women are as common as those of men, indicating strongly that the men intended to stay—there would be no place for women and children on board a fast raiding vessel.

The Norwegian origin of the settlers both in Orkney and Shetland, as opposed to Dane or Swede, has been well attested. All Viking expeditions to the British Isles from A.D. 793 to 803 were from Norway. In the case of the landing in Wessex and the sack of Lindisfarne it is specifically mentioned that the raiders came from Hordaland. It was during the reign of Beothric, king of Wessex, when three ships' companies came ashore at Portland and killed a reeve who had ridden from Dorchester to intercept them. Two years later in A.D. 795 the Vikings raided the island of Lambay off the east coast near Dublin, where shortly afterwards Turgesius with a great fleet established a stronghold by the Dubh-linn, the black pool at the ford of the Liffey, and became master of the earliest Viking state recorded in the west, while in Orkney the first Norseman known by name to subdue the islands was Ragnar Hairy Breeks, whose sons Halfdan, Ubbi and Ivar the Boneless were responsible for beginning the Thirty Years' War with England.

10. *The Viking Settlement*

By the year a.d. 800 the Shetland and Orkney islands were firmly under Norse domination, with Norse settlers staking claims wherever they went. Innumerable explanations have been given for their continued eruption from the land of their birth, including over-population, lack of agricultural ground, the laws of primogeniture which inevitably gave rise to family feuds and discontented younger sons determined to seek fame and fortune outside their own country. The Viking, like the Muslim, prided himself on the number of his sons and diligently contrived through the possession of under-wives, mistresses and concubines to scatter like Maker's image throughout the land. He would however at this time be the last to subscribe to the idea that he depended for his existence on the Christian Deity.

True, King Hakon the Good, the child of Harald Fairhair's old age and fostered at the court of King Athelstan of England, arrived in Norway a Christian which made such a bad impression on his people that he promptly reverted to paganism and in 960 when he died he was laid to rest in full armour and in richest array, his subjects praising him as the defender of temples and in splendid rites speeding him on his way to Odin, so that he might join his eight heathen brothers in Valhalla. After this short flirtation with Christianity it was not until Olaf Tryggvason came to the throne in 995 that Norway, officially at any rate, adopted the new faith.

In Shetland the priests or *Papae* were well established, their name perpetuated by the Norse, if not their bodily presences. The Vikings arrived prepared to fight for what they wanted and the early graves in Fetlar may well have been occupied by those who initially resisted them. After the first round of skirmishes, however, the country settled down and the first colonists pursued in the main an ordinary agricultural way of life both in Orkney and Shetland.

Seasonal activities varied little and at Jarlshof the Norse occupants used iron sickle blades, soapstone blocks for tethering cattle, they "kavilled" the lambs with bone bits, milking the ewes in the morning. Already showing their ability as craftsmen whose work was to become

88

Shetland ponies at Uyeasound, Unst.

A six-year old Jacob Ram introduced into Foula; now pure-bred sheep are seen in several areas of Mainland, bred from Eastern and Hebridean stock with very short wool. (Photo by Eric Isbister.)

Bonxie chick (Great Skua) once valued for its eggs and skin, now protected. Of the entire northern hemisphere count, 95 per cent now nest in Shetland.

Rafts of guillemots off the Noup of Noss which rises 592 ft above sea level. (Photo by J. Laughton Johnston.)

so distinctive an art form in wood, silver, bronze and gold throughout the entire Viking period, they showed an affectionate enjoyment of their children by making all kinds of toys for them to play with. Little miniature querns for grinding corn were contrived out of soapstone and the favourite playthings seem to have been decorated bones called *snoriben*, spun on a strand of wool, surely one of the earliest forms of diabolo or yo-yo. They ploughed the fields with an *ard* and wove wool on an upright loom, the warps hung from a horizontal beam weighted with stones or baked clay rings.

They owned boats, drawing graphic pictures of them on slate, although fishing seems to have been a secondary occupation, pursued when they wanted a change of diet. Finely decorated hog-backed bone combs, axe-headed and thistle-headed pins, beautifully carved, often with animal heads; portraits of Vikings on sandstone, one of an old man and the other a young bearded Norseman, emphasise the sophisticated and artistic qualities of the settlers. Machinery destroyed a warrior's grave complete with weapons when levelling the site of the control tower at Sumburgh Airport and drain-cutting destroyed another, although a bowl-shaped brooch was saved and is in the County Museum. During the building of the new enlarged airstrip in the same locality one can only hope that this time an archaeologist can be on the spot to avoid the ruination of an area that might prove rich in Viking or Iron Age finds.

Already the islands had been sub-divided into ten or eleven districts, the "governor" or magistrate known as the Great Foude of Shetland, appointed by the King of Norway. The Foude derived his authority directly from the king, entrusted with the maintenance of law and order, the carrying out of judgments and the collection of revenues for the Crown. He had assistance in each district by an under-foude and a lawrightman, equally trusted by the foude and the people and elected at the annual "Thing" or Parliament in Tingwall. The duties of the lawrightman included the regulation of weights and measures, especially those involved in the payment in kind of land taxes; he was also charged with the upholding of the general interests of the "herad" or parish, especially in the Lag-thing or Lawting, where he acted as assessor of the Lawman or Foude.

There were in addition, ten ranselmen (modern Norwegian *ransake*— to search), in whom were invested powers almost pertaining to those of the "Grand Inquisitor". The ranselman was quite literally authorised to inquire into all scandals and misdemeanours in his district. He had the right to enter any house within the parish at all hours of the day or night; to seach the house for stolen goods and if refused entry or access, to break open doors or chests; to examine the household's stores of flesh, meat, wool and yarn, and if necessary demand proof of their purchase or barter. He was empowered even to scrutinise family morals; the relationship between husband and wife, parents and children, to prevent, if he could, family quarrels or disputes with neighbours. His powers would appear to us to have been inordinately wide, increasing with the years, for later the ranselman could appear on the doorstep on Monday morning to find out why certain members of the family had not attended the kirk service on the Sabbath. Although the office was, perforce an invidious one, many were highly respected and their appointment continued up to the year 1836.

The land was held under udal tenure without obligation to chief, squire or laird. Land was the property of the first improver and any settler was free to choose as much land as he wished, the basis of value being the *merk*, denoting quality, not quantity. A merk of the best land might be roughly an acre, of the poor land four or five, but each merk was intended to be of the same value in crop or animal production.

Townships were enclosed by stone or *failey* (turf) dykes and beyond that lay the *scattald*, the common grazing. For the freedom to use the scattald for grazing and peat-cutting a land tax was levied, known as *skat* from the original *skathold* (again modern Norwegian *skatt*—tax), the tax payable on each merk of enclosed land. Every crofter had his share of good land and poor and the fields were carved up into long rigs separated by strips of grass. In the beginning each rig was worked by the farmers of the township in rotation, the system known as *riggarendel*.

Standing on the west road to Sumburgh above Bigton in summer is like looking down on an endless patchwork in permutations of greens and browns. Running down from Setter the long rigs stretch out towards St. Ninian's Isle in strips of cinnabar, light gold and pale ochre; away on the gentle slope of the hill below Ireland more rigs fan down at right-angles to Setter, beyond, the sea and Foula on the horizon. Look down on Spiggie Loch below Scousburgh where the rigs seem to run forever like fingers pointing to the voe and think for a moment of the men who first *delled* them. Uniquely preserved at Spiggie, Clavel, Rerwick, Setter, Ireland, they are all within a few miles of each other, all within the fertile lands of Dunrossness. There is nothing quite so salutary for the human soul as to see stretching out in front of one some visual evidence of history, not in monumental capitals, vault or architrave, buttress or spire, but in the humblest possible way, a simple piece of strip cultivation, surviving the elements that batten on and destroy the most exquisite of man's creations, still the same after nearly 1000 years.

Sheep grazed on the unfenced scattald, all lug-marked by their

90

27 Old hand quern lying in an abandoned croft: the upper stone with the "eye" through which the grain was fed with one hand while the other rotated the wheel by means of a wooden "handle" set into the stone through the smaller hole.

owners in an infinite variety of individual *cleeps*, *biddies*, *shears*, *bits* or *cross bitted*, so that one sheep would be marked on both ears with two *cleeps* or two *biddies*, another with one *shear* right or one *cleep* right and one *biddy*, so that even today each crofter can recognise his own sheep. The original Shetland sheep, and they would all be small in those days, was *rooed*—the wool pulled off by hand, an entirely natural process still practised with the hill sheep especially in Unst where the pure Shetland gives the fine wool of which the lacy shawls are made. Little effort is needed to divest the sheep of her wool in the *rooin* season; you will see half-naked ewes casting their winter fleeces almost spontaneously trailing behind them grey skirts and petticoats of fleece.

91

28 Williamsetter, near Bigton, Dunrossness in 1930. In the background is St. Ninian's Isle and the "Louse Head" (Loose Head) and Foula just visible on the horizon. On the slope above the long rigs is the village of Ireland which had obviously moved with the times as all the roofs are now made of slate. Today, only the small outhouses are still thatched. (Zetland County Library and Museum.)

When farming became too monotonous the settlers, both in Orkney and Shetland, relieved the tedium by sporadic raids on Ireland and the Western Isles. A primitive and divided country, Ireland was easy prey and although the Irish resisted with great vigour and courage the annals from 807 onwards are littered with battles and desperate struggles against the Norse pressing in from the sea. The first raids were, as usual, onslaughts on coastal and island monasteries, the fear they inspired described in a quatrain from a 9th century manuscript, revealing the relief of a scribe watching a storm at sea:

Fierce and wild is the wind tonight:
It tosses the tresses of the sea to white;
On such a night as this I take my ease;
Fierce Northmen only course in quiet seas.

In a Munster chronicle the writer lists the horrors of a Viking raid
in these words: "Immense floods and countless sea-vomitings of ships
and boats and fleets so that there was not a harbour a land port nor
a dun nor a fortress nor a fastness in all Mumha without floods of Danes
and pirates . . . so that they made spoil-land and sword-land and conquered land of her throughout her length and breadth and generally;
and they ravaged her chieftainries and her privileged churches and her
sanctuaries; and they rent her shrines and her reliquaries and her
books."

Throughout all the waves of peoples who lived in the Northern Isles
and used them for one purpose or another, it is from the grave goods
that we learn most about them, the epochs they dominated and the
places from whence they came. Although Shetland and even Ireland
are relatively short in burial finds, further excavations in Shetland are
bound to reveal in time many more settlements and burials.

The Norse seem to have run the gamut of most known ways of disposing of their dead. These included cremation; earth burial, being laid
to rest in mounds with or without grave goods; on level places with
boats real or symbolic in the shape of stones arranged to form the outline
of a ship, or no boats at all; in big wooden chambers and small coffins
and sometimes in neither. There have been found single graves; graves
for two, the one sometimes a woman slave, and communal graves.
Sometimes they show a mixture of paganism and Christianity, but Viking-Age burials were strongly affected by pre-Viking-Age customs and
regional distinctions. Christianity frowned upon the bestowal of grave
goods save of the simplest, but heathendom, especially in Norway and
Sweden, everything possible to make the after-life a comfortable and
honourable one. There were weapons, ships, wagons, dogs, horses,
adornments, utensils, toilet articles and even food.

The early Vikings of the Northern Isles did occasionally cremate
their dead, a custom associated with the mutilation or burning of swords
and weapons in a symbolic "killing", but so far as finds have revealed
inhumation seems to have been the most common, gradually replacing,
in the Iron Age, cremation, which was still particularly favoured by
Norway. Usually the remains were slid into the ground within a setting
of stones or sometimes placed above ground level and a mound raised
over them. There are examples of stone-built graves and interments
in already existing mounds. In Shetland the old Norse name for a stone

29 The Brothers—three great stones, one still standing. The story goes that three brothers fought over a woman and killed each other. The area was excavated and it appeared that someone had been buried on the spot. The Mill Loch below, and on the right the shoulder of Hamnafjeld.

pile or mound is *kuml*, pronounced in the islands, *komel*, a *stangkuml*, a green *kuml* used in the sense of a burial mound. "The Kummels o' Korkigerth" are the graves in the churchyard. In the Viking Age the word *kuml* meant a grave monument either of earth or stone and only in two places does it survive, in the Shetland Islands and in Iceland.

These stone *kumls*, rather in the nature of a cairn and tending to be found on hilly slopes or on the tops of hills, are numerous in the northwest Mainland, in Aithsting and Sandsting, but on the island of Unst there is what is believed to be one of the earliest places of burial in the islands. At Watlee, where the lonely bridge has long had the reputation of being haunted, a raised mound appears out of the moor, covered with boulders and rock in a manner suggestive of the hand of man although time and weather must have displaced many of them. It was said that in the beginning the dead were simply laid out here like the bodies left on a Parsee Tower of Silence for the predatory Black Backs and crows to pick their bones clean. On closer examination there can be traced just outside the circle of the mound itself a six-foot-long roughly rectangular depression surrounded by stones which could well be that of an early Viking burial site.

Earth mounds on the other hand invariably lie near farms or land that is or has been inhabited, often by the side of burns or lochs, as at the beautiful mound near the little loch of Asta in the Tingwall val-

94

ley. It has also been noted that these mounds occur in many cases on or near farms bearing the oldest type of Norse names such as Asta itself, Grista, Breibister, Setter, Huxter, Heglibister, Beosetter, which would have been the settlements of the earliest colonists from the Agder-Roga-land and More districts of Norway who had followed the old native custom of raising grave mounds to the departed.

So far, attested pagan Scandinavian graves are rare in Shetland and indeed only two have been excavated both in Unst, although Mr. Peter Moar of Lerwick has discovered at least 10 Norse house sites which he is certain belong to the same period. In a woman's grave at Clibbers-wick, Unst, two tortoise-shaped brooches of bronze were found and a trefoil brooch and a circular bronze box came from another woman's grave, also in Unst, but no closer record of the site has survived. The brooches would have been the standard adornment of a woman of the upper classes, fastening the loose flowing cloak of wool so that she could be free to display the alabaster whiteness of her arms. Another relic of the Viking Age was a gold bracelet of plaited wires found in a peat bank, photographed by Miss Arcus of Scalloway, but now lost.

Small personal objects have occasionally appeared such as a gold finger ring from Marrister in Whalsay, a gold bracelet from Oxna and a pennanular silver brooch of well-known Viking type found in Gulber-wick but there is no evidence at present to connect them with burials. They may simply have been lost and one can imagine the dismay, the hopeless search among the heather, beach stones or tall grasses, then the admission of carelessness or angry recriminations. Even as extraneous objects each must have its own small story to tell.

We could also include 10 glass beads found in a bog at Hillswick and a 9th-century war axe of iron in the churchyard at Whiteness, the latter probably of a later date when the Norsemen with certain reserva-tions were tending to accept Christianity, but still paid some homage, perhaps just to be on the safe side as it were, to the old Norse gods and customs. Many more burials have been discovered in Orkney, which together with the stray Shetland finds and graves indicated by Mr. Moar point to the immense possibilities of finds yet to be investi-gated in Shetland. Mr. Tom Henderson, Curator of the County Museum, has long suspected that two Viking longhouses exist on one of the offshore islands in Dunrossness, but again lack of experienced archaeologists is still the stumbling block as far as future digs are con-cerned.

In Ireland occasional ecclesiastical hoards were successfully hidden from Norse raiders, but by the 8th and 9th centuries an enormous number of priceless objects from Irish sources had already reached Nor-way. Norse burials with grave goods of Irish origin, already buried with

95

their owners, consist mainly of mountings from shrines re-fashioned into brooches; hanging bowls and escutcheons and reliquaries while a great part of the material of Irish origin found in Denmark came through Norway.

The Viking's greatest weapon was his undisputed mastery at sea. Amazing navigators, outstanding shipbuilders and superb sailors, all their major successful attacks were launched from the sea. They built ships for carrying armed settlers and their families, women, children and household goods; great roomy vessels for the transport of armies; swift traders and seaworthy craft expressly designed for long voyages of exploration. Some of the earliest, such as that found at Nydam in south Jutland, show a large open rowing boat without mast or sail and with only a rudimentary keel. Made of oak, it was 23.7 metres long with ribs of natural grown crooks to which the planks were tied clinker fashion through cleats made out of solid wood, but big enough to cross the North Sea; in fact, many an eighteenth-century privateer was no larger.

The first Norse sail, a small piece of cloth set high on the mast, soon developed along with a vastly improved keel into the great bellying sails of the later Viking ships, and by A.D. 790 it was obvious that northern shipwrights had evolved vessels of unsurpassed beauty and seaworthiness, like the beautiful Gokstad ship found in Norway, the culmination of centuries of ship-building as far back as the Bronze Age. Around the year A.D. 800 a leader of rank and means had at his command for ventures overseas a manœuvrable sailing ship some $76\frac{1}{2}$ feet long from stem to stern with a beam of $17\frac{1}{2}$ feet and a little over 6 feet 4 inches from the bottom of the keel to the gunwale amidships.

From the book of settlements, the *Landnamabok* came sailing directions for Norsemen without compass or sextant: "From Hernar in Norway one must sail a direct course west to Hvarf in Greenland in which case one sails north of Shetland so that one sights land in clear weather only, then south of the Faroes so that the sea looks halfway up the mountainside (an almost identical way of pinpointing a position to that of the Shetland meithes used by long-line fishermen) then south of Iceland so that one gets sight of birds and whales there."

Any seagoing people would recognise their proximity to land by the seabirds off-shore. They would see storm petrels in the open ocean or a shearwater anything up to 1000 miles from land. A hundred miles out the Arctic skuas would appear and around 50 miles off he might see the Great Skua or Bonxie. But during times of fog, which still beset the Shetland and Arctic waters for days on end, when even an aeroplane cannot land with all the modern aids to navigation, the Viking had only his sun stone. It was recorded in the saga of Olaf the Stout, later

96

St. Olaf, that one of his henchmen boasted that he could tell where the sun was through cloud or fog, locating it with a magic stone. Both Icelandic spar, crystal and tourmaline, found in Oslo Fjord, have light polarising qualities and in fact the scientific principle of the polarisation of light by Icelandic spar was first formulated in 1669 in Denmark by one Erasmus Bartholinus, leading indirectly to the invention of the Kollsman Sky Compass in use today on Polar flight routes.

The Viking's sun stone has been tried out by Captain Jorgen Jensen who took a Danish scientist with him on the flight deck on an investigation as to its accuracy. Captain Jensen used the Sky Compass and the scientist used the sun stone to examine the overcast sky. As he revolved the stone in the direction of the sun it changed colour from pink to pale blue, quite enough to locate the sun so that a Viking ship could keep on the right course.

Possibly because of the development of Norse ships into fine fast vessels, raids on Shetland became much more frequent after about A.D. 750. Expeditions from Norway were aimed firstly at appropriating land for settlement in Great Britain and Ireland. Danish princes were involved in trying to maintain their claims to dominion over the coast from Holstein to Frisia with consequent campaigns and interference in Frankish politics, sometimes as allies or mercenaries. But the great Viking armies that preyed upon France took no steps towards settling in the country as they did in England.

The colonies everywhere became the starting point of warlike expeditions to more distant lands, to southern France, Spain, Morocco and Italy in the same way as the Swedes from Russia infested the islands and shores of the Aegean. The three countries had completely different zones of interest, the Norsemen settling chiefly in Orkney and Shetland, the Hebrides and round the Irish Sea; the Danes operating within the Frankish Empire and crossing the Channel to invade England, while the Swedes found their way along the great Russian rivers.

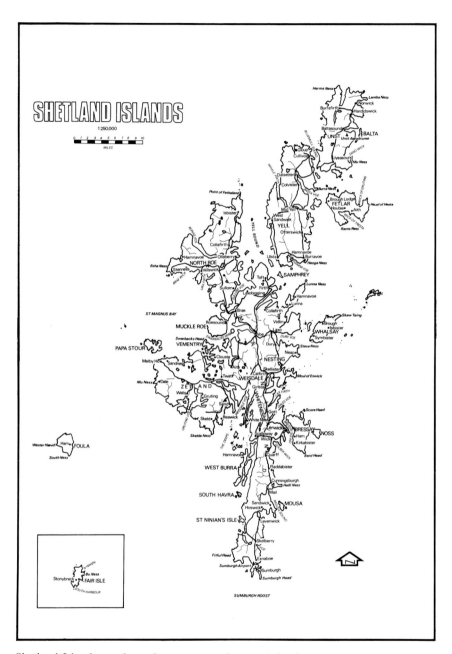

Shetland Islands: modern place names and communications.

11. *The End of the Golden Age*

ON A FLAT spit of land thrusting out into the bay wisps of blue smoke seeped upwards from the *skollas*. In the East Voe and the West Shore gulls cut intricate patterns across a forest of swan-necked *halfskip* and *karfi*. The wind that had furrowed the cornfields in the valley and combed the fleece of the grazing sheep had suddenly dropped with the evening. A light curtain of rain shrouded the maze of island, holm and skerry flung like a floating barrier between Scalloway and the Atlantic. Water met sky in a luminous haze, arrows of pale sunlight shafting down on a pewter sea.

A *langskip* nosed her way up the long channel of Clift Sound, arched prow drawn back, a sea-stallion, teeth bared, the men already furling the flapping sail carried on a single yard, red stripes on white wool lighting up the narrow entrance. A Viking with a yellow curling beard leant on the cross-bar of the rudder, upright like a vast paddle on the starboard quarter, while the crew prepared to bring her in under oar. Every foot of beach was crowded with small rowing boats belonging to the local inhabitants, *foueringr* and *sexaering* drawn up for safety high above the *shoormil*, for even in June the weather was unpredictable.

Inside the *skollas* Norsewomen, discarding the aprons and kerchiefs they wore outside, bustled to and fro in long woollen dresses over linen petticoats, holding them high off the trodden rushes, showing off white legs thrust into woollen socks and *rivlins*. They sniffed at steaming cauldrons, adding here a sweetening of honey, there a pinch of spices from the East, and complaining as women will over the temporary lack of home comforts, the glow from the peat fire glinting on bracelet, neck-collar and brooch, bright sparks of colour in the smoke-filled room.

Thrall women squatted on their heels, sweating over meat roasting on the spit or boiling in iron pots slung from a tripod, baking bread and oatcakes on flat stones laid across the fire pits, scooping dough out of wooden troughs, stopping only for a moment to push back lank dark hair with their forearms. Great bowls of curds, *blaand* and buttermilk were set out on makeshift tables along with home-brewed beer made from fermented honey and water, and wine imported from Europe and

99

Byzantium, ready for the men when they should come ashore.

And as they waited the women chattered, exchanging gossip from Dunrossness to Unst. Everyone was talking about the miracles wrought by the jarl Magnus who was now a saint and how the woman Sigrid from Unst, servant of Thorlak at Baliasta, had refused to stop her sewing on St. Magnus' Eve and they said she had gone raving mad, serve her right the stubborn bitch. Soft-hearted as always, Thorlak had taken her himself to offer money at the shrine in Orkney and there she had seemingly come to her wits. And yet another told of the man Sigurd, son of Tandri who lived out at Dale. He, poor carl, had become suddenly possessed of a devil so that they had sewn him up in a cowhide in case he did himself an injury and brought him to Kirkwall to St. Magnus the Jarl, where he was cured on the spot.

Then they fell to admiring each other's finery, the Chinese silks and brocades, sandalwood and filigrees, bringing forth their treasures and precious things and showed each other what their men had brought from Ireland, Spain and Italy. Ranvaig ran for her casket; it had come from a monastery she told them, where they called it a reliquary and she had got the smith to engrave upon it "Ranvaig owns this casket." Well, it had been long before they had had to become Christian, and she pouted a little pretending guilt. Helga had set aside her ribbon loom for tablet weaving. Feverishly she was putting the last stitches into Njal's *hlao*, the streamer-shaped ribbons with the gold embroidery he wore on his forehead when he went to the *Thing*.

All this time old Thorkel sat on a bench leaning against the wall, criticising everything he could think of, his great rough-coated hunting dog at his feet, his favourite hawk on his wrist. His battle wounds healed slowly and irked him so he vented his spleen on anyone who happened to be around. It was just his luck to be stuck in Shetland and then they had to drag him along to the *Thing*. He spat slowly and vindictively. How they were going to get him to Tingwall he had no idea. He had seen more *Things* than any of them. A lot of old fools like that *foude* Frakki, long-winded, pompous devil. They might even have to bury him here. If it came to that he would agree to be placed in the yard of the round-towered church of St. Magnus at the head of the loch. They were to lay him facing the east and just to be on the safe side he wanted his axe and his sword laid beside him. All right, he was old-fashioned, but who would ever know, and he had no family here to look after his grave mound.

They were no kin of his these oafs who had brought him back from Ireland. Suddenly the dog bayed, hackles up, and he gripped it by the iron collar. It was only the men, crowding in, shouting for food, curds and wine, for tomorrow was the meeting of the *Allthing* on the Law Ting

100

Holm up on the little island on Tingwall loch. This was the most important court of the year, the culmination of an assize which had visited
each parish in turn, minor courts presided over by the parish lawrightman and the under-foude. The chief foude had already arrived and
in the morning he would sit with all his officers on the ceremonial stones
inside the low wall that bounded the island and preside at the high
court of Shetland.

By this time there were *Things* in all the main districts of Shetland
but the court at Tingwall was the "Parliament" of the islands, held
once a year in that long and fertile, limestone-bedded valley, still rich
in pasture and arable land. Long after the last echoes of that first *Thing*
had died away in time the udal law, established by the Norsemen, lived

30   Looking up from Scousburgh Sands to Coubal and Vanlop.

on, surviving on its ancient site up to the sixteenth century. All over the islands other "Thing-steads" can be traced in names like Delting, Nesting, Aithsting, Lunnasting and Sandsting, and by the time of Harold Fairhair, who although as strong-willed and covetous of power and riches as any of his contemporaries, was also endowed with a keen sense of justice. Norsemen for the most part lived under the rule of local custom and *Thing-law*, and *Things* themselves grew in usefulness and importance.

At least part of the system had been established before Harald Fairhair came to power but the *Gulathing* owed much to his determination to control and pacify the Vestland. "With law shall the kingdom be built up and with lawlessness wasted away ... If we break the law we break the peace." Such sayings may appear to be a complete negation of all that the Vikings stood for, at least in the eyes of the world, but according to their lights they adhered to the law.

There was another vital matter that had to be agreed between king and freeman, provision for which was built into the later codes of the law when Harald's successor, Hakon the Good, formulated more elaborate regulations for the *Gulathing Law* and the *Frostathing Law*. This was coastal defence. It had always been the unquestioned right of the local chieftain to call on his people to resist attack from without. At news of marauders the summons went forth like a fiery cross and men took up arms and rations and hurried to the place of assembly.

Harold required more than just a local muster of men. His defence measures must be prepared in advance and he needed to have a fleet instantly ready at his command. The farmers were a peace-loving people who wanted only to be left alone to raise their crops and tend their livestock. The lands controlled by Harald were divided into districts and regions and it seemed fair enough that each one should contribute a ship and a ship's crew. The difficulty lay in deciding how to choose the men, how many and for how long. Harold finally chose to institute a kind of army or navy service rota, and in the later *Gulathing Law* it was laid down that three families of free farmers must put up one man between them, supplying him with rations of meal and meat for two months. When he stood down from service he was given provisions for two weeks, presumably to allow him to return to his home hale and hearty.

From Thingvellir in Iceland to Garder in the eastern settlement of Greenland and Tingwall in the Shetlands, all such *Things* underwent the change from heathendom to Christianity and their laws were first committed to writing after this change. Recourse to it was the prerogative of all free men and its operation a public one. The original designation of *herred*, a body of mounted men riding to an agreed place, is still commemorated in Yell, Fetlar and on Herrislee Hill between Dale's Voe and the Tingwall valley.

All the most common causes of disputes were catered for such as boundary marks, hunting rights, flotsam and jetsam, the felling of trees, and collection of firewood, infringement of grazing rights; laws on libel, satire, calumny, the making of love songs—although it is difficult to imagine just what could be arguable about such a gentle pursuit. There were laws dealing with sheep stealing, turning people's butter sour or wooing their bees, to offences against the person with an endless gradation of injury and penalty from cutting off a finger to cutting off a head.

Little was left to chance, for there were also laws concerned with the flouting of public morality, hurt to the community, and of course the good old Viking practise of *strand-hogg* which had now become intolerable; laws dealing with fines, death and outlawry, strangers, visiting nationals and trade. The law had an answer for everything, for religious observance, respect for holy places, and the property of married women.

It was significant of the times that the laws dealing with the taking of life included every possible permutation of the deed from manslaughter, self-defence, fair-fight, burning indoors (a favourite Viking method of disposing of one's enemies), killing under provocation, killing by night, in the king's presence, in a holy place, unavowed killing, infamous killing, to murder most foul.

Unfortunately the *Things* were almost powerless to halt the blood feuds which could go on from generation to generation unless the local people were prepared to risk their lives enforcing judgment. Bearing a striking resemblance to the Pathan of the North West Frontier, his hyper-sensitivity to personal honour and pride embodied in the one word *nang*, the Norsemen was equally ready to take offence on the slightest provocation. Insanely jealous of his good name, he regarded gossip as the worst crime. "The tongue that hurts most should be the most heavily punished", was his creed and an imagined slight, however trivial, led inevitably to bloodshed and bloodfeud.

"There is an evil custom in this land of Norway that when a man has been killed, his kinsmen attack whoever is considered to be the most important member of the murderer's family, even though the killing may have been without his knowledge or against his wishes. These people refuse to avenge themselves upon the murderer even though this could easily be done."

Another solution was the payment of compensation or *wergeld*. Each individual had his value and complicated tables of fines were drawn up, sometimes counted in silver, woollen material or cows, the guarantee that a man might not be attacked with impunity in his person, family, property or honour. For example, it was laid down that "When a man wounds another, he shall indemnify him at the rate of one eyrir for every cut, one eyrir for every broken bone, one eyrir for every cut that bleeds and four eyrir for every wound in vital parts", an eyrir being a Viking coin. As it was written in the Havamal: "Cattle die, kinsfolk die and we ourselves die. One thing lives on—a man's reputation."

There were, however, many laws expressly designed to help ordinary people in distress or misfortune. If a farmer lost more than half his cattle through disease he could claim up to half their value from the rest of the community. Likewise, if a man's house was burned down he could apply for compensation for any three rooms and their contents. Under all these heads, the law in Shetland as in Norway expressed the dignity of a society of free men. A small legacy still remains of this concern for the community, at least in the country districts. Immediately after some tragedy involving loss of house or stock, perhaps due to fire, a fund is automatically set up, collections being made from house to house. At Christmas children volunteer to collect donations towards the postman's Christmas box, a pleasant and thoughtful way of involving the community, in islands where personal suffering or disaster is invariably shared by every village and croft for miles around.

Before the Roman alphabet was adopted, runic inscriptions being too clumsy for code or chronicle, the body of the law had to be carried in the memory. First there were private individuals well-versed in the law, the lawmen, useful as advisers and consultants to those who had a case to plead or a cause to defend. The lawspeaker was an elected official whose business it was to memorise the law so that he might recite one-third of it each year for three years in succession at the main assembly.

On the whole the northern peoples were obedient to the rule of law, enjoyed its benefits in respect of property and person and found it a stabilising influence on social order from king and chieftain to bondi and thrall alike. Like newspaper reportage, seeking out always the most sensational, the bloodiest and most harrowing *causes célèbres*, the sagas played up the blood feud, the raiding and the battle. Behind this façade, however, existed a deep respect for the *Thing* and insistence on its public and democratic exercise was a distinctive feature throughout the whole of the Viking Age, standing out as an example of the advanced thinking of an enlightened people when compared to the narrow-minded and bigoted feudalism that was to come near to obliterating for all time the days of the Viking democracy.

Travel in these early days was naturally by sea. Shetland's rugged coastline and deeply penetrating voes, the lack of any kind of road or road transport, precluded land travel save for the shortest journeys, so that everyone who attended the *Thing*, and there were few who were excused, would naturally land at Scalloway. Its ancient name is *Skallava*, the voes of the *Skollas*, the temporary houses or booths erected to shelter the litigants and officials bound for the *Thing*, and it is still pronounced locally Skallawaa'. From here they would make their way in solemn procession led by the chief foude, followed by under-foudes, lawmen, lawrightmen and ranselmen, up the Tingwall valley to the Law Ting Holm, all down the years from the first Norse colonists who founded the udal system, right up to the reign of the notorious Stewart earls, when the annual Parliament was moved for the first time in its history to Scalloway itself and the castle that Earl Patrick built there in 1600.

In spite of the importance attached to the various *Things* and the democratic spirit underlying their meaning and observance, the kingdoms established in Denmark at the beginning of the ninth century, in Sweden some 50 years later and Norway a little before A.D. 900, were all formed out of a purely personal desire for self-aggrandisement, for wealth, territory or trade based on sea power. Although these were an undoubted improvement on the independent jarlships which had preceded them, there was nothing truly national about them. As late as the reigns of Knut or his regent in Denmark, Olaf Skotnung and Onand Jacob in Sweden, Harald Hardrada in Norway, there was no overall policy or form of administration. Men of significance in their day however, Godfred, Harald Fairhair, Harald Bluetooth, Olaf Tryggvason and Olaf Haraldsson, Svein Forkbeard and King Knut, all played a part in shaping the destinies of the countries they controlled.

Inseparable from Shetland's history, and commemorated in Haroldswick in Unst, was Harald Harfagri. A king in Norway such as the land had not known before, his reign lasted more than half a century. Battles were fought, kings slain and realms conquered until Harald found himself undisputed ruler of lands as far north as Gudbrandsal, enough to impress Harald with the meaning of power and to lay down the seeds of his continuing ambition.

Although many of his bitterest enemies were dead or in flight Harald could not yet trim his hair. For at least 50 years before the climax of his warmongering, the sea-battle of Harfsfjord fought about A.D. 870, there had been Viking activity in western Europe and the Norwegians had well-established colonies in the British Isles. It was obvious that in spite of northern tradition to the contrary great numbers of colonists had been arriving in practically all the Atlantic islands long before

Harold Fairhair came to the height of his power. Certainly many Norwegians now fled from his tyranny or became political refugees, and settling in Shetland, Orkney and the Hebrides at once began to practise Viking in reverse, and instead of spending their winters in Norway and their summers raiding the British Isles, they now lived out west and did their raiding back in Norway.

Ingolf Arnason had landed in Iceland when Harald Fairhair was 16 years of age, and by the time Harald was ready to deal with affairs outside Norway Iceland was largely settled and Harald's tyranny precipitated the last influx. Anxious to exercise some control over this new colony, Harold set a tax on the head of Norwegian emigrants to Iceland and to curb over-extensive settlement that invariably led to quarrels he gave forth an edict that no one should occupy more land than he and his crew could carry fire round in one day.

With Norway more or less under control, Harald was still encountering fierce opposition to his campaign against the "raiders in reverse" and finally, his patience exhausted, he sailed west-over-sea, with a great fleet, landing, it is believed, in Haroldswick in Unst. Putting all he caught in Shetland, Orkney, the Hebrides and Man, to the sword he laid claim to the earldom of Orkney and Shetland bestowing his prize on the family of the Jarl Rognvald of More, the first of his family to win a title to land in the British Isles and progenitor of all our kings for 900 years.

Earl Rognvald gave the new earldom to his brother Sigurd, notorious for his assaults on Scotland, the last of which culminated in his death at Dornoch fighting against a Scottish earl. He was succeeded by Hallad, son of Earl Rognvald, who blithely set up house in Orkney. His stay, however, was short-lived. Unusually for a Viking, he found no enjoyment in its occupation, inseparable as it was from continual harassment by local Vikings. Unable to support life under these turbulent conditions he quite lost his nerve and resigning the earldom—amid loud laughter, as the sagas relate—retired to the comparative peace and quiet of his country-seat in Norway.

His brother Torf Einar, of peat-cutting fame, ugly, one-eyed and the son of a thrall woman, succeeded to the earldom of the Orkneys. Base born he may have been but he was more than capable of keeping control and his devotion to his father, the Earl of More, was such that when the news of his death—by burning alive at the hands of two rebellious sons of Harald Fairhair—reached him Einar took awful and immediate revenge. Capturing one of them, Halfdan Longlegs, on the island of North Ronalsay, he cut a blood-eagle on Halfdan's back and being a poet as well as a ruthless Viking boasted of his deed in verse, sparing none of the gory details. King Harald took it all in his stride like the

106

redoubtable old warrior that he was, fined Einar a nominal 60 gold marks and left him to get on with ruling Orkney and its neighbouring isles of Shetland.

Einar's half-brother, Hrolf, meanwhile had been banished for life by King Harald for seizing cattle from a Norwegian farmer in the old manner of *strand-hogg* to feed his men when homeward-bound from a Viking cruise. Hrolf settled in France and became the first Duke of Normandy, the progenitor of William the Conqueror and thus an ancestor of our present Queen. The extraordinary thing was that the Norman conquest and its consequences, the imposition of the feudal system in England, was the direct result of King Harald's suppression of the Viking raiders in Orkney and Shetland and the establishment of law and order in Norway.

Orkney now because the centre of a semi-independent state which included Shetland and Caithness and from time to time Sutherland, the Hebrides and various appendages. The powerful earls owed nominal allegiance to the kings of Norway and Scotland but for the most part pursued their own autocratic policy, high-handed and in constant conflict with their overlords.

At the beginning of the tenth century a second farmhouse was built at Jarlshof and significantly the old temple, if temple it was, fell into disuse and was never replaced. Finds from the upper levels of excavation included at this time cross-headed pins indicative of the growing Christian influence and a bronze strap-end decorated in the Ringerike style of the same period. For the Scandinavians paganism was in its last stages and with Olaf Tryggvason, who came to the throne of Norway in 995, the country, officially at least, adopted the new faith.

Sigurd the Stout, earl of Orkney, had died in the battle of Clontarf, bearing his raven banner; Thorfinn the Mighty, for 20 years Earl of Orkney, died in 1064, the acknowledged ruler of the whole of north-west Scotland. Earl Thorfinn left two sons, Paul and Erlend, joint earls of Orkney who, dying left each a son, Hakon and Magnus. Hakon survived at the expense of the martyrdom of Magnus, that Magnus once trencher bearer to King Magnus of Norway, but who, psalter in hand sat on the king's ship singing psalms the battle through, steel ringing against steel and arrows flying to their marks like showers of hail. That strange man "who had no quarrel with any man here", a positively unbelievable remark for a Viking.

Earl Magnus, though wedded to Ingegord, born of the noblest family in Scotland, lived with her for 10 years and "satisfied neither his own lust nor hers, and was pure and unsullied from fleshly taint. If he felt tempted he bathed in cold water and prayed for God's help," all of which self-mortification set him apart from other men even during his lifetime. No one, however, has thought it important enough to spare a thought for his wife who no doubt married him in all good faith ready to share his bed and board. Though high-born she would be no less lusty than the women of her time. Did she in desperation take a lover or did she suffer her own martyrdom of the flesh crying out in the long cold night for an end to her virginity?

We shall never know, for Magnus pursued with ever-increasing fervour his pursuit of the unattainable, his final discipline in offering himself for sacrifice in place of his cousin. Commending his soul to God and praying for mercy upon his executioner he made his last confession. And in the end he fell, cleft by a great wound through the head at his own request, for he did not wish to die beheaded like a common thief, which smacks curiously of a most un-Christian lack of humility. After all, the Christ whom he sought to emulate made no such distinctions in His moment of death.

The deed, however, was done and Earl Hakon was free to rule the Orkneys and Shetland. The date of the murder was April 16th, 1117, and by the following winter Christ's Kirk in Birsay where Magnus was first buried had become as famous as Lourdes and all the sick, maimed and mentally disturbed in Shetland flocked to his tomb and Magnus' fame grew greatly. The Bishop of Orkney himself was converted to the belief in his sanctity and authorised the removal of the relics to Kirkwall where 20 years later Magnus' nephew Rognvald, then Earl of Orkney, put in hand the building of St. Magnus Cathedral in memory of his uncle, saint extraordinary of Orkney.

The end of the Golden Age was in sight and with Orkney's second saint, the gallant, adventurous and ebullient Rognvald Kali, nephew of St. Magnus, who died in Caithness in 1158, the last great figure of Norse domination in the islands, the saga ended. Strangely enough, although Orkney's history from the 9th to the 12th century is well attested, neglected Shetland came briefly to life during the reign of Orkney's last earl of any consequence, his apologia St. Magnus Cathedral. In penitence and for the good of his immortal soul, he also made a crusade—and enjoyed every minute of it. It was a great, poetic, romantic voyage lasting nearly two and a half years but Rognvald returned to the old problems of trying to keep the peace between dissident earls, friend and foe alike. Buried on his death in St. Magnus Cathedral he was canonised 34 years later.

It was on his way to Norway from Orkney in the autumn of 1148 that a great storm arose and Earl Rognvald was driven ashore. There was a rocky beach in front of them and only a narrow foreshore with cliffs beyond. All the men were saved but they lost much of their belongings some of which were thrown up on the shore during the night. Going

108

inland to look for inhabitants, for they were sure that they had landed in Shetland, they came to the house of Bondi Einar at Gulberuvik, "the bay of Gulbera", "the gold-bearing lady", a few miles south of Lerwick. Local tradition is contradictory as to the exact site of the wreck, as most of the bay would answer equally well to the saga's description, and the house of Bondi Einar, who took in the bedraggled party, may well have been the farm of Trebister.

Here they received great hospitality, the lady of the house bringing a skin cloak for Rognvald to wear as a kirtle. Food was prepared for them and as they were sitting round the fire a little Shetland maidservant, Asa, who had been sent to the well for water, fell in and returned dripping and shivering with cold. As she stood there with chattering teeth she muttered something but none of the men could make out what she was saying. The genial earl, who required no encouragement to burst into verse, immediately declared that he could understand her and promptly recited to the company:

> Warm by the fire
> You sit, but Asa
> —Atatata—
> Lies in water
> Hutututu
> Where shall I sit?
> I am frozen
> To the marrow.

And one can almost see him, a great bearded face, eyes crinkling, a drinking cup in his hand, his legs spread towards the glowing peat fire, watching the girl, well aware of her small body sculptured by the damp folds of clinging blouse and kirtle, and of the impression he is making, half-teasing, half in earnest, joking about her plight. There is no mention of any woman in his company but one is tempted to include Gulbera who gave her name to the little village of Gulberwick, the land she owned, either then or later, sitting slightly withdrawn, no doubt resigned to the irresistible attraction all women seemed to hold for Earl Rognvald and he for them. Perhaps it was she who lost her thistle brooch in boggy grass above the foundered ship.

Earl Rognvald seems to have spent some considerable time in Shetland. Incognito he went off fishing with a local bondi ending up in the tiderace off Sumburgh Head to the great distress of the old man who owned the boat. While the bondi prayed, earl Rognvald rowed, bringing them both safely ashore with a fine catch, the earl distributing his share among the poor.

By 1066, after two and a half centuries of world-ranging expansion, the Vikings, with the exception of their north Atlantic colonies, were literally back where they started, their great victories obliterated in the continual struggle for dominance at home. Olaf Trygvasson and Olaf Haraldsson, Svein Forkbeard, Magnus Olafsson and Harald Hardrada were all kings hopelessly impeded by internal wars. Vinland was abandoned, likewise Greenland, and with improvements in agriculture there were not enough men available or desirous of venturing overseas. Iceland became quite independent of Norway and even the duchy of Normandy cut free from its Norwegian-Danish connection and long before the end of the Viking age it was French in culture, language and politics.

As a maritime power Norway had everything against her at this time and what happened in Norway influenced Shetland. Climatically a change had come about, as it had done so long ago at the beginning of the Iron Age. After 1200 Greenland and Iceland were becoming colder. Over much of Europe the glaciers were advancing, eating up the treeline and for longer and longer periods the Alpine passes were sealed. Drift ice off Iceland became an increasing hazard to shipping and the same problem was apparent in Greenland. By the 1300's the old sailing route west had been abandoned because of Polar ice and on the west coast the Eskimo was reappearing, penetrating the north-

31   Ponies and sheep near Uyeasound, Unst. Uyeasound meaning the island sound (ON -y, island).

ern hunting grounds and hampering their use by the Norse Green-landers. By 1350 it was reported that "the Skaelings hold the entire Western Settlement". Pastures had been attacked by pest. The increased trade of furs and hides out of Russia, the growth of the English and Dutch cloth trade in opposition to the Greenland woollens, and the preference of French workshops for elephant ivory in place of the inferior walrus tusk priced Greenland out of the market.

Even in the thirteenth century Bergen had all the furs and hides it needed and the town, like Norway, was headed for troubles of its own. In 1349 the Black Death killed one in three of Norway's population. As though plague were not enough Bergen was twice burned towards the end of the fourteenth century by the Victual Brethren and twice sacked by Bartholomeus Voet. Finally the Hansa merchants secured a stranglehold on the town's trade and by 1400 on all of Norway.

After the Earldom of Orkney had been established, Shetland, Orkney and Caithness had had a common government until the luckless Earl Harald Madaddson, whose mother had eloped with Earl Erlend to Mousa, finally lost Shetland when it was annexed to Norway in 1194 after the rebellion of the islanders against king Sverre and their defeat at Florevag near Bergen. Norway, which had made such an impact on the world, like so many great empires was weakening. A culture, but never a civilisation, it lacked cohesion due largely to the innumerable jarls involved in perpetual family feuds and the demands of widely scattered dominions. These great adventurers had contributed greatly to trade, discovery and colonisation in such a diversity of achievement both at home and abroad. Outstanding in their day in the arts of seafaring, possessed of boundless energy, intelligent, fearless, and at the same time ruthless, careless of their own safety, they drove themselves and their nation inexorably towards its own dissolution.

12. *The Betrayal*

The line of earls ruling over Orkney and Shetland, for years practically half Scots, became wholly Scottish when Torf Einar's male line ceased with Earl Jon in 1231, after holding the earldom for 10 generations. In that year Jon was murdered in Caithness and one of Jon's sisters, having married Gilbert of Angus, brought the earldom into this purely Scottish family. The Angus line retained it till 1329 when through lack of male heirs it passed in 1379 in the person of Henry St. Clair to the St. Clair line, which held it until the mortgage.

After the indecisive Battle of Largs embassies were exchanged between Scotland and Norway to negotiate a settlement. Due to the time involved in communicating back and forth between the two countries it was not until 1265 that the parties came to an agreement, and the Norse and Scots met at Perth, where the final treaty was concluded in July, 1266. The king of Norway ceded Man and the Sudreys with all rights to the King of Scotland and in addition the right of patronage to the Bishopric of Man, though without violation of the jurisdiction of the Norse Archepiscopate. In return King Alexander III of Scotland pledged himself to pay 400 marks sterling and a yearly payment in perpetuity of 100 marks sterling each year in St. Magnus Cathedral. This "annual ov Norway", or rather the subsequent failure to pay it, was an important part in the mortgaging of the isles to Scotland in 1468 and 1469. It was expressly stated in the treaty that the Orkneys and Shetlands with various precisely defined rights were to be retained wholly and without reservation within the realm of the King of Norway. This treaty was subsequently confirmed by Robert Bruce and Haco of Norway on October 19th, 1312.

Some years after this the Norse King Erik married the daughter of Alexander III and their daughter Margaret's right to the Crown of Scotland held all Britain in an agony of apprehension and "The Little Maid of Norway" was callously betrothed to Edward son of Edward I of England. Sent off on her bridal journey her passage was a stormy one. Sick and ill with the relentless tossing on the wild North Sea she died of her misery before she could reach Orkney in the summer of 1290

It is difficult to dissociate Norway, Denmark and Sweden during these remarkable years so frequently referred to in Shetland history as The Golden Age. To the millions of unfortunates who suffered from raids and piracy they were all Vikings. For 300 years they had contrived to make their influence felt. Gradually there had come a distinction and Danes, Swedes, Norwegians in their trade and exploratory routes had taken very different directions. Shetland from the very first was associated with Norway but at a crucial moment in history Norway united with Sweden and in 1397 came the union of Denmark, Norway and Sweden under a Danish king. Shetland's whole connection with Norway, indeed her entire history, might have taken a different turn had Norway been able to maintain the balance of power, but with the Union the fate of the Northern Isles was sealed and although Shetland continued trading and cultural links with Norway up until the nineteenth century the islands were to become mere pawns in international politics.

After the previous war with Sweden, King Christian, the new King of Denmark, Norway and Sweden, realised that the "annual ov Norway", the 100 marks due each year by King Alexander of Scotland since 1266, had been long neglected and that an enormous sum had accrued. He demanded payment in full. It was King Charles VII of France who acted as intermediary and peacemaker and helped to arrange the marriage between Princess Margaret of Denmark and Prince James, soon to become King James III of Scotland. This scheme would immediately have reversed the financial positions of the Scottish and Scandinavian kings, making Christian the debtor to the tune of 60,000 florins for his daughter's dowry.

By the marriage treaty of 1468 the arrears of the "annual" were cancelled and the princess's dowry fixed at 60,000 florins of which 10,000 were to be paid within the year, the Crown Lands of Orkney to be pledged for the remainder. Only 2000 florins were paid within the agreed time and on May 20th, 1469 the Crown Lands of Shetland were pledged for the remaining 8000 florins, a stipulation in both cases being that the laws and customs of the islands should remain unchanged "in the meantime", a phrase suggesting that these measures were only temporary ones until the islands could be redeemed by King Christian. A clause in the marriage contract directed that in the event of James predeceasing Margaret and in the event of Margaret wishing to leave Scotland thereafter then Margaret was to be paid 120,000 florins (as representing one-third of her marriage portion) from which the debt of 50,000 florins for her dowry was to be deducted, and Orkney (and *a priori* Shetland) was to return to Norway.

In both groups of islands at that time were four classes of land; the ordinary udallers' lands, the earls' estates, the church lands and the royal estates. It was therefore solely the royal estates and the accompanying sovereignty of the islands in each case that King Christian pledged, for it was only these that he owned, which goes far to explain the difference between the Orkney and Shetland amounts pledged. When in 1470 King James III of Scotland and Earl William Sinclair exchanged the earl's lands in Orkney and Shetland for the king's estates at Ravenscraig in Fife King James automatically became the rightful earl of Orkney, an hereditary position, so that even if the pledge had been redeemed and the sovereignty restored to the Scandinavian king the position of earl, which was actually a far more powerful one within the islands than that of king, would have been held in perpetuity by the King of Scotland and his family. An Act of Parliament was passed on May 11th, 1471 to ratify the exchange and on March 31st, 1486 the Town of Kirkwall was erected into a Royal Burgh with power to elect a commissioner to Parliament.

The choice of Shetland as the second bond in the payment of the dowry had undoubtedly a geographical basis. Of all the outlying possessions of the Dano-Norwegian kingdom, these islands lay within reasonably easy reach of Scotland and had long afforded shelter to pirates who molested the adjoining coasts. Secondly, from the thirteenth century when the Hebrides were absorbed from Norway after the Battle of Largs, Scotland was striving to reach to the natural limits of her kingdom, and to obtain permanently the land described by Charles II as "so great a jewel of their Crown". Scotland was quick to seize her advantage, for James III was married in July, 1469 and by November of that year the Bishop of Orkney, significantly one of Scotland's ambassadors to the Court of Denmark, was appointed a constituent member of the Parliament of Scotland. Four years later the Crown, by virtue of an Act of the Scottish Parliament, took over the Earldom.

In spite of the "take over" of the Orkneys and Shetlands by the Scottish Crown, the ancient Law Ting continued to regulate life and government, still under the spiritual, if not the physical, aegis of Norway. A regular digest known as "The Buik of the Law" formed the ruling authority in the Courts of Justice similar to those of Norway. The ties of 200 years were yet strong enough to ensure that Shetland's first loyalty was to her Norse forbears, stubbornly surviving the systematic infiltration of Scottish or "foreign" law and the pressures of Church and commons for over 130 years. In Orkney, Norse manuscripts end in 1426 but still occur in Shetland as late as 1607. While in 1439 the Orcadian lawman was writing his evidence in Scottish, its use does not appear in a single Shetland document until as late as 1525. In 1485 we find

114

an agreement with regard to the possession of certain lands in Shetland made in the court at Bergen when a lawrightman of Shetland was present in person, while 50 years later a judgment given in a Shetland court "according to the *Gulathing Law*" was confirmed in Bergen.

The chief civil positions in Shetland continued in foude and lawman. The foude summoned the courts, presiding over them but taking no part in the deliberations, his duty lying in carrying out the courts' decisions and playing some part in the choice of assessors. The Lawting still tried all the more serious cases of crime, settled major civil actions and made general regulations and laws. In making his circuit every summer the foude collected the taxes, paid in *wadmel*, a rough home-woven tweed, butter and fish oil. He issued licences for trading to the ever-increasing number of German merchants and to residents leaving the country. He set the prices of goods imported by the foreign merchants and had jurisdiction over wrecks. Whatever the crime, no one was ever confined in prison; the loss of personal liberty, the most commonly used deterrent in our so-called enlightened age, was quite unheard of and would have been wholly abhorrent to the Shetlander of the fifteenth century. An elaborate system of fines was imposed and the ultimate punishment was exile.

The foudes continued from Norse in the thirteenth century in one Sigurd, representing Duke Haakon, son of King Magnus of Norway, to names in the fourteenth century like Thorvald Thoresson of Papa Stour, Giafladr Ivarson, Hakon Jonsson and Malise Sperra of Tingwall until in the fifteenth century the Scots arrived with John Sinclair, son of Earl Henry St. Clair, and the English in the person of Thomas Inglis, factor of Bishop Andrew, who was given, significantly enough, the "feudal right of removing tenants at will and entering others in their places", the Church already setting the example of what was to follow.

Towards the end of the fifteenth century came Sir David Sinclair, Captain of Bergen Castle in Norway and Dingwall Castle in Scotland, a "go between" of the kings of Denmark and Scotland. He is buried in Tingwall. He was followed by Thorvald Henderson of Brough Nesting; then came the two brothers James and Edward Sinclair who usurped power after killing the Earl of Caithness at Summerdale in the last battle fought on Orkney soil. For a few years a William Sinclair held the position of foude, then Olaw Sinclair of Havera (the little island off Maywick on the west coast) and Broo, (the old spelling of the loch of Browe in Dunrossness). Fleeing before raiders from Lewis he fell from the cliffs at Sumburgh Head, lost an eye in the process, and his reputation not long after when he entertained the notorious Earl of Bothwell. With Laurence Bruce of Cultmalindie, half-brother of Robert Stewart, a Scots upstart whose illegal actions and oppressions became the subject of an inquiry by the Regent Morton in the year 1577, the ancient position of foude came to an end.

Although in 1540 the islands had been re-annexed to the Scottish Crown and granted a year later to Oliver Sinclair with instructions to judge fairly and not to oppress the people, a caution which does not speak too highly of his reputation, the words were scarcely worth the paper on which they were written. The lordship was declared to be of the value of £2000 (Scots) a year, the rent, at least in part, to be paid in kind, flour being delivered regularly to Tantallon Castle. The Scottish Parliament could self-righteously point to its own specific finding that both Orkney and Shetland should continue to enjoy their own laws and not be subject to the common laws of Scotland, paying lip-service only to the terms of the marriage contract of 1468, an empty gesture to which no one paid the least attention.

The manner in which Scotland's "peaceful penetration" of the islands began, with innocent sounding overtures that gathered momentum with the years, finds a curious parallel in twentieth-century central European history, the first lessees being the spearhead of ultimate domination. Bemused by the phraseology of Scottish feudal law, couched in a tongue with which the ordinary Shetlander was as yet scarcely familiar, inundated by a constant stream of legatees, lords, commoners and bishops, each making his own subtle contribution to the dissolution of the traditional way of life, the islanders awoke one day to find their freedom gone, the ancient laws twisted and bent out of all recognition, the "unholy" Roman churches razed to the ground and themselves in thrall to a series of despotic landlords.

By the time Bishop Andrew had been given the lease of the islands it was obvious that the Scottish Crown was regarding the law in Orkney and Shetland as not being too dissimilar from that adhered to in Scotland, and in 1489 when James IV granted a lease of the islands for 13 years to Henry, Lord Sinclair, his terms of office included that of "judiciar, foude and bailie, together with the power of uplifting escheats." The latter is defined as "property that falls to the feudal lord or to the state for want of an heir", a far cry from the old udal law which recognised no superior.

Things were taken a step further in 1541 when Oliver Sinclair of Pitcairns received a grant under the Privy Seal making "the said Oliver and his heirs, male justices, sheriffs, admirals and baillies" of all our Sovereign Lord's lands and lordships of Orkney and Shetland, with power "to the said Oliver and his heirs male (to set) courts of justiciary, sheriffship, admirality and bailliary" to call suits, to fine the absents, to attach and to arrest, to uplift escheats and, finally, to apply all

116

32 At the peat banks a pony is being loaded with peat to take home. On its back is the *flackie*, the straw packed saddle, then the *clibbers*—made of wood, the horns just showing: the *meshie* is the net made of straw rope which is hooked on to the *clibbers* and holds the *kishies* (baskets) one on either side. (Zetland County Library and Museum.)

escheats and unlaws "to their own use, utility and profit . . . and if need be to poind and distrain therefor".

No dictator could have had more sweeping powers and nothing approaching such distraint had ever been known in Shetland before. By the end of the fifteenth century there had been indications that Scotland was awakening to the benefits she might extract from her newly-acquired territories. There are frequent references in the Exchequer Rolls of Scotland and the Accounts of the Lord High Treasurer to the visits of falconers: ". . . the xxxvllj day of Aprille, giffin to Alexander Law the falconer, to pas in Cathnes, Orknay, Schetland, for halkis to the King." The trade in hawks continued but at the end of the sixteenth century, along with a growing reluctance on the part of the islanders to pander to the king's demand, a complaint was lodged that the falconers had a difficulty in acquiring hawks owing to the "evill handilling of his Majesteis servandis and falconaris".

117

Nevertheless the trade continued and in the middle of the eighteenth century, when "A True and Exact Description of the Island of Shetland" was printed in London, the writer notes that "the finest Hawks in the World are bred in this Island, and whether it is by Charter or not, I cannot tell, but the Inhabitants are obliged to provide the King's Faulkiner (who commonly resides in Edinburgh) with so many every Year, for which Purpose, a proper Person is sent out to receive them, who maintains them in their Passage from Zetland to Leith with Dogs Flesh which he buys up in the Islands and kills occasionally on the Voyage".

This small pamphlet was written in 1753 and by 1841, in the New Statistical Account of the Shetland Islands, the minister for Tingwall, Whiteness and Weisdale was commenting in an extremely full account of his parish on all the burdens of taxes that his parishioners are burdened with: ... "The land mails or rents", he notes, "were anciently paid in *wadmell* afterwards converted into money or butter. The merks land rated at 6 penny, 12 penny etc. The tenants also paid one fowl for every house or reek to feed His Majesty's hawks. This claim has again been set up by His Majesty's falconer for Scotland but resisted by the Shetland gentlemen and a process in regard to it is now pending before the Court of Session."

In fact, this levy had been responsible for the introduction of stoats or whitrits into the islands. There came a year when the crofters flatly refused to pay the falconers his hens and the next time he came to Shetland he "slipped" a pair of stoats into the islands, no doubt hopeful that they would feed on the crofters' hens, and to this day these animals are quite commonly seen in the countryside.

In 1491 also occurs the first mention of a skin trade: "for Orknnay Skynnis (?marten) to line it (a gown)". The goods of a Shetland heiress were considerable. She may well have lined her gowns with marten in the cold winters but a record is preserved in the list of goods belonging to one Gudrun Sigurd's daughter, wife of Arnbjorn Gudleikson, residing in the Faroe Islands. Besides her land rent from Shetland she brought as her dowry: "a headdress valued at 13 or 14 ore; a full dress suit decorated with shields down to the waist in front and on the loins: a great silver buckle and a rosary with silver beads: a small buckle from Courland of silver gilt or of gold; a finger ring of gold and two silver bowls (which may well have resembled those from the St. Ninian's Isle treasure); two cloaks and gowns with buckles; bed ornaments and curtains, silk, red and green and numerous bright ornaments. It was noted that on Fridays she resorted to a coarse cap instead of her brilliant headdress, and one wonders whether this humble attire had been a kind of penance, or whether on that day she supervised the making of wine,

118

baking, or cleaning of the house? She possessed five or six beds and pillows, with covers of precious workmanship and fringes, and a large furnished chest; basins and bathing tubs on two feet (tuifot); dishes, cans, pots, kettles and goblets beyond number; brocaded and lace coverings (for saints or relics) a truly magnificent plenishing of household goods and personal apparel." Soon the Crown was receiving from the islands supplies of salt marts (cattle carcases) and salt swine, for Orkney and Shetland were now expected to supply provender for the Royal household. Shortly after that butter makes its appearance being exported from Orkney and probably, since butter was in use as one of Shetland's taxation payments, from that island also. Not good enough, however, for the Royal household, it was designated as: "Orkynnay buttir ... for the artalere ..." the fusiliers either being credited with less delicate palates or the "buttir" was used to grease their matchlocks.

The real landmark in the transition period was the first charter of May 26th, 1564 in which Mary Queen of Scots granted to her half-brother, the bastard son of James v, Robert Stewart, for a feu charter of £2006 13s 4d (Scots), in return for an annual duty of 3000 merks payable to the Crown, the following: "the earldom and crown lands of Orkney and Zetland with the isles belonging thereto and castles, towers, fortalices, woods, mills, multures, fishings, tenants, tenandrie, service of free tenants, superiority of free tenants and advocation and donation of churches, chaplainries and benefices thereof and also the office of Sheriff of the Sheriffdom of the Foudrie of Zetland". At the stroke of a pen Mary signed away the birthright of a group of islands of which she knew nothing, unaware of its lack of woods, castles, fortalices or towers, her half-brother leaning over her shoulder, making very sure that his sister left out nothing in the document, that his would be full and unquestionable control of whatever these Northern Isles might contain to his benefit.

Illegal though it might be, and Robert Stewart in no way in the line of royal descent, it left the Shetlands helpless in the hands of a Scottish earl with little to stop him from dreaming up innumerable methods of increasing his revenue while still remaining on the right side of the law, and acquiring as much as he could in the way of rents, dues and fines. Unlike the Norse earls, who seldom visited Shetland, Robert Stewart built a mansion at Sumburgh and had a house at Wetherstaa in the parish of Delting. In 1576 the last foude was appointed and by 1580 Earl Robert was administering the Norse Law through his sheriff deputies. The offices of lawman and lawrightman were dropped although under-foudes continued to play a part in the local government under the Scottish title of bailie well into the eighteenth century and ranselmen were appointed as late as the nineteenth century. Along with Robert Stewart had come his half-brother, Laurence Bruce of Cultmalindie, who obtained the office of Fowdrie of Zetland, built for himself the castle of Muness in Unst and so managed his affairs in Shetland that he was able to leave an estate worth £4000 when he died in 1617, a fortune in those days.

By now the Shetlanders, caught in a web of oppression between Robert Stewart and Laurence Bruce, were on the verge of open rebellion. In the Records Office in Edinburgh is the official record of the "Complaints and Probations of the Commons and Inhabitants of Zet-

33 Muness Castle, Unst, a 3-storeyed fortified building begun in 1598 by Laurence Bruce of Cultmalindie, half-brother of Earl Robert Stewart. Bruce, Great Fowd of Shetland, was apparently as tyrannical as his half-brother. The castle "a most finished and scholarly piece of architecture" was designed by Adam Crawford, who was also responsible for Scalloway Castle which is now being restored.

land" received and taken up by Commissioners appointed by the Regent Morton in 1576 to inquire into the "many high attempts, inordinate oppressions, and new exactions daily committed upon our peaceable and obedient subjects, the inhabitants of our country of Zetland".

The Commissioners sat at Tingwall in February, 1577 where from day to day the men of the different parishes appeared before them to recount the "divers wrongs and extortions" they had suffered when "after the coming of Lord Robert Stewart, feuar of Orkney and Shetland, to the dominion of the said countries, Laurence Bruce of Cultmalindie obtained of him the office of Fowdrie of Zetland".

Shetlanders have so often been accused of an abysmal resignation to their lot, of lack of initiative or the guts to rebel, but when courage was tested to the limit, their every attempt at redress quashed, the final peripatetic attitude is wholly understandable. As always, no redress was forthcoming. Bruce, although ordered to remain south of the Tay by the Privy Council itself, either disregarded it with impunity or the order was rescinded, and all that happened was that Lord Robert was created Earl of Orkney and Lord of Zetland, to be succeeded by his son Patrick. Mary, Queen of Scots, in creating Adam Bothwell Bishop of Orkney, had made it possible for Earl Robert to exchange his own bishopric of Holyrood for Bothwells's Shetland one, thus taking possession of the Bishop's rents and so became not only the sole proprietor of the Crown rents but also of the Bishopric's.

Things went from bad to worse. Earl Robert found a new "exactioun" in sheep and ox money: "one ox and twelff scheip" from every parish towards the expenses of the annual Lawting Court at Tingwall, which was later to feature in the list of complaints against Bruce of Cultmalindie. Matters were complicated by the break-up of church estates at the Reformation when relatives of churchmen in Orkney arrived to add their demands to a bewildering and ever-mounting series of dues payable to either earl, bishop or minister. The ministers in fact got the worst name of all, their voracious appetite for lands and payment in kind leading to the bitter remark that all Shetland got out of Scotland was bad meal and greedy ministers.

In addition to the weight of unorthodox and shady double-dealing from foude and earl, the crofter was besieged and bewitched into disposing of his lands to "gentlemen of Scotland" who came to settle in the islands . . . "these incomers found no great difficulty in purchasing land from the poor simple inhabitants . . . They began to lay aside the Shynd Bill and to use dispositions and sasines and thereupon followed that long train of conveyances filled with all the clauses and quirks that the lawyer and notary could invent, for lengthening the writing and making it so intricate that the true sense and meaning thereof might only be known to themselves; so that it came to pass in a short process of time ". . . whereby the ancient simple udallers were turned out of their old inheritances, and obliged to improve that ground for others that they had foolishly neglected to do for themselves."

It is apparently not widely known and certainly ignored by Scottish historians that time and again the Danish kings had made formal representations by letters to the Scottish Court and to the sovereigns of England and France and on more than one occasion by special embassies, to recover the Orkneys and the Shetlands. During the years from 1549 to 1660 no less than eight attempts were made with offers of repayment of the sum pawned.

For the last time in the middle of the eighteenth century, King Frederick v demanded the restitution of the islands. It would appear that even yet the right of redemption under existing arrangements remains with Denmark, because, according to Goudie, when Denmark and Norway were disjoined in 1814, Denmark retained the islands of the North Sea, which may well be held as including all rights of reversion to Orkney and Shetland. While the position now remains *in status quo*, it is interesting, that Scottish historians have ignored these episodes, clearly documented not only by the Danish historian Thormodus Torffaeus but throughout Europe from Elizabeth of England to the Spanish king.

122

13. *Earl Patrick*

FROM THE STRAGGLING hamlet of skollas and sketchy lodging houses grown up around the bays since the first Norse *Allthing* sat in the Tingwall valley Scalloway was soon to become Shetland's capital. As the centre of government it could scarcely claim even village status, but it would grow, dominated for all time by the grey walls of the turreted castle of Earl Patrick Stewart. Inheriting a grandiose but none the less elegant taste in architecture from his grandfather, James v, Earl Patrick was not impressed by the family seat of the Old Haa' at Sumburgh. With a lavish extravagance for which Shetland was to pay dearly, he employed as his architect Adam Crawford, designer not only of Muness Castle in Unst for Bruce of Cultmalindie, but also the beautiful Bishop's Palace in Kirkwall. Crawford died in the first decade of the seventeenth century, his fine tombstone preserved in a vault in Tingwall kirkyard, perhaps fortunately not surviving to see either the abuses to which his inspired creation was put nor the eventual execution of his patron.

As Shetland's only village, apart from the castle itself, Scalloway was a modest, unimpressive collection of small houses, its only residents of note being one or two officials and people in the Earl's service. The entire population of Tingwall parish at this time was only about 1150. There were a few skippers, as would be natural in a sheltered seaport, and one or two tradesmen; George Mitchell and James Schort, or Schortus, who were tailors; John Ross, a mason; Alexander Gray, a "cordiner", or shoemaker, and Archibald Murray, a wright whose apprentice Francis Inglis boarded with one Lilias Boyd at the rate of 4s per day. As in other ports there would be a booth or trading place; in each parish a manse and here and there a laird's haa' hoose. Apart from these the country was thinly scattered with isolated farmhouses and an occasional cluster of cottages.

Over the islands the distribution of the population, while fairly even, meant that some places had fewer people than today and some a larger population in the seventeenth century than in the twentieth. Fetlar for instance boasted about 500 inhabitants as against today's figure of 92,

34 Abandoned planti-crubs like tilted saucers in the olive parks—the small, shallow depressions once stone walled where cabbage seeds were planted out and well away from the cultivated area so that they might be kept free of disease. In the distance is the top of Fitful, the highest point, then Noss. Only one is still in use on the extreme right.

and many of them lived in parts of the island now abandoned. The tiny island of Bigga, long deserted, was then in occupation, while the north-west quarter of Yell, between Lumbister and Gloup, together with Mousa, Papa and Hildasay, was empty except for shepherds and yet in the nineteenth century the islands had 12, 23 and 30 people living on them respectively.

The Scottish immigration was still in progress and in May, 1604 the Earl issued a proclamation announcing "in lurid terms" that "beggars, vagabonds and immoral persons from the Scottish Highlands and other barbarous parts", had entered Orkney, devouring its substance and associating with the idle and immoral among the natives and now intended to proceed to Shetland "where they hope to have liberty to live wickedly according to the appetite of their filthy flesh" and where "they proposed to establish a house of ill-fame in Sumburgh".

Evidently Sumburgh was already a place of ill-repute, its position as a commercial and fishing centre attracting "vicious persons" and the Orcadians in Dunrossness had a bad name as thieves. Even after Earl Patrick's day it was still "hevile complaint be the inhabitantis of Yetland of the great resoirt and repair pairtlie of sturdie beggaris and partlie of puir vagabondis from Orkney, Caithnes and utheris forren places".

Shetland life under Earl Patrick is not only documented for all time in the Court Book of 1602–4 but in Professor Gordon Donaldson's brilliant and meticulous account of every facet of a crofter's existence during this period. Society was divided into well-defined classes. The wealth of the islands without exception was in the hands of Scotsmen, most of them incomers who had rapidly acquired substantial although scattered estates. Easily the richest of these were the Sinclairs of Brough with lands in Nesting, Delting, Sandsting, Aithsting, Walls, Whiteness, Weisdale, Northmavine, Bressay, Burra, Dunrossness, Unst and Fetlar and in most of these districts tenants owing them rents and dues. The possessions of Robert, son of Hugh Sinclair of Brough, were valued in 1617 at £26,486 6s 8d and the debts owing to him amounted to £5640. He organised fishing on a commercial basis, owned 13 boats and had his own "great boat for passage". By today's standards he would be worth about a quarter of a million.

Bruce of Cultmalindie, who died in 1617, was another landed magnate but not even he could match the fantastic standard of the Sinclairs. In the same category as Bruce was the minister Pitcairn. Ministers in general appear to have accumulated quite excessive estates, their remote country manses often being luxuriously equipped. Robert Swinton, minister of Walls, left a remarkable list of household plenishings including: "36 pairs of blankets, (£3 each); 16 pairs of sheets (£3 each); 5 feather beds, 6 bolsters, 20 cods of pillows, 12 coverings or bedcovers; a quantity of buird cloths or tablecloths, serviettes, towels and 12 cushions". He also owned boats and it was hinted broadly that he may well have been the first on the spot when a well-furnished ship broke up on the shores of his parish. As Sir Walter Scott remarked in *The Pirate* "a ship ashore is a sight to wile the minister out of his very pulpit in the middle of his preaching".

The great bulk of the population in Earl Patrick's day, and for at least a generation after it, consisted of a middle-class of small landholders, neither rich nor poor but relatively comfortable each with his ponies, cattle and sheep, crops of oats and bere. Many of them were udallers but among them quite a number were tenants either of the Earl or one of the larger landowners.

The humblest folk could rarely aspire to property worth more than £20 to £30; a tiny estate in Whalsay worth £23 included: "ane auld coo, ane bull and a quoyack, ane stirk and twa yowis". Agnes Olasdochter of Aithsting was worth only £20 3s 4d with half a mare, two cows and seven sheep. Everyone, however, would have some arable land, probably enough to feed himself; grazing for his animals and peats for the fire and yet most people with estates valued at under £100 could keep servants. Matthew Sutherland at Funzie in Fetlar, whose goods were valued at only £58 8s had two servants, Ola Magnesson and Janet Thomasdochter, while Alexander Forrester at Northerhouse, whose estate was less by £1, had four servants, Magnus Olason,

Walter Forrester, George Williamson and Christian Erasmusdochter.

The number of paupers was infinitesmal and significant of the general humble but adequate economic status of most of the inhabitants. The passing of a law whereby the finder of beggars and vagabonds was adjured "to take the plaidis from them or their uppermost clayth" and deliver them to the baillie of the parish to be punished in the stocks and jougs, certainly did not encourage idlers. There was only one pauper in Lunnasting for example; in Unst two women and four men; Walls and Sandness four men and three women; in Aithsting and Sandsting one man; in Dunrossness two men and two women and one woman in Bressay. Those people who perhaps through age or infirmity could no longer look after or support themselves were cared for by the traditional practice of "upgaistry". In this manner anyone possessing udal land could, with the consent of his heirs, dispone his patrimony to any person willing to support him for the rest of his life.

Occasionally this led to complaints that the disponent was not always being kept "in the manner to which he was accustomed", as we find in the case of James Sinclair of Norbuster.

It was, however, becoming increasingly obvious that during Earl Patrick's ill-starred reign conditions were steadily worsening and the variety of taxes and fines imposed on the islanders systematically drained away any possible profits they could be expected to make, in order to fill the exchequers of laird and Earl alike. The Althing had been moved to Scalloway Castle; the very fact of entrance into the great hall synonymous to the udallers with acknowledging their now feudal state.

By 1602 the building of the castle was so far advanced as to allow it to be used for the first time in Shetland law as a prison for one Henry Wardlaw and in the following year a German merchant was also held "in sure firmance" within its walls. While the old myth of eggs being used in the making of cement or maidens' hair being incorporated in its building was totally untrue the legend in an obscure way epitomised the feeling of compulsion under which the islanders laboured, as though in fact their very life blood and the sinews of their being were cruelly extracted in "biggin my lordis castle". The daily prosecutions that resulted in an ever-mounting list of fines, which of course went into the Earl's pocket, were indicative of the growing anger and unrest felt by the people bereft of any personal freedom of choice, a liberty held sacred since the first *Thing* had given to all men a constitutional right in ordering their lives as each one thought fit.

There was no doubt that such strictures merely encouraged the subversive element in the population to further acts of obduracy. In 1602 there were proceedings against John in Caldback, Delting, and James

126

Barnetson and Adam Cromarty in Dunrossness for disobedience "in non passing to my lordis wark to Scalloway as they wer derected". In 1604 "the haile inhabitantis of the bankis " (Scalloway banks) were suspected of theft of "my lordis timmer" and Captain Knightson and others were ordered to search "the haile houssis, greit and small, for my lordis timmer, new or auld". The smiths of Tingwall and Weisdale were accused of theft of the Earl's iron and John Smith and "the smith of Weisdale" in particular were suspected of stealing a hammer, a riddle and a crook of my lordis.

In each of the 10 or 11 district divisions of Shetland was an under-magistrate, still known by the Norse term foude, who could give his decision or "doom" for payment of debts, rents and other dues, the erection or upkeep of dykes and *grinds* (gates) and the protection of crops and pasture from destruction by animals. Normally a licence issued by a foude was sufficient authority for anyone to leave the country but labour became scarce, which is not to be wondered at, and it was ordained that shipmasters should carry no one from Shetland who had not a permit from the Earl or his deputies. One can imagine the difficulties involved in trying to obtain such a permit—no prisoner in the Alcatraz could have been more securely confined, the sea a natural but insuperable barrier to freedom.

The other district officials were the "officer", the "lawrightman" and the "ranselmen". The officer, a deputy of the foude, had the duty among others of marking any animals which had been forfeited to the Earl. The lawrightman, along with the foude, was custodian of the official weights and measures and many a complaint was made of the falsifying of the traditional "cannis, buismeris and cuttellis". The can was the measure of capacity, the bismar a weighing apparatus, still in use up to the end of the ninteenth century, and the cuttell the cloth measure. To the lawrightman also fell the duty of "riding the slaps" (inspecting broken-down dykes) and reporting the person at fault. The ranselman had the odious task of searching the houses in the detection of theft.

Anyone accused of a crime, either at a local court or at the Law Ting, was commonly given a chance to absolve or "quit" himself by bringing forward honest neighbours who would support his oath that he was innocent. In the "*larycht aith*" (*lyrittareidr* in old Norse law) the accused had two men, one appointed by the judge and one nominated by himself who could, by their oaths duly "quit" the accused. The second oath was known as the "*saxter aith*" (*settareidr*), the sixfold oath, and thirdly came the "*twalter aith*" the twelvefold oath (the *tylf-tareidr*).

The kind of oath required was apparently determined by the gravity of the crime. Treason and arson demanded the twelve-fold oath, sorcery and thefts above a certain value the sixfold, and petty thefts the three-fold. The system was a curiously complicated one and it might be that a person who had failed to produce friends to quit him by the *larycht aith* might then find himself facing the *saxter aith* and so forth until the chances of successful acquittal diminished as the number of oath helpers increased. In addition, the fine which was the penalty for failure to "quit" increased with the relevant oaths and anyone who had the misfortune to die "under quittance" would draw his last breath in the painful knowledge that all his wordly goods would be forfeit to the crown. The same penalty would fall on someone who had failed miserably in the "twalter aith of befoir".

There was little in either the old Norse law or the Scottish feudal law that Earl Patrick failed to turn to his own advantage. The anonymous author of the *Historie and Life of King James the Sext* remarked that Patrick "behaved himself with such sovereignty, and if I dare say the plain verity, rather tyrannically by the shadow of Danish laws, different and more rigorous than the municipal or civil laws of the rest of Scotland, whereby no man of rent or purse might enjoy his property without his special favour, and the same dear bought".

Even old half-forgotten breaches of the law were somehow exhumed so that a fine might be imposed. The lengths to which those in power were prepared to go in order to further line their own pockets border on the ludicrous when we read that Laurence Bruce of Cultmalindie, unearthing some 30-year-old offence of a purely technical nature, which had indeed been passed over when it was committed, dragged it up into the light of day and had the audacity to impose a stiff fine on the miserable culprit.

The economy of the islands at this time was based on the land on which the Shetlander grew oats and bere from which he made his meal and bread. On it he pastured cattle which gave him beef, butter, milk and cheese and the sheep produced not only mutton for food but wool which was "cairded", spun and knitted into stockings and shawls or woven into cloth, but the balance between cattle and sheep was vastly different from the picture today. Large flocks of sheep were found only on the "holms"—small, grassy uninhabited islands—usually owned by Earl Patrick himself or some other wealthy landowner.

Among the Earl's holms were Papa and Hildasay, conveniently near his castle of Scalloway. Even so, in 1597 about 150 sheep were stolen from Hildasay and 80 from Papa. Suspicion fell on four men who had been to Hildasay to gather bait. On the grounds that it was illegal for them to land on the island except under stress of weather the court at Whiteness declared their goods forfeited and ordained that in future

128

a gibbet be placed "in ilk greit holm or yle" for the execution of trespassers, whose goods were to be forfeited and a third of their possessions
to go to the person who had informed against them.

The gibbets on the holms proved no deterrent, for in 1603 the court
of Dunrossness had to pass an act generally forbidding trespassers on
the Earl's holms and particularly denying the right of anyone to "frequent the yle of Musa nor travel thairinto with boitis" without the
advice and company of David Ked whom the Earl had placed in charge
of his holms. In the same year the Earl's shepherd on the island of
Vementry was suspected of illicit dealings in wool and sheep.

The sheep wandered free on the common grazing and the court had
to ordain the foude to "mak everie ane of them to haife ane kenning
mark by utheris, that everie ane of them may ken thair schepe by
utheris". The term "kenning" is still used in the Faroes in this connection. No doubt the marks were permanently made by cutting the ears as
is still the practice today but an animal could be marked temporarily
by affixing a rag to one of the ears. We read of a "yow" which was
"lugmerkit with ane peice clayth". It was understood that the marking
of lambs should be done in public and the law could be invoked for
redress in the case of mismarking whether by error or with criminal
intent, reckoned a form of theft or "stowth". Besides being entitled to
mismarked sheep the Earl had a right to sheep going unmarked. It
is not unusual even today to see sheep going around with a coloured
rag attached to their fleece looking rather like pampered poodles.

Dogs were used for driving or "caa'in" the sheep but from very early
times it was forbidden to own more dogs than were necessary for working purposes and these could only be kept by persons either chosen or
approved by the foude and the parishioners, so there were many prosecutions for keeping dogs unlawfully. Wool was removed from the sheep
by "rooin" or plucking and the custom has survived in the case of the
real Shetland sheep, especially in Unst, the fine wool under the neck
being traditionally used for knitting the delicate lacy shawls.

Sheep stealing continued to be prevalent in every part of Shetland,
the largest number of cases occurring in Unst and Delting. Margaret
Petersdochter who had no sheep of her own stole one of her neighbour's
"in plain hunger and necessity" but in spite of the extenuating circumstances was sentenced to banishment; Ola Manson was accused of stealing a sheep from his own mother; there were notorious sheep thieves
in Papa Little and the tenants of Olnafirth were accused of the theft
of 48 sheep while Christopher Johnson of Scatsta had made away with
29.

The main difficulty very often lay in the disposal of the carcases and
in one instance the ranselman whose job it was to search for stolen

property found a gigot hidden under the bedclothes. Sometimes it was "reistit" mutton that was stolen, cured mutton for winter use, and in Papa Stour we find a reference to "twa birskettis" (breasts) of sheep. Beef also attracted thieves and removing cattle without leave of the owner was called "gripster" rather than "stowth". It was even found that cows were milked without permission, an offence which was "counted stowth". Butter was also another temptation, being barrelled and kept often for long periods so that it could be used in payment of dues to the Earl and the minister. In actual fact of course the Court Books only recount crime and that mainly of a petty nature, and many were the allegations of deliberate provocation by the Earl's men such as discovering a dead sheep in someone's park. If a man was found slain, the land on which he was found was confiscated. A few swine were kept and Bruce of Cultmalindie as foude of Shetland imposed a fine on everyone who kept swine and many killed them off. The oppression was eventually withdrawn but swine were notorious for the damage they did in cultivated ground. In 1603 the court of Walls approved a "doom" of the foude that the swine of Papa Stour should be "snypit and ringit", muzzled and ringed in both summer and winter so that people would be free from damage to their corn and grass.

Ponies were used, equipped with meshies or nets attached to klibbers harnessed on their backs, to carry peat and hay. As usual any pony for which no owner could be found was a perquisite of the Earl. An illicit journey on anyone else's pony meant that the rider was fined according to the number of scattalds—an area of land pertaining to the number of houses—that had been covered. The Country Acts of 1615 laid down that the fine for riding another man's horse was £6 within the bounds of the parish and an additional £6 for each further parish ridden through. Horse tails were rooed for hair for fishing lines and probably as in Faroe, twisted together to form ropes.

Peats were cast in the same way as they are today and the supply of peats for the use of Earl Patrick was a major operation. The people of Dunrossness were obliged "veirlie to leid and carie to my Lordis hous in Soundbrughe the quantity of twentie four faddom peitis . . . and to be placit and stakit . . . at whatever place was appointed . . . under the paine of ane angell nobill". The house at Sumburgh was built by Patrick's father and later given into the custody of William Bruce of Sumburgh.

Then there were the ferries, from Unst to Gutcher; Unst to Reafirth; Reafirth to Fetlar; Lunna Firth to Fetlar; across Yellsound by Bigga; across Yellsound to Northmavine and so forth all round the coast from Scalloway to Maywick; Maywick to Scalloway to Houss, Bressay Sound, Whalsay Sound. The people of Burra were under a particular

130

obligation to keep their boats on the east side of the island while the Earl and his deputies were in Shetland in order to convey his lordship and his staff whenever they wished. They were also responsible for flitting strangers and passengers from their island to Scalloway or to Maywick and were commanded to subscribe among themselves for the purchase of a ferry boat for this purpose which seems the last word in autocracy. This duty to provide water transport for their lord when called upon to do so was known as "flit and fuir" and one of the complaints against Bruce of Cultmalindie was his excessive demand for this service.

The constant search for bait also led to dispute and the old udal phrase "from the highest stone of the hill to the lowest in the sea" takes on new meaning when we find Magnus Robertson, officer in Whiteness, accused of taking bait within William Sinclair's ebb in Ustaness, for it is plain that property extended to the shore between high water mark and low water marks. There was also an act forbidding Sunday fishing, the General Assembly in 1602 blaming the fishing for the poor church attendance. Another act was decreed that "for the weal of the country, that no person or persons shall fish, lay or shoot lines within any voe of the country from Beltane to Allhallowmass yearly"—that is from the 1st May to 1st November—in order to protect the fishing in sheltered waters during the time of year when it was relatively safe to fish at sea and also when fresh meat was available.

At this time there were probably not more than 12,000 people in Shetland, and Lerwick was not yet in existence as a settlement although the use of Bressay Sound by the Dutch was already beginning to attract the natives to its shores. In 1615 an act was passed that "no persons shall repair to the sound nor isle of Bressay for furnishing of beir, vivoris and uther necessaris to the Hollanderis and utheris forreineris committing thereby villainy, fornication and adultrie, under paine of twentie pundis".

The court also dealt with moral lapses which elsewhere fell within the province of kirk sessions. In Papa Stour in 1602 poor old William in Hougoland was accused of "leading his life in fornication with Marion Hucheonsdochter these twenty years bygone" which surely in Scots law would have automatically been regarded as a true "marriage by repute" and in Nesting in 1604 Thomas Sinclair was brought before the court "for being ane relapsit person with Marion Manisdochter".

This was an age not only in Shetland when fear and superstition were rife, men and women were tried on the most absurd charges and in the name of God burned to death with true Christian zeal on a hill overlooking the village of Scalloway. Nearly every district in Shetland has its gallows hill. In Walls, Paul Watson and his wife were suspected

35 The waters of the Sneug, Foula, are believed to have medicinal properties. This tiny basin is tucked away in an overhang on the steep northerly slope of the Sneug (1369 ft.).

of "the stowth of their nychbouris profeit of butter, in respect that thayr is mair butter fund with them with twa or thrie ky nor with thair nychbouris quhilk hes sevin ky" and were ordered to clear themselves with the saxter aith "becaus the actioun is wechtie". How dangerous it must have been to strive through honest good sense and hard work to improve one's milk yield and then have jealous neighbours attribute it to witchcraft. In fact the chance to quit oneself through the larycht aith may have saved many a poor woman from a fate which in Scotland itself she would have no hope of avoiding.

Perhaps Shetland's most famous so-called witch was Marion Pardoun of Hillswick, burned as a witch in 1644, one of the many charges brought against her being that she had appeared in the form of a pellack whale and upset a fishing boat whereby four men were drowned. It was stated that apart from her evil tongue her eye was no less baneful. "She looked upon a neighbour's cow and it crapped tagidder till no life was left in her." She also cursed Janet Robertson of Hillswick and accordingly pains and fits fell upon her.

It was believed that witches, in league with the devil, were able to command the assistance of demons, who having been driven out of heaven took shelter in old ruins, in old mills and under brigs in burns. The forms in which these demons appeared, with whom the witches in Shetland communed, were those of the raven, that familiar of the old Norse gods, whose language the ancient diviner boasted she could understand. In like manner Marion Pardoun was seen going from Brecon to Hillswick while devils who were her own familiars appeared in the likeness of two crows that followed beside her all the way—her only

132

friends to whom she had been accustomed to throw bread and crumbs. As this appearance was solemnly maintained in the Shetland Court of Law to be contrary to the nature of wild fowls, this formed one of the charges against the unhappy woman at her trial.

At a court in Hillswick, Marion Pardoun was accused and found guilty of witchcraft and was brought to the place of execution on the Hill of Berrie and burned to ashes at the stake on the afternoon of March 21st, 1645. The judge at the trial was Olaw Magnasson, Moderator Nicol White, Clerk Robert Murray.

A Shetland witch could not only change her form at will into a variety of creatures but she could also "take the profit from a cow" by merely touching it, cause crops to fail by crossing her neighbours' fields, drawing behind her a rope twisted from grasses plucked from her neighbour's land. In Shetland old women in their dotage and people with physical abnormalities were always suspected of being witches. There were elaborate precautions to be taken when an animal was believed attacked by a witch, in addition to discovering witches. A suspect might be thrown into a loch. If the poor creature succeeded in swimming ashore she was undoubtedly a witch and was taken to the hill and burned alive.

Right up to the beginning of the present century, although never admitted, all kinds of complicated precautions were taken against witchcraft and trows. In a byre alongside the *veggl*, the stake driven into the stone wall and used as an anchor for the cow's headband, a steel knife was stuck. Trows were known to fear cold steel so this prevented them from taking the milk. Above the entrance door on the lintel would lie an old Bible to ensure that no evil spirits could cross the threshold, and hanging from the crossbaaks or rafters would be tufts of coarse hair from cow's tails and scraps of hide, shrivelled with age. When a beast died or was killed it was the custom to keep a bit of hide then "you can be sure that where one has been another will be".

14. *The Hansa Traders*

THOUSANDS OF YEARS had passed since the first human voice splintered the ancient stillness of voe and moorland piercing the cloud flowers of whirling seabirds, shattering wind sound and wave sound; since the first furrow was broken, the first seed planted. In the beginning man turned anxiously to the sea for some means of staving off the hunger pains until the crops could ripen, grateful for the small offerings the shores provided. The dune dwellers of the second millenium B.C., laboriously fashioning their quartz scrapers and split-pebble knives, gathered cockles, limpets and mussels. Watching the long rollers climbing the tilted rock platforms of Scatness, Fitful and Sumburgh, curling pale emerald to pour into the West Voe, they had waited, eager for the ebb, combing the beach for what the tide had left them, wood and wrack, tangles and beach stone, with now and then, perhaps, a stranded whale or seal.

On Whalsay the priests and their acolytes had walked between the Benie Hoose and Yoxie, tramping the island searching the pools under the pink quartz rock for *yoags*. In all the voes and sheltered coastal waters, from the green serpentine of Unst to the red sands of Ronas Voe and Stonga Banks, they had ventured cautiously forth bringing back sillaks, saithe, cod and ling. From narrow catwalks on broch towers eyes had swept the horizon watching too the boats riding the swift currents with net or line. They pounded fish bones with "knockin' stanes", a practice still continued in the remoter islands up to the nineteenth century when times were hard, to eke out the meagre diet of corn meal.

Centuries passed and the voes and beaches echoed to the ring of steel and the waves spewed up flotillas of high-prowed galleys filled with boisterous rough Norsemen continually coming and going, the sea their own peculiar highway. Even their first colonists appear to have used the shores as a source of food solely to vary a diet of meat, meal and vegetables. The sagas, concerned with greater things, scarcely mention such a mundane occupation as fishing. In Egil's Saga Grimm goes off herring fishing in winter along the Norwegian coast "taking many

134

house carls with him". In late spring they moved further north but still in the beginning herring was only part of the activity. In Njal's Saga the Bjorn Islands in Breida Fjordur owned by Thorwald Osviffson, from which he got dried fish and flour, were a recognised fishing station which was a fine place to gather and exchange news.

By now Shetlanders too were venturing further off the land and in April, 1136 a Norwegian called Uni took with him his three sons and fished off Fair Isle. In the party were "three Hjaltlanders" and they took a six-oared boat, some provisions and fishing tackle which seems to indicate that they might have been line fishing. Earl Rognvald's expedition with the bondi near the island of Horsholm off Sumburgh Head emphasises the fact that fishing was quite a usual occupation when food was scarce. The old man was terrified at the tide race, and his only thought to return safely with this mad stranger who laughed at the wild seas, bringing back enough fish for his wife and children. The adventure ended happily with what was obviously the usual "share out" among the crew.

Although a number of stone "sinkers" have been found in Shetland it is difficult to say whether all of them were used in line fishing, for many could equally well have served as loom weights or door-lock weights. The Foula crofters who "cavilled their lambs" just as the early Norse colonists in Jarlshof had done, coined the word from the Old Norn "kavlin tree" a wooden implement for taking the hook out of a fish's mouth—so there must have existed some kind of a hook.

The invention of the cod line is attributed to a More farmer in 1680, who probably learned about it from the English or the Dutch who were using long lines at the turn of the century. The salmon must have been familiar to the Norsemen, its presence in Shetland attested in place names like Laxfirth, Laxdale—Laxo from the Norse word *laks*. They were undoubtedly eaten but were not used as a regular part of the diet.

Earl Rognvald's friend the bondi was most likely fishing for saithe, using the dorro or hand-line, one man rowing against the tide—*andoin*, as it is still called—while the other sat aft and did the fishing. Although never far off-shore they caught fairly large fish. Information as to trading in fish is scanty but some kind of processing did take place in Scandinavia, for again in Egil's Saga we learn that Thorolf prepared a ship on the south-west coast of Norway and sent it to England with a cargo of "dried fish, skins, tallow, grey fur and other furs and all this was of great value ..." The ship was then loaded for the return journey with wheat, honey, wine and cloth. In the tenth century the Saga of St. Olaf records a boat passing laden with salt or herrings.

As early as the great days of Imperial Rome, Roman merchants in

Utrecht had traded in herring between the Rhine delta and the southern provinces of Europe. Between the eleventh and fifteenth centuries Shetland had some trade with Bergen in fish and other commodities but the two events consequent upon each other which turned the peasant farmer into a fisherman and made the name of Shetland almost synonymous with "herring" came later and both from outside the islands. The first of these was a simple natural phenomenon of migration, as unforeseeable as an earthquake and equally irreversible. Before these extraordinary happenings the herring was unknown in Shetland although the earliest reference to it is dated A.D. 709, when we find in the chronicles of the Monastery of Evesham an invoice for salt herrings purchased for the monks' larder. At the time of Domesday Dunwich paid 60,000 herrings annually to the king. Herring appeared on the corporation seal of Yarmouth and Dunwich so when Henry I created Yarmouth a burgh the price of the honour was another annual payment of ten millards of herring. From that day onwards this insignificant fish assumed the importance of a status symbol. The Mayor and Sheriffs of Norwich were allowed to hold so many acres of land in return for the peppercorn rent of carrying 24 herring pasties to the King wherever he might be.

By the end of the twelfth century fishermen from every part of western Europe between the Skaw and Ushant had made Yarmouth a fishing rendezvous, led by the Dutch, who had developed fish processing to a fine art. The English, sceptical at first, eventually became resentful of Dutch successes. Feeling ran high and Henry I was forced to pass an edict allowing the Dutch to fish for herring at Yarmouth and forbidding the English to molest them. Herring was big business and Matthew Paris writing at St. Alban's in 1238 noted a glut of herring that year at Yarmouth because the Scandinavian merchants who normally marketed their catch in the Baltic were deterred from the venture for fear of the Mongols, the power of the great Chinghiz Khan from Karakoram even affecting the marketing of the humble herring.

The Barons of the Cinque Ports had the right of holding a Fair on the seashore between Michaelmas and Martinmas and about 1270 the great herring fair lasting the traditional 40 days was instituted, occurring for nearly 50 years. The place became the Marseilles of Britain with all the crime and loose-living of a cosmopolitan resort, so much so that the Barons were forced to send officers to keep the peace. The same story was to be repeated in Bressay Sound when by order of the Scottish authorities the Dutch Fair was burned to the ground. The series of wars between England and Holland was in point of fact the first step in Britain's struggle for supremacy at sea, which in practical terms meant control of the herring fishing in the North Sea.

At this time the power of the Hanseatic League was at its peak. It was a league of merchants which was to have a profound influence upon Shetland's whole economy and most of the trade in northern Europe was organised through one of its kontors. Originally founded as a merchant company, the Hansa began in the humblest way possible, by setting up a modest collection of booths outside a monastery or castle. Convenient for the owners and inmates, the small shopkeepers seemed able to provide whatever goods they might require. In no time at all the insignificant traders were rich enough to be in a position to lend money to their clients, who were in constant need of funds to finance the wars in which they were involved.

Unlike the Jews, the Hansa merchants demanded no interest. Instead, with infinite cunning they merely requested some small privileges, perhaps hunting or fishing rights which the Barons gladly allowed them. Then they pressed for the right to bear arms, a reasonable enough request as the countries through which they were forced to journey were infested with robbers and the seas with pirates. Following on this came the privilege of holding City Councils and finally the demand for a City Charter by which they might manage their own affairs without interference by an overlord. It was the first step towards a far-reaching civic power that became powerful enough to dictate to kings and emperors.

They reached the zenith of their power at a time when the demand for fish was so great as to be almost unquenchable. Both the Roman Catholic Church and the Greek Orthodox Church, with their numerous fast days and Lenten feasts, were ready to buy all the fish that could be provided. With this in mind it was natural that the Hansa turned its eyes to the flourishing trade off the Baltic coasts. With the aid of the salt deposits around the Baltic the Danes had invented a method of salting fish so that it could be carried, a trifle high in odour, but edible, across the seas and far into the countries where the demand was greatest. In no time at all the Hansa were in control. Their vessels carrying cargo for Lenten feasts were not bound as other vessels by the laws governing sailing ships and each voyage meant a return trip with ever more valuable cargoes. Even women played an active part in the commerce of the Hansa merchants and were recognised as accredited agents.

During the Middle Ages the strong links between Shetland and Norway were strengthened by the fact that Bergen was the most active trading city for the north and west Scandinavian provinces. By 1186 the city was a growing centre for the dried fish trade, its merchants coming from Orkney, Shetland, the Faroes, Iceland, Germany and England, but a law passed in Bergen by special legislation to protect the rights

36 The old Kirk of Lund, Unst, with the House of Lund on the hilltop. The church is said to have been a place of burial since the twelfth century. Inside is the gravestone of Segebad Detkin, merchant and burgher of Bremen who died in 1573, while outside on the grassy slope overlooking the bay of Lunda Wick lies Henrik Segeleken the elder, also of Bremen, who died in 1585, only two of the many German traders who began coming to Shetland in the late fifteenth century, corresponding with the decline of the Hanseatic League. Also known as the Wick Kirk (St. Olaf's, Lund): in use until 1785.

of local traders, including Shetlanders, came too late. The Germans by this time were complete masters of the Norwegian export which included re-export of goods from west Scandinavia, Shetland, Faroe and Iceland.

Little by little, however, the League began to find itself threatened on all sides. Denmark, Norway and Sweden grew ever more restless under the rule of the German merchants who denied them even the right to fish in their own Baltic and tried in every possible way to exclude them from all participation in the lucrative herring industry. The fortunes of the Hanseatic League had been built up on a foundation of herrings. The arms of Schutting, the House of the Herring Fishers of Lubeck, show three herrings on a plain shield and on the arms of the League itself were half the Lubeck eagle and a dried stockfish surmounted by a crown.

Suddenly the teeming herring shoals, which year after year with unfailing regularity had spawned off Scania and Pomerania, vanished from the entire Bohuslan coast. That seemingly unending iridescent

138

swimming multitude that had cascaded year after year into the Hanseatic coffers like a rain of silver coins had suddenly and inexplicably diverted itself to new spawning grounds in the North Sea. Like sea swallows, following some strange predestined route, their migration succeeded in one move where Empires had failed, and sealed the downfall of the mighty Hanseatic League.

Impotent to prevent the one thing over which not even their great power could prevail the Hansa found themselves attacked on every side. Between the embittered Dutch, Frederick of Denmark and Gustav of Sweden, the fuse was laid which was to undermine politically and physically the future of the Hanseatic League. The English harassed the Germans in both the Baltic and the North Sea and then succeeded in opening up a sea route to Russia via Archangel, which did away for ever with the necessity for employing the Germans as middlemen for overland transport of merchandise to Novgorod and the North.

The misfortunes of the Hansa provided a golden opportunity for the Dutch, splendidly placed to take full advantage of the new spawning grounds in the North Sea, who found the markets lost by the Germans ready and waiting to be filled, and it was also a momentous stage in Shetland's history. Corresponding with the slackening grip of the Hanseatic League in Europe as a whole, the first known German merchant appeared in Shetland. In the late fifteenth century a Bremen shop keeper took up residence in Yell. Their numbers increased rapidly and in the early sixteenth century Boece was writing that "the merchandis of Holland, Zeland and Almanic cumis yierlie to Schetland to interchange uthir merchandyis with the people theirof . . ." the effects being felt all over the islands.

Between May and August each year vessels arrived from the three most important cities of the Hanseatic League—Bremen, Hamburg and Lubeck. The German merchants either rented ground on which to build booths or had houses specially built for them by the landowners, easily the best preserved of these being the famous *Bremen Böd* at Symbister on Whalsay. Jutting out into the bay, surrounded by water on three sides, it was designed so that boats could come alongside, the merchandise being winched up into the Pier House itself. Another booth stands back from the harbour at Uyeasound in Unst and many more, or at least their remains, can be traced all over the islands. Here the "Dutch" as they were known in Shetland, a confusing title corrupted from *Deutsch*, displayed their goods for sale or barter: "Brandie and strong waters of all sorts", hooks, lines and herring nets, corn and flour, a kind of bread called "cringel bread", salt, fruit, mead, hempen cloth, linen and muslin, Monmouth caps, "Bisket", and tobacco, a veritable treasure house of mouth-watering luxuries for islands cut off from the main sources of supply. Although much of the trade was conducted under a barter system the North German merchants for the first time introduced money into the economy and in the late sixteenth century Shetlanders were actually able to buy houses and furniture, pay their rents and even buy a considerable part of their food. By the mid-seventeenth century the currency was mainly in Hollands and Dutch.

After 1600, for about 100 years these German merchants held sway in the islands breaking the power of the small local traders and leaving behind them numerous exotic place names in the hitherto exclusively Norse islands. Blaew's "Sea Mirror" of 1625 refers to Sandwick Bay as "Hambourgh Haven" or "Bremenhaven" and in 1640 the Pool of Virkie in Dunrossness was known as the "Dutch Pool", while people still point out the "Bremenstrasse" in Whalsay.

To buy all these exciting new delicacies the Shetlander simply launched his boat and caught ling and cod from the abundant shoals that then frequented the voes. The fish were landed at the booths of the merchants who organised the splitting, salting and drying of the catch for shipment to Germany, hiring from the local landowners stony ayres or beaches where the fish could be spread to dry. Curing consisted either of complete wind-drying to produce "stockfish" or part-wind part-salt curing to make *klippfish*. The saithe liver oil was collected in barrels and sillak livers boiled on the spot. The Germans were always prepared to buy woollen cloth, knitted stockings, seal and otter skins, beef for salting and also butter and fish liver oil in which taxes were paid.

There were still barriers far greater than the sea separating Scotland from her most northerly islands and little control was exercised by the Scottish Crown. The islands were laid waste in 1524 by the English and the lessee, William Sinclair, was granted £80 as compensation. In 1539 James v made a voyage to Orkney and his pilot, Lindesay, drew up a "Pilot" used by the French squadrons in 1547 and 1548 when they took the north-about route to help the anti-Presbyterian movement in Scotland, for the English were then controlling the North Sea. There seems to have been another invasion of Shetland in 1539, this time by the Earl of Caithness, and the islands narrowly escaped being ravaged by Henry VIII's Commissioners at York who were, fortu-

37   Old Bremen Böd.

nately for Shetland, too fearful of the unknown dangers to which they might be subjected.

It was in 1542 when Henry commanded his Commissioners to ravage the Iceland fishery but referring to the islands of Orkney and Shetland "wiche his highness pleasure is we sholde cause to be invaded after our arrival in Scotlande, in case the great enterprise (against Iceland) were not facible ...", the Commissioners listed all the reasons against the expedition which plainly shows their ignorance of these remote islands. They proceeded to plead that "no man dare go thither at this time of year and cannot tarry longer than St. James' tide ... There is one passaige that they must go through called Pentley Frijthe, wiche is reckened the most dangerouse place of all Christendome ... And as to the Isle of Orkney, the place is also very dangerouse and full of rocks though it be not so far off as Shotlande is, (Shetland), wiche standethe for the most parte by fysshing and nothing or litle there to be devasted saulve otes and litle other grayne, the people lyveing theire most by fissche and suche fewe beastes as ar theire be so wylde as they can be taken non otherwise but by dogges ..."

Contemporary Scottish opinion of conditions in Shetland were indicated by George Buchanan who wrote that the inhabitants of Fair Isle were very poor "for the Fishermen which Sail that way every Yeare, coming to fish from England, Holland and other Countries near the Sea, do plunder and carry away what they please. The maritime parts of it (the Mainland) are, for the most part uninhabited; but to the inward parts no Animal comes but Fowl ..." Of Yell he maintains that it is "so uncouth a Place that no Creature can live therein unless he be born there ..."

By the time of Earl Patrick the Dutch merchants had been long established bringing further revenues to the exchequer of the acquisitive Earl. Apart from the rents accruing from booths and ayres, their presence in Shetland was of tremendous benefit for many of the dues and taxes paid by the islanders were settled in kind and the Germans were always willing to ship away the butter, oil and cloth paying for them either in hard cash or commodities not locally obtainable. Both Earls Robert and Patrick therefore regularly granted to an individual German merchant the monopoly of trade at some particular port so that each trader had his own sphere of operation within which he could be free of competition.

If there were no convenient booth on shore the merchant used his ship lying at anchor in the voe as a floating mart, flit boats acting as carriers between the boat and the shore, which they continued to do up to within the last 20 years or so until piers were built where the steamer serving the Northern Isles could tie up. German merchants occasionally appear in the Court Books either in connection with proceedings to recover debts due to them and at other times themselves accused of falsifying weights and measures in their own interest. In 1602 it was for the second time "heavilie complainit be the gentilmen and haill commonis within the countrie of Yetland that quhair the Dutche merchandis and utheris straingeris repairing within the countrie ... bringis to the countrie and sellis thair wairis with unlawful mettis (measures) kannis, busmeris and wechtis, quhairbe thai ar greitlie inritchit and the haill inhabitantis depauperit and hurt thairby ..."

In Dunrossness Germans were established both at Virkie and Bigton where a spring at Brake is still known as "The Dutchman's Well". Geert Hemelingk had been in the district in 1567 when the Earl of Bothwell used his ship, the *Pelican*, to escape from Shetland. This same merchant was still in Shetland in 1602 and indeed several of these traders died in the islands, two of them being buried in the old Kirk of Lund in Unst. Inside the ruined building which looks out over the wide bay of Lunda Wick is the flat tombstone of "Segebad Detken, Burgher and merchant of Bremen. He carried on his business in this land 52 years and fell asleep in our Lord in the year 1573 on the 20th day of August. God rest his soul."

Outside, on the slope facing the bay to the east of the tiny church, lies a second lichen-covered stone in memory of another Bremener, the lettering almost indistinguishable: "In the year 1585 on the 25th July being St James' Day, the worthy and well born Henrik Segeleken the elder, from Germany and a Burgess of the town of Bremen fell asleep here in God the Lord. May God be gracious to him".

The traders did not deal only in ordinary goods, for in 1557 the owners of a Scottish ship called the Angel had fitted her out for naval operations. Off Shetland she ran out of victuals and ammunition and the captain obtained from "ane man of Breme callit Henry Schroder, 3 pieces of artillery, 8 barrels of beer and 2 barrels of tye meal". In Iceland mention is made of metal goods and hardware, pots, pans, knives and horseshoes, swords and kettles, purses, girdles, gloves, needles and thread and yarn for nets, which would almost certainly be available also in Shetland, providing the islands with a variety of goods which they were reluctant to lose.

In 1662 when a stricter line was taken and all were to be banished, the people of Shetland, dependent on them not only for luxuries but for their livelihood pleaded, that the Act should not be implemented otherwise most people would starve, three-quarters of the island's corn alone being bought from the visiting Lubeckers, Hamburgers and others. In 1663 compassion prevailed "seeing traffecting with forraners is the only means of their lyvelyhood".

142

The German merchants finally disappeared in the first decade of the eighteenth century but during their stay Scots, English and Hollanders had obviously been trying desperately to break the monopoly. As early as 1594 English merchants are recorded in Shetland and by 1603 Edward Cross from Southampton was buying and curing fish at St. Ninian's Isle. No trace of booth or drying shed remain, only the uncertain name of the spit of rock on the Bigton side of the ayre joining the mainland land to the isle. The rock is called Skeoclett and although *skeo* is the old name for a drying shed and *clett* a rock local tradition says it means simply "a sea rock".

In 1580 a Scottish vessel came from the North Isles to Dundee "ladent wi' herrings" and in 1594 Fife merchant fishermen were granted permission by Earl Patrick to erect houses for the "mailing, paiking and drying and wynning of fische." In 1625 Blaew's Atlas is calling Levenwick the "Scottish Haven" and by mid-century not only do ships from Dundee have close trading connections with Grutness but special trading rights have been given to the Edinburgh merchant Gideon Murray to buy the countrymen's fish in preference to the Germans.

In the sixteenth century English ships were active in Orkney and Shetland waters and London fishmongers reported that 7 score and odd ships went to the Iceland fishery, about 80 "crayers" to Shetland and 220 crayers from Scarborough sailed to the northern seas. The important industry that had drawn the boats ever further north was, however, on the decline owing to the abolition of Catholic fish days in England. At the beginning of the reign of Edward vi an inquiry was made into the demand for fish and it was found that in 30 years the number of crayers visiting Shetland waters had fallen to less than 10. An Act was passed in England limiting the purchase of fish to those fishing grounds frequented by the English, including Iceland, Scotland, Orkney and Shetland, Ireland and Newfoundland.

Shetland itself still took little part in this lucrative industry, although the greater part of its historical culture and economic development for the next 200 to 300 years is inextricably bound up with the securing of fish to supply contemporary markets. The old agricultural way of life disappeared as the islands were exploited by Hollander, Scots and English, aided and abetted by every petty laird from the Stewart Earls onwards. During the reign of the Hansa merchants, and probably earlier, Scots had been acquiring ownership of land, the English and Scots fishing for cod and ling, the Dutch taking over from the German merchants the role of Europe's suppliers of herring.

15. *The Grand Fishing*

IN THAT CURIOUS way in which history repeats itself the birth of Shetland's two capitals, so far apart in time, had much in common. Just as the Norse udallers made their way every June to the Scalloway banks to attend the *Althing* in the Tingwall valley, their descendants, four or five centuries later, at the same time of year, gathered on the site of Lerwick to celebrate another annual event: the arrival of the great Dutch herring fleet. As in Scalloway where the skollas had been erected to house the temporary invasion, so along the scattalds of Sound huts and booths sprang up ready for the Dutch Fair at the Buss Haven in Bressay Sound.

By sea and land, everyone who could be spared from the crofts, old and young, excited as children on their way to a party, headed the same way. Women knitted as they walked, kishies on their backs filled with woollen stockings, caps, haps and gloves. Barefoot boys led shaggy ponies almost hidden under bulging meshies (panniers) of butter, *reistit* mutton, salted beef, eggs, hens and geese. Some threaded their way across the moor by way of the old broch of Clickhimin to the east Ness of Sound where their menfolk were busy cobbling together ramshackle huts, driftwood shelters and rough canvas tents, while others from north and west gathered at the Hollanders' Knowe between Scalloway and Bressay Sound.

Fresh-faced, nubile country lasses, trigged out in their best, strong-legged and lissom, released from milking kye or raising peat, their backs yet unbent with delling the pitiless soil nor hips broadened with continual child-bearing, they chattered like starlings. The old, nodding in rusty black, heads decently covered, blinking in the bright sun, predicted with bitter wisdom that there would be "mair heard o' this". They had seen it all before but nothing would have kept them away and needles clacked in twisted hands even faster than their tongues.

Matrons sorted out their wares, bairns clinging to skirt and apron. They flyted and gossiped and joked, eyes sharp with curiosity and heads turning at the sight of Marion or Janet, back again this year and still no better than they should be. Here and there a young wife shifted

144

a bawling infant from one hip to the other ready to lash out at her man whom weary experience had taught her would be roaring fou before night.

In all the whispered tales they had to keep a check on their words for the courts were packed these days with folk taken up for slander. Yon Dunrossness carles never cared what they said. James Brown had called Elspeth Bu a harlot and Laurence and John Rendall used the same word of John Scott's wife while John of Ringyista slandered Catherine Linkletter of harlettrie.

Robert Acheson joined one of the groups. He had brought down some selchie skins—"Skin Robbie" they called him—and recently he had had to pay dear for his loose mouth too. Slander at four merks a time was an expensive business but the courts, realising that cash payments were far from adequate amends, occasionally ordered that there should be a formal request for forgiveness. Robert who had slandered David Foster in Lunn of the theft of sheep had not only to pay eight merks "to the king" and eight to the party slandered, but had also to "ask the said David forgifnes in face of the court and siclyk (the same) at the paroche kirk upoun Sonday nixt before the minister and haill congregatioun convenit for the tyme".

Garvell in Cumlawik had said that Magnus in Channerwick was "ane skolk" and Annie Mansdochter who had been there at the time told them all that someone had to be called to explain to the court what it meant . . . "ane skolk, quilk is said to be ane loun or ane dissaver (deceiver)". The old Norn words died hard and my lordis court at Skallawaa had a hard time trying to understand them.

Three hundred and fifty years ago boats were used as the most natural way of travel and some of the men were down to the shore tying up for the night those small boats that kept their families supplied with fish. Ola Jacobsen was coiling up his *buchtys of lynis* (hanks of lines) for he had a mind to put out himself later that evening. Erasmus Scott was telling him of some of his own cured fish, with his mark on them too, stolen from his *skeo* the day before. Both ling and saithe were fished fairly extensively and most Shetlanders were engaged in fishing for herring, some of which were for their families and some they managed to sell to Scots and Danes. Even the minister Mr. Robert Swinton, that wealthy man of God, organised quite an extensive herring industy which he pursued with an apostolic zeal even greater than that which he devoted to his parishioners.

However small, the industry was important, and the men complained bitterly of time wasted in providing water transport for the gentry. The Earl expected them to be always ready at his bidding for "flit and fuir"; he and Bruce of Cultmalindie were two of a kind. Hugh

Tarrell had indeed been accused in court of usurping the king's authority by ordering the inhabitants of Whalsay to "flit and fuir" him to Reafirth. Nicol Olason and Thomas Johnson were of a mind to buy a boat between them if the Hollanders could be persuaded to pay cash for their mutton and beef. Prices were high though, a fourareen could cost anything from £4 up to £20 and a sixareen from £8 to £40.

Thomas Manson absentmindedly thrust his hand into his pocket, forgetting his siller had long gone and wondered whether the Hollanders would ever come. Life had changed for the worse since these Stewarts had come upon the islands. A man dare not even touch a wreck any more. Even the 800 barrel staves that came ashore in Fetlar and 200 in Yell were all ordered to be taken to Scalloway for the Earl's use. "Black Pate" they called him in Orkney which was a mild way to describe yon tyrant. Out of five barrels of pitch washed up at Lunnasting, three went to "my lord's wark". Aye, and what about the wreck found in Weisdale? "The haill timmer" was taken to the castle— except that the Earl waived his claim to "some small parts quhilk will do na guid". Magnus Huchesoun had told them it was scarce good for firewood.

Suddenly a ripple ran through the waiting crowd like wind stirring a field of bere. One can imagine the excitement, the news passed from Trebister Ness all along the Voe of Sound, in through the Ness. Sails bellying in the wind betokened the first of the Dutch busses. From their home ports of Brielle, Rotterdam, Delfshaven, Schiedam, Vlaardingen and Maassluis, from Enkhuizen, Hoorn and De Rijp, Scheveningen, Marken and Katwijk bustled the great fleet of three-masted busses, a square sail on each mast and a topsail on the main. Totally different from the elegant Norse langskips that had once swept up the Sound, they rode the waves, squat, sensible as the wooden clogs in which their crews clattered ashore. Although they sailed under strict orders from the Placart that "no person shall set their nets in the sea or begin fishing before the Feast of St. John the baptist on June 24th" the fleet had left their home ports three weeks before so that they would have time for trade to buy or exchange their commodities for fresh meat and provisions and for the hosiery for which the islands were already famous.

In 1614 the fleet was said to be over 1000 strong of which more than 600 were "great busses" of 100 to 120 tons, the main catching units, with a crew of 16 to 24 in each. The rest of the fleet was made up of small vent-jagers or fast carriers and tenders of different kinds. Before the great expansion of the herring fishing at the end of the sixteenth century the Hollanders had been active round Scotland and probably Shetland for some time. Estimates vary enormously as to their numbers at any given time and one must allow for a natural tendency to ex-

38 Dutch doggers coming into Lerwick around the turn of the century. (Zetland County Library and Museum.)

aggerate when such very large fleets are under discussion.

Tobias Gentleman numbers over 700 boats fishing *by line* in 1614. The fleet then consisted of quite a variety of vessels with intriguing names like "doggers", "sword-pinks", "flat-bottoms", "Holland Toads", "crab-skuits", or "welboats". Lying in the fishing grounds they used a drove-sail (a form of sea anchor) while fishing by hand-line for cod. For the first period at sea they used live lamprey for bait and when that was finished nets were used to catch herring. It is obvious that right from the beginning the Hollanders were predominant in these fishing grounds for besides all these pinks, welboats and others the Hollanders had continually in the season another fleet of fishermen in the north east head of Shetland ... "and these they call Fly boats and these do ride at anker all the season in Shotlande (Shetland) in the fishing grounds and they have small boats within them which be like into cobles, the which they do put out to lay and hale their lines and hookes whereby they do take great store of lings".

By the middle of the seventeenth century the size, organisation and importance of the herring fleet became so vital to Dutch commerce that a squadron of naval vessels often accompanied it. The North Sea was by no means safe from privateers or even pirates and the fleet, fishers and all, were armed, keeping convoy position all the way north. In 1641 a fleet of 1900 busses had 36 men-of-war with them.

Although for the Shetlanders the arrival of the fleet was a signal for general rejoicing, it was otherwise regarded by the authorities. Simon

Smith in a report on the "herring buss trade" published in 1641 explains that if the Dutch arrived before 24th June, "then do they put all into Shotlande ... into a sownde called Braccies Sound, and there they frolicke it on land, untill that they have sucked out all the marrow of the Mault, and good Scotch ale, which is the best liquor that the land doth afford".

The first arrivals moored to a suitable berth on the sandy beach, willing hands stretched out ready to catch the ropes and make them fast; the next made fast alongside and so on until a bridge of busses extended well out into the quiet waters of the Sound. Soon the great army of Hollanders with some Flemings, French, Prussians and Danes, all bent on making the most of every minute of their stay, poured ashore and the prelude to the yearly carnival had begun. As the Dutch put it "The herring keeps Dutch trade going and Dutch trade sets the world afloat."

Trading was not confined to Bressay Sound or the Ness; Levenwick and Quendale are also mentioned but the second most important gathering place was a small hillock beside which the roads between Lerwick, Scalloway and the south Mainland join, still known as Hollanders' Knowe. Here the Shetlanders brought their ponies and the Dutchmen, out for as much fun as they could pack in before the serious business of fishing commenced, were easily persuaded to hire these apparently docile little animals at a stiver a mile or sometimes a penny a ride, the wilder the pony the shorter the ride. The stout, phlegmatic Dutchmen, throwing decorum to the winds, bestrode these tiny creatures, legs dangling to the ground, continually, to their own bewilderment and the hilarious enjoyment of the natives, finding themselves rolling most indecorously in the heather, their mounts gazing down at them through windswept manes with suspiciously innocent brown eyes. Up they would get again, good-humouredly fishing out another stiver, the whole proceedings enlivened to no small extent by the copious supply of brandy and Hollands gin.

It would require the pen of a Rowlandson or the palette of a Breughel to do justice to the infinitely less innocent amusements on the Ness of Sound ... "of the great abomination and wickedness committed yearly by the Hollanders and country people, godless and profane persons repairing to them at the houses of Lerwick ..." From all accounts the "Dutch Fair", as it came to be called, appears to have embraced a Bacchanalian orgy of such immensity that Sodom and Gomorrah might by comparison be considered veritable fortresses of virtue. Drunkenness, swearing, bloodshed, murder, robbery and immorality, lust and fornication flourished like the seven deadly sins.

It is difficult to assess from the Court Books of the period the exact

148

morality of the Shetlander at this time. Certainly during the rule of the Stewarts there must have been extracted more than the usual number of fines, justifiable or otherwise. Little example was set by the clergy, many of them with moral standards only appreciably higher than those of their parishioners. At the close of the preceding century there were only two ministers and nine readers for the 11 ministries in Shetland, and their miserable stipends forced them into all manner of shady but profitable dealings. Both John Sutherland, the reader in Aithsting and Sandsting, and William Hay, Archdeacon of Shetland and minister of Tingwall were found guilty of assault. In 1603 a Cunningsburgh man was accused of using the church there as a cow-byre, and of the reformed church in Shetland it was said that "it is no wonder that, with such shepherds, the wolves invade the flock of the Lord and ruin all".

Even as late as the eighteenth century the clergy were accused of "celebrating the orgies of Bacchus" with the "cornwater" smuggled in by their parishioners. The smuggling trade in which they were extensively engaged had "a most demoralising effect on the people." According to Cowie "The gentry when they met spent their time in drinking punch and playing cards and profane swearing was awfully common even among ladies of the best position."

Church discipline was just beginning to take over from the court, a discipline fanatical in its pursuance of wrongdoers, the Bishop himself urging kirk and session "with all rigour" to punish with stocks, the jougs, branks, ducking in the sea and as a matter of course the perfectly justifiable Christian persecution of witches. The last person to be imprisoned in the stocks (outside the Tolbooth in Commercial St. Lerwick) was John Henderson, labourer, at 16 convicted of petty theft and forced to sit in the stocks daily from November 17th, 1824 until March 15th 1825. A complaint was made in the general assembly of the Church that discipline was not sufficiently effective in the north. It was solemnly stated that over 600 persons in Shetland had been convicted of incest, adultery and fornication. Although strangely enough tea was yet unknown in Shetland, the most common beverage being buttermilk, kirn milk or *blaand*, beer must have been a fairly common drink. The brewing of ale flourished in Dunrossness, probably because grain was most plentiful in that fertile area, whereas throughout the islands generally the grain was required for bread, which was part of the staple diet. In 1604 we find 35 persons engaged in the industry and three acts of court were promulgated to control it. Maximum selling prices were fixed and inspectors appointed to test the quality each week. The ale which they considered "insufficient" was given to the poor. Brewers who violated the regulations were to lose their "brewing lums."

It was a bizarre anomaly that fishing began on the Feast of St. John the Baptist, June 24th, Midsummer's Day, which gave an opportunity to give vent to a long-suppressed desire for uninhibited merry-making. In spite of all the ale from Dunrossness and the not-infrequent venture into lusts of the flesh, life was generally bounded by the croft, its precarious yield, the never-ending demands for taxes, dues, rents, fines and debts. The light summer nights, busses riding at anchor with gently-tilting masts, the exotic fascination of foreign tongues, the bargains made, washed down with fiery unaccustomed spirits simply swept everyone off their feet. Tomorrow would be another day.

Complaints were bound to reach the authorities about bawdy houses, brawls and licentious behaviour of all kinds. Previous ordinances of 1602 and 1615 had stated categorically "that in all time cuming no persones or persone sall repair to the sound nor isle of Bressay for furnishing of beir, vivoris and uther necessities to the Hollandaris" and the owners of the ground were ordered to demolish all houses already built "nor sall suffer nane to be bigit nor make residence thair".

When James V had visited Orkney in the fifteenth century a deputation from Shetland was there awaiting him to complain of the disgraceful goings-on at what was described as the Dutch Fair at Bressay Sound. Later Earl Patrick Stewart issued an edict regulating relations between the people and the Hollanders but according to one writer it was like Satan regulating sin, and had little or no effect. With the Union of the Crowns complaints about the Bacchanalia still pestered officialdom in Edinburgh. In 1625 an edict demanded that the houses and booths on Bressay Sound must be destroyed. Condemned as a den of vice, they were one and all burned to the ground. In addition it was forbidden that any woman "of quartsumeur rank or qualitie sall repair to the said Sound for selling of sockis to the said Hollandaris or bying of ncessaris from tham Bot sall cause thair husband thair sons or servandis sell and buy fra thame".

The value of the herring, however, was immense, and the old Dutch saying that Amsterdam was built on herring bones could well have been applied to most towns in Holland at that time, its trade being greater than the wealth of the Far East. The fleet brought in "Hempe from the ports of Leisseland and Prussia. Pitch and tarre from the Balticke seas and Norway. Barrel boards and willow hoopes from Hambourgh and those parts. Deale boards, Masts and Sparres from Norway and firewood. Lixboan salt and salt upon salt made in England ... Normandy canvas for sayles and Ipswich canvas. Barke and Ashen trees for tanning the nets. Seacoles for heating the Copper for tanning. Corke and Rosen from Burdeaux ..."

At the same time all this gave employment to local labour "for the

150

stronger to beat the Hempe, the lame to turn the wheels, the children to spin the Twine, and the women to braid deepings (weave nets)". The busses did not carry small boats and each required a yawl for her own use while in the Sound. As the fleet grew the annual demand increased until yawl building became a staple industry in the isles, flitting the Hollanders back and forth between the shore and the busses.

Punctually on June 24th the great fleet sailed for the fishing grounds. First they fished off Cullivoe in Yell, then to Noss for about two weeks before spending the next three weeks off Fair Isle and then steadily fishing their way south. The seabed sloping eastward from Baltasound in Unst to Yarmouth in the south is known as the most suitable spawning ground for the herring, in all the seas of Europe. Sheltered as it is from the ground motion attributable to the heavy Atlantic swell and also from the deep-streamed ocean currents which sweep in from the west, "The Grand Fishing" as the Dutch called it after 1580, was first established through the discovery of the correct "cure" for the preservation of the fish. Beuckels, a native of Zeeland, was responsible for the improved method of curing which enabled the Dutch to bring the art to a state of perfection never surpassed. Independent of foreign bases they combined the process of capture and cure afloat.

The busses were not fast ships but were built for their carrying capacity and seaworthy qualities. With its two entrances, Bressay Sound was ideal in any wind and safely inside the great natural harbour ships could effect repairs or shelter in bad weather. After the nets were out came the job of making all snug for the night. The square yards would have to be unshipped and placed fore and aft along the deck. The fore and mainmasts were lowered, swung bow on to their drifts with a tightly-stretched mizzen to keep each in position during the night. It required a remarkable sea sense to find room for 200 miles of drift nets on a coast only 70 miles long but the fishing operation was carried on in almost the same way as by modern Shetland drifters.

A curtain of hand-woven hemp nets was hung from the surface of the sea, held up by small casks or buoys and weighted below by a strong hemp rope, usually tarred, now known as the "buss' rope. This rope was wound round a capstan manned on the busses by six men who took most of the weight of the nets by hauling them up to the ship on the rope. They were then lifted aboard and the herrings shaken out by three other men while one man took the nets and stowed them out of the way. Another man stood by with a dropstick (landing net) catching "Cods for the Kettle" and the master stood in the cabin wells catching herring which had dropped out of the nets.

One boy held the "way" or heavy rope to the capstan and another coiled as it came in. Once the herring were safely aboard they were gutted, salted and packed as quickly as possible, one man gathering them into baskets while nine men gutted. Except for the fact that the herrings were cured afloat, the method was the same as that used in Skanor and Falsterbo six centuries before.

First the herring were lightly salted (roused) by a boy and then put into barrels by four packers. Depending on the time of year, the salted fish were either transferred to carriers or stowed below. Most of the tenders to the fishing fleet were fast-sailing jagers which vied with each other to take home the first cargoes and gain the highest prices.

One jager was allowed to every 10 busses and if the weather permitted the herrings were transhipped at sea; if not, busses and jagers had to run into Bressay Sound. The catch was estimated in "lasts", a last consisting of 17 barrels. Ten barrels of the first catch were considered worth the run to Holland where these fish were regarded as food with a medicinal value and fetched £50 a barrel. The vent jagers ran the salted herring to Holland until July 15th after which the busses fished and cured on board.

At the end of the voyage before the master was allowed to break bulk he had to take the oath that the regulations had been complied with: "The Captains of the men of war attending to this fishery are allowed to arrest any Master of a buss selling herrings to Zeelanders or to any inhabitant of the United Provinces not of Holland, or to any foreigners. The first-caught herrings are not to be sold until they have lain ten days in pickle." In default a fine of 300 guilders was imposed, the alternative being imprisonment.

39   Three little Dutch boys in traditional clogs at the Bressay Slip: early 1900's. (Zetland County Library and Museum.)

In spite of the burning of the booths on Bressay Sound, eight years later busses, vent-jagers and men-of-war gathered in the Sound ready for another season's fishing. It is a curious fact that in spite of the English accounts of anything up to 2000 busses in Bressay Sound, Dutch historians state categorically that the whole Dutch herring fleet never exceeded 500 vessels at any one time. The whole affair had grown to such proportions that England was forced to take notice. James I made strong representations to the Dutch. Holland forbade Dutch fishermen to fish near, among other places, the coast of Shetland under penalty of a fine of 300 florins for each buss. But still they came. The islanders themselves had no quarrel with the Dutch. With the change from the old Norse rule to steadily encroaching Scots feudalism they must often have felt that they were living in occupied territory, and they had not the least compunction in evading and even breaking the new Scottish laws. They admired the skill of the foreign fishermen, their ships were immaculate and what was more they brought with them the temporary solace of brandy and gin besides all kinds of other small luxuries.

Smuggling, too, was a lucrative business and few there were even among the gentry who did not indulge in a practice even winked at by the customs. Shetland's prosperity attracted small cargo boats from Orkney bringing in corn, meal and malt. Dutch stivers and half stivers circulated in Shetland for many years. There were other coins too, occasionally palmed off on the islanders, old or devalued, and useless as currency. Many were the parish ministers viewing the collection plate through half-closed eyes while piously consecrating it to the Lord's work, who would later angrily demand an explanation from the kirk session.

In the meantime Bruce of Symbister, a native of Fife, as were several other landlords in Shetland, had brought an action against Patrick, Earl of Orkney. Earl Patrick was eventually confined in Edinburgh Castle, mainly through the pressures exerted by Bishop James Law, who by commission was now appointed sheriff and justice of the islands. The Privy Council, obviously referring to Patrick Stewart recorded that "Some persons bearing powers of magistracy within the bounds of Orkney and Yetland have these divers years bygone most unlawfully taken upon them for their own private gain and commodity, to judge the inhabitants of the said countries by foreign laws, making choice sometimes of foreign laws and sometimes of the proper laws of this kingdom as they find matters of gain and commodity ... therefore that in the light of previous enactment that all subjects of the King should be governed by the King's own laws and by the law of no foreign country, the King's Privy Council proscribes the said foreign laws in all time to come." It was eventually found that in addition to his oppression and extortion, Earl Robert, along with his son Patrick who had tried to raise a rebellion in Orkney to help his father, was guilty of treason and both were executed in Edinburgh in 1615.

After the removal of Patrick Stewart, Orkney and Shetland were annexed to the Crown. In 1643 Charles I granted the islands to yet another court favourite, Douglas, Earl of Morton.

Meanwhile the English became more and more concerned about the growth of the Dutch navy which the Hollanders claimed was vital for the protection of their shipping. Preyed upon by Dunkirkers, British privateers and Scots pirates alike, both the herring fleet and the Dutch East Indiamen, forced to take the northabout passage, required constant protection. One of Cromwell's first actions on coming to power was to frame the Navigation Act of 1651 and in the following year the first Anglo-Dutch war broke out. For the next 26 years Shetland could be said in twentieth-century parlance to be "in the news" in connection with the constant struggle for sea power. Battles raged all round her coasts, even in Bressay Sound and from the Skerries to Burra Isle wrecks continued to litter reefs and voes.

Battle was nearly joined off Burra Isle between Admirals Robert Blake and Maarten Harpetsz Tromp. The Dutch fleet under Van Tromp had just been sighted by the English who were about to give chase when a violent gale arose from the nor'nor-west. One of Van Tromp's fireships was lost with all hands on the west coast of Burra and two fireships and a warship foundered on the Burra Haaf, the remainder taking shelter until the storm abated among the small islands to the north of Burra.

On June 15th, 1640 at the zenith of the Dutch herring industry, four Dutch men o' War lay at anchor in Bressay Sound waiting to rendezvous with the returning fleet from the Indies. Although outward bound, Dutch East Indiamen sailed in pairs, they returned from the East in convoys of up to a dozen at a time, to be met off Shetland by an escort of Dutch warships to guard them on the last lap of their journey home to Texel. The Dutch conveyers, the *Haan, Jonas, Reiger* and *Enckhuijsen* were at anchor waiting to join up with the *Retourvloot*, daily expected. Suddenly, taking the convoy ships completely by surprise, 10 fast, heavily armed Spanish frigates sailed into the harbour, specially armed at Dunkirk for the express purpose of destroying the escort and capturing the homeward bound fleet.

Both the *Haan* (the cock) and the *Reiger* (the heron) were sunk in Lerwick harbour, their crews fighting until the ships sank under them. The *Enckhuijsen*, battered and bloody struck her colours and only the *Jonas* escaped through the north entrance of the Sound but ran ashore at Brunthamarland, Nesting, where she was blown up by her crew.

154

Even in defeat the four ships had given such a gallant account of themselves that the Spaniards, after a brief token cruise westward, limped home to Dunkirk without their prize and badly damaged.

Nearly 300 years later during dredging operations at Alexandra Wharf in February, 1922, four guns, about seven feet long were brought to the surface along with some heavy oaken timbers in one of which was embedded a cannon ball. The guns were identified as part of the armament of the *De Haan*. One was mounted and stood for many years at Albert Wharf and when dock extensions took place it was transferred to Fort Charlotte.

One of the most interesting under-water explorations taking place today is that on the wrecked *Kennermerland* which in 1664 was one of the Dutch East India Company's newest ships. She was sailing from Holland to Batavia with a cargo of wine, cloth, oil and coins to the value of 120,000 Dutch florins. As England and Holland were still at war she took the usual northabout route to avoid enemy warships in the Channel. It was a pitch-dark December night, when running before the wind in a southerly gale she struck Stoura Stack on the Out Skerries and broke in two. The foremost mast fell on the land enabling three men on the rigging, one of whom was the pilot, to escape, the only men from the 150 crew to survive. A salvage vessel, delightfully named *De Rommelpot* (The Rumbling Pot), sent out to investigate did not find even a single plank from the ship. The *Kennermerland* is known in Scotland as the Carmelan and still current in the Skerries is the following rhyme.

> The Carmelan fae Amsterdam,
> Cam on a Maunmas Day,
> On Staura Stack she broke her back,
> and in the Voe she ca,
> and the Skerry folk got a prey.

Maunmas Day was the feast day of St. Magnus of Orkney and so many kegs and casks of wine and spirit were washed ashore that the male population were drunk for "three weeks and a day".

By all accounts the *Kennermerland*s forepart had sunk in the deep water off the stack. Her stern, where the treasure was reputedly stowed, was first cast up on Bruray and then swept out by the strong tide into the South Mouth. Three chests of gold and silver numbered 1, 2 and 4, were salvaged and privately sequestered by the Earl of Morton, then Lord of Shetland. King Charles II, whose extravagances had almost emptied the Exchequer and led the country to the brink of ruin, was furious, the more especially as on his restoration he had graciously returned the islands to the Earl of Morton, who had been stripped of them by Cromwell. The King immediately had the wreck declared a prize of war, claimed the treasure, and once again the Morton family were deprived of their estates in Orkney and Shetland. Later, he bestowed the remains of the ship and her cargo on the Earl of Kincardine.

In 1971 an expedition was planned by the Aston Sub Aqua Club. With the help and guidance both from the Curator of the County Museum, himself an expert on Shetland wrecks, and local knowledge which proved to be incredibly exact, the Club found and plotted evidence of the wreck both in the deep water off Stoura Stack and in the shallower water of the South Mouth. Some of the finds including the ship's bell, her compass and three seventeenth-century earthenware "greybeard" flagons bearing the Amsterdam city arms are now in the Shetland County Museum. Two years later in 1973 a second diving expedition was planned by the Sub Aqua Club of Aston and Manchester University in collaboration with various other student bodies, in order to continue the work and hopefully raise further articles of archaeological interest for Shetland's museum, already rich in finds from these once-valuable ships. Led by Mr. Richard Price, the patron of the 1973 attempt was the present Earl of Elgin and Kincardine who may well be the legal owner of what is left of the *Kennermerland* and her cargo.

The finds, taken at once to Shetland County Museum for expert examination and treatment pending eventual disposal by the Receiver of Wrecks, included an incredible collection of small personal belongings which apart from their archaeological value, span the centuries in a way that no treasure chest of gold or silver could ever achieve. The amazing thing is that they had survived at all. Embedded in a large lump of conglomerate, partly composed of pitch, were four small tobacco boxes, a gold ring, six rings of a baser metal; a man's brass thimble; a small pair of dividers, 16 bone dice and about 50 coins.

The gold ring, well worn, narrow, with a raised engraved band round the middle, has no initials or hallmark. The tobacco boxes, two made entirely of brass and two of brass with copper sides, are oval and engraved with characteristic Dutch designs. The coins were contained in two small bags. There was one piece of eight, a thaler from Cologne, silver ducatoons and what Mr. Henderson the curator described so evocatively as "small change". Probably the coins and all the other unimportant intimate possessions and articles of daily use had formed the contents of a private chest or ditty box belonging to one of the ship's officers, or maybe a passenger.

Perhaps the most unusual objects of the whole find, however, are four brass bodkins, used in some form of lace-making, weaving or

40   Mr. Tom Henderson, Curator of the County Museum in Lerwick, with a Bellarmine flagon from the wreck of the *Kennermerland*, a Dutch East Indiaman wrecked on
the Out Skerries on December 20th, 1664. These flagons or "Greybeards" as they were
often called, are a product of the Rhineland ceramic industry probably made at
Freuchen, near Koln. Three were found, all having the typical iron-washed "tiger-
skin" finish of salt-glazed stoneware and carrying applied oval body plaques. Flagons
2 and 3 had been used to carry mercury, listed in the cargo of the *Kennermerland* and
shipped by both the Spanish and the Dutch to their colonies in large quantities, where
it was used in an early process for the assaying or extraction of gold and silver from
their ores.

157

tapestry. About five inches long, curved, they have what appear to be eyeholes just below the ornamental heads which represent human hands. They may have belonged to one of the crew who, like many sailors, whiled away the weary months from Holland to Batavia in some artistic pursuit, a picture for his wife or sweetheart, a tapestry chair seat or a lace collar so often portrayed in Dutch paintings. Whalers used to carve the most delicate objects from walrus ivory or whale teeth. Someone aboard carried his tobacco in these small brass tobacco boxes and smoked a clay pipe, nine inches long and still unbroken. Among other things the divers found a small Bellarmine jar with some plum stones still remaining from a favourite conserve. The thimble may have been used along with the brass bodkins. And what game did they play with the bone dice that black December night?

The rich East Indiamen with their legendary cargoes, a constant source of speculation and temptation even today, irritated the impoverished King Charles even more. Then when all seemed hopeless and the country heading towards bankruptcy Samuel Pepys wrote on April 17th, 1665 that "news is brought the King that the Dutch Smyrna fleet is seen upon the back of Scotland and thereupon the King hath wrote the Duke (of York) that he do appoint a fleet to go Northward to meet the enemy coming round ..." With the capture of 45 prizes, including treasure ships, the fleet—and the King—were jubilant, the fleet receiving the congratulations of the Naval Lords from Lord Sandwich attired in his nightgown.

With the second Anglo-Dutch war well under way and the Buss Haven even more important to the Hollanders, John Mylne, King Charles' master mason received orders to begin the building of what was later to be called Fort Charlotte. That massive pentagonal fort, designed after the manner of Vauban, the great French military engineer, covering finally over two acres on a cliff, still dominates the Old Town.

In 1667 a Dutch fleet under Lt. Admiral William Joseph van Gent entered Bressay Sound with invasion orders, but although Fort Charlotte was almost entirely ungarrisoned no action took place. During the first Dutch war, according to Gifford of Busta "his Majesty was pleased to send over here a garrison consisting of 300 men, under the command of one colonel William Sinclair a native of Zetland ... with 20 or 30 cannons to plant upon it for the protection of the country. There was a house built within the Fort sufficient to lodge 100 men; the garrison staid here three years; the charge whereof, with the building of the Fort, is said to stand the king 28,000 pounds sterling."

It is difficult to determine just when the first house was built in Lerwick. For a long time "from Holmsgarth to the North Ness and again southward by the 'wick of Lerwick' to the South Ness no man's dwelling was". The communicating link at that time between Bressay and Sound was from Ham to the beach below Westhall and it was from there that people tramped across the moors to Scalloway and to the then more populous area on the West side. Early in the seventeenth century a settlement of booths was established round the little bay known as Leir vik (the muddy creek) and when Gifford of Busta was writing his historical description of the islands in 1733 he notes that he has known old men who remembered when there was not one house there but "now there are about 200 families in it, abundance of good houses and fashionable people as are to be seen in any town of Scotland of its bulk," an incredible transformation from the days of the Dutch Fair.

The Dutch continued to be unfortunate in their visits to the isles. During the second Anglo-Dutch war in December of 1674 *Het Wapen Van Rotterdam* (the Rotterdam Arms) owned by the East India Company of Amsterdam arrived for shelter in the deep bay of Ronas Voe. The British sent two ships chasing after her which blockaded the voe and overpowered her. The many members of the crew who died in the battle were buried on the southern shore of the voe, the site still known as the Hollanders' Grave. The third and last Anglo-Dutch war brought another enemy fleet into Bressay Sound and in 1673 Fort Charlotte and part of the town were burned. The peace of Niymegen in 1678 brought the busses back to Bressay Sound.

The Sound, however, was far from seeing its last naval encounter. About the year 1700 the war of the Spanish Succession brought France and Holland into conflict. On the night of June 22nd–23rd, 1703, some 160 busses convoyed by a squadron of Dutch cruisers had made Fair Isle on their way to the Buss Haven when they were intercepted by a superior fleet of French warships. In this attack the Dutch ships based on Enkhuizen sustained especially severe losses with more than 100 vessels from that city utterly destroyed by fire. The fishermen, reduced to beggary, received a small payment from local funds and the authorities took pity on the widows and orphans.

In 1722 there was a second French attack on the herring fleet in Bressay Sound. On this occasion the Hollanders had locked off the bay with a chain the outer rings of which can still be seen on both sides of the Sound, but nothing could prevent disaster, and the fishery never really recovered from these blows.

As far as Shetlanders were concerned little attempt was made to emulate the scale or methods of the Hollanders although they used the same type of net. They continued to consider the herring fishing as a subsidiary or incidental activity and even by 1774 there was reported to be only one local herring buss. Sporadic attempts throughout the years

159

were made by kings and governments to build up a British herring industry but with little effect. The Stewart kings had done nothing towards its formation and little to control the Dutch. James I had levied
a tax of one barrel of herring on every buss fishing in British waters,
but the delineation of what constituted British waters simply aroused
derision. Then the King replied by forbidding them to fish "within a
kenning of land as seamen do take a kenning..." Harmless to fishermen
who cured afloat it was altered to a 14-mile limit which nobody
observed around the northern isles.

Charles I founded the first herring fishery company ever formed in
Britain but he subscribed only royal patronage. Then Charles II
imposed heavy taxes on imported fish, followed by a complete prohibi-
tion of foreign-caught herrings, haddocks etc. Then the liberty to raise
lotteries was granted and the right to collect money in churches in aid
of this second herring venture. Some years later the Royal Fishery of
England was set up and seven busses bought from Holland and manned
by Dutchmen. Hardly had they begun fishing when they were captured
by the French who were at war with Holland.

After the Restoration, projects were revived for a Royal Fishery of
Great Britain and Ireland. The king offered £200 to every one sending
a buss to the fishery. These busses were to sail from the Shetland Isles,
to take the privilege of fishing before other nations, for the Dutch prose-
cution of ling fishing was another grievance ... "so great the staple
ling, taken indeed only by the Hollanders, but got about the islands
of Scotland, Sheteland, Orkney and wherwith they serve all Christendom, is called forsooth by the name of Holland ling".

Beyond the passing of an Act during the reign of Queen Anne, granting export bounties on herrings, nothing more was done till about 1750,
until the Act for the encouragement of the herring industry granting
a bounty of 30 shillings per ton on every fishing vessel built and operated
in Great Britain. As far as the Northern Isles of Orkney and Shetland
were concerned this was absolutely untenable for the minimum tonnage
on which grants were to be paid was 20 tons, a size far above that of
the average sixareen.

The next move was the founding of the society of the Free British
Fishery in London, also in 1750. Over £200,000 was subscribed and
four keels laid down, the plans taken from a Dutch buss hired for the
purpose. The authorities had to send messengers to go to Holland to
engage persons "experienced in the sorting, curing, gypping and barrel-
ing of herrings". Three Danish skippers were sent for and examined
as they had lately arrived from Holland, "as to several particulars rela-
tive to the fishing". Later two Dutch skippers and 12 seamen also from
Holland were engaged as part of the crews for the two busses being

160

built at Southampton.

The *Pelham* and the *Cartaret*, the first busses to be launched, sailed for Bressay Sound on June 3rd, 1750 accompanied by a jager each and a sloop-of-war, the *Spy*. The busses carried English masters as well as Danish skippers with mixed crews of British, Danes and Dutch. The British masters were given precise if voluminous instructions and naive exhortations: "Doe you direct perswade the most sedate and ingenuous parts of your English crews, nay bribe them by a gallon or two of Brandy to learn the Dutchmen's secrets in gypping, salting, packing and curing of herrings ..." Besides master and skipper, the *Pelham* had a crew of 15, nine of these being gyppers who cut the herrings' throats and take out the guts, filling the full herrings into one basket and the shotten (spent) into another.

The other two busses were sent to Stornaway and all appear to have had a successful season. Some of the cured catch was sent to Hamburg, most went to London where one barrel and six half-barrels fetched £75 11s at the Royal Exchange Coffee House. In 1753, 38 British busses fished from Bressay Sound but due to defaulting subscribers corruption crept in and the society fell into bankruptcy.

Yet another attempt was made 30 years later by decreeing that the tonnage bounty be increased from 30 shillings to £3 the ton, with an extra £1 per ton for the first 30 vessels that reported themselves in Bressay Sound. But there was no benefit whatever to the Isles. Hemp had risen to a price without precedent, and a drift of nets for a 50-ton drifter cost over £600. Second-hand drifters and nets did not exist in the islands and a capital expenditure of thousands would bring only a certain revenue of £200. One record exists for 1809. Dr. Edmonston tells us that only one Shetland vessel entered the tonnage bounty in Bressay Sound that year and that otherwise she had indifferent success.

As far as Shetland was concerned, then as now, the Shetlanders took fish from local grounds but with a small scale of industrial organisation. The percentages of herring caught by local and Dutch boats in 1660 was probably near that taken by Norwegian and Icelandic purse-seiners and the Shetland drifters in 1965. The effort expended by pre-eighteenth-century foreign line fishers has been compared with that of the German, Russian and Scottish trawlers today. Then, as now, the full advantage of the resource exploited around Shetland did not come to the local fishermen, rather it came to the local traders ashore who provided for the foreign vessels while in port.

161

16. *The Bitter Years*

THERE WAS A Shetland saying, current at the end of the nineteenth century, which is still remembered: "There are bad crops once in every seven years and bad fishings once in three, but the lairds are aye bad." From the year 1712, when the Salt Tax priced the foreign fish curer out of the market, for the following 150 years the Shetland crofter faced one calamity after another. Caught up in the "truck system", with 40 days' notice to quit, eternally in debt, he was frequently on the verge of famine when crops and fishing failed simultaneously. More than usually vulnerable to epidemics and disease against which he had no immunity, press-ganged into the Navy and finally driven to ruin or emigration by "the clearances", he was changed out of all recognition from an agricultural tenant making what livelihood he could, to a serf whose very existence depended upon his landlord. The entire era was overshadowed by the powerful figure of the landmaster-trader, his dominance never to be forgotten. Corrupted in many cases by absolute power, like dictators their deeds lived after them and even today there are few Shetlanders who cannot tell personal stories of the hardships suffered by their families up to the very end of the nineteenth century.

For the past hundred years or so incoming Scots had acquired large areas of udal lands so that at the beginning of the eighteenth century the Shetlanders from being masters of their own lands became merely tenants burdened with taxes. The crofter not only paid his share of the Scottish land tax of cess, 3d for each merk of land, but continued to pay the ancient Norse land tax of scat, in spite of the obvious injustice of the double imposition. The islands had been restored to the Morton family in 1707, which in turn sold its rights to Sir Laurence Durrdas, ancestor of the Earls of Zetland. To these gentlemen the crofter paid, as well as scat, also the watle, sheep and ox-penny which together varied from 4d to over 1s for each merk. To his landlord he paid rent, three days unpaid labour and a fowl for each merk.

The minister also was entitled to three days free labour, plus corn teinds and casual teinds. Corn teinds were paid in cash at the rate

162

of 8d or 10d for each merk. The casual teinds were paid in 2–4 marks, (about 2½ lb of butter for each cow); 1d for every sheep, payable in lambs and wool. There was also a new boat teind of 12 ling for each sixareen, paid by the crew. Towards the salary of the parish schoolmaster the tenant paid 2d for each merk of land, although returns appear to have been disappointingly slow for in the island of Whalsay in 1862, of 486 persons between the ages of 8 and 80 only seven could read, write and count.

Shetland's isolation caused grave delays in transport not only of people but of goods, although there are many islanders today who would question just how much improvement there has been since the Earl of Morton agreed in 1716 to freight a ship for the carrying of butter. Although the butter in question was intended for lubrication and not human consumption there were risks that even so it might depreciate

41 The herring fleet in Levenwick Bay circa 1908 with the old Netherton graveyard in foreground. Like the great majority of Shetland burial grounds it has been placed as near the sea as possible. Often these are quite some distance from the church itself. (Zetland County Library and Museum.)

by a year's wait in Lerwick. To be certain of reaching Edinburgh in time for the General Assembly of the Church of Scotland in May the Rev. James Grierson had to leave his manse in March. He first took ship to Hamburg, and thence to Leith. By the end of the century there were still only 10 ships a year between Shetland and Scotland.

Within the country itself until about the end of the eighteenth century there were no roads. Boats had always been the principal means of transport with ponies carrying peat, manure and the occasional person. The wealthier inhabitants owned horses which could be hired in 1733 at one shilling (Scots) a mile and "something for the boy". The people themselves thought little of walking long distances, perhaps from Noss (in Dunrossness) to Lerwick with a cow, a distance of over 25 miles, resting halfway for the sake of the cow. To serve a season on a Peterhead whaler men coming across from Papa Stour had to walk from Sandness to Lerwick, a distance of about 30 miles, their sea-chests on their shoulders.

As for post offices, letters might be weeks on the way. In most places when a letter was sent or received someone had to be sent to Lerwick who was paid one shilling and sixpence or two shillings for 16 miles depending on the state of the weather.

For years the islands had depended on the German and Dutch merchants and fish curers to buy their salt fish, butter, fish oil, stockings and worsted stuff, supplying in return hemp, lines, hooks, tar, linen cloth, tobacco, spirits and sometimes cash. The system had worked admirably. The landlords not only drew dependable revenues from fishing böds or booths rented to the merchants, with now and then a backhander for monopoly of trading in a certain district; rents for beaches or ayres where they dried their fish, but the merchants in their turn relieved the landowners of the oil, butter and cloth in which the tenants paid their rents and taxes, paying cash for these commodities.

The effect of the Salt Tax on landlord and tenant alike was cataclysmic. The bottom fell out of the economy, and both landlord and tenant alike were left helpless, hanging like a fish in a skeo. The only possible remedy was for the landlords themselves to become fish merchants and general traders. They had some small encouragement from the government which offered a bounty of three shillings per hundredweight on all home-cured fish exported.

When the lairds first entered into the exporting of dried fish to the Catholic countries of Europe they were hampered by lack of experience, a limited knowledge of the market, a small working capital and strong opposition from the German merchants with the result that more than one landowner found himself bankrupt. Thomas Gifford of Busta appears to have dominated the early dried fish trade in Shetland and

164

through his letters and writings we learn a great deal about the country at the opening of the eighteenth century. A letter from his son in Edinburgh gives some idea of the problems of marketing and also refers for the first time to the method of curing fish which came to be universally adopted and was responsible for the high reputation of Shetland dried fish later in the century.

"If you please to make a Tryall of four or five hundred ling and Cure them after the new method, that is just fresh out of the sea Right Spekked, prest, Little Salted and hard dried ... it be fact that fish thus cured will give far better price at any markett. ... I hope the herring venture Shall be better with you this year than formerly and that the fishing will afford to send a ship up the Straits (of Gibraltar) but ... do not send them to Lisbon at least the Merchants here that have Dealt that way think it the worst Mercatt in the Straits ..."

By 1726 in addition to the difficulties of marketing his fish, prices having slumped due to the Newfoundland fishing begun by the French, Gifford was complaining that fishers in the islands would rather sell to small traders than to him. These small traders would finally in the nineteenth century emancipate the Shetland fisheries from the yoke of landmaster control. The first evidence of the beginning of this control is shown when in the same year, Gifford, having trouble selling herring in the Hamburg market, ruled "that he would only buy herrings from those who were also white fishers ..."

A couple of years later and summer brought a good return of line-caught white fish, coinciding with the opening of the Spanish market which was until the end of the nineteenth century the largest consumer of Shetland-caught and cured white fish. With this impetus a considerable quantity of goods were imported from Bergen for the fishing industry.

Fishing was still carried on inshore with only four-oared yoals and no sixareens (six-oared boats) were being imported. However, by the 1740's the larger-boat fishery was developing rapidly and Gifford's next import order includes 8 sixareens and only 24 fourareens, all brought from Bergen.

This was the beginning of the rise of the haaf fishing, an era of unprecedented success for the landlord and a desperate struggle for the crofter fisherman, when men and boys risked their lives daily, out at the "far haaf" putting their slender open craft to the most severe test possible, to seek the fish which due to some climatic change had left the inshore grounds for the wild open sea. Books could be written and have indeed been written solely around the haaf fishing of the eighteenth century. Tales of superb seamanship and unsurpassed courage, of monumental disasters when the sea claimed all the able-bodied men

165

42 Old boat noosts, the Ness, Foula. Boats used to put out from Foula in the nineteenth century from a small cobbled beach below—all that is left now are broken shells.

from one parish in a single night and the roots were laid.down of a particular brand of skill and endurance that was never equalled in the long history of seamanship.

The Ness yoal, one of the oldest boat types surviving round the British Isles today, was, at least up to 1817, the universal fishing craft of Shetland. Clinker built, with a sweeping sheer, amazingly supple. and graceful but with a resilience all her own, the yoal was designed for the turbulent inshore fishing for saithe, off the headland of the dynning röst. Frail as she looked, it was just this deceptive elasticity that was her greatest virtue, the same sea-kindliness of the Gokstad ship whose replica Magnus Andersen sailed across the Atlantic in 1893. Captain Andersen noted that "she showed a gunwale twisting out of the true by as much as six inches ..." and yet she remained completely seaworthy. That great expert on Shetland boats, Mr. Tom Henderson, Curator of the County Museum in Lerwick, said almost the same thing about the Ness yoal when he wrote comparing the two vessels: "She is a mere shell and so supple that when standing on a beach by shaking her stem you can make the other horn oscillate backwards and forwards at least six inches."

It appears that the sixareen was evolved after the middle of the eight-

166

eenth century to meet the needs of the Shetland deep-sea fishing—the *far haaf* and by 1791 they were universally used in the Isles. The proportions of the sixareen were not so very far off those of the yoal, but between the slender hull of the yoal and the deeper fuller one of the sixareen there is a world of difference. It was, nevertheless, in these slim graceful yoals that the Shetland men of the eighteenth century had to venture out, so far off "as to almost sink the land".

At the beginning of the inshore fishery in yoals in the tide races, off Sumburgh Head, Skaw in Unst and all the fast sounds that ripped through between the islands, the nearest grounds were called *saets*—a fishing place—and the boats used hand lines. The offshore grounds were called *reiths*, an area of sea bottom which was known by certain landmarks called *meiths*. As well as defining each area of the sea they indicated physical peculiarities of the seabed itself, which determined a good fishing place, shoal, hard or soft bottom and so forth. The accuracy of these cross bearings where landmarks could be seen and the height of water up a headland gauged, with probably two headlands in line, were of enormous importance and as good as a written chart to men who knew every spot around the islands.

As economic pressures grew on landmaster and tenant-fisher to produce more fish so the industry grew in scale and range. At first the efforts of the landlords had been directed towards sustaining themselves and their tenantry, in a way keeping them both suspended in the vacuum created by the disappearance of the foreign merchants. It seems reasonable to suppose that in the hazardous experimental days, in order to be able to count on a sure supply of fish it had to be a compulsory condition of tenure that the crofter would fish for his own landlord exclusively and sell him all his catch. No doubt in the desperate measures to salvage all there was little thought of the future. As soon as the situation began to improve, largely due to the appearance of British merchants from London and Greenock willing to contract for the fish for re-export to Barcelona, the landowners realised that the more fishers they could command the greater the profit. The result was inevitable, an intensification of what came to be known and hated as "the truck system" and all the consequent miseries endured by the practically captive tenant-fishers.

The industry now developed until it became the pursuit of the entire male population of the islands, and with larger boats required and longer fleets of lines the landowners became boat-owners as well. Already they owned the crofter's house and land; they had set themselves up as merchants and bankers and finally emerged with complete monopoly of power over their tenants, which few could resist turning to their own advantage. Occasionally the landlord rented the farm at what was supposed to be a low rent in return for preference as buyer of the tenant's fish and other produce, but in the main, as the condition of tenure, the crofters were compelled to sell their fish, surplus eggs, butter, hens and knitwear to the landlord at a price lower than that which they could receive elsewhere and in addition pay a higher rent.

It was a custom in Shetland, where the land had earlier been the mainstay of life, that no young man could take a wife until he owned a piece of land on which they could settle. The landlords now subdivided the land into smaller portions which certainly encouraged earlier marriages but also brought young men and their wives into districts short of crews for the fishing boats and ensured a future supply of the same commodity.

The landlord could also give notice to quit, usually 40 days, with, needless to say, no appeal. If any crofter succeeded by sheer industry and perseverance in improving his home or croft the landlord congratulated him and put up the rent. Not only was the crofter forced to fish for the laird, but he must buy meal, groceries, boots, and any other household necessities from the landowner's shop at his prices. Once caught up in this vicious circle, where accounts were settled once a year, the crofter was continually on the debit side and there was no escape. Part of his right of tenure included so many days working at his landlord's peat and crops. He was bound to sell his animals to him as well, or at least give him the first option of purchase. If for any reason he could not pay his rent the factor came and removed any animal which he considered equivalent to the debt. Two years arrears of rent and the family was evicted. In one case the factor came and removed the one cow which was the main sustenance of a blind father and a young family of seven, and widows losing the breadwinner at sea could expect little sympathy. A young man escaping for a year to the whaling in order to earn perhaps £2 for the season came home to find his family had been levied a guinea for his absence.

At the beginning of the eighteenth century the population was estimated at about 15,000 over the whole islands, of which 700 to 800 lived in Lerwick. During the eighteenth and nineteenth centuries these figures fluctuated enormously, certainly one of the reasons for decreases being the almost regular outbreaks of smallpox which decimated the islands each of these outbreaks accounting for the loss of about one quarter of Shetland's population. In 1700, 90 persons were prayed for in one day in Lerwick out of a total population of 1000. In 1720 it was called "the mortal pox" and of about 200 people living in Foula only five or six were left to bury the dead. During the epidemic of 1760 inoculation was introduced but owing to the high fees charged for this

168

service, two to three guineas, only 10 or 12 persons availed themselves of it. At salaries of £2 a year for a housemaid and perhaps £4 for a fisherman it was scarcely surprising. Again in 1769 inoculations were more widespread followed by the usual results, fewer deaths but a continued spread of the disease.

With mortality still very high, there appeared one of those natural geniuses, John Williamson, who invented an improved method of inoculation. Dr. Robert Cowie, MD, who followed his father in the practice of medicine in Lerwick and wrote his Thesis on Shetland, describes Williamson's method as told to him:

"He is careful in providing the best matter and keeps it a long time before he puts it to use—sometimes 7 or 8 years; and in order to lessen its virulence he first dries it in peat smoke and then puts it underground, covered with camphor. Though many physicians recommend fresh matter, this self-taught practitioner finds from experience that it always proves milder to the patient when it has lost a considerable degree of its strength.

"He uses no lancet in performing the operation but, by a small knife, made by his own hands, he gently raises a very little of the outer skin of the arm, so that no blood flows; then puts in a very small quantity of the matter which he immediately covers with the skin that has been thus raised. The only plaster that he uses for healing the wound is a bit of cabbage leaf. It is particularly remarkable that there is not a single instance in his practice where the infection has not taken place and made its appearance at the usual time. He administers no medicine during the progress of the disease nor does he use any previous preparation ... several thousands have been inoculated by him and he has not lost a single patient."

Williamson, from his various attainments and superior talents, was called Johnny Notion among his neighbours. Under this cognomen he is spoken of by his countrymen to this day. To his attainments in medicine and surgery he added the arts of shoemaker, tailor, carpenter, cutler, farmer and fisherman.

Cowie remarks that "Is it not strange that, at the very time when the most learned and able physicians in Europe treated most inflammatory diseases by excessive salivation, bleeding, purging and blistering, this poor, unlettered empiric in the Shetland Islands refrained from the use of medicine altogether? He applied to his lancet wound simply a piece of cabbage blade, while his contemporary Mr Bromfield, Surgeon to Her Majesty and to St George's Hospital London, dressed his larger wounds with 13 layers of applications placed on them at the same time."

The Letter Book of Thomas Gifford of Busta is sufficient to give us

169

some glimpses of the conditions of Shetland in the eighteenth century. Shipping was delayed by storm and other hindrances. His son John who went to Hamburg in a Hollands ship that Gifford had freighted there with fish was frozen in along with a Zetland vessel. Two Dutch ships carrying Shetland fish were lost. "This winter" he writes, "is said to be the worst within the memory of man."

A letter to his cousin tells that "Farquar who writes me from Lerwick that he was taken by a Privateer of Dunkirk of 12 Carriage Guns and 16 Swivels . . . and after having plundered him of everything that was in the ship worth taking he ransom'd for £110 stg." Despite the weather and the pirates Gifford conducted a fairly large trade on his own, and in one season this single merchant shipped to Hamburg 54,430 dried ling, 1320 cod, 12 barrels of herring, 3 barrels of fish oil, 81 barrels of butter, together with over 1000 pairs of hose, but John was no longer to write from Hamburg.

Although Thomas Gifford of Busta was easily the most influential landowner on the islands, in spite of his undoubted wealth and position, the House of Busta was the scene of one of the greatest tragedies and mysteries ever to happen in Shetland. The first mention of Busta is in a deed dated 1488. The house was already 100 years old when it was bought by Robert Gifford, the younger son of a family which originated from the Lothians in Scotland and settled at Wetherstaa. Robert one of 24 children, had to leave Wetherstaa and moved across the narrow sound of Busta Voe. These Giffords of Busta, as they came to be called, built on Muckle Roe a new and larger house alongside the old one, strong, plain and solid, designed to stand up to the cold stormy winters of Shetland.

By 1742, Thomas, grandson of Robert, was Steward Depute to the Earl of Morton, administering law and justice throughout the islands and involved heavily with estate duties, the fishing industry and foreign trading. His wife Elizabeth was the daughter of John Mitchell, who became Sir John Mitchell of Westshore, Scalloway. Almost from the beginning, in spite of wealth, position and all the comforts of the landed gentry, the Giffords seem to have been singled out by the Fates. They lost five of their children in two years during the smallpox epidemic but were still left with four sons and four daughters. Cursed on a dark night by drunken John Oliphant, whose father James had been in debt to Thomas Gifford who had a "wadset" on his lands of Ure, Thomas threw him out of the house with Oliphant's words ringing in his ears . . . "may your sons never live to inherit your stolen lands . . ."

Lady Busta, as Elizabeth was called in the manner of the day, was autocratic, high-handed and determined that her son John should make a good match and inherit the lands of Busta. When Thomas Gif-

170

ford, her husband, taking pity on Barbara Pitcairn and her sister Ellis, Lady Busta's distant relatives whose father had died leaving them in impoverished circumstances, invited them to stay at Busta, Elizabeth while giving lip-service to the wishes of her husband, treated Barbara more as a ladies' maid. Unknown to her, John Gifford, her son and heir fell in love with Barbara and persuaded his cousin John Fisken, an ordained minister to marry them secretly. The marriage lines he gave to his uncle Patrick at Wetherstaa to keep them safe from Lady Busta until such time as he could announce the fact that Barbara was now his wife.

As soon as Barbara confessed that she was about to bear his child he promised to bring back the lines and confront his mother with the truth. That night of Sunday May 22nd, 1748, John along with his three brothers and John Manson who was in charge of the cattle at Busta House, were all five drowned in Busta Voe. It was a fine, calm night. They were returning from a visit to his cousin the Revd. John Fisken at Wetherstaa. In the morning the empty boat was found floating in the voe. John's body was recovered and Barbara, stricken with grief as she was, slipped the marriage lines from his pocket, only to have them stolen by Lady Busta as she lay on childbed. Gideon Gifford was brought up by Lady Busta and scarcely saw his mother, who eventually was persuaded to take up lodgings in Lerwick on the promise that her son would inherit Busta. Long after the death of Elizabeth, Lady Busta, the lines were discovered in an old mahogany chest by Lady Symbister one of the Gifford daughters along with a letter from Elizabeth confessing her treachery.

In spite of a long and protracted lawsuit brought by Arthur of Ollaberry who claimed to be heir in line, Gideon Gifford's son also called Arthur still remained laird of Busta, and although the costs of the case amounting to £40,000 crippled the estate, Barbara Pitcairns's name was cleared. Arthur Gifford left no heirs to inherit and eventually the estate was bought first by the Hon. Brigadier William Fraser and finally by Sir Basil Neven-Spence. Sir Basil died in 1974 but his words at the end of a play for radio written round the ill-fated house of Busta by Jenny Gilbertson still remain in the last paragraph of the script: "Sometimes I look from the window across the Voe to Wetherstaa, and ponder on the mystery that surrounds the tragic death of their four sons and on that quiet night in May 1748. Sometimes the gentle spirit of Barbara Pitcairn seems still to pervade the ancient house. The curse laid by Oliphant of Ure has died away." It may have died, but in the tragic life of Sir Basil Neven-Spence himself, some echo of the curse on the house of Busta seems to have lingered on.

In 1758 and for the next few years some "pestilential fever" broke out, succeeded in 1761 by smallpox, between the two killing more than 200 people. That year there were more severe frosts and loss of livestock. This dreadful tale was repeated 11 years later at the same time of year. A series of bad crops and bad fishing about the year 1781 reduced the crofters so far below the poverty line that Nova Scotia emigration agents moving through the country were able to persuade numbers to emigrate. This, in addition to a further emigration of 280 persons from Caithness and Zetland in 1774 was a serious drain on the population, soon to be further reduced by the "Pressgang".

Britain, apparently never happier than when engaged in several wars at once, had taken on America, France, Holland and Spain and desperately required men for the navy. It was a long way to go but these were partly procured in the Shetlands by an official government agreement with "the Gentlemen Proprietors of fishing in Shetland". The agreement read rather like an order for so many cattle: "to receive an hundred seamen and fishers belonging to the said Island, fifty to be delivered immediately and fifty in August next", which must have been a sore temptation for the local lairds to get rid of any particularly troublesome crofters.

The other method of procuring seamen for His Majesty was by the direct method of the Pressgang and scarcely a district but has its stories of escape and searches. In a house at Williamsetter two Goudie men from Clumlie in Dunrossness were rudely interrupted in the middle of their tea one Christmas Day. While seated at the table enjoying themselves a thunderous knock came at the door.

It took only a matter of seconds for them to escape through the back door into the barn and out through the barn window. The night of course being pitch black their progress was slow, but at last they came to their laamhus (lambhouse) at Trotta Knowe. The roof had fallen in but the langbands were still there (part of what might be called the rafters), so creeping in they managed to cover themselves with wood.

As they had, rather stupidly one might think, made straight off in the general direction of home, it was scarcely surprising that about half an hour later they heard the panting of their pursuers. The officer in charge walked all round the building and drawing his sword plunged it several times into the pile of wood but mercifully without wounding either of the men. "There's nothing here but old wood" they could hear the Press men say, and so they departed. In the morning the two Goudies made their way to Clumlie and with the rest of the Clumlie men went east to De Un, a cave at Ramnibanks, where they lay hidden for three weeks, their wives bringing them food every night until the Pressgang had left the islands. There are still "Goudie men" at Williamsetter.

172

43 The Gospel Ship: once found hanging in many croft houses, an extraordinary model composed entirely of quotations from the Bible.

THE GOSPEL SHIP.

There were men who spent months living in a peat stack and being fed at dead of night. Anything was better than to have to leave your wife and children fatherless, perhaps forever. Whalers returning from Greenland were often relieved of half their crews and even men in little rowing boats close inshore went in fear of their lives. After Trafalgar it was estimated that 3000 Shetland seamen were in the British Navy, out of a total male population of less than 10,000. Once impressed these men were asked to "volunteer" to fight "for King and Country" and kept in solitary confinement without food until they decided to "volunteer". Those who survived to be discharged were paid off at Portsmouth and had to make their own way home as best they could.

The usual procedure in Shetland was for the naval vessel to land a party of armed seamen which went straight to the "Gentleman Proprietor of fishing" and received from him a list of men who could or should be pressed. The party then went to the nearest house and demanded guides. If the request was refused one member of the household was impressed. Whether the officer who came to the House o' Gairdie had previously visited the local landowner we do not know but the story of the Six Men o' Gairdie has come down to us from Sandness on the west coast.

At the House o' Gairdie lived a widow with six stalwart sons, all fine-looking men of whom she was inordinately proud. In small communities news travels fast and in no time at all she heard that the "Press" had been at Waas. She knew where the next stop would be. She managed to hide all her sons away and sat down with her knitting. Soon the Pressgang came to the House o' Gairdie, the remains of it still standing, and informed her that they were there to stay until she produced her sons. She knew very well that they meant what they said and that there was little hope of getting rid of them. So finally she said that she would make a deal with them.

The lieutenant accompanying the men was young himself and appeared a reasonable kind of person. So she said to him: "I've always heard it said that you prefer a volunteer to an impressed man", to which he agreed. "Well," she replied, "I'll give you one volunteer instead of six impressed men, if you will keep your side of the bargain." Waiting her chance she slipped away to where the boys were hidden and returned with her youngest son, who was then about 18. "Here's your volunteer" she said "provided you go and leave my other five sons," reminding him that he was supposed to be a gentleman and would honour his pledge, which he did. The boy served all through the Napoleonic wars and came safely home again.

It was during the Napoleonic wars that for an annual retainer women in straitened circumstances pledged the service of their male children

174

to the navy when they reached the age of 12. A Lunnasting man and his son returned from fishing one day to find two naval officers waiting to take the son away for naval service. The mother had made the agreement without the man's knowledge when the child was born and had spent her yearly pittance in complete secrecy. It is not surprising to know that the poor man was beside himself with grief and the couple parted in consequence.

The main cause of the poverty at the root of these and similar cases was the total dependence of the Lairds on a single industry run on a shoestring, by craft too small for the waters in which they operated. Even the method of fishing was incapable of giving fishermen adequate returns for the amount of work and the dangers involved. Although many Shetland families emigrated most of the people were too deeply "sunk in poverty and famine" to leave the islands. In 1784 there were again agents in Shetland "who have orders to emigrate as many of the inhabitants or the whole if they can to Nova Scotia and that Transport shall be sent for them whenever they find it convenient to Ship themselves".

Meanwhile there had been a steady decrease in the size of the crofts. The number of ploughs fell since nearly all the arable land could be dug with a spade. The minister at Delting noted that it was common to have four families on a farm which 20 years earlier had only one. The fishing grew at the expense of the agriculture and at the end of the eighteenth century small farms known as "outsets" came into being. The method was to build a stone or failey (turf) dyke round a few acres of moorland and then turn it over with a spade. Several thousands of acres of arable land were cleared in this way causing complaints from crofters who lost grazing land without compensation from the landlord in the form of reduced rent. The outsets were doomed to failure from the start. Given to a young couple with no family to assist them, no funds with which to buy the stock whose manure would have been essential in cultivation, they could not keep up either the rent or the work.

Then came failure of the potato crop, a recent introduction to the islands where hitherto people had preferred cabbage. The disastrous harvests of 1846, 47, 48 and 49 reduced the islanders to the brink of starvation. And so began the first network of roads in the Shetland Islands, forever to be known and remembered as "the meal roads". The Edinburgh section of the Board for the Relief of Destitution in the Highlands and Islands of Scotland resolved to aid them both with meal and money on condition that they entered into some kind of work. Roadmaking was chosen as being the most urgent public improvement which would provide lasting benefit to the community.

175

44   Old mill, the Ness, Foula, the burn strewn with yellow Iris.

The Board agreed to furnish two-thirds of the money required on condition that the landed proprietors put up the other third. Many entered into the scheme and then the local Inspector for the Board, later Admiral Craigie, argued that it would be better to construct main trunk lines rather than small side roads and persuaded the Board to give a larger grant. Everyone who was fit laboured on them for a peck of meal at the end of the day, worth about three pence, although there were in some districts those who refused to accept any kind of charity work. Over 100 miles of road were constructed, the people carrying gravel in kishies on their backs, the youngest a boy of nine, sole support of his widowed mother, all under the direction of a contingent of sappers and miners from the army.

By the 1840's the landlords found that farming could be more profitable than fishing and they began to drop the system of fishing as a condition of tenure. The crofters lost the market for their fish; they could no longer barter them for meal at the landowner's shop and many moved to districts where fishing was still part of the tenure. The lairds did not re-let the vacant crofts but laid them down as pasture for sheep. And then began the clearances. Landowners could not wait for empty crofts and often gave the tenant notice to quit. It has been said that "the clearances", as they were known, were equally as disastrous if not worse in Shetland than in the Highlands of Scotland.

When the valley of Veensgarth in Tingwall was cleared in the 1850's to make room for sheep 21 families were removed. In 1874 the entire lands of Garth were cleared by the laird of Quendale, the houses being stripped and in some cases burned as soon as the tenants stepped out. Not a living human being was left in Garth, Quam, Corston or Neeflan. Land which had been worked for a thousand years had been laid down to sheep and the names of once busy townships erased from the map. All over the islands, and Unst was particularly badly hit, one can see

176

in certain lights the faint outline of rig and park and maybe a rickle of stones or sheep sheltering in some abandoned croft. At Bigton, one of the two seats of the Symbister lairds, the other being in Whalsay, only a few remember the names of the little crofts of Ratchel and Buegel, Whistlebere, Kettleneckit, Cauldhame, Upper and Lower Lowrie, Vessamers and Windhouse, all lost within a space of less than three miles. The Windhouse folk moved their cottage stone by stone, carrying them in kishies out of the estate about half-a-mile down the road from where the old Bigton house now stands.

Today the planning schemes for Unst and the Council's proposals for the arbitrary zoning of good crofting land for oil development projects, naturally came up against bitter opposition from men whose parents remembered the last evictions in Cliff and Burrafirth. The flow of emigrants increased to a torrent and in some places the lairds encouraged it. The owners of the Garth estate in Dunrossness helped to arrange assisted passages to New Zealand and emigration was also encouraged by the laird of Fair Isle. Some of the people there left for Orkney and in March, 1862, a total of 148 passengers sailed from Fair Isle for St. John, New Brunswick. Between 1871 and 1881, 4640 Shetlanders left the islands.

Then the landowners cast covetous eyes on the scattald—the free grazing land. A circular that was sent to all the tenants on an estate in Unst shows the change following the removal of the scattald from the people. They would still be allowed to graze animals but charges would be levied of 9d for each sheep; 1s 6d for a cow and 3s 6d for a horse.

In one way or another whole areas, small fertile islands, became deserted, given over to the sheep and the seabirds. Lights went out one by one until only the oldest residents were left, finally to be dispersed among relatives if they had them, if not they "were put on the quarter". This was a traditional Shetland way of relief for the poor. If a person applied to be put on the quarter, the minister announced it from the pulpit and if no objections were raised on moral or economic grounds, he received immediate assistance. He was taken in by each croft in turn and looked after for as many days as the number of merks of land occupied by the family, moving on within his own small circle, but always sure of meat and bed, the weekly offering at church being used to buy his clothes.

17. *The Far Haaf*

It were as if the mould
was the trough of a wave
taken by the eye to the land
and by the hand filled around
with larch. First with adze
he carved out the wooden keel
to lie as heavy flotsam
against the drag of the sea,
and then with template bowed
the strakes like swans' wings
from stem to stern, and finally
he cut the ribs—a wishbone
for their flight.

From the same wave she was made
as the Gokstad ship, but Willie's hand
and Willie's eye saw only
the haaf grounds and the mind
to reach them and return
with the speed of the gull
before that wave
reclaimed its stolen shape.

Laughton Johnston.

The remains of inshore fishing stations litter the voes from Sumburgh to Burra Firth, but the hives of lodges for the far haaf were plotted only on suitable beaches nearest the grounds. Shelter from wind and weather was a secondary choice, a fine drying ayre more important, where the sixareens could haul out like seals on an easy sloping shelf of small grey stones. The stations began on the west side of Bressay opposite Lerwick and on Noss at the voe of the Mels, the boats being nearly

178

as large as the west side boats, but not carrying so many lines, the Bressay men going to the Bressay Haaf, now known as The Forty Mile Ground.

Further north Nesting had in addition an important winter sillock fishery and at Grif Skerry, Whalsay, Out Skerries and Fetlar, boats fished up to 40 miles, according to Goodlad, off at the Fetlar Haaf, although it is considered that a sixareen would put the Pobies of Unst (Saxavord) under at 35 miles and "Da Pobie's dippin" was understood to be about the furthest limit to which a sixareen was asked to go. From Haf Gruney, the green serpentine island off Uyea sound in Unst, Haroldswick, Norwick and Skaw, the most northerly point in Unst, the men of the 1780's were regularly rowing as far as 30 miles off to the haaf, and from the end of the century to the last days of the sixareen fishing in the 1880's, Goodlad again mentions record trips of up to 50 miles from land. Occasionally men from Unst might meet up with Norwegian *attrings*, larger than the sixareen with eight oars instead of six, and now and then they would catch a glimpse of a white-shouldered mountain rising behind Möre and Trondelag where centuries before men had set out west-over-sea, ancestors of both the haaf fishers and their craft. Far out at the Pobis of Unst, da Bank Haaf, just before the continental shelf drops steeply, all they could see of Shetland was Ronas Hill "sitting like a kishie upo da water".

On the east side there was a small station at Woodwick, a fine beach but a dangerous landing and there was an important haaf station at Gloup in Yell where the sixareens joined the fleet from North Mavine coming from stations in Fedeland and Uyea, from Heylor and Stenness, Cullivoe and Hamnavoe in Papa Stour. By the time of the first Statistical Account, North Mavine was the main ling fishing parish in Shetland with over one-third of its boats at the haaf, using more lines than any other district, up to 80 *baukts* per boat being recorded. By 1774 this

45   Wood Wick, Unst, once an old haaf station and now, owing to tides and its narrow entrance, a veritable treasure cove of driftwood, a rare sight in Shetland where every piece thrown up is valuable, but here in Unst the road through the valley is a mere track, hilly and boggy, through which no vehicle could pass.

was up to 100 and the stations of Fedeland, Uyea, Ronas Voe and Stenness were the most important in the islands. By 1785 boats of 20 feet keel, 30 feet overall, were going up to 50 miles off-shore with 120 *baukts* of lines.

From all the long years of the far haaf little remains. High on a ribbed shoreline wide-bellied sixareens yawn spilling open, rotted by sun, wind and sea. The thwartship rowing benches that once supported men leaning on oars, their life blood sweated out of hands swift on line and sheet, these tafts that once divided the flying sixareen's rooms have long come adrift. Where the stern has sunk into nettles and sea grass you can see the shott hole where a skipper fought to drive her, helm against his weather shoulder running the seas in the tails, his whole being intent, depending on his own inborn sense to keep her from taking the water she cannot hold. Weeds thrust through the run where big cod and ling arched, spent and flapping, waiting the *kavlin tree* to gouge out hook and bait, guts to fly over the gunwale for the waiting gulls, heads, maybe some at least, kept for the family. Rainwater swills in the owseroom for'rard of the run where the bailer might be baling the water two gallons at a time in heavy seas. Then came the midroom, in fine weather used for shooting and hauling the lines, six or seven miles of baukts alive with struggling, kicking fish. You might find the rusted remains of a fire kettle and pot in the foreroom, the peat long dissolved, and along the gunwales *kaibs* spiked like broken teeth.

On other beaches are outside lodges and drying sheds, on lonely crescents of shelving stone, no sheltered harbour their's, but shallow where a boat can be manhandled up from the tideway, wet seaweed, whale ribs or useless halibut strewn as *linns* or runners for the keel, skeletons of sixareens lie forgotten as the yellowing photographs of their crews. Seven men are there. They might be any of a hundred men, not big but well-built, eyes crinkled and crossed with weather lines under small round peaked caps, thick striped sarks, a waistcoat with a chain, a precious watch in its pocket. Line and sheet-hardened hands laid loosely on thigh, but fine-boned like their faces, bearded, tanned.

On a bright May morning the thin rigs delled and planted, the planti crubs netted over the cabbage seedlings, the peats cast, the men set off for another season relentless as the wind that filled or rent the sails, flattened the swaying crops and stamped its mark on the women's faces who watched them go. A nod over the shoulder as the croft fell away into the distance; a hand raised helpless like a prayer above children's voices suddenly stilled. The eyes of the old mirrored tragedies. The wind whipped an unshed tear from their dimness. Black figures turned. Kye had to be milked, peat raised, bairns fed. Emotions, love, small tendernesses had long been beaten out of them. Empty as

180

a shell a silent grief paraded like a cross, thrust constantly before their sons' young wives, bright-eyed, eager, flowering briefly only to wither under the weight of years.

The men shifted wooden rafters from one shoulder to the other, cracked a joke and plodded on along the track to where the bare walls of last year's lodges waited for the pones and divots to be cut and replaced, their only refuge for the season unless they were lucky enough to get home for a *helli*, a week-end in the middle of the fishing. They carry to their stations two lispunds of meal; two ankers of potatoes; a pork ham or a smoke-dried sheep and half a lispund of dried bere which they will pound in a stone quern to make broth. The young boys walked, blyed, excited, laden with oilskins, hooks, lines, pails for the bait. Some of the men would have a little cheap smuggled fiery spirits that might keep someone alive one night, but their usual drink is water, unless they bring from their homes a small cask or jar of *blaand*.

46   Sixareens at Fethaland in the 1890's: their lodges can be seen on the opposite bank and it would seem that the boat in the foreground had just returned from the fishing, her shott full of fish. (Zetland County Library and Museum.)

They were allowed by law to build their huts on any unenclosed or uncultivated land at a distance of not more than 100 yards above high water mark. These lodges were re-occupied year after year, dismantled at the end of the season. In 1726 on the Skerries there was a great fight between the Sinclairs and the Giffords over possession of a booth. The Giffords of Busta came armed and a siege took place. Magnus Flaws, champion of the Sinclairs, mounted the roof and swore to make entrance. Not surprisingly he was promptly shot, and the Sinclairs abandoned the dispute. For years afterwards it was remembered as "The Skerry Fight".

The men began as feid boys, with a fee for the season, their food and the catch or takings of a baukt, 60 fathoms, 60 hooks, which they were free to choose from anywhere along the lines. But however young, 12, 13, 14, they had to be able to pull an oar and take their part in man's work. Their feid days lasted till they were considered fit to go as a share hand. Earnings from the haaf fishing in 1809 were calculated to be about £1 12s per man or just about enough to pay the year's rent. For food a man depended on the lesser spring and winter fishing, his croft and when there was not enough to go round credit from the landmaster was the only means he had of sustaining his family, so that as the population increased and food shortages became more acute the landlord's position grew even stronger.

The first duty of the crew, usually six men and a boy, was to catch piltocks or haddocks for bait by handline in inshore waters. In good weather, setting out for the haaf in the morning, they rowed in pairs, the companion boat known as "the ranksman", *kemping*' or racing each other to the grounds. It was a crazy expenditure of strength, a game of prowess that lightened the long row of maybe 12 hours, and reaching the fishing grounds in the evening they began to lay their lines.

The lines duly laid, they were left for about three hours in which to *tide* or fish, while the crew rested or had some supper, and then the *hale* began. One man hauled the line over the starboard side, one *kaevilt* or *kavilled* (taking the fish off the toam) throwing the fish aft where they were gutted and headed. Depending on the weather, one, two or more men were required to *ando* to the line which meant usually little more than row the boat up to the line against weather or tide. If the haul was meagre and the weather set fair they might set the lines again, but if a good fishing had been taken from the first *sett* (the complete cycle of shooting and hauling the lines), or the weather showed signs of deteriorating, the boat would be back at the station by noon the next day.

The sight of the first flashing white bodies under the water were by tradition referred to as "light in the lum"; the next as "light below

47   Lerwick harbour and Bressay Sound with Shetland drifters in the foreground and Dutch doggers filling the Sound. (Zetland County Library and Museum.)

that", varied by "white again" or "white in under white", the general sea term for fish being white and the ling known as the *hwida*. They never bragged about the catch, it was "ill done" and three score of ling might be deprecatingly referred to as "twartree", two or three. When big cod and ling appeared, and they could be up to 30 or 40 lbs each, they often swallowed hook and bait together so then the man with the *kavlin tree* was kept busy. A halibut could weigh up to two cwt. and after taking the bait the fish had to be played to wear it out. The Unst fishermen fearing it might break the line, shouted "alta-gongi" (ON-stop running). Every now and then they might hook a gigantic skate. With the help of all hands and the *huggistaff* the great fish was secured fighting and threshing wildly, a fearsome battle in a small boat, but both these fish could be used to lay on top of the smaller fish to keep them from escaping. Strange as it may seem now, halibut was at that time useless commercially; it would not take the salt so it was used by the crews or laid down as runners on which to haul out the boat.

One might have imagined that these boats had been designed by some master craftsman literally fitted into the seas they had to be able to take. Each one was different, each had to be handled, gentled and run like a racehorse, all with their own peculiar temperaments. Stability was essential so the bilges were much fuller in the sixareens than in the yoal. Some required a ballast of as much as a ton of beach boulders in addition to the lines and gear. These were cast overboard when the fish were caught, for when the water came pouring in over the gunwale, a *run* full of fish meant less water and more stability.

Next the midroom was the foreroom, headroom and bow space. In the foreroom were kept the fire kettle and pot and the peat fuel, while the headroom and bow served as the galley. A sea-chest, the lid covered with a tarpaulin, held bere, meal, bread or bannocks and maybe a tot of spirits. For'rad in the headroom two water beakers were stowed and when not in use the sail was kept in the bows, its folds being useful as bed and blanket if necessary. On the oar bench abaft the mast trunk the sailman and his helper were ready to hoist or lower, urge or ease. Much of the fishing was done in rough weather and that meant keeping the boat running down the falling face of a wave as long as possible, so the keel length of a sixareen was greater per foot of overall length than it was in boats operating in calmer, inshore waters.

Before the nineteenth century the sail had only been run up as an auxiliary when the wind was fair but after that it came to be used automatically whenever the wind was strong enough. Running before the wind was infinitely faster and more comfortable than rowing. For tacking, the sail developed from an almost square "lug" to one having a pronounced peak.

At the shore stations, old men, their days at the haaf over, and young boys too young yet to go to sea, waited for the catch ready to wash, salt and dry it on the ayres. As the fishing expanded some of the ayres became too small and were built up artificially as at Symbister, Whalsay and Hildasay. First the splitter cut the fish open from the head to the tail, removing with the flick of a knife half the backbone next the head; then the washer with a heath brush and sea water cleared away every particle of blood. Once split and washed the fish were allowed to drain. The salter then packed the fish skin-side undermost layer by layer with salt in a great wooden vat until the chest was filled, heavy stones laid on top keeping the fish in the pickle.

After a few days they were taken out, washed and brushed again from shoulder to tail and put up in small heaps called *clamps* to let the

184

Voar (spring) ploughing at Bigton.

A Shetlander and his boat.

The Holm of Heogland looking towards Fetlar.
The Burgi Broch, Scatness. A blockhouse type, its only counterpart is that of Dun Beag in S.W. Ireland. Across the West Voe rises Sumburgh Head and the lighthouse designed by the father of Robert Louis Stevenson.

water drain off. The fish were next spread out exposed to the sun; again clamped and again spread out and turned until dry. Afterwards the fish had to be built into a large stack called a *steeple* which for the sake of equal pressure had to be taken down again and rebuilt so that the fish undermost in one steeple then became uppermost in the next, a process known as *pining*. At the end of this long and laborious task the fish acquired a white efflorescent appearance termed *bloom*. They were only then collected and cellared in the landmaster's böd to await shipping.

This was when everything went well, but it is easy to forget in the many great tragedies at sea the hundreds of lesser personal struggles fought out from dawn to dusk, day in day out, year after year, for a catch that had a mere 30 per cent maximum efficiency and an average of 10 per cent. In the season it was rare that more than 18 trips to the haaf were made, each catch averaging about five tons of wet fish. Using modern methods, as much fish as was then caught in a season can now be landed in a single day by the same number of men. The fishery began about May 20th and finished about August 12th to 15th at Lammas.

The great disasters strangely enough came in July, more Shetland lives being lost in gales during that month than at any other time of the year. These summer storms continually struck without warning, often when boats had lines out so that they were too light and it was essential to get in weight if their course to land was to be close hauled, the only hope being to persevere and haul the lines. In the flying spindrift, boats lost sight of each other so that little help could be given.

In the gale of July 17th, 1832, 105 men were lost, 42 from Nesting and Lunnasting. Thomas Laurenson of Lunning's boat was at the Skerries *haaf* the day before with his crew of his son-in-law, Robert Robertson, known as Muckle Robbie, Robert Pearson, Laurence Irvine and two feid boys. They had already set their lines but before they could even begin to hale the wind struck from the west, nor'west. All they could do was to hurriedly get in what lines they could, hoist the sail and set off in a southerly direction. Off the island of Mousa the wind eased a bit and they sighted the sloop *Matchless*, belonging to Robert Bruce of Simbister with two sixareens in tow. They finally decided to accept a tow themselves as their food was about done. The crew got down the mast and the sail, stowing it as well as they could and throwing the fish aft to lighten her bows succeeding in getting a rope aboard from the *Matchless*.

"Muckle Robbie took the rope around the *stammerin* and made fast the end with a clove hitch around the *horn*, and a cast of the main rope over the horn also and all the men got safely on board." The wind

185

took up stronger than ever and the *Matchless* stood on for Fair Isle. Just off Sumburgh Head one of the boats filled with water and was cut away. The cast around the horn of the other boat came adrift and the *stammerin* pulled out and she was lost too, but Muckle Robbie's hitch held and the 18 men got safe aboard their boat and landed on the isle. It was a week before the storm broke and they could get a fair wind for home, their women watching the churning seas hopelessly for the sight of a boat lifting out of the troughs.

The week must have seemed endless. No telephones or radio to let them know their men were safe, but the wives of the Sweening boat, John Hughson skipper, had to wait three months for their men. The crew had been taken aboard another vessel and landed at Aberdeen. No word was heard, the men having worked at the harvest in Aberdeenshire before they could get a boat home. The four Gray brothers of Lunnaness and their brother-in-law never returned. Their boat along with two others was last seen being towed by a Dutch buss. This quite natural habit of families or relatives sailing in the same boat gave rise to all the saddest disasters when fathers and sons, brothers and cousins, all went down together.

In the great storm of 1832, from Nesting seven boats were lost, each widow receiving annually £3, each child under 14 10 shillings and parents dependent on sons £2 from 1832 to 1843. From mid and south Yell four boats were lost and of their whole crews numbering 30, only three men were saved. These were all men in the prime of life and left behind 23 widows and 61 fatherless children under 14 years of age.

Of the Whalsay boats in the '87 gale seven men died leaving 34 dependants and James Williamson and Laurence Moar received awards from the Shipwrecked Mariners and Fishermen's Society. Even today the son of the man who brought the remnant of his crew into Lerwick, himself an old man and nearly blind, can speak with difficulty of that dreadful night.

The morning of Friday December 9th, 1887 was fine and frosty but a heavy swell prevented several boats from setting out for the haddock grounds. By mid-day, eight crews decided to leave their noosts, four going south and four northwards. About three o'clock in the afternoon the wind rose without warning to gale force and heavy snow began to fall. In Lerwick itself, even in sheltered places, people dared not venture out of doors and within a few hours six-foot drifts were building up.

Of the four boats fishing to the north of Whalsay, Andrew Barclay and his crew of three had left the ground before the storm struck and were actually weighing their fish at Symbister when the wind rose. Magnus Williamson was lucky too—meeting the gale north of Sym-

186

bister, he made the north bight, drew in their boat and walked home.

James Williamson's crew, off in a new boat, only a fortnight old, were caught with their lines unhaled. Driven on to a rocky shore one of the crew leapt ashore, two were pinned underneath the boat and Williamson somehow in a last burst of strength as the boat lifted with a wave succeeded in getting them out. Struggling to a nearby house in blinding snow, a local man skilled in first aid tended one of the crew with a broken jaw and severe head injuries, stitching up his wounds. Sandy Kay and his crew were having the same trouble but near the shore at Vevoe not far from their own noost a great wave lifted them and left them in a cleft of rock from which they were able to scramble ashore.

The four boats fishing in the south were faced with the grimmer prospect of either attempting the well-nigh impossible in rowing back to Whalsay in the teeth of a gale or drifting before it towards Bressay and Mainland. Matthew Robertson of Hamister was an old haaf man and experience and calm assurance helped to bring his boat safe home. He told the men to keep her head up to wind, to row steadily but not to burst themselves and he would bring her in. Frequently the boat was half filled with water, but they kept baling and rowing until after eight hours or so they came to lee water. Matthew still wouldn't attempt a landing and headed out towards rough water again. Almost completely worn out they at last recognised the approaches to Symbister and made their own noost in North Voe.

James Arthur and his crew rowed against the storm, but driven before it, came into Beosetter, Bressay in the early hours of the morning. The crew got the boat ashore, hauled her up and went to a nearby house for assistance. When they returned Arthur was dead. Robert Williamson and his crew, a brother, cousin and another young man Gilbert Polson, all young and powerful men, never came back. It was assumed that they had either spent themselves in trying to regain the isle or had broken oars and been capsized in the murderous seas.

The remaining boat fishing south of the isle was skippered by Laurence Moar with three brothers, Andrew, Laurence and Thomas Anderson as crew. They were fishing off the Hoga Neep when the storm struck and managed to hale one line before conditions became so bad that they had to cut loose the remainder and head up into wind for Bressay. They lay on their oars until Andrew Anderson, a man of 60, fell from his taft (seat). Then Laurence collapsed. With the intense cold, blinding snow and bitter wind the two brothers must have died very quickly. Moar and Thomas Anderson realised the hopelessness of two men attempting to ride out the storm with oars and somehow they set

187

the mast and got a sail on her. Running before the wind they came down on Bressay but Moar thought of the two men who might conceivably be still alive and would need attention so he headed for Lerwick. About five o'clock on Saturday morning, 14 hours after the storm had struck, they came into Hay's dock. As Anderson was lowering the sail he too collapsed and Moar took the boat alongside. Somehow he managed to reach Hay's shop where he found someone up and about who helped to revive the two survivors.

Of all the disasters that dogged the men of the haaf fishing, in terms of human suffering alone, not one was less terrible than the others, but one of the most poignant must surely be the Delting Disaster of Christmas, 1900. The story was told many years later on sound radio by old people of the district, who as children had lived through those terrible days, and re-told as though it had been yesterday by the last living survivor, William Nicolson who died at the age of 92, three days after the recording. The almost total recall of those quiet voices came across the air like gentle ghosts from a district whose whole future was wiped out within the space of 48 hours.

Mossbank, Toft and Firth is the area ironically described by the planners as "a scattered community with many abandoned crofts" and ear-

48 Andrew Moar of Whalsay, son of the famous Laurence Moar, hero of the gale of '87, who along with James Williamson received awards from the Shipwrecked Mariners and Fishermen's Society. At 86, Andrew still remembers that dreadful day.

188

marked as a development site for Shetland's oil related communities. Throughout these ruined cottages, over 74 years ago, 15 widows and 61 other dependants mourned the loss of four fishing boats and 22 young, vigorous men in the prime of life. Delting was never a rich crofting area. The barren ground could only support a small number of tiny crofts, each one little more than "three acres and a cow" so that the men of that area were forced to "drive the fishing" as they called it, risking their lives in all weathers just to keep home and family alive.

In the late eighteenth century Firth was a tightly knit community where everyone knew everyone else and the rhyme woven around those long lost names familiar to every child in the district.

> Pund a Lut, Peerie Lut, Muckle Lut and Holla
> Da Whilbigarths, da Tiptigarths, da News, and Upper Scolla,
> Da Bonny Hoose o da Bergens, da Giltic at day rose,
> Gostaw and da Punds a Firth, and next tae dat da Crus,
> Fluccads lies oot ower a knowe, and Sandgeo hit lies lonely,
> Mongra Clett lies in a blett and Villance breeds only.

Before the disaster the women remembered the "cairdins", the old women who came along and spun: the lasses with their maakin and the men winding simmants for the thatching. There would often be someone there with a fiddle and maybe before their supper at 11 o'clock the younger ones would put by their work and join in a reel. Every now and then, after a wedding in Lerwick, they would have what they called "hamefers" when the bridal couple came back to Firth for a homecoming of happiness and celebration to which everyone in the district would be invited. Three weeks before Christmas John Hay had married Maggie Nicolson, but that was the last "hamefers" in Firth that anyone could remember. Three weeks later he was lost along with his father-in-law Charles Nicolson and his four brothers-in-law, William, John, Peter and Charles.

In March the men would go to the spring fishing; to the herring all summer; then come home and take in the harvest and then they would be off to the winter fishing around the Skerries. All the other work of the croft was done by the women. It was a wild bit of sea from which they had to wrest their livelihood, bounded by the southern tip of Yell with Fetlar to the north. To the south was Mainland, "The Bonnie Isle" of Whalsay and 20 miles off the rocky Skerries. To the east there was nothing between them and Norway, only the grey heaving waters of the North Sea. Like all Shetland fishermen they accepted the fishing not only as a way of life but as a dire necessity. Often their

189

boats were owned by local merchants, who practically owned their lives as well.

The story was told of two of these merchants talking together and one says to the other: "Boy, what's this I'm hearing that you're *fantin* the fishermen?" (literally keeping them at starvation level). "Well" replied the other merchant "I can't afford to sell them flour and meal. They're all in debt to me. They just haven't the money to pay for the goods." The first one nodded his head. "Yeh, yeh, dat's what I'm tellin dee. . . . Get them in debt because the only fisherman that's of any use to you is a fisherman in debt."

Sitting by the fireside old William Nicolson recalled the times when all they got was 6s 6d per cwt. for ling and cod and 3s 6d a cwt. for haddocks, all gutted. His father, who must have been a courageous man demanded 5s a cwt. The merchant gave him four. The boat William's father took out that winter's morning was *The Happy Return*, LK 774, a fourareen with only a 15-foot keel, a jib and mainsail rigged fore and aft and a crew of five. For three weeks wild seas had kept them at home and it was a case of no fish no money. The westerly gale had died down and they left the shore between three-thirty and four o'clock in the morning, bent to the oars, rowing out into Yell Sound with a great swell coming from the south-east but no wind. Meeting their cousins' boat they asked what the weather was going to be like. The answer was: "I don't know, but there's something more to come out of this."

They had shot four great lines when William's father decided not to shoot any more although the haddock were coming in faster than anyone could remember. Then young William felt a breath of wind coming down from the north and looking up he said it was just the same as though someone had spread a big white sail round the Horse o Burrafirth. "To tell you the truth," the old man said, "I'm not telling you any lies, it wasna five minutes from then till the gale struck and with the heavy swell from the north-east, nothing could live in it." Close by in the great troughs of the waves was a sixareen. One minute she was there and the next a huge lump of sea had struck her and that was the first one they saw lost.

Back home in Delting the gale hit the houses with such force that it took two people to shut the doors. Within seconds the whole voe was a seething cauldron of white water almost invisible in the great cloak of blinding sleet. *The Happy Return* flying before the wind, close-hauled was struck amidships by sea and wind. William saw his father at the tiller, the sea like a white mountain around his shoulders. Seizing the water keg, once smuggled home from Torshavn full of spirits, he stove in one end of it and picking up the ousekerry (the baler) shoved it into his cousin Tommy's hand. "Tommy," he says, "For God's sake, if ever

190

you wrought in your life ... work this day ...." They came down across the sterns of two other boats running for Fetlar but both were lost soon after.

Young William managed to set the compass on his knees and found they were heading straight for the open sea. Then through the blinding snow and spindrift he caught a glimpse of the Skerries light. Somehow they got down the mainsail and using the jib as a spinnaker managed to get the helm round and make for the Skerries. And all the time they ran dodging the great lumps of water, as they called them, something every Shetland fisherman feared, baling for very life.

On the hill at Swinister women leant against the gale desperately trying to pierce the blank wall of sleet, with salt stinging their eyes thinking maybe the boats had been driven off and were still at sea somewhere between them and the Skerries. Others gathered along with the old men at Tiptigarths, the home of Mrs. Laurenson who was then a child of ten. They begged the steamers' agent in Lerwick to let the *Earl of Zetland* go down to the Skerries to see if any had arrived there but he refused. On a fine day they could have seen the Skerries, these three main islands of Housay and Bruray joined by a bridge. The north mouth was a difficult entrance with three reefs of baas as they call them sending mountains of water high into the air as the seas struck them. As *The Happy Return* fought her way in William saw Johnnie Laurenson's boat go down, and it must have seemed to the five men on that small fourareen that their turn must come at any moment.

But someone saw them. An old woman on the Skerries out looking for her kye saw beyond the white line of breakers crashing on to the reefs a boat. Hurrying to the house of an old skipper, Willie Sutherland, she battered her way into the house and cried out: "Willie, Willie, my Lord, is du standin here an a boat perishin in the north mouth?" He knew that no Skerries boats were off and he told her that there would be no boats out from Delting in weather like that. "But man," she says, "the boat is there ... tak the men and go ...." His son Alec believed her and struggling into his oilskins hurried down to the beach telling all the men on the way.

So near to safety *The Happy Return* caught in a following sea was lifted almost clean out of the water and a great sea poured in over the stem head. Somehow she righted herself and William's father felt the boat answering the helm again but the seas had carried them broadside on only a matter of 10 feet from the cliff face. The Skerries men, watching from the cliff-top lay down, their faces on the turf. Not one could bear to watch, sure that the boat was gone. All except John Henderson, a great tree of a man well over six feet. Running down to the beach he caught one of the "burrups", a fine line that they set their lines with and coiling it round his arm he made for the outer end of the beach. Tying a piece of stone in the rope, he battered his way out among the breakers, the water right about his neck and threw the loaded rope out to the men. William caught it and somehow *The Happy Return* was hauled to safety.

A telegram came from Mossbank to say that one crew was safe. Another boat came in about dinner time and every child got a piece of what they called "banks fish", the customary fish they got when the boat landed. But no one could give them news of the other five boats still missing. On Sunday morning a single sail was seen crossing the Skerries Firth but no one knew whose boat it might be until William Nicolson's grandmother, helped out to the gable of the house took a short look and said: "Yes ... that's wir boys' boat ..."

But the relief of the few whose men had returned was forgotten in the grief of others. The women crowded down to the shore crying "Did you see wir men ... did you see wir men ..." Mrs. Laurenson even as a child crept about the place white-faced as some of the women were carried in; some of them fainted and others stood "as though carved in stone".

After most of the big fishing disasters of the nineteenth century funds were set up which helped a little but the amounts allowed for each dependant were pitifully inadequate. The last refuge of a poor person was the parish relief and the consequent loss of the only remnant of pride. Grants were made that Christmastide of £5 to each widow. There was £1 to every child under 14, £3 to the widow, £1 10s to each daughter and £1 5s to each son in respect of mournings with aged dependants getting £1 10s each. But the district of Delting never recovered. Some people gave up their crofts and took rooms somewhere and others emigrated. Mrs. Nicolson who had lost her husband, four sons and a son-in-law said at the time: "Well, you see, they werena mine. The Lord gave them to me for a time and then He took them back again." Life had to go on but for the Shetland fisherman-crofters' womenfolk death was seldom far away.

18. *Light in the Lum*

A GLIMMER OF HOPE, as eagerly awaited as the opaque glint of a struggling fish on the *toum*, "light in the lum" and "light below that", came to the Shetland crofter-fisherman. A mundane yet crucial step in the islands' history was taken with the passing of the Reform Bill in 1832. At long last the franchise was extended to all proprietors and tenants occupying lands of an annual value of £10, and by 1847 Shetland had found a champion for her cause, a voice to speak for her in Parliament, the voice of Arthur Anderson. From an insignificant beach boy whose sole job it was to help to turn, pile up and turn again the drying fish on the beaches of Lerwick, he became Liberal M.P. for Orkney and Shetland. He was also co-founder of the Peninsular and Orient Steamship Company and the guiding spirit in providing Shetland with a regular steamship service to and from Scotland. With his gift of a fine lace shawl to Queen Victoria in 1837 southern eyes were opened to the beauty and craftsmanship of Shetland knitwear and by 1893 the industry was worth about £25,000 a year.

In 1847 an appeal, signed by 7000 Shetlanders against the Corn Laws, through the agency of Arthur Anderson, was read in the House of Commons and the Corn Laws repealed. He established on the island of Vaila the Shetland Fishing Company, drying fish on wooden "flakes" instead of beach stones, giving the Shetlander for the first time employment in his own islands with reasonable remuneration and without restraint from curer or merchant. The venture unfortunately did not survive for long but the experiment showed what could be achieved. Anderson also produced the islands' first newspaper, *The Shetland Journal*, enlarged to the *Orkney and Shetland Journal* in 1837. In 1862 he gave Lerwick the Anderson Institute, now an academy comparable with any secondary school in Scotland and three years before his death he erected the Widows' Homes.

Other "free" merchants in Shetland followed his example and prices for fish, farm produce and knitwear slowly began to rise, the demand stimulated by more frequent shipping services. Mr. Hoseason of Aywick had re-introduced kelp manufacture in 1845. Only 11 tons were

49 The island of Vaila with Vaila Hall and below the old fishing lodges and the beach where Arthur Anderson began the first trial of "free" fishing, drying the fish on wooden laths instead of cobbles and paying the fishermen a fair price: the beginning of the long struggle to free themselves from the landmaster trader.

obtained the first year as folk disliked working in the west, but in 1851 152 tons were shipped at £3 5s a ton. Cattle were now exported "on the hoof" instead of being sold to Lerwick merchants at Martinmas to be killed and salted, and the price rose accordingly. The price of eggs went up from 1½d to 7d a dozen and in the 1840's the Shetlander, crossing Blackface and Cheviot sheep with the small local breed, gained nearly 3lbs in weight per fleece.

Lerwick itself was growing and with ships from many ports fishing in her seas foreign coinage was circulating to such an extent that fear of unrest and revolutions in Europe induced 46 merchants of Lerwick and the islands to address an appeal to the bank in Edinburgh in 1846 "to direct your agent here to receive foreign money at the rate of exchange with the respective kingdoms of France, Holland, Belgium, Spain, etc. which would be a great benefit to Shetlanders in enabling them to continue their dealings with foreigners".

In spite of all these visible signs of improvement the crofter still remained basically in the same position, the system of barter fundamental to life and trade. It was yet impossible to eradicate the sporadic cases of what we would today bluntly call "blackmail". The wife of a Shetland crofter-fisherman, selling one dozen eggs to a nearby family, immediately got a notice from the factor, claiming a fine of 2s 6d from her husband for the transaction, which he was forced to pay or leave at the first term.

It was not until 1872 that an official attempt was made to investigate conditions in Shetland in the shape of the Truck Commission, its name deriving from the extent to which barter was used in place of wages. Not one commercial concern in the islands escaped a searching scrutiny, the intention of the Truck Act which followed being the emancipation of the Shetland crofter from the crushing power of the landlords, few of whom escaped censure in the report. Its enforcement was another matter. Far too many lairds still insisted on their tenants handing over their catch, the alternative 40 days notice to quit; in other cases punishment for misdemeanours or petty crimes against the landlord was banishment.

It seems incredible that this almost medieval state still persisted. The offenders were never again allowed to set foot on their island, their families being quickly called to account should they connive at secret visits. The story is still remembered in Whalsay of the man who got notice from the laird to quit. In the dead of night his friends rallied round and moved out every scrap of furniture from his cottage; killed his pig for salting, gathered his few cattle and somehow succeeded in flitting him across the sound to Nesting and moreover used the laird's boat for the passage.

Landmaster traders continued to refuse to pay cash for eggs and hosiery and if a knitter insisted on money instead of goods a reduction of 25 per cent was made on all her knitwear. As late as 1908 Lerwick merchants were being fined for this form of abuse.

At long last came the Napier Commission which led to the Crofters' Holdings Act of 1886, establishing security of tenure, compensation for improvements and a guaranteed fair rent. With the setting up of the Crofters' Commission in 1889, expressly convened to hear appeals against the landlords and landowners throughout the Highlands and Islands of Scotland, some real progress was made. The Commission began its Shetland sitting in Dunrossness on August 24th. The islands were in a ferment. As soon as the news got around the islanders flocked to the south end. Word was somehow sent even to the fishing grounds. Lines were haled, empty or full, and men rowed for the shore. The Editor of the *Shetland News* recorded that the crofters "gave their evidence as a rule in an unhesitating way, like men who knew their rights and meant to have them". This required no mean courage on the part

195

of crofters who must have realised that should their appeal fail they could expect no mercy from their landlords.

Although the Crofters' Holdings Act which followed did perpetuate a system of uneconomic holdings, freezing the distribution of the land into the pattern still obtaining today, it established in perpetuity the civil rights and liberties to which every man was entitled. Unfortunately the Act did not follow the advice of the Napier Commission which had drawn the Government's attention to the great need for more arable land and the creation of new townships. As happened so frequently and still occurs, an English Parliament sitting in London was hopelessly out of touch with affairs in these remote rural districts, of whose existence they had barely been aware, and merely authorised the enlargement of the scattalds. At the time the innovations were at least sufficient to release the crofter from his years of bondage and the Act itself was the Shetlander's Magna Carta.

Meanwhile the rise of the merchant-fisher class, following on Arthur Anderson's experiment on Vaila and a newly-developing cod fishery, provided a long overdue escape from the dangers and misery of the far haaf, with opportunities to fish for herring or cod from the larger-decked boats. The example set by fishermen from Buckie, who came to Shetland with a fully-decked sailing vessel equipped with long lines, showed the Shetlander the difference in the size of the catch. Used as long-liners at the haaf, for cod with hand-line or herring with drift net, the versatile half-decked boats could be used for whichever fishing proved most profitable at the time.

It took many years before the new type of fishing became successful. In spite of the bounty paid of £3 per ton of fish caught in 1819, the average profit per vessel was only £5 5s. There were bad years. There were many who could not afford the size of vessel necessary to qualify for the bounty, but gradually, through prize money taken into the country by Shetlanders who had served in the Royal Navy or the Merchant Navy, and those who had managed to scrape together some money from the Greenland whaling pooled their resources and several cod sloops came to be owned by the men who manned them, a feature of the Shetland fishing industry which is today the most common method of boat ownership.

For nearly 100 years Shetland cod smacks, vessels larger than a sloop, rigged fore and aft with one or two masts, gaff mainsail and bowsprit with two or more headsails, reigned supreme in the cod fishing. From the home grounds the larger vessels ventured further and further afield, and by 1820 trips of a week to 10 days were being made, the cod cleaned and salted on board. The entire area became famous as "The Faroe Smack Fishery" or the "Banksmen" as they were known, ranging from

196

50 A sixareen's crew at Fethaland in the 1890's: Back row, left to right: Andrew Sinclair and William Johnson, both Westsandwick; Laurence Johnson, West Haa', Lochend. Front row, left to right: Charles Ratter (Skipper) Setter, North Roe; Basil Sinclair and James Thomson, both Westsandwick; and Gideon Anderson, Fethaland. "Seven men are there . . . outside a lodge . . . line and sheet hardened hands laid loosely on thigh, but fine boned like their faces, bearded, tanned . . .". (Zetland County Library and Museum.)

the Davis Straits to the North Cape.

The first documentary evidence of cod fishing from Shetland seems to have appeared in Hibbert's *Zetland Islands* (1822). In January, 1819 he wrote a paper on the subject having noted while in Hillswick a sloop coming into the harbour belonging to Mr. Gifford of Busta laden with cod from a bank recently discovered to the west of Foula later identified by him as the Regent's Fishing Bank. At Ollas Voe on Papa Stour he also encountered sloops returning from the cod fishing and noted that up to 40 vessels were employed every summer.

Fishing agreements were stringent. "The Sloop shall have a master and eight hands. Ninc in all, of which seven shall be share hands the other two being fee'd or hired by the sharers." In return for one-third of the tonnage bounty, one-half the value of the entire catch, one-half the fish and oil bounty, these seven men had agreed to bring the vessel to Reawick at the beginning of the season, ready and fitted out for the cod fishing, provide themselves with provisions, stores, hooks, lines and bait at their own expense.

Roughly speaking, for the sum of £133 6s 8d the seven sharers had, in addition to the foregoing obligations, to engage two hired hands whom they had to pay and feed whether they themselves earned anything or not. They had to catch the cod, split, clean and salt them down in bulk on board, become liable for the salt used to cure the owner's half; keep the vessel's sail, tackle and all equipment in order, beach and clean her bottom between voyages. The owner paid for half the curing stock used, but only after the fish was sold at the end of the season, on a no fish—no settlement basis.

"The Master must also see that the fish caught by each man are numbered and the numbers entered in a book. Whatever whale, wreck or driftwood salved by the vessel during the fishing, shall be equally divided between the owner, Master and crew. In the event of any damage to the vessel her sails, materials or anything belonging to her being carried away or lost, or if any of the cables, sails or ropes being rotted by disobedience, obstinacy, neglect or carelessness of the crew, they shall be bound to make up such loss or damage and shall be liable to have the amount retained by the owner out of their half of the proceeds of the fish and oil bounties." The skipper was not allowed to leave the sloop unattended while in harbour and at their own expense the crew were bound, without fee or reward, to bring her round to Lerwick, unrig and lay her up at the end of the season, having already shipped the fish on to the waiting vessel.

In 1823 a new clause was inserted into the agreement forbidding smuggling and laying down heavy penalties should she be found in possession of dutiable goods. This implied that she was almost certainly

198

fishing in foreign waters, most likely Faroe, a smuggler's paradise for years to come, where *Faera brandi*, scents and tobacco were available for those who cared to take the risk.

By 1829 the tonnage bounty was taken off vessels fishing for cod and many owners were in such dire straits that the industry declined immediately. By 1840 there were no boats fishing on the Faroe grounds and it was nine years before they returned, between times fishing off the David Straits and the Disko bank and along the Greenland coast. After the 1850's Icelandic grounds were fished right up to the beginning of the present century.

There were still the inevitable hazards and tragedies. Even the smacks, so much more seaworthy and comfortable than the old open sixareen, were helpless against the mountainous seas off Iceland, and by the mid-nineteenth century smacks owned by curers were setting off for the home grounds in late February so that they could safely run for home in bad weather. For the rest of the year small boats exploited the home grounds, the smacks fishing Faroe, Iceland and Rockall. The first trip of the year to Faroe took place in April to the Faroe Banks, 45 miles south-west of Suduroy after the vital call at Torshavn for provisions which could not be had "duty free" in Lerwick. In the middle of May the men would be home for 10 days and back again on the midsummer trip till the middle of August. In autumn Shetland smacks fished off the north Iceland coast from Langaness to the North Cape, the fish eventually being exported to Bilbao where the demand for Shetland cod and ling was far above that for Norwegian or Newfoundland fish.

The method of fishing was relatively simple, the tackle consisting of about two feet of strong wire with a hook on a *toam* at each end and a seven lb. lead weight in the middle to which the line was attached. The hooks were baited with yoags—horse mussels—dredged up from the voes at Bixter and the Skap of Trondra and each man looked after his own line. The cod, which might weigh up to 40 lb. each, were hauled aboard and the line rebaited, the crew member cutting off the barbels of the cod to record his catch for payment. Frequently fragments of bait coming off the hooks would attract more fish so that the hooks were snapped up even before the lead had time to touch bottom.

By one of those strange compulsive phenomena of nature the fish became frenzied and would bite at anything, so that a tuft of white wool or even a bare shiny hook would be enough to act as a lure. This "lust" in a dense school of fish was known and taken advantage of when fishing for sillaks in "craig seats" around the coast or in small boats. The fisherman with his rod and line had a large supply of half-boiled limpets which he chewed to an oily pulp before spitting them out into

199

the sea around the boat or craig seat to *sö* or lure the fish. As the oily *vam*—the smell of seaweedy shellfish—spread, sillocks were attracted to the area and when the lust grew nothing more was needed but the bare hook. The same initial attraction is used on tuna clippers with live anchovy as a lure.

If the catch was heavy the men had to stop fishing to get the fish below decks in bad weather and after 1850 many of the smacks had wells built into their holds so that the cod could be carried back alive. Although it reduced the carrying capacity higher prices were obtained, but the mortality rate was high and only about 80 per cent—perhaps about 1000 large cod—survived.

Several of the most prolific banks were discovered quite by accident. In 1788 a Shetlander, John Slater, master of a merchant ship from Bergen to Ireland was becalmed 35 miles south-west of Foula and during his enforced stay within a few hours he had taken 250 cod on his line. It was not until 1817 that the bank was fished commercially, rediscovered by a local sloop driven off course by a gale. In 30 hours they took 900 cod and "The Home Cod Grounds" or the Regent Bank remained the main fishing ground for smaller vessels until its failure in the 1830's. It was the failure of this "gold mine" on the west of Foula which first sent the smacks further afield to Faroe, Rockall and Iceland, and the first Shetland smacks actually went to Faroe in 1833.

One of the most important cod banks was again found by a Shetlander in 1889. Several smacks had been sheltering from a south-west gale in the wide bay north of Langaness when one of the skippers, Johnson of Garriock's, familiarly known as "Old Heglie", tired of constantly having to keep a look out for other vessels while they manœuvred inshore, hove to and let the smack drift seaward. When the gale abated after several days the smack had drifted "land down"—so far out to sea that no land was visible, and soundings were taken. Old Heglie used the traditional "banksman's cast", a fishing line with two hooks baited, and found the depth, only 30 fathoms on soft bottom, alive with fine large cod, and in 10 days his crew had used up every grain of salt on board on over 20,000 heavy cod, on what came to be known ever after as "Heglie's Bank".

An added advantage of the Icelandic grounds was that it was comparatively easy for the smacks to carry a few drift nets which they set during the night thus obtaining with the minimum of effort the necessary bait—herring. In fact by 1905, when the herring fishing had become all-important to Shetland, a large smack was fitted out as a dual purpose cod-smack herring-buss in an attempt to sustain the cod fishery but the high cost of the double gear gave poor results.

After 1860 more than 1000 men were employed on smacks, roughly one-third of the island's fishermen. On the distant grounds most smacks carried 12 to 15 men, the home fishers, 8 to 10. The younger men with fewer family ties went to the far banks and the older men to the home grounds, typical of modern Faroese fisheries. The sea dominated all activity and unemployment was rare, the cod fishing period the only one in which Shetlanders, fishing in their own vessels, developed what might be regarded as a large-scale mid and distant fishery. Indeed during the nineteenth century, the Shetland fishing industry attained a peak in number and size of vessels, the amount of people employed and a variety of work which has not been equalled since.

There was also, from the 1850's to the late nineteenth century, always employment for Shetlanders not engaged in home fishing or sailing in the Merchant Navy, or indeed the Royal Navy, as hands on whalers from Hull, Dundee and Peterhead. Initially Shetland took part in the industry only in sporadic drives of "caa'in whales" (*Globiocephala melaena*), an annual event in the Faroes, the blubber being stripped and boiled for oil. These mammals were never regarded as a source of food in Shetland although in the famine of 1741 whale meat was quite often eaten out of sheer necessity, especially in North Mavine. The numbers killed must have been colossal. In that year 360 whales were driven ashore at Hillswick the record being taken at Quendale in 1845 when 1540 were despatched within two hours.

The lairds were quick to seize this opportunity of obtaining their share in spite of the protests of the tenants that whales were invariably killed below low-water mark, in the sea itself, and therefore outside the laird's property. This custom, however, continued until the famous Hoswick case of September 1888. Over 300 whales were driven ashore and auctioned for £450, an enormous sum in those days. The two land-owners in the district claimed their share, but the men refused. Taken to court in Lerwick, Sheriff Mackenzie ruled that the landowners had no rights to any share in the profits.

Not content with his decision, such was their determination and greed, the lairds took their case to the Court of Session in Edinburgh. Naturally the crofters were panic-stricken at the thought of the costs they would be forced to pay should the case turn out against them. A fund was immediately established, contributions pouring in, a large sum coming from New Zealand. To the great joy of the crofters and indeed of all Shetlanders their Lordships upheld Sheriff Mackenzie's ruling and all proceeds were to go to the fishermen alone.

Inevitably the Greenland whaling came to an end through over-exploitation, but with the invention of the explosive harpoon in 1868 the Norwegian whaling industry was in full swing. Again the grounds were hunted to depletion and by 1904 whaling on the Norwegian coast was banned and the Norse looked to Shetland. Norwegian companies received permission from the British Government to establish whaling stations in Shetland at Ronas Voe, Collafirth and Olnafirth at the head of the voe where the old wooden buildings, latterly modernised by Adie's of Voe, still stand. Even at the tiny harbour of Cumliewick, at Broonie's Taing, on the east coast near Sandwick, men still remember whalers coming alongside the pier, which is now completely unrecognisable, overshadowed by the great aluminium storehouses of Hudsons' Offshore Enterprises, oil supply ships and dredgers lying within the greatly extended breakwater, a strange and dramatic transformation.

There were many protestations, the herring fishermen maintaining that the whaling would be the end of the herring industry, and nearby crofters complaining bitterly of the stench and pollution of the beaches. In 1907 there were large anti-whaling demonstrations and the following year an appeal direct to Mr. Asquith, then Prime Minister. On the other hand, although the herring fishing was at its peak there was unemployment in the islands and a letter from the people at North Roe to the Shetland M.P. of the time defended the Norwegian whaling stations, declaring that they were a Godsend to the people as they employed up to 100 men although there were also herring stations in the parish.

The size of the Norwegian operation was vast and the numbers of whales killed staggering. In 1908 with 142 British employed in its shore force, 651 whales were killed, yielding oil, whalebone and cattle food worth £63,000 and in 1914 the catch was 599 whales. Exhausting the more distant areas, Norwegians were allowed to hunt nearer and nearer to Shetland and by 1928 the whaling industry in Shetland was finished.

In the Antarctic Christian Salvesen and Company of Leith had begun operations in 1908 in the Falkland Islands and later at South Georgia. Between 1945 and 1963 about 200 Shetlanders a year were employed in the industry and in 1950 Shetland was receiving about £200,000 a year in wages. Again the stocks declined, which was scarcely surprising, the astonishing thing being that any were left at all, and by 1963 British ships found it an uneconomic proposition to hunt in the Antarctic.

Most British whaling vessels called at Lerwick to complete their crews and in 1808 with 600 men engaged in the Arctic whaling some £7000 was paid out in wages but at the end of the eighteenth century £2 a month or £12 for the season was considered good money, to rise by the end of the nineteenth century to £24. It was one of the most hazardous of all fishing enterprises, the journeys north and home being made during the stormiest seasons of the year. In 1830, 19 vessels were lost

202

and on March 8th, 1866 the steam whaler *Diana* left Lerwick for Greenland and the Davis Straits with a crew of 51, about half of them Shetlanders, 10 of them in their teens, two of whom were 15 years of age and one only 14. Over a year later she limped into Ronas Voe with 13 dead or dying, the remainder helpless with scurvy or dysentery. Nine Shetlanders were among the dead.

Shetlanders were highly valued in those days as crew members not only because of their unsurpassed seamanship but for their hardiness and steady character, far less given to drunkenness we are told than the Scots or English. Twenty-six signed on and the *Diana* sailed on her first stage, a sealing trip to the Jan Meyen area east of Greenland.

After an abortive and gruelling voyage they returned to Lerwick on April 28th with "a clean ship". After a week's rest the *Diana* sailed again on the main part of her expedition for whales in Baffin Bay. On June 10th the ship was well up the Greenland coast and the rich whaling area of Melville Bay. Edging westwards to the Baffin Land coast there was no escape from the wilderness of pack ice. Their only hope was to drift south with the grinding mass, which continually threatened to crush the ship like matchwood. The surgeon in his diary described the nightmare:

"We listen to the rearing rushing rasping noise of the ice ... now rattling exactly like a mill hopper, now roaring for all the world like an express train through a tunnel, now hammering with regular blows, as it broke up. ... We felt the perpetual jump, jump, jump of the ship, resembling to my fancy the pulsations of the heart of some huge creature in the extremity of torture. Now a shuddering vibration would run through her whole frame as though she felt herself trembling on the brink of dissolution. All the while 50 poor souls were quaking with terror, knowing that their fate was sure and certain should a single timber give way."

And give way it did. The forestem gave and with water rushing in it was decided to abandon ship and pitch an improvised tent on the ice. The pumps were manned and the men, weary, famished and depressed, struggled 24 hours a day to control the leak. The water gained on them and she would certainly have foundered had she not been so securely nipped in the ice. "Chippy" succeeded in caulking the main leak before the ice split and once again the *Diana* inched southwards.

It is almost impossible to imagine the conditions of the men, the intense cold penetrating heart and lungs when the breath froze and eyelids could scarcely lift. The crew had been on emergency rations since September: three biscuits and two ounces salt beef per man per day, for three months with no ventilation, no means of washing. On

December 26th old Captain Gravill died. Two Shetlanders followed him in February and by March 7th 40 men were stricken with scurvy, half of them quite incapacitated.

The men from Shetland being the last to join had got quarters 'tween decks where there was no heating. In February the sides and ceilings of their quarters were covered with solid ice, the frozen moisture from their breath. Thirty-five bucketsful were scraped off. Only then, after almost six months did they get a fire, and then with coal rationed for only part of the day.

On March 17th the ice began to break up and with a westerly wind the *Diana* once more heeled over to her sails. Leaking badly, the remaining crew manned the pumps day in, day out, until they fell at their task. When they eventually sighted land on April 2nd, only six men were able to be on deck and when she dropped anchor in Ronas Voe two days later only three men were fit to clamber aloft and stow the t'gallant. Thirteen men had died and many were so severely injured that they remained semi-invalids for the rest of their lives.

In spite of the fact that the name of Shetland was to become in later years almost synonymous with that of the herring, rivalling even the great early days of the Dutch fishery, it was a long time before Shetland-owned and manned boats could compete with the Dutch, Scots or English fleets. Until well into the nineteenth century, with an economy scarcely above subsistence level, there was insufficient capital available in the islands to purchase and fit out craft of any size, range or seaworthiness suitable for the deep sea herring fishery and perforce the Shetlander continued to pursue the cod, ling and tusk.

At last, owing largely to the growing Scottish fleet constantly replacing its outmoded craft, half-decked second-hand boats could be bought at a price which Shetland could afford. Messrs. Hay and Ogilvie of Lerwick, then the largest fishing company in the islands, came to own or finance 100 boats and gave their fishermen good credit. A man could enter into an agreement with the curer who provided the vessel and nets and took half the earnings towards repayment while the crew received the other half as wages, and when the whole sum was repaid the boat belonged to the fisherman.

It was a brief period of success. In the 1830's the capricious shoals almost deserted local waters. In 1831 the fishing was a complete failure and the worst storm in living memory resulted in heavy losses of gear and vessels. At the turn of the century herring had been in great demand in the West Indies as food "for the negroes" but by 1883 the now "emancipated" consumers had apparently lost their taste for salt herring. Due to the Irish potato famine and the consequent mass emigration another market was lost, bringing a surplus of British and especially

51 Regatta Day in Lerwick at the beginning of the century. Crowds throng Victoria Pier and the waterfront and on the right H.M. Revenue Cutter the *Active* is dressed overall. (The late Mrs. Abernethy's Collection via Jack Keddie.)

Scottish herring to the European market. In 1840 a storm caught the fleet at sea with the loss of 30 boats, at least five with all hands and in 1842 the fishermen's bank at Lerwick collapsed. No credit was to be had and the men had no option but to haul their hard-bought craft ashore.

Forty years later the total cured had risen to 59,586 barrels and the fleet to 276 vessels. The tide had turned and three years later 300,117 barrels were cured from 932 fishing craft. The new herring fishing round Shetland drew men and boats from Scotland to East Anglia, the Isle of Man and Ireland like a marine gold rush. Although few Shetland curers took full advantage of the rapidly-expanding industry, Scottish curers leased areas, erected stations and engaged Scots fishermen to fish for them.

Lerwick became a boom town and up to the outbreak of the First World War Shetland hummed with life, bright as the silver shoals that poured ceaselessly into farlin and barrel. At the height of the season in Lerwick harbour Shetland boats rubbed shoulders with Irish and Manx smacks with elegant yacht-like lines; steep-stemmed West country rigged Peelmen with a dipping lug and a standing mizzen lay close to English smacks with boomless mainsail and a gaff topsail; Scots

205

52   Hollanders from the fishing fleet stroll above Bain's Beach in Lerwick—about 1905. (Zetland County Library and Museum.)

lugger, Fifie, Scaffie and Zulu lay gunwale to gunwale with Dutch doggers from Vlardingen, and Schveningen, *boms* and steam doggers.

After 1866 there had been a revival of the Dutch fishing industry. At Boulogne a new type of vessel had been introduced—the herring lugger. At the same time the fishing nets, once made from hemp, were replaced by cotton nets. Both innovations were taken up by the enterprising Dutch fleets and by the end of the century 200 luggers mainly from Vlaardingen were engaged in the industry. The fishing villages along the coast at Schveningen and Katwijk which lacked a harbour used the *bom*, a type of vessel developed from the old *pink*, which could easily be pulled up on the beach. The season lasted as before from St. John's Day till late autumn and Dutch ties with Shetland became stronger than ever.

The old Dutch fishermen knew Bressay Sound as "The Bay" and museums of Vlaardingen, Schveningen and Katwijk still have souvenirs of Lerwick. In Lerwick new cemetery are no less than 25 graves of Dutch fishermen of that era, mute testimony to the deep sentimental ties between the two countries. Picture postcards with Greetings from Lerwick, portraits of Queen Victoria and King Edward, found their way to Holland and pottery can still be seen in the cupboards of houses in Marken. Milk jugs, coffee pots, teapots and sugar bowls of brown earthenware decorated with brightly coloured flowers graced tables and Dutch fishermen adopted the "Hitland" nightcaps with their coloured brims. English flour of excellent quality was bought by Hollanders and sold in white cotton bags of 14 lb. In Holland as well as in Scotland and England the fishermen's wives made buttonless sailors' blouses from the bags, put into the tarnish kettle along with the herring nets. The Dutch *bom* did not survive the period of 1914–18 and was

206

almost entirely replaced by the sailing lugger and by 1919 there werc already about 600 of these in addition to 66 steam luggers, comprising a fleet of enormous catching capacity.

In Shetland the fishing drifts had first been hauled by the primitive process of muscle power. Then came line-haulers for the tows and Iron Men for the nets, both hand-driven but a great advance on the old hand-hauled lines. In 1886 the last clinker-built smack built in the Isles was launched from Hay's yard at Freefield. Fishermen wanted the bigger, faster carvel-built boat with a capacity for a longer drift of nets and finally the innovation of the *Excellent*, built in 1892 by James Smith of Sandwick, brought the so-called "floating nets" to Shetland for the first time. She might almost be designated as the first Shetland buss in that she re-established the use of the buss rope on its ancient herring grounds, and the next two years saw the entire Shetland fleet swing over to floating drifts.

The large Scottish-built decked herring smacks provided the necessary impetus for the start of the great days of the herring fishery. Since a far larger labour force than the local community could supply was required at the curing stations vast numbers of men and women were engaged by the curers in Scotland before the season began. Huts were built to accommodate the floating population of workers and in bases such as Baltasound and Lerwick these amounted to good-sized villages all of which meant increased trading for the local community.

For years the North of Scotland boats were packed with gutters coming to Shetland for the herring season, sleeping on the decks, singing half the night. Like nomadic gypsies they trekked north, then south, following the herring. Many of the shore workers arriving in May came from the Western Isles, often speaking the Gaelic. Visiting fishermen came from the Isle of Man, Schveningen, Gothenburg and Alesund. Only the British fishermen used the islands as a fishing base, the others coming in for shelter or supplies.

In 1904 Lerwick and Baltasound both landed over half-a-million crans, a cran weighing $3\frac{1}{2}$ cwt., and by 1905 the sail fleet had reached its maximum. That same year saw herring records broken in Shetland, perhaps for all time. Well over one million barrels were exported but hardly one-quarter of that cure stood to the credit of the islanders. Besides the latter, 1000 British and foreign sail and nearly 300 steam drifters landed their catches at 170 stations from Boddam to Baltasound. By the end of the century herrings were being auctioned at Lerwick, Baltasound and Scalloway instead of the fishermen selling their fish at agreed prices beforehand. More facilities required for landing and auctioning fish led to the Lerwick Harbour Trustees constructing the Alexandra wharf and the Fish Mart, first used in 1907. With the advent of the steam drifter at the beginning of the twentieth century, with big catching power and apparently limitless markets on the Continent, the Shetland fleet was greatly reduced, the expensive steam drifter being beyond the capital resources of most owners and fishermen in Shetland.

In the record year of 1905 when 1783 sail boats and steam drifters manned by 21,201 fishermen caught fish amounting to over one million barrels cured in the Shetland area the whole catch was sold for over £500,000. There were 174 stations distributed over 27 districts, 46 in Baltasound and 36 in Lerwick alone, the shore workers totalling 2483, of whom 1985 were women gutters and packers.

Although most Scots brought their own teams of gutters up to Shetland, all over the islands around the month of February representatives from Shetland curers toured the villages to engage girls for the season. They paid them *arles*, £1 in advance which booked them to work for that curer for the season. Huts were provided for them, 16 rooms to a block with six girls in each room, the beds divided off by partitions giving them some small personal privacy. Usually the coopers in charge

53 A souvenir photograph of the crew of a large herring station in Lerwick. In the front row are the gutters and packers dressed up in their best for the occasion. Behind them stand the coopers and foremen. (Around 1900.) (Zetland County Library and Museum.)

of the gutters arranged for a fire to be lit for them at least before the end of the day and a pan of hot water for washing was ready waiting. Even so, the girls had rarely more than 15 minutes off before meals in which to prepare their food so that in some stations a stew would be left by the fire all day to be ready for dinner time.

As the boats came in to their stations one of the crew would lift up his arms, say five times, indicating a catch of 50 crans. The whole process was geared to as near automation as possible, a continuous chain of movement from ship to gutter. Fresh herring scooped up from the holds with wooden shovels flashed into basket and barrel, were pushed on trolleys from jetty to station; lightly "roused"—sprinkled with salt to keep them from spoiling—then tipped into the *farlins*, the shallow wooden trough-like boxes from which the women in crews of three gutted and packed from morning till night.

After two or three days the herring shrank and the barrels had to be topped up with fish of the same day's catch and size. They were then "headed" left to stand 10 days or so, a hole drilled in the barrel and half the brine allowed to run off, more herring packed in to replace it, the hole plugged and the barrel re-topped with the same brine then stacked with others to await shipment.

The older women in villages all over Shetland have still vivid memories of the "gutting", of work that must have been cold, hard, and hours that would be unthinkable to the present generation. But the lasses were young, imbued somehow with a zest for living, a capacity to work till the small hours of the morning and still look back with a gleam in their eyes, full of stories of the "foys", the dances, the fun and the singing after the week's work.

While gutting the girls worked in pairs with a third packing. The speed with which they picked up the fish from the farlins and in one movement slit and removed the guts was like some incredible sleight of hand. In this split second they had to be able to grade the fish and toss each one into its correct tub ready for the packer: Fulls, Mediums, Matjes or matties, small herring caught early in the season and Spent which had spawned. If the heads were not intact, the eyes not right or the fish had been bitten by dogfish they were no use for salting.

The crew of three got paid 1s for each barrel of herring gutted and packed, or 4d to each girl. A good crew could work three barrels an hour with approximately 900 herring to a barrel and a really fast gutter could get through 40 herring a minute. Everyone was paid a minimum wage of 15s to £1 in addition to the money per barrel and in Lerwick at the height of the season Mrs. Laurenson from Bigton and her co-worker Mima Lizzie remember working till two o'clock in the morning.

209

In stations like Baltasound in Unst Mrs. Priest and Mrs. Mouat, still living in Haroldswick, during the summer season in the years between the wars, from mid-May till the end of September, had to rise at 4 a.m., dress, and take bread and fresh milk with them, about an hour's walk from their home to the station at Uregarth, to be ready to begin work at 6 a.m.

"Packing salted herring, we would get 4 pence an hour and mind you it was cold mornings, then it might be raining and we would have our skin jackets and Baltic boots up to the thigh; cut-off Shetland stockings as high as they would go to protect our legs above the boots; a short skirt above the knees covered with a black oilskin *bratt* (or apron) with bib and straps that came down just over the tops of our boots. We had woollen jerseys and headscarfs and if the herring was coming in fast, which would be very often, we would be clearing up at midnight. There were no fixed hours then....

"You see the worst of it was we got sore hands ... my hands are still marked, the holes seemed to go to the bone and that was the only thing we sort of complained about. There was never any blood poisoning, the salt disinfected them I suppose, and if we could just set our teeth together at the first then the pain went. We worked with rags round our fingers (a usual practice with all gutters), and I can remember when we worked on Bressay there were two lady nurses who came. They were very kind and if we could manage to walk they would attend to our hands ... but oh, it was really jolly!"

54 Packing herring, Lerwick, early twentieth century. After the herring have been gutted and graded by the "gutters" the packers take over and fill the barrels in neat layers lightly sprinkled with salt. The girl on the extreme right has a half filled barrel in front of her which she is filling from the old barrel on her right, into which her helper is putting gutted herring ready for packing. (Zetland County Library and Museum.)

And Jackie Mouat and Lizzie Priest nodded with nostalgic joy describing the fun they had at Bressay where they worked for several seasons. "Usually the coopers, the men who were over us, were very nice too and when on Monday nights there was no fresh fish we got in to our rooms at 6 o'clock and had some fun. There were four men and one of them played the melodeon and we would all go down and dance ...

"Yes ... yes ... I remember on Bressay the boys from the factory (a fish meal processing plant at Heogan), were going to have a 'do' in the Bressay Hall and we were invited to this you see. We should have worked straight on till maybe midnight but the foreman said he would let us off at 8 o'clock. 'Remember,' he said, 'you have to be out at 6 o'clock as usual in the morning, and when you go just you slip along behind the dyke and then the buyers won't see you going off!' So we got back to where we were staying and got dressed and kept down behind the dyke for we didn't want to get into trouble you see....

"And we had to walk, I think it would be about three miles, from the north end of Bressay to the middle and we got to the hall before 10 o'clock. We had over three hours of dancing and we left there at the back of one and home again about two o'clock and I suppose before we got our clothes put away and into bed it would have been well on to three and we had to be out again at six. It seems silly now, but we were awfully pleased. We wouldn't have missed it for anything. The boys were just waiting and we were always on the floor, dancing Highland Schottisches and the Lancers and Shetland Reels. ... No, there wasn't much drinking in those days, just an occasional refreshment you know. I always wonder nowadays why the men can't drink at another time and just dance with the lasses. It's an awful pity to put it like that just down the drain..."

Every now and then a Government Inspector would make random checks on the barrels and if all the herring were considered perfectly cured and packed they received the Crown Brand mark, without which they would command a much lower price in the Continental market.

There was plenty work for the coopers too. The barrel staves, all cut to the correct length and supplied in different widths, came from Norway, and when unloaded were built up into piles. Steam-driven machinery was used for shaping the staves and there was a cutting and bevelling machine for shaping barrel ends but the actual barrels were made in the cooperage by hand. The trussing hoops determined the capacity and the barrel was built up inside them with a skill and craftsmanship acquired over years of experience. When it was finished the barrel was placed over a basket fire and as the wood softened the staves

211

55 Number one station at the North Ness, Lerwick, about the middle 1890's. The gutters are "at the farlins"—the long wooden boxes continually replenished—behind them the tubs into which they toss the gutted herring, grading them expertly into Fulls: Mediums: Madjes: Matties and Spent, which are discarded.

were driven tighter and tighter together by driving on iron hoops from either end towards the centre where the barrel was widest. As each barrel was completed it was plunged into water and air blown into it to ensure that it was tight. It was all piece-work; the materials were supplied but the men owned their own tools and a good cooper could turn out about five barrels a day.

Once both sides of the wide voe of Baltasound were stacked high with barrels tier upon tier; barrels full of salt for curing in layers of two. Timber houses for 2500 fish workers lined the banks and on Saturdays the nets were spread to dry in nearby fields, brown lacy curtains stretched one on top of the other with rows of corks separating them, two feet apart. Timber and iron churches were erected at each side of the voe where all the fishworkers and fishermen, maybe 4000 of them, sang on a Sunday till the roofs rang. Steamers were anchored in the voe waiting to discharge more barrels and unload salt; Dutch fishing boats with brown sails stood off-shore, an anchored hulk or two with drifters alongside waiting for coaling first thing on Monday morning. Old sixareens were used as flit boats to take the barrels out to the steamers, coming and going all the time. Out beyond lay the mission schooner *Albatross*, sometimes called the Gospel Ship, together with the old wooden gunboat *Ringdove*.

Where once the busy station hummed with the chatter of the gutters, the ring of the cooperages and all around rich fields bright with the waving flags of bere and oats, the spectre of the new oil industry haunts the islands; storage sheds of glittering aluminium, chemical plants and tankers obliterating all memory of that famous herring station. Instead of the creak of oars of the old sixareens, the brown sails like butterflies winging their quiet way in and out from the banks laden with shoals of silver herring, oil dredgers and supply ships will churn up the lovely voe and for people like Lizzie and Jackie Baltasound will never be the same again, and neither of them want to see it.

212

19. *Land and Croft*

ONCE IT WAS said that the Orcadian was a crofter with a boat, the Shetlander a fisherman with a croft. The Orkneys too underwent years of their own dark fishing sagas but, singularly blessed with rich farming soil, longer and closer ties with the mainland, they had almost a head start over the wilder peat-blanketed islands of the north, where for centuries Norway was closer than Scotland, German and Dutch merchants and fishermen more familiar than British. Over the span of 300 years Shetland's fortunes ebbed and flowed with the fishing round her coasts, the bulk of her population caught up in its elusive pursuit, a way of life opened up to the islanders since they first caught fish to sell to the Hansa traders, then to the Hollanders and finally, in order to keep house and home together, forced into fishing for the landmaster traders.

For all the seas' harvest, it was not enough. From the croft had to come food to feed the family and even 100 years ago the area under cultivation was more than twice that of today. It was a precarious way of life, crofting and fishing, bound together by sheer necessity, the fortunes of one inseparable from the other. Only latterly, when conditions had improved, although few could lay their hands on actual cash, at least a generation ago they "aye hed enough".

The seasons and the weather dominated and directed events from the *voar* to the *hairst*. Hampered by uncertainty of tenure and dependence on both land and sea crops, bound by the runrig system, almost the same at the end of the nineteenth century as it was when the Norse first colonised the islands, agriculture generally was as uneconomic as it was possible to be. The townships came to be an arable area, settled in the pattern of strip cultivation, separated from the hill or scattald by the toun dyke. In 1840 the general size of holding was only two to three acres arable and none was above six acres. Although a distinctive and essential feature of Shetland rural life the scattald had its drawbacks. Scrub sires roamed the hills and ran with the township's animals, resulting in hopelessly uncontrolled breeding, usually of inferior stock.

56 The Gray family outside their home in Foula; of the seven brothers and sisters two are missing. Taken about 1916.

The udal system of land tenure, family holdings, where a man held the land from the highest stone on the hill to the lowest on the seashore, gave him the right to valuable driftwood and seaweed for fertiliser, winter grazing on the beach as well as peat cutting and grazing on the hill. The unit of land measurement was the merkland, which was originally the land to support one cow. In 1741 there were in Cunningsburgh 34 merks of land divided into nine or ten pieces. As a merk measured only about half-an-acre, an animal breaking its tether or scrambling through the turf dykes could soon do a vast amount of damage.

Various Acts were issued to try to keep order, one of which "Anent Guid Nichtbourhead" (good neighbourhood) laid down that good neighbourhood be kept among neighbours in each parish in all time coming in "bigging of thair dykis zeirlie (yearly) and putting of thair swyne to the hill befoir the fiftein day of Apryle keiping and hirding of thair sheip befoir the first day of May under the pain of fourtie shillingis monie..." Swine were the greatest offenders and one broken dyke was enough to allow them to escape and rampage through a neighbour's rigs.

Should an enterprising crofter wish to experiment with a new crop, perhaps maturing later than that of his neighbour's, he was helpless to prevent the old custom of "slipping the okrigirt" at the stated time—allowing animals access to the township to glean what they could from the ground where the usual crops had already been harvested. Any suggestion that the animals be kept out longer was bitterly resented by the rest of the community. In the nineteenth century the heritors who had replaced the udaller had their ground "planked"; that is, surveyed and divided so that each heritor had all his grounds in a township together and not scattered among the town lands. The tenants, however, mostly had to cultivate unfixed rigs.

Although the potato came in to supplement the grain food staples in the eighteenth century, and turnips were adopted in the nineteenth century occupying some 10 per cent of arable land, the main crops grown in the long rigs were oats, potatoes and bere, more important even than oats because of its greater yield in grain although its straw was much inferior as fodder. Cabbages, introduced by Cromwell's soldiers stationed at the Fort in Lerwick, still formed a large part of the staple diet of the poor at the end of the eighteenth century. Known as "long kale" the cabbage seeds were planted in the month of June in *planti crubs* on the lower slopes away from the rigs. These stone-walled enclosures protected the young plants from the salt winds and the cold and were fertilised only with peat ash which reduced the rate of growth and prevented weeds. The plants were then moved to the infield in spring. Cabbage was used a great deal as food. Chopped, it was packed in wooden kegs in alternate layers with fat or dripping, oatmeal or groats, salted and sometimes spiced, then a weight placed on top to consolidate it. When required, a piece was cut off and boiled, producing a tasty and nourishing soup.

Even in 1840 there were few ploughs, mainly belonging to the proprietors. Up to the end of the Second World War all the ploughing in Fair Isle was done with oxen. One of the last teams was still used in Fair Isle in the 1950's. The Shetland plough, however, was not strong enough for stony soil and most of the ground was prepared with the Shetland spade, a narrow implement of iron, stepped, so that it could be driven into the earth with the foot, almost all the land being cultivated by "delling" teams of women. In the middle of the eighteenth

215

century it cost 8s to have an acre of ground dug at the rate of 6d a day for each woman, and amongst the essential equipment for starting off married life was the fish basket or büdie; fishing rods or waands for the craig seats; along with a cow for milk, a spade, a tushkar for casting peats, a pot, a rug and a blanket.

Even the Shetland spade, however, proved useless against the tough wiry heather which of necessity had to be removed as crofts grew smaller and any kind of ground was better than none. The heather was first burned, and all over the islands the word Brenna (ON to burn) appears, indicating those areas. It is still extant in the croft of Brinna in Bigton, the Bruntlands in the next village of Ireland, Brenna in Fladdabister, Brenyens in Walls, Brenhoull in Sandsting and Brunthamersland in north Tingwall, names which perpetuate those areas burnt out for settlement.

The parish ministers constantly endeavoured to advocate improvements in agriculture and certainly experimented themselves with a fair amount of success, their glebe usually consisting of some of the best land in the district. They were also in touch with new methods, and although their actual salaries were low they could command three days' free labour from every crofter plus all the various teinds. The Rev. John Turnbull, parish minister in Tingwall, one of the most beautiful districts in Shetland where the limestone floor produces rich green fields, experimented with sown grass and clover; introduced turnips; imported agricultural implements from Scotland and induced the crofters to build stone dykes in place of the old *failey* or turf dyke.

Many landowners, too, did their best to ensure a definite crop rotation and in 1818 Mr. Ogilvie of Quendale, in another area notable for its good soil, was rotating turnips, bere, clover and oats, an experiment which demanded the enclosure of land, still anathema to the Shetland crofter, so that it was virtually impossible to persuade him to follow suit. For centuries his animals had had the freedom to wander where they would after the crops were in, grazing on the seashore or the stubble fields of the townships. A stranger visiting Shetland might almost believe that the same method was practised today. Sheep lamb by the roadside where they continually graze and in many parts where long stretches of moorland border the road Shetland ponies foal unattended and wander where they will.

In contrast to the practice in the Gaelic-speaking Highlands there was no restriction on the number of animals kept by individual crofters and the Shetlander of last century with three or four acres would have four to six milking cows with calves and yearlings, two or three ponies, 30 to 40 ewes, at least one pig and often hens and geese. Shetland has retained its native stock to a much greater degree than any other croft-

216

The long sandy ayre joining St Ninian's Isle to the mainland is one of
the most beautiful tombolos in the world. In winter storms the ayre
is often covered for days on end.

Winter sunset in Bigton.

The hills above Bigton, Dunrossness, in winter.

The harbour at Symbister on Whalsay.

57　Behind the neat cottages at Williamsetter cabbages are being planted out in small patches of cultivated ground. In Shetland, spring (the voar) is well over a month later than in Scotland, and the lambs in the foreground have been born in April or May.

ing region and until cross-breeding was introduced Shetland's domestic animals were all small and only the hardiest survived. The Shetland pony, probably the best known of indigenous animals, although tiny, is perfectly proportioned. The skeleton of one these animals found in the midden of the broch at Jarlshof and the carving of one on the Bressay stone suggest that the Shetland pony existed in the islands at least in pre-Norse times. The original horse of Mainland was only 11–13 hands and the Sumburgh midden pony under 12 hands.

Out all winter in snow and gales they had to find what they could to sustain them from the hills and shore. Hay, peat and passengers were carried on their backs. The tails and manes of the ponies were used for spinning into fishing lines by means of a "spinning mare" and the Country Acts finally had to constitute it an offence to take the hair from another man's pony. The inventive ability to employ whatever was at hand was again demonstrated in the use of sheep gut for spinning wheels, washed, spun on the wheel and dried.

There were several varieties of pony on the islands; the finest according to O'Dell was found in Fetlar which showed affinities with the Arab. A grey Arab ridden by the famous General Bolivar at his last battle was presented to Captain Arthur Farquhar R.N. who later sold him to Sir Arthur Nicolson and the horse was crossed with the Shetland Fetlar ponies from 1837 onwards. Later there was another cross on Fetlar of a second Arab and an Orkney garron which produced ponies of from 11 to 12 hands. The way these ponies bred true confirmed the suggestion that the Shetland pony had an Arab strain in its composition.

217

From 1870 to 1899 the Marquis of Londonderry established a stud farm on the neighbouring islands of Bressay and Noss. Noss was used as a centre for stallions and at Maryfield on Bressay the mares were kept, so for the first time in Shetland's history the breeding of ponies was absolutely under control. The stud was dominated by one definition "as much weight as possible and as near the ground as it can be got" virtually to produce a pony which had the appearance but not the prohibitive size of a Clydesdale, for use in the pits of Northumberland. There was no cross with other breeds. The Londonderry stud obtained as sire "Jack" and he and his three sons sired in 10 years 248 foals and 160 were sired by his eight grandsons; 36 sired by Oman and only 46 by sires totally unrelated to Jack.

The first volume of the Shetland Pony Stud Book was issued in 1890. Characteristics of the best ponies in the last century were height less than 42 inches but not less than 34 otherwise there was no power in the back legs for leverage. The ponies had to have hardihood, stamina and even tempers. The standard aimed at by the Londonderry stud produced good pit ponies but poor riders as they had short straight shoulders. The thick coat was well known, the colours varied but traditionally dark brown was preferred. Piebald and skewbald were avoided except for circus ponies as they had a reputation for short tempers. The price of ponies went from £1 in 1743 to £30 for horses in 1920 and £12 in 1930. Mares fetched £5 but after 1913 to 1930 they were unsaleable.

The average Shetland pony is the smallest European pony, its gentle docile character making it easier to train for pit work than the more turbulent Welsh ponies. Even by 1913, when machinery had displaced the use of ponies on the main roads of the pits, the Shetland pony was still in demand since it could draw a load along a passage scarcely four feet high. The Mines' Act of 1911 ameliorated their conditions and the use of ponies under four years old was banned. Mares were never used because of the difficulty of working horses and mares together.

As far back as 1737 Shetland ponies were known and used as children's ponies, later to be adopted by the American market for this purpose. Just after the Great War the Russian supply of pit horses closed and the crofter had a boom period in selling, then the price slumped and became too low to justify breeding. A valuable Norwegian stallion was introduced to Unst by Mouat in 1808 and he wrote that "the larger horse is coming into use". The Department of Agriculture then granted premiums to subsidise approved stallions and by 1939 one of the finest herds in Shetland was the Mousa stud. By 1968 the record price of £598 was paid for a Shetland pony and today, although prices have dropped considerably, buyers come to the annual pony sales from all over the Continent and even from America.

218

58   Newly born Shetland foal
by the roadside, Unst.

Some form of control, however, is still badly required over the mating of large stallions with these small ponies, experienced help, readily available during foaling and a great need to protect young animals such as geldings and foals from vicious attacks by these extraordinarily mettlesome animals. No one is quite happy about colts bought for a song and shipped out of Shetland by dealers whose motives apparently may not be questioned. A premium of £60 is placed on ponies exported to the Continent, their value assessed by the local auctioneer whose duty it is to make certain that pedigreed animals are not bought merely for horseflesh. This is backed, of course, by the local Shetland Pony Association. Ponies in Shetland are becoming big business and like all businesses are liable to exploitation.

The pure-bred Shetland cattle, like the ponies, are among the smallest in the world, and alone of all cattle are resistant to tuberculosis. They may have been brought into the islands by Norse immigrants, derived from the Celtic shorthorn or come of ancient and old-established Galloway stock. At first they were exported as salt carcases and hides were sold to the Lerwick merchants; meal, flour, biscuits barley and other articles were bought in return. In summer there was overstocking and with the approach of winter they either had to be sold or many died of sheer starvation. The result of this overstocking meant that they could not command an adequate price if sold at Whitsunday, owing to their miserable condition, nor did the milk yield repay even the expense of their half-starved keeping. All the cows were horned, of every colour, and no attention was paid to the development of a proper breed.

Finally the Department of Agriculture loaned bulls and gave grants in aid to various societies. The only drawback was that with larger offspring there were complaints that byres and doorways were too low and too small for the new generation of cows! By 1920 Dunrossness and Tingwall had mainly cross shorthorns while in the north the small Shetland breed tended to remain. In Unst, Aberdeen Angus were

219

crossed with Shorthorns and in 1912 a Shetland Cattle Herd Book was established to raise the status of the breed. Shetland was the first county in Britain to become free of bovine tuberculosis and now an all-out effort is being made to eradicate brucellosis. Few crofters now keep cows to supply milk. In 1970 the number of cattle was 7033 including 1135 dairy cattle. Milk for Lerwick, Scalloway and Burra comes from Dunrossness, Tingwall and the outskirts of Lerwick itself. It is taken to Lerwick for pasteurisation and thereafter delivered to the outlying districts in plastic bags.

The true Shetland sheep is unmistakable. Small, almost dainty, with a neat head and a distinctive intelligent expression, it varies in colour from all shades of natural to moorit and Shetland black. Somehow able to subsist on the bare hill grazing, the very sparseness of its diet is believed to produce finer wool. The original breed had short tails the ewes light goat-like horns while those of the rams were heavy, curved but not spiral. In both Soay near Skye and Shetland, the sheep are the descendants of very early varieties, the Soay sheep resembling the "peat sheep" (ovis aries pulutrus) of Neolothic man and the Shetland sheep the wild Mouflon of Corsica. These Turbaries or peat sheep, found in midden heaps and in broch deposits, were slender-limbed, 22 inches at the shoulder but light and extraordinarily agile. From Neolithic times to the Middle Ages the Turbary sheep formed the backbone of the Scottish woollen industry despite the fact that the breed gave less than a pound of fleece as contrasted with the Cheviot. The Shetland sheep can fetch twice as much, weight for weight, as Blackface wool although the fleece weight at 2 lbs is only about half that of heavier breeds.

Just before the end of the eighteenth century a southern ram was introduced into the islands with a view to increasing the size of the local breed. Unfortunately it also brought in scab, hitherto unknown in Shetland. In 1791 Blackface and Cheviots arrived and in North Mavine every seven years the crofters crossed with a Blackface which is said not to coarsen the wool. The equivalent of the Shetland sheep is found in the Faroes, Iceland, Brittany, Auvergne, Alpes Maritimes, Ardennes and parts of Siberia. In 1915 and again in 1917 a Siberian ram was sent to Mr. Gordon of Windhouse, Yell. The first cross was a nearly pure Shetland ewe and the resulting lambs were hardier while the second cross had an improved lustre on the wool. Siberian Shetland wool is a rich brown colour with a breaking strain of 330 lbs.

In 1969 Shetland's 129,000 breeding ewes and gimmers were divided into 2225 actual flocks, 75 per cent of the breeding sheep being native Shetland, the others Shetland crosses, mainly from Cheviot and Blackface and Cheviots on the better hills and improved pastures. The total

220

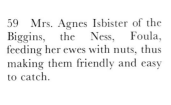

59 Mrs. Agnes Isbister of the Biggins, the Ness, Foula, feeding her ewes with nuts, thus making them friendly and easy to catch.

weight of the clip averages about 400,000 lbs its value around £100,000, of which some £80,000 to £90,000 represents "good" Shetland and Shetland first cross with Cheviot. By 1970 a subsidy of £1.60 was paid for each breeding ewe and gimmer.

Mr. R. D. Winton, late of Kergord, produced the Pettadale sheep, the result of a programme of crossing based on Romney Marsh rams and Shetland ewes. The result initially seemed to produce a greater meat weight, with 5 to 6 lb. fleeces worth about £1.50 each. His experiment was largely inspired by the attempt to combine a Shetland type wool with more actual meat. The Shetland breed itself is now considered largely uneconomic because of the small carcase and the fact that the wool clip must be light if it is to remain fine. The greater part of this clip is sold for cash to wool brokers in Shetland or sent to woollen mills in Scotland and its original unique character and specialty value is rapidly diminishing, only a small proportion of the wool clip returning to Shetland as hosiery yarn.

Recently in Foula the first Jacob ram was brought in by John Thomas Ratter and crossed with Agnes Isbister's ewe. Now there are several pure-bred Jacob lambs, white with black and black with white. The wool is very short and the sheep are believed to have been bred from Eastern and Hebridean stock.

Over the centuries little has changed in the handling of sheep. The cross-breds are kept in the home parks or occasionally tethered to a wooden stick like a tent peg stuck in the ground, to which is attached the rope round the animals' neck, their small area changed twice a day. Because of the lack of good grazing they are hand-fed in winter with cabbage, hay and neeps. A "borer"—a sheep which is continually

60 Shearing in the *crö* near Mail, Cunningsburgh. Held between the legs this Shetland black ewe is having her winter fleece removed.

61 The hill sheep have been gathered into the *crö* and each crofter, who has probably tramped miles over the hills that morning in the annual *ca'in* of the hill sheep, now collects his own and marks the lambs before shearing or *roo'in* the Shetland sheep.

managing to push its way through fences—wears a wooden collar known as "a grind", "trees" or "beogs". Three pieces of wood giving a triangular hole in the centre for the neck, the ends projecting, prevent the animal from getting through between the wires. The pure Shetland sheep's wool is roo'd, or plucked; the fine neck hair is used in Unst for the knitting of the delicate lacey shawls capable of being drawn through a wedding ring.

While the cross-breds are pampered animals the Shetland sheep must survive on the sparsest of diets. It is noticeable too in some districts that the sheep are being kept on the hill largely for the £2·875 subsidy they carry. Little effort is expended on caring for them, a sign of the times, when the hill is seldom visited except for the caa'in.

Until the end of the nineteenth century conditions changed little. With the men at sea the women worked the crofts in back-breaking delling teams, raising and bringing home the peats, making butter and baking bannocks, infinitely resourceful, inventing a hundred different ways of using the most ordinary food, not a scrap wasted. The beautifully-restored croft house of 100 years ago in Dunrossness is typical, its design unchanged since Norse times. The stones would have been gathered in from the nearest source, quarry, broch or Neolithic settlement, taking the same amount to build it as to fill it. Everything was done *sungaets*, building with the sun, starting in the north east corner. Even a boat at sea is never turned against the sun. Until the late nineteenth century the croft house was built of rough stones and dry mortar, about 28 to 30 feet long by 8 to 10 feet wide, house and byre under the same roof although partitioned off, allowing the crofter to look after his animals even in the depth of winter. At first there was a central fireplace in the living end of the long buildings, like a Viking longhouse, and later one in the ben and one in the but end. King Olaf Kyrre of Norway is recorded as the first person to have removed fireplaces from the middle of rooms in the eleventh century ordering the erection of chimneys and stoves.

The roof was the most complicated part of the building, requiring a patience and expertise now rarely found even in the islands. Thick laths called rafters were fastened at the top by a wooden peg and they rested on the inside of the wall head. "*Ta helliks*", or edging stones, were laid against them along the wall head and a series of rough wooden laths, the *langbaands*, fixed across, parallel to the ridge or *riggin*. The tie beams were known as the *twartbaaks*. The *pones* forming the roof, cut from hard topsoil and oblong in shape, were laid, each one overlapping the other starting at the waa' head, sometimes laced down with heather *simmands* like ropes, and pinned with a wooden peg.

The thatch was then begun. Bunches of straw *tekkin strae* or *gloy* were

223

cut, opened up and spread out, tops uppermost on the roof of pones, overlapping to allow the rain to drain off the eaves. Starting at the eaves the men worked upwards and at the ridge the bunches of *tekkin strae* were folded over each other to make the roof watertight. Held in place by straen simmands stretched from gable to gable, wooden pegs were driven into the pones to keep the thatch vertical. Next came a layer of drawn strae and finally the windlin strae. As soon as a section was completed it was covered with an old fishing net. Finally the entire roof was securely tied down with straw ropes called links crossing the thatch vertically and horizontally like an enormous meshed net and weighted down by loop stanes resting in the bight of extra thick ropes known as gors simmands. These roofs had to be renewed every two or three years when a new layer of thatch was added to the old one after any growth of grass or weed had been removed.

Although at first smoke from the fire filtered through the roof from the "*hert-stane*", four to six feet in diameter and laid a little more than halfway from the door, the Shetland croft house was vastly superior to the "black houses" of the western Isles and very early in their construction included a but end and a ben end with a fire at the wall end. Tiny skylight windows, often set in flagstones, depending upon the availability of suitable stone, were covered in the beginning with a membrane of animal fat or a scraped lambskin in place of glass.

The main fire was "rested" at night, banked or "*smoored*", so that in the morning it was an easy matter to waken up the still-glowing peat. Cooking pots, muckle kettles and cauldrons could be suspended at any desired height above the fire by means of crooks and links, a chain of round iron links, itself hung from the *crook baak*, a square log of wood centred over the hearthstone and running the length of the room from waa head to waa head. Directly on the fire could be placed a brandiron on which oatcakes, scones and brandiron bannocks were made. A kind of half attic was usually incorporated in the but end like a great shelf— useful for storing all kinds of articles from ropes and nets to kishies or wool.

When the fire was placed centrally, one of the most important furnishings of the cottage was the *reist*, really derived from the word to *roost*, applied to a cock or a hen. The *reist* proper consisted of laths, rods and *simmands* netting laid down on top of the tie beams with several *reps* running across the width of the room both inbye and ootbye the fire. The meat or fish to be *reisted* or smoked, was carefully arranged on the netting and hung from the *reps*. Another appliance in the ootbye reist was a large rectangular framework of wooden boards on which cowhides were stretched and cured before being made into *rivlins*, the raw hide shoes worn by all the family. During late autumn and early winter the reist would be packed with kail seed, stocks, floss baets, mutton tees and shooders, spaarls, pork hams, shitterlins, piltocks, troots, saithe, skate, hoe and of course the rivlin hide.

Around the walls or separating the but end from the ben end, were the typical box beds, usually with sliding doors, which ran in wooden channels top and bottom. Occasionally two doors were fitted which could be closed or opened with the fingers pushed through holes cut for the purpose, often carved in the shape of a heart, diamond or clover leaf, which served both as door knob and ventilator. The females of the family would be in one box bed and the boys in another. There would be a kist or two, a *restin-shair*, an uncushioned wooden sofa six feet long with arm rests at each end, the back closed to half its height and standing against the wall opposite the *hert-stane*. The top half was sometimes ornamented with carving or turned pillars and occasionally closed in to form a storage chest for linen and blankets, but more often underneath the restin-shair was the favourite place for one or more of the family's collies. There were almost certainly a couple of wooden chairs, home-made, one hooded with a drawer underneath the seat where granny kept her "*makkin*"—her knitting and wool—and one or two small stools or *creepies* used by the children. Many of the early crofters also possessed a *straen shair*, a tall canopied chair something like the wooden one but made of straw laced together on a wooden frame like a peat basket but much closer in weave so as to be completely draught-proof and often used by the older members of the household. The old people of 100 years ago would never have imagined in their wildest dreams that these well-used, ordinary pieces of furniture would become "collectors' pieces", or that the prices paid for them today would be enough to keep them in comfort for a year.

Near the door of the croft house was kept the water *baenk*, a rough, wooden or stone bench on which stood the *hevel dafficks* holding the water supply and refilled from the well daily. There used to be a kettle or some receptacle for storing "Shetland soda", which, apart from being the sole available washing soda at the time, added to hot water was the only effective way of removing the fish oil (*creesh*) from hand spun worsted before being knitted or woven into woollen goods.

Hanging by the fire was a *strae* bag for salt, nearby a jumper board, the most efficient way of drying and stretching woollen sweaters, together with a leg board for stockings. The number of hand-made implements connected with the croft was endless. There were *sivs*: sieves made from a sheep's hide, a wet skin turned round a hoop with straw to keep it in place until it stretched and dried; a *bismer* for weighing meal while *ootbye* would be the *knockin stane* and *mell*, muckle kettle, *peerie* kettle, (*peerie* the Shetland word for small), brandiron and so forth.

225

62 Mrs. Jane Sinclair (grandmother) sitting by the fire knitting a lace openwork sweater in the horseshoe pattern. At her feet sits her grand-daughter Kathryn, aged $3\frac{1}{2}$, winding wool from a wooden wool winder made locally. In one corner a finished *kishie* holds the peats.

No croft would be complete without a spinning wheel, the small upright one known as "the spinney" and the bigger Norwegian type as "the wheel". Apart from the wool rooed from the sheep, they would gather bits caught here and there on walls and posts, *"henty leggits"* as it was known in Unst. First cleaned of bits of heather and grass it was then *"cairded"* on two flat pieces of wood with teeth like a brush on one side of each, before it could be spun.

Young farm animals shared the warmth of the living room. Perhaps a young pig or, in the spring a calf, would be brought into the but end and given a *bol* on the ootby floor until strong enough to be moved to an enclosed stall in the byre or barn. In early summer *"caadies"*— lambs that were orphans or whose mother was unable to feed them— were bottle-fed inside on cow's milk. A clockin' hen often hatched out her brood in the comfort of the but end until the chicks were nimble enough to look after themselves in the byre.

Entering the croft house, on the right was the byre, on the left the entrance to the but end and directly in front was the door to the barn. Inside were kept the hand quern and all the implements of crofting; the Shetland spade, the tushkar, meshies and clibbers for the ponies, peat baskets and so forth. In one corner the kiln was built. In the Dunrossness district the kiln was circular and inside it was a rectangular box crossed with ribs of wood, on top of which was spread the straw and then the grain. In one corner, below the kiln was the *kilnsluggie*, a kind of funnel inside which the fire was lit to dry the grain, the smoke escaping through a flue in the back wall.

When the bere was cut it would be set up in small stooks, called *bullies* in Foula, then built into *dusses* and carried into the yard where it would stand in *skroos*. Quite often the actual threshing was carried out in the barn itself. First the sheaves would be laid on the floor of the barn, their heads together in a heap, then threshed with a wooden flail to separate the grain from the straw. The flail was made up of two pieces, the handstaff to which the *souple* was attached by means of rawhide thongs to give it greater elasticity. Then the grain itself was heavily

63   The little village of Fladdabister in the 1930's. Although most of the roofs are now either slate or tar this village has still preserved a beauty of its own. It lies on the East coast of Mainland about 5 miles south of Lerwick. (Zetland County Library and Museum.)

threshed to remove the loose husks, *beards* or *anns*, a process known as *hummeling*. After that it might be taken outside, or a *flackie*, a straw mat, was laid on the floor between two doors and the grain thrown up in the air so that the chaff was carried away in the wind. In some districts a man might stand with a *kishie* or basket on his shoulder pouring out the grain. Each district had its own methods and individual names for all the varying processes and implements used. In the winter, sitting by the fire, the men made kishies which many still do today, but no longer of necessity; the kishies are made from reeds or Shetland oats and are designed for use as waste-paper baskets, laundry baskets or to carry logs.

After milling, two sieves made of sheepskin stretched on wooden frames, one coarse and one fine, were used to separate the *sids* from the meal. The coarse remains were fed to the cattle and the remainder again divided into two by means of the finer sieve to separate bere meal. Small quantities of grain could be bruised and husked on a knockin stane and meal ground in a hand quern, but water mills, built on the Norwegian system with horizontal wheels, were common on every burn, sometimes half a dozen in a row.

From the meal all kinds of scones were made; the hot water bannocks, baked with hot water on the open fire with a brandiron on top so that they didn't rise but kept flat, spread with home-made butter and kept warm; then there were the brandiron bannocks; pan bannocks; fat bannocks made with a little fat from the pig heated in the pan, then brünies and scones with oatmeal and fat brünies with mutton fat put in a pan with a little water then poured into oatmeal little round cakes were made and cooked like oatcakes so that although the ingredients were almost the same they were all different. "Burstin brünies" from *brunt* stane fed the family at hard periods when there was no meal in the house. The tops were threshed off the sheaves and the husks pounded off, dried in a pan over the fire and ground on a hand quern.

Of course there was simply nothing the Shetland wife couldn't do with fish. With the livers they made *stap* and *crappen*. Fish livers were scalded then oatmeal added to them and mixed up with a fork until it was soft; seasoned with salt and pepper and then the mixture stuffed into a fish head, or put into little muslin bags, dropped into boiling water and boiled for an hour, when it comes out it is almost the same as what they call a *crookie* dumpling and that is *crappen*. *Stap* consists of boiled livers laid on top of boiled fish with all the bones removed, mashed up with a fork and seasoned.

Two old ladies in Unst, Jackie and Lizzie, remembered all the things they had which didn't have to come out of the shop. "We had plenty of potatoes, plenty of turnips, and then we had a big pig. We had milk

228

and our own butter. The boat was just lying below the door and we had all the fish we wanted, May piltocks, and before that it was sillocks. We would have fat from the pig, the sillocks rolled in a little flour and with meal and potatoes it was just lovely! We had fresh mackerel and what we call young tatties ... that's our favourite meal yet if we could get the chance of them. We had buttermilk from the churn what we called *blaedick*, that was awfully good for the grice (pigs), better than blaand. That's made by putting boiling water in what we called the blaedick, that's just when you are taking off the butter and then you get the blaand. It goes to the bottom and then you get what we call kirn milk, just like cheese. The blaand would come to the top and the pig would get that and sometimes they would get too fat. Everyone had a pig then and the legs of the pig, they were salted and hung up above the old Shetland stove. The peat reek made them just like kippers and we'd have that with bannocks."

Veevers was known as tasty food—perhaps shop biscuits. *Vivda* was meat wind-dried in *skeos* and eaten cut in small slices which must have been very like South African biltong. In times of famine, following crop failures or when bad weather prevented fishing, folk were forced to "*bluid da kye*". A vein was opened at the back of the cow's head and a measure of blood drawn off. This blood was mixed with "burstin" meal and cooked like a black pudding.

Different foods were associated with certain days. On Beainer Sunday (the Sunday before Christmas) an ox head was hung in the chimney with which to make broth; on Jol E'en or Christmas Eve, *sowans* formed the supper. On Christmas Day itself breakfast was the main meal at which all kinds of meat were available. Fastern's E'en was a movable feast with a supper of brose and half a cow's head. On Bogle Day, about the end of March when delling began, a supper was served of cakes named bogles, and on Lammas Sunday milgruel was made for breakfast and next day the meadows were mown.

Shetland folk always used to eat fish with their fingers, a vastly more sensible way than "*trivlin*" hopelessly around in a genteel fashion with knife and fork. A great dish would be set down out of which each one helped himself. There was liver flakkie, two "sooket" piltooks split and laid one against the other with liver in between and roasted. There was oily muggie, the stomach of a fish stuffed with liver and boiled. For liver heads the head was washed, the gills kept in, washed livers put inside the head and the mouth closed by stitching. Cooked in boiling salted water, it was drained, laid on a hot plate and all the bones removed, then the whole thing chopped up together. The muggie is the stomach of the fish and ling muggie is best for liver muggies. No part of an animal or fish was ever wasted.

64 Taking home the peats, *kishie* on her back, leaving her hands free for her "*maakin*" or knitting. Around the end of the nineteenth century. (Zetland County Library and Museum.)

Almost all the clothing made for the family was sewn at home. A day's work was literally a day's work from before dawn till after dark. The two sisters, Lizzie Priest and Jackie Mouat, who worked at the gutting and whose father was postmaster on Unst, described a day at the beginning of this century. "On Monday morning the steamer came to Uyeasound and father had to be there at eight o'clock. He got up at four to feed the horses, he kept two, that was one of the rules. Then he came back for his own breakfast and it was a good walk to and from the stable. Then back to harness the horse and set off for Baltasound where he had to be on the dock at 6.45 in the morning. He could shoe the horse himself, that helped him a bit, and when it was frosty he would go out in the early morning and put frost nails into the horse shoes, so that the horse wouldn't slip. He could mend our shoes, all our boots, half sole them and patch them, then he could sit at the table and make little trousers for the boys and he had a little oil lamp hanging from the roof above the table so that he could sew at night.

"For breakfast it was fresh fish, hot bannocks and home butter or another morning our own eggs or porridge. We would have potatoes in their jackets and fish or tattie soup, mutton and our own turnips or a big potful of potatoes and turnips and reistit mutton about Christmas. We had a pig's head on Christmas morning, and then through the day, well I don't know how many friends would come in and see us and there would be fiddlers ... All the boys came from round about and we would maybe dance a Shetland reel in the middle of the day, or at night there would be dancing at different houses. At Halloween, what we call Hallomass, then there would be dancing *grillocks* (dancing

230

guisers) six men and their fiddler ... I remember the year that the First War finished it was either seven or eight *swedes* ended up at our home. There was seven in every *swede* counting the fiddler for there had to be six for the Shetland reel, and we danced till four o'clock in the morning. Just this past winter a man said to me that he would always remember that night and your Dad going to bed something like after 12 o'clock and I said 'Jimmie John, you'll not get much sleep tonight with this din going on' and he just replied 'Just you enjoy yourselves, I'll sleep if I get my head down'."

In the First World War which ended up with the dancing and the fiddlers in Unst, more than 3000 Shetlanders were involved, and in the Merchant Navy and the Royal Navy, even according to Admiralty reports, they were not excelled. Some of them were attached to the Gordon Highlanders and later in the 3rd, 15th and 51st Highland Divisions they fought alongside with Scots, so that between army and navy experience and meeting with Scottish fishermen the bitter memories of 400 years of Scots domination began to fade.

The 10th Cruiser Squadron was established at Swarbacks Minn and Lerwick and it was categorically stated that the great submarine menace, accounting for 12 million tons of shipping, would have cost us the war, but for this squadron's efforts. In 1914 the *Oceanic* came to grief on Foula, but to this day Foula folk cannot account for the wreck. The ship was seen, not on a foggy day as was reported, but clearly from the shore, heading in the direction of the Hoevdi Grind on which she finally struck. In February, 1916, within sight of Muckle Flugga, the 16,000-ton *Alcantara* went down taking with her the German raider, *Greif*. One bright June morning a few miles off Lerwick, a German submarine suddenly surfaced in the midst of a peaceful fishing fleet and proceeded methodically to send 15 to the bottom with shell fire, leaving two to take back the survivors.

By the end of the war Shetland had lost 600 dead, one out of every 35 inhabitants while the British Isles had lost one out of every 45.

Between the Wars, in spite of efforts to help, the extent of land was limited, seamen found themselves unemployed and the new crofters had to keep up houses and rents on a falling market. In the late 1920's it was not unusual for a crofter to send a score of lambs to Aberdeen to find that after paying freight and feeding he had lost by the transaction. Ponies could scarcely be given away and many had to be shot. Fishing fleets were depleted and the wool and hosiery industry almost non-existent. In proportion to its population Shetland had the largest number of old age pensioners of any county in Scotland, about one out of every 14 persons, and in the 1950's over 17 per cent were over 65.

Then came the Second World War. A smashed lifeboat from the *Athenia* drifted ashore at Sound and again the islands were inundated with servicemen. The last incident of the war was the sinking of the final submarine to be destroyed in the European theatre, hit off Shetland by a plane from the islands an hour or so before Germany capitulated. The great majority of Shetland soldiers were in the 51st Highland Division. There were Shetlanders, too, in the *Royal Oak*, the *Hood* and the *Rawalpindi* and as always hundreds of men from the island were manning small ships all over the world. Sullom Voe was established as an R.A.F. base and batteries manned by the Royal Signals were built at the entrances to both Lerwick and Scalloway harbours. With the fall of Norway the islands became the base of one of the most remarkable exploits of the war and "The Shetland Bus" became legendary. Based first on Lunna and later at Scalloway, Norse and British kept up a constant service between Shetland and Norway.

Norwegian patriots arrived in the islands in every craft that could float, some of them barely seaworthy, sometimes three and four boats landing in one day, somehow making the crossing. Seven young men arrived in Baltasound after a two-day sail from somewhere north of Bergen with no compass, no log, but a good watch, just enough fuel for a straight run, and Old Axel. "The best seaman in the world," smiled the lads pointing to the veteran. But the old man shook his head. He had expected to sight Saxavord dead ahead and had been nearly 10 miles off course. He showed his hand-made log, a bit of wood, curiously fashioned and controlled, and one thought of Leif the Lucky and Flokki of the ravens who had quite possibly used a similar device.

Norwegians sailed their fishing vessels across the North Sea to their Nazi-occupied homeland to land ammunition, radios and saboteurs, returning with refugees. Two hundred and six missions were undertaken; 192 men and 383 tons of military stores landed; 73 agents and 373 refugees brought back with 10 boats and 44 crewmen lost. Fishing boats were fitted out as a Q-ship's minelayer. Boats were stolen by Norwegians even down to food, oil, charts, bedclothes and even a new suit of sails from under the very noses of the Nazi occupants, the whole story retold in *The Shetland Bus* by David Howarth who was based in Shetland, and also in another epic description by Neils Larsen.

232

20. *Sea Route to the Northern Isles*

AT THE BEGINNING of the eighteenth century Shetland was the most difficult of access of all the outer isles, and it is recorded that the Rev. James Grierson, minister in Shetland, had to make elaborate and wearisome arrangements to be picked up by some passing smack, leaving his manse in March, in order to be certain of reaching Edinburgh in time for the General Assembly in May.

Although the generation of intrepid English adventurers who diligently explored Arabia, Africa and Hindustan had never heard of Shetland, the ordinary Shetlander was as familiar with foreign ports as he was with Lerwick or Scalloway. In the Merchant Navy or the Royal Navy he had sailed the seven seas; to Shetland came fishermen from all over Europe, their base Bressay Sound. For generations communications with both Orkney and Shetland were largely determined by exports, the only travellers the unfortunate ministers whose diaries reflect the tribulations of their calling, necessitating endless miserable and hazardous journeys to and fro by trader from Leith to Kirkwall, a four-day journey; from there hiring a sixareen and frequently storm-stayed in Orkney's island of Sanday for a couple of weeks.

Smacks and sloops bravely battered their way north and south with fish from Shetland and corn from Orkney bound for the West Highlands, Norway, Holland, Ireland, Spain and Portugal. From Norway the return cargo consisted of timber for boats and buildings, staves for herring barrels; flax from the Baltic, salt from Spain and Portugal, while from ports in southern Scotland coal was imported into Orkney. Orkney was in addition, a port of call for ships from the American colonies, bound to put into a British port on their way to Bremen, Hamburg, Rotterdam or Amsterdam.

Wherever their route lay these tiny sailing craft were faced with a passage through one of the worst pieces of water in the world. At either end of the Pentland Firth lie the Bore of Duncansby and The Merry Men of Mey, while in its centre churns the oceanic whirlpool of The Swilkie, where as every Shetland schoolchild knows, Grotti Minni and Grotti Finni endlessly grind salt on their magic millstones. Long ago, so legend tells, the giantesses were captured by the captain of a pirate vessel harrying the Shetland coast. Southbound under full sail, bent on making his fortune, the foolish fellow having set Grotti Minni and Grotti Finni to work, forgot the words that would command them to stop and his ship sank under its load of salt in the Pentland Firth. After the Firth come the turbulent waters of the North Sea with its 70-foot waves and finally the Sumburgh Röst where even on the calmest day a slight swell betrays its presence.

The history of transport at sea provides a story in itself, a Conradian tale of wreck and gale, described in detail in Professor Donaldson's entrancing book *Northwards by Sea*. Before the eighteenth century Lerwick was a relatively unimportant settlement until Shetland lairds found it convenient to build town houses there and merchant landlords set up in business to feed the growing port. By 1762 a vessel from Lerwick was busily engaged in supplying the haaf station in Fetlar with meal, gin, tobacco, napkins, hemp, horn combs and "Casteel" soap; cloth of various kinds, red and black "shag"; red plaid for women; English cotton for vests or petticoats; Zetland cloth and "Knap's"; spotted cotton for vests, the gaudy waistcoats that were obviously the rage in Fetlar as well as everywhere else. There were kettles, lispunds

65 Loading the Mails circa 1900 outside the old Post Office at the Tolbooth. In the background left is part of the Queen's Hotel building. The mail cart is a wagonette. A gig has stopped so that its driver can chat with a friend and a four wheeled wagon stands outside John Tait & Company's Wholesale and Retail Warehouse. (The late Mrs. Abernethy's Collection via Jack Keddie.)

of Norroway bark for fishing nets, ankers of brandy, meal, wool, salt, haddock hooks and ling hooks ground lines and toum lines and hemp, all stowed together in an *oyl* barrel; sugar, tea, butter, Annise seed, "Rock Indico", Table Blue, thread and buttons. From Fetlar in return came the inevitable ling, 2905 of them; cod, tusk, barrels of oil, butter, calf skins, hides, stockings and eggs.

In 1790 there were two decked boats in Unst of 10–15 tons plying between that island and Lerwick. Almost everyone in the islands possessed some kind of a boat and internal transport consisted of local fishing boats, the lairds having their own "great boats of passage". Recognised ferries were supposed to be available between the islands but first the owner of the boat had to be summoned from the fishing, the ploughing or his peat banks; wind and weather considered, by which time the strong tides might well hold up the traveller for days.

While Orkney at least had the pretensions of a regular mail service, Shetland had none. In 1750 it took a letter 50 days between Leith and Lerwick. A government grant of £60 was made to Leith merchants to carry mail "five times a year", but even so they were often six months late in arriving and there were angry complaints. Shetland landlords pressed for a subsidy in view of the growing value of the islands, not

66   The crew of the old Foula Mailboat at Walls, probably 1910 before the engine was installed. In the bows is Thomas Isbister, catechist, or missionary as it is now called, on the island, who died in 1934.

67 The Christmas mail being winched up to the light at Muckle Flugga slung on a twin cable way of steel ropes. 195 feet above the sea, during a storm, one of the doors was broken open ·by the strength of the waves.

only as a stepping stone to the Archangel and Baltic routes, but because of Shetland's importance as a supplier of wool, stockings, butter, hides and men to Britain.

Their demands were eventually met and in 1810 there were 10 mails a year "wind and weather permitting". The Leith mails were carried in an 80-ton smack and local trade by a 30-ton schooner. By 1833 Shetland mail was despatched and received by chance coasting vessels at the rate of a penny a letter but the "wind and weather" clause being the operative phrase the service was so erratic that six weeks often elapsed between opportunities. Usually only a moment's notice was given and a bellman rushed off to tramp the streets of Lerwick while feverish attempts must have been made to complete a sentence, seal packages and carry them to the impatiently-waiting ship.

Before the advent of steamers, oddly enough, between Shetland and Orkney there were no trade communications whatsoever. In 1832 the first steamer was seen in Shetland waters and in 1836 the paddle steamer *Sovereign*, built for the North of Scotland and Orkney Steam Navigation Company, arrived in Lerwick harbour, carrying mail from Leith. In spite of the arrival of steam, however, sailing vessels still dominated traffic with the islands for the next half-century. In 1838 a government contract was obtained for carrying mails to and from Shetland, once a week in summer (April to October) by the North of Scotland Company and the week-end boats remained the primary service to

236

Orkney and Shetland for 101 years. It was not until 1847 that the first steam vessel was seen in the North Isles of Shetland when Arthur Anderson entered a certain voe in Yell in his steam yacht. A great deal of noise was occasioned by blowing off steam and two unsophisticated islanders gathering limpets on the shore gazed at the "fire ship" in blank astonishment. At length the more strong-minded of the two handed his snuff horn to his terrified companion with the exhortation: "Oh Jamie, tak du a sniff for du'll snuff nae mair wi me till we snuff together in Glory!" He had imagined that the great day of wrath had come and that on board the steamer was the angel blowing the last trumpet.

A journey by steamer to the most northerly town in the British Isles suddenly became a novel attraction for adventurous travellers and in 1814 Sir Walter Scott came to Shetland, the visit remarkable for his subsequent novel *The Pirate*, in which he bestowed the name Jarlshof on the Old Ha' Hoose at Sumburgh. The name remained, quite obliterating his own connections with it, the inspiration of a moment, to remain forever as the title of the world-famous complex of prehistoric settlements now known collectively as Jarlshof.

Sir Walter found the streets of Lerwick full of drunken sailors returned from the whaling, noting in his Journal with astonishing naïvety that the thousand Zetlanders who had accompanied them "made a point of treating their English messmates who get drunk of course and are very riotous. The Zetlanders do not get drunk but go straight home ..." Entertained by Scottish lairds and ministers it was little wonder that he confessed "I cannot get a distinct account of the nature of the land rights. ..." but in some verses written later he is obviously well aware of the conditions of the crofter fishermen.

Scott set the precedent for a positive influx of tourists and travellers of one kind or another whose comments, together with a spate of literature from resident ministers, provide a wealth of material on the islands all through the nineteenth century. Walter Calverley Trevelyan on his way to a geological survey of the Faroes in 1821 found Lerwick a clean town, commenting on its narrow flagged streets and the houses built into the sea; climbed the Ward of Bressay twice and went on to see Noss Head. Here he saw "the spot where a kind of bridge is formed across a chasm 160 feet above the sea by means of a cradle of wood in which sheep are carried over to a holm ..."

For over 200 years 12 sheep continued to be pastured on that tiny green platform on the Holm of Noss, the shepherd crossing in a kind of bo'sun's chair carrying one animal at a time, a man standing by on the Noss side to haul him back by a rope attached to the cradle. From the 400-feet high Sheep Craig on Fair Isle to tiny islets and

68 Family group, Shetland, around the turn of the century. Even the little maid has been brought in with newly starched white apron, and it is likely that four generations are represented. (The late Mrs. Abernethy's Collection.)

pocket-handkerchief squares of turf lying off-shore, sheep are ferried out, carried back and forth in the same manner today, for all round the coasts of Shetland every scrap of grass is precious, the green holms, fertilised by colonies of sea birds, particularly rich in pasture.

From Walter Trevelyan's account book we find that his entire stay in Shetland cost him about £8 10s including the cost of sending his luggage to Laxfirth by boat and then on to Weisdale Voe by cart to catch the boat for Faroe. His passage in the smack *Coldstream* from Leith cost him £1 11s 6d, less than the price of one first-class sleeping berth today from Aberdeen, which includes neither passage nor food. The accommodation, like Hibbert's before him, was humble but its shortcomings well compensated for by the warm welcome and kindly care of the captain. At his lodging in Lerwick Trevelyan paid 1s for his bed; 1s for breakfast; 1s 6d for dinner and 1s for supper. He noted that a calf sold for 3s and a hen for 8d while eggs were from 1½d to 3d a dozen and a preparation of ale and toddy for his farewell party set him back the considerable sum of 2s 8d.

As Robert Louis Stevenson's father had designed both Sumburgh Light and Muckle Flugga it is not surprising that on occasion his son should accompany him on a tour of inspection. R.L.S. was not impressed. After a desultory exploration of the Broch of Clickhimin, where he peevishly complained of having to creep on all fours through stone passageways, he walked a short way up the south road out from Lerwick. The cottages disgusted and repelled him, thatched and "bearing every sign of desertion and decay, except the curl of smoke from

238

the place where the chimney should be and was not …"

George Borrow on the other hand had been so fascinated by the Broch that in spite of the fact that it was winter, with snow on the ground, he took off his shoes, stockings and trousers and waded all round the buildings, examining every inch of them. He was later to be seen striding about wearing a cotton shirt and loose open jacket, seemingly impervious to the cold and was afterwards remembered in Shetland, not as the author of *Lavengro*, but as "da man at waded aa aroond da Broch i da hert o winter".

Tourists and visitors vary little over the centuries, their observations rarely pleasing to the inhabitants. Drawn northward in ever-increasing numbers as sail gave way to steam and then to aeroplanes they have nevertheless returned again and again, attracted by some subtle alchemy inherent in the islands or to enjoy briefly and vicariously the toil and hardships of others. Television teams descend with increasing regularity to report the strange and the outlandish and occasionally the reality. Each one has his own idea of what Shetland should look like and willy nilly that is the image that is projected.

Embarrassed natives are pressed into resurrecting an ancient Shetland spade to *dell* uncomfortably, well out of sight of gleaming harvester or harrow; sheep are awkwardly dipped in the stern of a decrepit fourareen where a few inches of water swill over the reluctant animal, again the modern concrete *crö* ignored. In one recent film about Fair Isle the producer makes the extraordinary discovery that Fair Isle women "use a belt when knitting". In one publication sheep were discovered to be "tethered" on a particular island. The women of Shet-

69   In the winter evenings Laurie Work is kept busy making peat baskets but now these are sought by visitors to the islands to hold logs, knitting or laundry. His youngest daughter, Kathryn, aged 3½, winds the wool for Granny's knitting.

land from Sumburgh to Muckle Flugga, not one of whom would knit without the traditional "belt" a leather pad pierced with holes into which one of the needles is firmly stuck—its ancestor a tightly twisted cone of feathers—and the numberless crofters who have tethered sheep and cattle since time immemorial can only mutter in helpless rage.

Ployen travelled south on the *Sovereign* described by one Catherine Sinclair who went north from Wick in 1839 as "a fine, large, well-grown steamboat". Alas, her return journey must have been a stormy one for the only passenger capable of sitting down to dinner with Captain Phillips was Christian Ployen himself.

The winter services to the isles continued to be almost non-existent, which is scarcely surprising with a fleet of paddle steamers wholly unsuited to the conditions of the North Sea and the abysmal lack of lighthouses en route. The acquisition of the screw steamer *Queen (II)* which made her first trip to Lerwick on November 9th, 1861 at last made winter sailings feasible although the company was still to invest in two more paddlers, and in the early 1860's, summer and winter alike, there were only two-steamer services weekly, one from Leith to Aberdeen, Wick and Thurso and the other from Leith via Aberdeen, Wick, and Kirkwall to Lerwick.

In 1881 a third weekly run began from Leith on Mondays, to Aberdeen, Stromness and Scalloway, the west-side service going on from Scalloway to other ports on the west side of Shetland, a service that continued with variations until 1939. Inevitably there was a personal side to these sailings and Captain Nisbet who skippered the *Queen of the Isles* a small schooner serving the west side before a steamer was put on, proved a key figure in the island service with his long experience of the dangerous passage up the west coast of Shetland. It is told that, when master of the first west side steamer, the Captain organised all kinds of private arrangements before the erection of official lighthouses. A lamp in a crofter's cottage guided him through Vaila Sound into Walls and a lamp in the staircase window of Melby House helped him negotiate Papa Sound, a service which he acknowledged with a blast on the ship's whistle as he passed.

Although the penny post had by this time been introduced all over Britain, Shetland was the last district to benefit from regular mails. One of the best known and most successful of the sailing ships which rivalled the steamship for many years was the *Matchless*. Built in Aberdeen by Alexander Hall & Co. at a contract price of £2000 for the Zetland New Shipping Company, she plied between Leith and Lerwick from 1846 to 1882. Her accommodation included an unheard-of innovation, a Ladies' Cabin with four berths. Her record run of 24 hours from Lerwick to Leith was never beaten by a sailing vessel and in spite of the

240

competition of steam she was able to continue trade between the two cities for nearly 40 years.

For many years there were no piers at all and flit boats, usually old sixareens surviving from the days of the far haaf ferried livestock and humans to and from the steamer, a precarious transfer of baggage, calves, sacks of coal, fertilisers and groceries that changed places at every port. The North Isles Service was at the mercy of every passenger and local traders, even to the extent of making special calls, and no one knew quite where she would sail next. At Burravoe, where she was liable to appear as early as 10.30 a.m. everyone had to be ready. Before the days of telephones, which reached the North Isles only in the mid 30's, an obliging postmistress kept in touch with the ship's movements by telegraph. "Tinkle, tinkle ..." went the machine and one was informed that "she left Uyeasound at 8 o'clock", or that "she was at Cullivoe at 10 o'clock", or "she's not come to Cullivoe yet", or the blessed news that "she left Mid Yell a little ago".

70 Waiting to find out whether the mail boat is leaving and when. She has been lowered into the water from her concrete noost. In the foreground lobster creels—practically the only kind of fishing now pursued off Foula since the Aberdeen trawlers cleared her banks of fish. Two Burra boats have put in for the night, obviously knowing the weather is set fair, for in a storm they would be smashed to matchwood in the tiny voe.

Up to just after the Second World War the atmosphere on any of the North of Scotland boats was one of intimate cameraderie. On the old *St. Clair*, where one enormous cabin served as dining room and sleeping quarters with bunks ranged in tiers around, discreetly draped by dark green curtains, dressing and undressing was a major acrobatic feat; the china at the single table of gargantuan proportions. Small boys were welcomed on the bridge and wearing the Chief Officer's hat rang the great brass bell for tea.

The Earl herself and all her successors have become almost legendary, part of the island image and her masters some of the most likeable of characters. The first *Earl*'s career was punctuated by a series of mishaps and adventures surviving 70 years of service with neither echometer nor radar, wholly dependent on the skilled judgment of her Master. We are indebted to Professor Donaldson for recording one of her mishaps commemorated in verse:

> She gaed on Robbie Ramsay's Baa,
> In Baltasound she brak in twa;
> They put a bit into her middle
> And made her fit as ony fiddle.

The lengthening of the ship actually took place in 1884 but not because of the mishap in Baltasound which line we must accept as poetic licence. The best-remembered incident connected with her long career happened one foggy day in 1912 when she stranded on Lunna Holm. When the vessel came to rest on the grassy islet a local worthy on board turned to the mate and asked: "Boy, is du tinkin tae gie her a corn i green girse i da mornin'?" ("Boy, are you thinking of giving her a little bit of green grass in the morning?"—as one would to a cow.)

The word "boy" used to grown men is always puzzling to southern ears, as is the peculiarly Shetland habit of referring to almost everything as being of the masculine gender. The clock, a doorknob, an iron, are all referred to as "he". "He needs a bit of oil" or "he's fast now . . ." and even bitches are invariably addressed as "boys". There used to be an old story of the man who had three wild and tomboyish daughters. Looking at them with pride and a smile he was heard to remark: "Wir lasses, der de boys!"

In spite of the many hardships involved in travelling on the old *Earl*, the only sleeping accommodation being a tiny ladies' cabin with male passengers forced to kip down in the Saloon except during the tourist season, when a temporary Gentlemen's Cabin was rigged up in the 'tween decks beside the after hatch, no competitors ever usurped her status as the North Boat. Her main rival became eventually the new "overland route" which always strikes one as a strange description for

242

a trip involving two ferries. The crossing of the sounds, Yell Sound from Toft to Ulsta and the Bluemull Sound from Gutcher to Belmont could both be hazardous especially in open sailing boats, the roads across the islands little more than tracks.

It was not until 1930 that motor ferry boats and improved roads challenged the service of *The Earl*, and were largely responsible for her new sailing on Tuesday afternoon to connect with the Aberdeen boat arriving in Lerwick that morning.

By 1939 a new *Earl* replaced the old one and it says much for the affection in which she was held that the occasion was marked by considerable ceremonial. A fortnight later came the Second World War and the new *Earl* was requisitioned for service in the Pentland Firth. Re-named *Earl of Zetland II* she served under that name throughout the War and finally, sold to a Panama company, she ended her days running illegal immigrants into Palestine while the gallant old *Earl* came back to serve the North Isles of Shetland till the end of the War.

The War years saw tarmacadam roads, larger buses and a regular overland service with safer piers for ferry crossings. On the steamer route the old sixareens which had acted as flit boats for so many years, adding excitement to the trip for those who liked it, were falling apart and the piers which began to be built were too late and in some cases hopelessly inadequate. The Mid Yell pier proved useless at low water and the pier at Symbister on Whalsay was not completed until 1966. Gradually schedules altered to carry goods before passengers, although for summer tourists the leisurely journey by sea is still incomparable and occasionally during winter snows the *Earl* came into her own again. Today with the roll-on roll-off ferries and inter-island air services the journey to Unst and back can be made in a day. The scenery is still magnificent even by road but nothing can quite compare with those early days.

Leaving Lerwick in the early morning for Fetlar, Yell or Unst, the quiet sound of the steamer was like a single note of music among the enclosing islands, its sharp bow sending a long ripple into the sea's flat brilliance; or beating up the Sound the taste of salt on the lips, solan geese (gannets) diving like a plumbline and a trawler appearing and disappearing like a toy ship in the troughs. Hilarious moments came when strong arms lifted passengers and calves alike into the heaving flit boat, the while local gossip was exchanged and the rugged weather-beaten face of the skipper Willie Sinclair, who had served as mate for more years than one cares to remember, now retired as Master, beaming down, always ready to help, to put himself to no end of trouble to make one comfortable.

243

A delightful story illustrates the total informality of the trip. Jenny Gilbertson, the first pioneer to put Shetland on the map with her film "The Rugged Island", but never the best of sailors, elected to travel south from Unst on the *Earl*. Coming aboard, the Chief Engineer—everyone knows everyone else in Shetland—suggested that should she feel queasy she could have his bunk. Jenny struggled manfully on until she felt that she could stand it no longer and accepted his kind offer. He gave her an arm down the companionway, set her on his bunk, the lower one; tenderly removed her boots and covering her up with a rug, jerked his head upwards to the top bunk, remarking in a comforting voice: "You'll be all right here. The 'Cruelty Man's abune ye but he'll no harm ye'."

In the early 1930's for those of us who were fortunate enough to have experienced the delightful cruise-like atmosphere of the long trip up from Leith via Kirkwall, strolling through the streets, meeting friends and re-visiting the magnificent rose-red St. Magnus Cathedral built by Earl Rognvald, and returning by Stromness and St. Margaret's Hope, it was something never to be forgotten. Although the boats must obviously have kept to a schedule, there was an element of timelessness about the whole voyage. At Stromness ponies were taken aboard with canvas slings around their bellies. It took three men to hold the furious, nervous and reluctant animal while the sling was put into place, then came the breathless and humiliating elevation—a miniature war charger being hoisted aboard. Arriving at St. Margaret's Hope, commemorating the little Maid of Norway who died on her bridal journey, at five o'clock on a summer's morning:

Pale yellow like flowers
The dawn opened before us,
Stillness lay, breathed softly,
Enclosed us, so that the ship
Stole through the waveless water
Noiseless like an owl
Blinded by the morning.

Little boats hung on the surface
Poised like resting birds
Each with a pale light
Glimmering on the swaying mast.
Gently we slipped like thieves
Into the secret harbour.

Walking the sleeping streets
We could hear the noise of cranes,

244

Hoarse voice, like knives
Tearing the silence into silk;
While behind the walls the sleepers
Alone or arms entwined
Turned at the sound
And covered themselves against the light.

Above the rigging the last star
Fled from the sky behind the islands,
And as the long daylight
Poured in a white flood
Into street and window,
The ship churned up the still water
And pushing the quays and buildings
Into the shimmering distance
Slid slowly into the black caves of Scapa.

One hundred years after the first steamer service the air route to Shetland was opened up, force of circumstances inaugurating the first mail to be sent to the island by air in January, 1937. More than a week of unprecedented gales held all shipping storm-stayed in Shetland. The *St. Ninian*, arriving in Scalloway on the Wednesday, made Aith, struggled back to Scalloway on Saturday where she remained until the following Friday. The *St. Catherine* on her passage north from Aberdeen on the Wednesday was forced to heave to south of Fair Isle and taking 30 hours to the journey lay in Lerwick harbour for 24 hours while a trawler took off her passengers. It was Friday night before she could come near the Victoria pier. For five days she tossed and strained, breaking a succession of hawsers, steaming for most of the time to ease the strain and keep her from being battered against the pier.

The *St. Magnus*, having lain at Kirkwall for four days, finally berthed at the same pier. No ship left the islands for 10 days and when all three finally sailed Aberdeen harbour was closed and the ships were forced to proceed to Leith. By the time the weather had moderated there was no ship available in Aberdeen to take the mails, and the Post Office chartered the first aeroplane to carry letter mail to Shetland on Friday, January 30th.

There are still those who remember the first pioneer of that air service from Dyce, Gandar Dowar; the Rapides, seemingly fragile little flying machines looking as though a gust of wind might blow them apart; the vital concern over each extra pound of weight, occasionally obliged to jettison part of the baggage or even a passenger or two before take-off for the bird-like bumpy flight north.

It seems ironic that a service inaugurated under such circumstances

71   Arriving in Foula by Loganair: about 13 people from the south end of the island have tramped out to the airstrip, constructed by the islanders themselves, to meet the plane. The sole transport, one mini, a motorbike and a small tractor.

should now take second place in reliability of schedule. Since the Second World War the larger and more powerful ships rarely miss a trip. Equipped with radar they are able to get through when the planes are grounded due to fog or crosswinds at Sumburgh, not only one of the worst possible approaches to the islands, the awesome heights of Sumburgh Head and Fitful looming on either wing like Scylla and Charybdis, but the last spot to clear in fog. The Viscounts have never been able to maintain the same regular service as the smaller Heralds which preceded them, not only with a lower ceiling but whose pilots flew the same route day after day, and knew every trick of wind and weather. In an effort to overcome the difficulties of landing, radar tests are being carried out with demonstration equipment which it is hoped will eventually prove effective together with the new longer landing strip.

We enjoy with amazement the arrival of roll-on ferries which now happily replace the old cargo vessels where the sight of a new car winched on board to disappear into the hold among cattle and sheep, dogs and refrigerators, strikes terror into the hearts of visitors, and where "rained off" dockers quaff tea while helpless passengers, impotent without transport, might wait for hours for the unloading. It has yet to be seen how the new transport ships will cope with winter gales.

246

21. *The Northern Capital*

LERWICK, GLIMPSED FROM the deck of the *St. Clair* at five or six o'clock on a midsummer morning, rises from the sea like a Northern Venice, a gigantic film set, its frontage firmly planted in the water that for centuries has washed the massive grey gable ends of its buildings, historic lodberries and tiny slipways. Through a gently-swaying forest of masts and rigging the houses climb like a backcloth, narrow lanes threaded upwards to the high ground, so steeply sloped that some are stepped and most have iron hand-rails to which to cling in icy weather; above them the square tower of the Townhouse is silhouetted against the skyline, all the monstrosities of the south side blessedly invisible.

Brown nets and orange floats sway like an endless kaleidoscope; trawlers and seine netters nose their way to a berth low in the water,

72 Lerwick from the *Earl of Zetland*, the Town Hall on the horizon.

laden with a night's catch, others off to the fishing grounds stringing one by one up the Sound. The street borders the quays with shops and houses less than 100 yards from the ship towering above. Gulls scream, swoop and wheel as boxes of fish are winched ashore; packed tight on roof ridge and gunwale, clinging precariously to flagpole and stem jack, swaying on yellow feet ready for take-off in a whirling greedy snow-storm of white and brown; scattering like leaves before the occasional predatory bonxie, swinging in like a dive bomber to the attack robbing them of their newly-caught meal with consummate ease.

Men in Norwegian and Fair Isle *ganzies* are busily mending nets, yards of silver-scaled lattice work, torn by the teeth of rocky shelves, bitten by the dogfish lurking like hyenas on the edge of the trawl. Boys shovel tinkling ice into buckets to top up boxes being sent to Fraser-burgh or Aberdeen by carrier. Fenders of old rubber tyres separate the close-jammed boats, their names and numbers picked out in an exciting flourish of curlecues in gold-embroidered lettering known generally in Shetland as "variorem", like the decoration on old sewing machines; *The Ocean Reaper*, the *Amethyst, Harvest Gold* and *The Bairns' Pride....*

Gone are the days of the hazardous line fishing from open boats. Today the fishing fleet is an efficient catching unit of diesel engined vessels nearly all built since the Second World War, equipped with echo sounder and radio, radar and television sets, showers and toilets. To the fishing grounds off Shetland's coasts come ships of all nationalities as they have always done, lending a cosmopolitan air to the capital. Lying in the midst of some of the best fishing grounds in the world, the islanders have been strangely content to allow other nations to reap the harvest of her seas and ships of more than a dozen countries fish around the Shetlands, and on her eastern banks, Bressay, Viking and Bergen banks. There are Scottish seine netters of 70 to 80 feet from Peterhead, Fraserburgh and Buckie, leaving their home ports at the beginning of the week, returning to base at weekends. The smaller Scottish boats frequently call at Scalloway and Lerwick in bad weather especially in winter, many of them taking on ice in Lerwick.

Since the development of power block purse-seining in 1965 the Nor-wegian fishing fleet has taken more fish from the Shetland area than any other nation—herring, dogfish, ling and tusk. Denmark has built up a large modern industrial trawl fishery, herring taken off the Danish coast and blue whiting and sand eel west of Orkney and Shetland, operating from the south-east of Bressay to the Continental shelf edge, south-west of Foula.

The days when Shetland herring were exported to the Baltic ports are over. In the 1950's the U.S.S.R. began to appear, operating trawlers and drifters about 130 feet long and coming from Kaliningrad or Murmansk. Fishing in flotillas of catching, processing and service vessels, the industry is highly mechanised and supply tankers buy large quantities of water from Shetland every year. In spring the fleet can be seen standing out north-east of Foula and off Fair Isle in the autumn, supported by the mother ship, a factory processing unit of 17,000 tons.

Lerwick's harbour visitors come from Germany, Poland, East Germany, France, Belgium and even Israel. Of the fish, caught by Norwegians, Russians, Scots and English together with all other foreign nationalities, a conservative estimate of the share taken by Shetland vessels would be less than five per cent.

Backstage, however, Lerwick's southern aspect faces the visitor who arrives by air, and it must be one of the most depressing sights in the whole of the islands. Certainly Lerwick houses roughly one-third of Shetland's population of about 18,000, but was it necessary even in the beginning to erect the grim rows of council houses across the road from the town's rubbish dump. No doubt one day the rising generation will be able to play tennis and picnic in a park built out of layers of tin cans, dead dogs and plastic containers, but for years rats and gulls have fought each other day in day out for scraps alongside a street where children play, and gates are perpetually open for animals to do their own scavenging.

Not content with these atrocities, in an age when towns *can* be planned, Lerwick is spreading out to Sandvein and Sound in a haphazard maze of concrete housing estates, looking more like some vast factory complex composed entirely of ventilation shafts and as far removed from the architectural charm of old Lerwick as it is possible to be. Some years ago a tiny scheme hidden away near Queen's Lane, received a Saltire Award. One wishes that there could also be available some public Black Mark for the newest schemes.

Thomas Manson, well in advance of his time, commented in his book *Lerwick During the Last Half Century*, first published in 1923, on the "deplorable lack of planning by the Feuars and Heritors of the town" with workshops and stores and gasometers littering the shore area. "Why should such erections", he asked, "be planted at the very throat or entrance to the town?"

Today, Richard Gibson, now an independent and imaginative young architect working in Lerwick, proposes "that every effort should be made to use derelict or under-used property; that a policy encouraging the use of vacant land within the town be introduced, even on the basis of building single houses and that an effort is made to integrate the new housing into the old herring stations along the north shore ..."

What is apparently not appreciated by any builders in Shetland is

249

73   From the Town Hall tower looking across to Bressay and one of the world's finest natural harbours. On the eastward side of the Steamer Stores lies the *St. Clair*, the passenger and cargo vessel plying twice weekly between Lerwick and Aberdeen. while on the near side of Victoria Pier the *Earl of Zetland* lies at anchor, the steamer once serving the North Isles. The roof on the right is the new swimming pool, an uncomprising concrete anachronism in the midst of so much dignity and history. To the right of the *St. Clair* is the small boat harbour into which the Bressay ferry comes and full of locally owned sailing boats.

that it is impossible to camouflage new erections, hiding them with trees as might be possible in the south and landscaping estates with green areas planted with flowering shrubs. Everything that is put up stands out stark and naked, frequently ruining views of surpassing beauty. The Civic Society protests, individuals complain, but they appear merely as faint voices crying in the wilderness. The transformation of Lerwick even in the last 50 years has been inconceivable; what it would look like to the Rev. George Low, who came to Shetland in 1774, one cannot imagine.

Sailing up Bressay Sound he remarked on 400 vessels lying in the harbour, about 200 Dutch, the remainder Danes, Prussians, French

250

and Ostenders with two English, one Scots and one local boat. Lerwick he describes as "a small, irregularly built village" containing about 140 families. In Dr. Cowie's day the "country village or *toun* of Sound was a mile and a half from Lerwick, supplying milk and peats to the capital". Overcrowding in Lerwick itself even then seems to have been remarkable for "among the lower orders the dwelling of each family consists of one room ... 10 to 12 feet square and seldom more than 7 feet high, and in addition to a family of from 5 to 10 people, there are two or three lodgers. Tenements constitute lodging houses for sailors and 'the peasantry' from the surrounding districts. These one-roomed lodging houses are generally much more overcrowded than the ordinary family dwellings although this can scarcely be credited." The astonishing good health of the citizens is attributed by Dr. Cowie to the fresh air and exercise involved in kishieing peats from the Staney Hill, about two miles from the town, although Cowie added that typhus was not unknown.

In 1762 Lerwick was largely occupied by merchant landowners exporting ling, tusk, cod, oil, hides, beef and mutton, woollen stockings, caps and rugs and importing groceries for exchange or sale, with a nice sideline in good Hollands gin and Hamburg brandy. The Day Book of a merchant of that year is crammed with sidelights on all the worthies of the day, their petty debts, illicit transactions and various addictions. "Twenty ankers of gin landed at Cruister of which 5 pints or thereby was delivered to Anne Gray and two taken this day to Hogan with 2 boxes Tobacco and 1 to ye house." A regular trade was carried on with a Captain de Munich and a Captain Boyson, the one specialising in gin and the other in Hamburg brandy. There was little stigma attached to the smuggling trade, the entire islands entering into the spirit of the game and delighting in evading the Customs in every possible way.

Faroe brandy was brought back by the fishermen and Captain McKinnon of the Revenue Cutter *Eagle* had his work cut out to come upon smugglers unawares in the long nights of the simmer-dim. One foggy night the captain cunningly concealed the cutter behind one of the islands and took off in his gig. The smuggler fishermen just had time to tumble a big sack of tobacco overboard and when the captain boarded the vessel the scuppers were awash with brandy while a man below was still staving in the remaining casks. One of the best-known characters, nicknamed "Preaching Peter", had worked out a splendid way of disposing of his illicit liquor. When he returned from Faroe with a goodly supply he sent round handbills which were distributed throughout the islands announcing his arrival and the dates on which he would be preaching at various centres. "After he had much prayed and much preached, he gave the benediction, the signal for all who knew the ropes to gather round. Orders were taken and both the needs of the flesh and the spirit satisfied."

As soon as the government imposed a duty on goods smuggling was the result. Shetland, far from the seat of officialdom and constantly frequented by foreign fishers, had always been a smuggler's paradise, only a fraction of the goods ever being detected. An unusual haul, however, was made by the Customs in two days in 1885 from Dutch vessels consisting of: tobacco over 2000 lbs: Geneva Rum, Liqueur Brandy, Perfume, Spirits, Dutch Drops and Riga Balsam, Bitters and Eau de Cologne.

The well-known *Sibella*, bringing a cargo from Hamburg in 1752, listed in her Customs returns: "salt, lines, iron and tar" but she also carried other delicacies such as corn brandy—used at the haaf fishing— French claret, cognac and a large variety of wines including Rhenish, all of which made up half the cargo valued at £6,000 Scots (£500 sterling). Even the Customs House itself was not above shady dealings and smuggling became almost a full-time business. A few were actually caught *in flagrante delicto* but there were many who managed to evade retribution. Later the landowners left the smuggling to merchants who appear to have been extraordinarily efficient, between 1790 and 1820 bringing in not only tobacco, spirits and tea, but also timber from Bergen and Christiansund. A sloop would land at Lerwick, be cleared by the Customs for Norway and then make for Holland where she loaded gin and tobacco, later to be put ashore at some well-concealed cove in Unst or Foula. Towards the end of the Napoleonic wars every leading merchant in Lerwick was "in the trade".

The old lodberries, of course, played a vital part in the landing and concealment of illicit cargoes and many a cask would be quietly flitted in at dead of night alongside these slips with steps and a door opening into an open court or cellar where boats drew in, passages under the street leading to subterranean store-rooms with secret cupboards, recesses in ceilings and tunnels from house to house which still lie concealed on the hillsides. Eight old smugglers' caves lie under Commercial Street alone. Murray's Hol was a well-known haunt where a joiner had his workshop. A smuggler escaped one night up the passage under part of the Queen's Hotel, below Scott's Hall Court and opening out to the South Kirk Close. Chased by preventive officers armed with revolvers, he squeezed his way along the dark tunnel, the home of rats and wild cats. In the planning and building of houses near the sea the citizens of Lerwick invariably made for the safe disposal of anything dutiable.

In those days the street, or shore, was a mere pathway running along the line of what is now Commercial Street. From the rock at the

Widows' Homes steep banks continued along the foreshore and a beach covered the site of the Market Cross. From this point the beach meandered northwards to the steep shelving banks below the Fort. Down Mounthooly Street ran a burn entering the sea at a slight dip just north of the present pillar of the Cross. Later it was known as "Miss Heddell's Burn" which could be jumped across by the more agile, or in heavy weather traversed on a plank from bank to bank. Within the southern arm the cliff line curved in between Stout's Pier and the Old Tolbooth. In this smaller bight are two beaches known now as Bain's Beach and Craigie's Stane.

Above the sea front the ground climbs towards the Knab and north Hillhead with the valley of Mounthooly Street between them and in the houses fronting the sea from Leog to the Fort lived about 700 people. One of the ancient landmarks now demolished was Twagios House, a kind of farmhouse haa' of 10 rooms on three flats with walls six feet thick. The great kitchen with its flagged floor had a spit for roasting whole animals with a "gravy pit" let into the hearthstone. There was a dairy, peat and coal store and a wash-house bathroom with a great copper boiler, plunge bath and its own water supply from a well beneath the floor. Occupied latterly by Ronnie Sill, the house had already become the nucleus of the Shetland Folk Lore Society and Mr. Sill tells of many curious experiences of mysterious footsteps, knocking on doors and airs played on a fiddle; of bells ringing and a dog which suddenly became frantic with fear, and bolted for home taking refuge under a bed where it lay whimpering for several hours before it could be persuaded to leave its hiding place.

In the Day Book nothing is hidden. All the small peccadilloes, debts, indulgences are carefully recorded. The Truck System is apparent in the excerpt: "To Ursilla Malcolms dr. 2 Bottles Wine, 2 oz sugar and 3 Doses Bark qr. upon Recd a Ewe from her Husband and promises of a beast next year."

The Old Manse in South Commercial Street must be at least 230 years old and the space of the north courtyard was once occupied by a two-storey house; next to this is the building which still stands with its gable end opposite Gellie's Pier. The only real pier in the town at that time besides Patrick Torry's pier was the Cockstool Rock which lay straight in front of where the steps now lead down to the Esplanade at the end of the Old Post Office, and round about this part lies the nucleus of old Lerwick. Where the present Masonic Hall stands, the land was known as Bullister—*Bolla Saetr*, a homestead dating from Viking times. The Market Cross was all beach and rubbish, with boats drawn up, stormy seas lashing the edge of the houses and slapping against the gable of what is now known as "R & C's" the grocer's shop, the old part of which, built in 1690, was at that time the Royal Dutch Hospital.

The crofters of Sound, a udal settlement before Lerwick existed, were of ancient stock; Laurence Erasmuson in Trebister; Malcolm Halcrow in Shurton, Margaret Johnsdaughter in Trebister and Adam White in Vatsland, to mention only a few. They cast their peats on the Staney Hill at Holmsgarth, skippered boats to the ling fishing, warded sheep and cattle in the scattald, giving kishies in return for flails and receiving meal and tobacco for their hard-won fish. In the old Day Book we can trace their economic problems, every detail faithfully recorded and the lean years see James Smith borrowing "a pint of Oyl" for his kolli, its light desperately needed in those dark February days and in spring before the outdoor work had begun he was forced to borrow 30 shillings Scots to pay the Scat.

The Anderson Institute built in 1862, the gift of Arthur Anderson, is mentioned by Mr. Manson as being notable for the fact that the Twageos Parks where old Dr. Spence's cows once chewed the cud "is now a rudely yawning chasm where water and sewage pipes are being laid to drain the Institute and villas are to be built above it ..."

The Widows' Homes, also a gift from Arthur Anderson, where Miss Annie Manson was once matron, was opened in 1865 and is now converted into a block of nine flats, near it the Smiddy on the Knowe where bare-armed smiths hammered horseshoes into shape. In 1867 Upper Leog was fresh and the new Lower Leog denuded of its upper storey, but a fine modern roadway ran from below to the paved street with its concrete sea wall. Visitors strolling below the charming little houses for elderly people living alone, can still lean over Gellie's Pier and admire the Old Manse above, now the home of Mr. Tom Henderson, curator of the County Museum, whose hotel at Spiggie will long be remembered with affection by all who frequented it.

Opposite Ross Court was a gig hirer, one of the first to have such a conveyance in Lerwick, above it Kveldsro House and Quendale House built in 1865. Bailie Robertson's old shop high up on a rocky point overlooking Bressay Sound was occupied by Fred Irvine, R.S.A. Queen's Lane, or North Kirk Close, as it was called, is the only lane wide enough to take a single car and until recently was still in use. Ascending or descending was inevitably a hazardous business, hoping against hope that one might not suddenly encounter a vehicle coming the other way. It led to the Free Masons Hall, to St. Olaf's the Parish and St. Magnus churches, to Lovers Lon and the Knab. At the time of its erection the Market Cross was without Anderson's shop and at that time was the narrowest part of the street, so that even an ordinary country cart could scarcely negotiate its passage.

254

The Cross itself still stands but the old pump has gone, likewise the elegant lamp standard now removed to Victoria pier. Here the people would gather with their *dafficks* to fill them with water and exchange the latest gossip of the town. Dutch Fadders and Kleine Youngish were tormented by the children for "a prime o tabak" which the boys smoked with a mixture of Dutch "hurl", tea leaves, dried "dottles" and a bit of twist if they were lucky. British Naval vessels were frequently in harbour and there would be dancing and singing to the strains of a melodeon or concertina; round the Cross "packies" and cheapjacks sold their wares to sailors grown generous with spirits. There was a hurdy gurdy, an Italian complete with monkey playing "The Anguish of my Heart"; Jeems Williamson and Blind Mansie "lashing away at the fiddle", his wife bringing him to plant him on a seat at the Cross where he would play for hours "The sailor ower da Rough Tree"; "Ahint da Daeks o Voe" and other Shetland reels. Today "the Cross" is still a landmark, "Meet you at the Market Cross" a recognised and easily-found centre and no New Year's Eve is celebrated unless there is dancing and singing, arms linked in a great circle round the Cross at midnight.

The late "Goudie and Son, Ironmongers" was one of the oldest businesses in Lerwick, established in 1821, and continued in the same family, like many more of Lerwick's establishments, for over 100 years. The present Union Bank buildings were erected to replace those burned down in 1903 but in 1867 another fire broke out on a Sunday evening

74 The old Union Bank of Scotland's buildings demolished by fire in 1903—ironically advertising in its one remaining window "Fire Insurance". (The late Mrs. Abernethy's Collection via Jack Keddie.)

during church hours in the premises of Mr. Dalziel, grocer, whose cellar was stored with a barrel of gunpowder, paraffin, linseed oil and other highly explosive and inflammable matter. Hoses were unknown, for the waters of the Sandy Loch had not been piped into the town at that time, and buckets of water had to be fetched from the sea, wells and pumps, and handed from one person to another.

As the news spread, citizens poured out from church or Sunday bed, leaving ministers preaching to empty pews, and everyone lent a hand to move goods and household effects to safety. It must have been quite a blaze for one Mary Norrie who lived near the foot of the Steep Close, quite lost her head and rushed out of her house in the scantiest of clothing, up the lane and into the *yatts* crying at the pitch of her voice: "Da last day is come, da last day is come, fly ta da mountains! Fly ta da mountains!"

Lerwick grew over the years, but 100 years ago there was still no water supply, no New Town, no Esplanade and the only street was Commercial Street. From Prospect House west to Burgh Road cattle, sheep and pigs grazed. From Hay & Company to the North Ness was a pebbly beach except for the various lodberries, Morrison's Pier and a few stone jetties. To a Mr. Harrison at North Ness goes the credit for opening up a new market for halibut, the import of ice from Norway and the chartering of a special steamer. Before that an enterprising fisherman, having secured a halibut in his catch, informed the inhabitants by bell of his intention to sell and proceeded to cut it up retailing it at 1½d per lb. "Now", says Mr. Manson in 1923, "the citizens of Lerwick actually survive the shock of being asked to pay 9d a pound for haddocks ... all I can say just now is that the present price of fish is diabolical ..."

At the Freefield Well and pump, before the water supply reached Lerwick, people sat up all night to get as much water as would make a cup of tea. It was a regular sight in summer to see the Baker's Close packed halfway down with people waiting their turn from early morning till late at night for the clear icy water. Every household had its *dafficks*, wooden pails and wooden "girds" carried on the shoulder, a pail depending from each end. Women took their knitting and gossiped while they waited their turn. Every now and then the well would run dry and a *peerie* keg which a boy could carry on his shoulder was used and the child sent off to the Ness of Sound or Gremista. Visits even had to be made to Bressay when all the public and private wells gave out. When a big washing had to be done all the family with tubs and *sayes* and *dafficks* tramped out to the loch of Clickhimin, the children having a holiday from school, *japplin* in the tubs to wash the blankets with their bare feet under the shadow of the old broch.

256

The Grand Hotel has arisen from the old building known as "Stoot's Hoose". Some of the old walls still remain and at the south end Mr. Leask had his business, the principal shipping agent in town, with considerable interest in the Greenland vessels. His office was so often packed with men waiting to sign on that the steps at the foot of Pitt Lane were packed; so were the stairs leading to the drapery and clothing establishment, the shop itself and the inside office. Below were licensed premises where a steady business was done with otter skins purchased as a side line. Leask who owned docks at Garthspool, was a large smack owner with fishcuring, chandlery and sailmaking businesses. Although proprietor of the estates of Seafield and Sand and with a property in West Yell he was a considerate landlord and firmly opposed to evicting his tenants to make way for sheep.

The Medical Hall diagonally opposite has a long association with medicine. In Manson's young days a Dr. Petrus Loeterbagh kept the shop. Dr. Petrus Dorotheus Loeterbagh was a ship surgeon belonging to Dordrecht who as surgeon of the convoy which accompanied Dutch vessels to the island regularly visited Lerwick in the late 1850's and 60's. In the block of houses known as Charlotte's Place the north chimneys are secured by iron stanchions, a precaution necessary owing to the vibration caused by the firing of guns at the Fort until the battery was removed to the North Ness.

It is a pity that Fort Charlotte has not been better preserved—one of the finest views of Lerwick can be had from its ramparts.

The road below Fort Charlotte was at one time a narrow dangerous track, the embankment running steeply down to Sinclair's Beach below and only after the mail gig fell over was a wooden paling erected. The gasometers which were such an eyesore to Mr Manson were erected in 1856 and from the gas works would be filched a cask or two of tar which was set alight and dragged through the streets by guizers with blackened faces around Christmas time, the precursor of the festival of Up Hella Aa'.

Perhaps the real spirit of old Lerwick is still at its best in the old narrow lanes, hopefully to be preserved. In a house at the foot of Water Lane (recently demolished) Bothwell, consort of Mary, Queen of Scots, took refuge. Some of the oldest include Law Lane, Tait's Close and Park Lane, Pitt Lane, Fox Lane, Pilot Lane, Burns Lane and Hill Lane where famous characters spun yarns of the whaling in the Davis Straits when every man would sit with his oar drawn across the boat, tightly grasped ready to spring should the boat be drawn under the ice by the harpooned whale. There was Jerome Anderson, a Fetlar man who went to the Californian gold diggings and to Sacramento to the salmon fishing; Daa Binnie, Robbie Snuddie, and Joanie o Muckligirt who

75 Law Lane, Lerwick, with steps leading up between the houses climbing steeply from the main street and a little barefoot girl carrying her milk can in the foreground. First World War period. (Zetland County Library and Museum.)

never referred to the death of a person or animal—he or she just "gude away". In 1885 Captain Adams of the *Maud* brought back an Eskimo who sat with him on the platform when the Captain lectured on Arctic life. Although the weather was cold the poor Eskimo sat through the performance in "a lock o sweat". Larger than life, their endearing eccentricities, their ebullient personalities, haunt the ancient lanes they made their own.

In spite of all the changes, the lost character and more strange faces on the street every week, some of the atmosphere of old Lerwick still survives and every January in place of the old tar barrels from the gasometers a splendid new Viking galley is built for Up Helly Aa', and

258

something of the soul of Lerwick is briefly resurrected for one night in the year. On a fine winter's night with a brittle sprinkling of frost, the procession starts off from the Town Hall, torches flaming, led by the galley and the Guizer Jarl's squad in elaborate and authentic Viking costume.

In 1974 the Guizer Jarl elected to represent King Magnus the Good who apparently succeeded in projecting an unusually virtuous Viking image, ruling over Norway for 12 years and Denmark for five before he died. Born to St. Olaf by his *frilla* Alfhild at Yaroslav's court in Russia he was named after Charlemagne—Karla Magnus; good he may have been, brave he certainly was, his major battle fought without his coat of mail, clad only in a kirtle of red silk, swinging the battle axe Hel which had been St. Olaf's own, leaving 15,000 Wendish corpses strewn on the field. He was proclaimed king at the Viborg Thing and ruled over two kingdoms after the death of Hordakanut. His kingdom was true to tradition and the times in which he lived. He died "of accident or sickness, by land or water in Jutland or Zeland in the autumn of 1047".

His re-incarnation in Lerwick in 1974 was a memorable one. Resplendent in purple cloak over silver mail, a black tunic caught by silver clasps (designed by himself as Art Master at the Anderson Institute) Guizer Jarl James Kerr could well have been the young Magnus, for one night a Viking tried in battle, surrounded by his lesser jarls in black cloaks lined with white, fur-trimmed scarlet tunics, brandishing aloft like their leader battle-axes, imbued in imagination at least, with the blood lust of their ancestors.

After a spectacular and rousing march through the town dragging the dragon-headed galley, a replica of reality from prow to stern, the long winding trail of torches twin columns of fire and smoke, singing the Up Helly Aa' song, a modern composition but well calculated to stir the blood already laced with a spirit no less fiery than the fury that roused the lusty crews arriving west-over-sea so long ago, the entire procession ends up in the traditional burning in the town's park. Singing The Galley Song—"Floats the raven banner o'er us Round our Dragon Ship we stand"—based on a traditional Norse tune, the torches wind and flicker snake-like round the swan-necked prow then at a given signal the burning brands are thrown in arcs of flame into the lovely ship, setting it alight. The rigging, the dragon prow, the entire beautifully constructed vessel, suddenly bursts a-fire; sparks like shooting stars fly upwards, a raven headdress etched briefly against the glow, the smell of pitch, the shouting and the excitement all providing a brilliant, unforgettable re-enactment of a Norse burial ship.

Then the heroic figures come down to earth, hurrying into buses, each squad to perform their burlesque acts around the halls and hotels of Lerwick where hostesses arrange a seemingly unending feast of soups, sandwiches, cakes and coffee for those who have been lucky enough to be offered tickets and for the hundred or so squads accompanying the Guizer Jarl and his men. Each group represents some aspect of Shetland life, skits on well-known public figures, topical events, in a motley troop of grotesque stumbling Teddy Bears; divers with bottles cunningly concealed in the oxygen flasks strapped to their backs; hefty fishermen shrugged into miniskirts, close-shaven cheeks simpering under wild blonde wigs; Spanish dancers in tight-bottomed flared trousers, clicking heels in an enthusiastic if doubtfully authentic *zapateado* around a male Gypsy Rose Lee undulating awkwardly in false bosom and whirling petticoats; a strip act that brought the house down with a muscular young Shetlander in suspender belt, black stockings and bra continually and selfconsciously hitched upwards; brilliantly executed musical numbers; a confrontation between Heath and Nixon; and pseudo Shetland crofters, shawls clutched close over long black skirts, the men shouldering tushkars and Shetland spades capering with painfully life-like arthritic movements, their faces ancient and repellent in skin tight masks, wrinkled, lascivious, grey locks circling bald heads incongruous above the patently virile if momentarily bent young bodies.

It is almost as difficult to find a berth on the ship to Lerwick or a bed for the night of Up Helly Aa' as it is to get a ticket for the World Cup and the entire country is hurled into a night of riotous enjoyment until the pale dawn sees the last stragglers picking their way unevenly through the deserted morning streets.

It is all a spectacle on the grand scale, wild, warm, uninhibited, a crazy fiesta of half-play, half-nostalgia, when old and young, to infants set on their fathers' shoulders, turn out to see the procession. Even the schoolchildren have their own small galley made by themselves, their own imitation Up Helly Aa', a strange Walpurgis night with a re-awakening of old Norse ties, wholly spurious, or wholly entrancing whichever way one looks at it, but wholly Shetlandic.

22. *Pattern of Islands*

THERE IS A distinctively deceptive appearance about the map of Shetland. You might imagine that it consists of three major islands, Mainland, Yell and Unst. Bus services, ferries and steamers ply between them. You can leave the south of Mainland early in the morning, take a car across the sounds on two ferries, stand on the wind-scarred platform of Hermaness and look down on the hog's back of Rumblings, Tipta Skerry, Little Flugga and Muckle Flugga, with Britain's most northerly lighthouse crowning its highest point. A short way out, north and slightly east lies the Out Stack, Oetsta, beyond that nothing but ocean between it and the Polar Mass. Later, re-crossing the sound from Belmont to Gutcher, you drive south in a long loop round Basta Voe, over Yell's loch-spattered brown landscape crouched over its great bed of peat to Ulsta and that night you can sleep again within sight of Sumburgh Head.

But south, east and west are other islands. No two are the same, these outlying holms thrown off Mainland, carelessly floating like scraps of torn paper on the Atlantic or North Sea. No matter how isolated, how awkward of access, how small, each has its own individual quality

76   The *Grima* alongside the landing stage at Toft on Mainland. Cars roll on and off within seconds for the 20 minute trip to Ulsta in Yell. Designed in Faroe it so happens that alongside her is lying the *Munkur* from Torshavn.

of life that can be found nowhere else. The slender thread that binds
their children to them stretches out over the years in space and time
like a natal cord, an emotional and physical link seldom expressed,
rarely understood by even the Mainland Shetlander, and only occasionally put into words like those of George Peterson, poet, teacher,
scholar and native of Papa Stour:

Oh my hert's awa hame,
Awa ower da sea!
My hert's awa hame,
Dear Papa, in dee!
Regairdless o saeson,
Fool wadder or fine—
Wharever I am
Aald Papa, I'm dine!

Whin da grun swell packs
Da caves wi a 'Boom'!
An Skarvie Head smoors
In a moorie o skoom;
Whin da sky meets da Erd
An whin Winter's mad ree
Rips aff da lum cans,—
Aald Isle, I see dee!

An whin Voar comes alang
Wi a ree an a brak,
Or a pretty still nicht
Whin da fish winna tak;
An da heddery fire glöds
Maks strips ower da sea—
Dan I tink i my mind,
Aald Papa, o dee!

An dan whin da Simmer
Melts tar po da röf
An aff i da Bist
Lies a shirk i da skröf;
An da simmer mirr shimmers
Ower knowe an by shore—
Dan I lang ta be hame,
In Papa wance more!

Whin da Hairst mön ower Saaness
Lift her muckle red face—

An da ekkered corn stands
Laek folk sayin grace;
Whin da wadder is coorse
An der puddins an brö—
Dan oh! ta be hame,
Whit wad I no dö!

Neddersheens and Klinkhammer
An deep Bennie Gio
Da Leowds an da Braesdelds
An lee Culla Voe;
Regairdless o saeson,
Fool wadder or fine—
Wharever I am,
Aald Papa, I'm dine!

A tearing channel of green silk and a small boat with a cargo of paraffin, coal, fencing posts, flour and meal, "wives fae Lerrick" with their shopping, a child, a calf, all stowed with the forethought of years, rides the swell in a canter out by the Holm of Melby, taking the wide tideway of the Sound of Papa. Slit eyes and weather-brown faces watch with the bright calculation of a hawk the flood tide running south towards Watsness and the ebb north into St. Magnus Bay, meeting in a streak of white froth, knowing just where to strike, feeling the boat's trim like wings.

Skerries split the röst, the dark stacks of Brei Holm and the Maiden Stack, a chimney of rock looming giddily over the torn seas; cormorants in a black frieze drying their wings like bats on brown tilted slabs, listening unafraid to the small noise of the *Venture's* engine, puttering above the crack of wave shipping the reefs. Puffins scutter across the water; seals lean lazily against the lifting sea. With an instinctive caution like a man guiding a ploughshare, his eyes set on the Pass, the narrow boiling channel that skirts the underwater reef of Staacka Baa, the skipper waits for the moment, holding back the quivering boat, a sea horse, impatient, until the "full ahead" signal and the calculated sprint into the bight of Housa Voe.

It might be a journey to any of Shetland's islands; Whalsay, Fetlar, the Skerries, Fair Isle or Foula, Vaila or Bressay each separated by its own peculiar tideway, few with more than one safe anchorage. The *Good Shepherd* fights its way through Sumburgh Röst to Fair Isle's deep water pier at North Haven; the Foula mailboat bringing out a cargo of lambs is waited for at Walls, taking in everything from seed potatoes to Bobbie Isbister's new tractor, its landing at Ham Voe the most

263

dangerous of all. In the old days lines were often stretched across the narrow voe to drag her in; oil was sometimes poured on the water, and more than once the islanders rushed into the boiling seas to save their one link with the mainland. Now winched up after every trip, hauled back on a cable secure in her concrete noost, she is only lowered when it is sure that the weather will allow her to take off.

The twentieth century has brought airstrips to almost all the outlying islands, practical if rough, bulldozed out of the bare moors, providing a lifeline or an escape route, whichever way you care to look at it. The Loganair pilots who fly in and out in anything but the very worst weather are very angels of mercy, but somehow one never quite knows what might descend out of the skies. Aeroplanes are for people in a hurry. But the plane is a measure of security, an exciting means of acquiring vital supplies, a bonus from the sky. There are scheduled twice-daily flights to Unst by Tingwall, Yell and maybe Fetlar, but when someone hires a plane to come into Foula, like a bush telegraph the news gets round and the lines are buzzing with orders for groceries, spare parts, knitting wool, medicines and perhaps a few precious bottles for celebrations and emergencies.

One of the saddest things about islands, is the imminent spectre of depopulation. Islands die like people and however remotely related the tragedy is unforgettable. Even on the tiny island of Havera off Maywick on the west side, which once boasted the only windmill in Shetland, nearly 30 people sustained some kind of life on its few acres until the 1920's. It had to come to an end; the miracle was that it lasted so long. The cliffs are so dangerously steep that small children had to be tethered like animals lest they fall over. There was no electricity or running water, and yet it was home for hundreds of years; even having a school where one of the Goudie's from Geosetter taught for some time.

Fair Isle was literally saved by its birds. In 1796 in spite of the small-pox epidemic 100 years before, the population had grown to 221 and by 1860 the number had risen to well over 300, far more than the island could possibly support. Their plight was pitiful and in 1862 assisted passages were provided for as many people as wished to emigrate to Nova Scotia and New Brunswick. One hundred and thirty eight persons left Fair Isle at one time, more than one-third of that small and closely knit community. For Fair Isle it was one of the darkest days in its history.

Over the last 50 years numbers dwindled and apart from lighthouse keepers and their families barely 40 now live on the island, its survival made possible by its 3000 species of migratory birds. In 1948 George Waterston bought Fair Isle from Robert Bruce of Sumburgh and the bird observatory, planned by George and a young Edinburgh lawyer, Ian Pitman, fellow prisoners in Crete, came into being. Eventually handed over to the National Trust, the Fair Isle Bird Observatory became the leader of its kind in western Europe. In 1958 a deep water pier was constructed at a cost of £9000 borne between the National Trust for Scotland and the Zetland County Council. Each summer the hostel is full. There have been incomers to the island, the lighthouses must continue to be manned and its future is assured.

Papa Stour on the other hand, only two miles from Mainland, narrowly escaped having its Post Office removed within the last year or so, inevitably the final stroke that signs an island's death warrant. In 1901 there were 270 people on Papa and 50 years later only 69. After the First World War many of the crofts were put down to grass and by 1958 only 30 out of the 170 acres of croft land were cultivated. Between the wars the population dwindled as the younger generation sought employment elsewhere and the Education Act depleted it still further when in 1944 compulsory education drew the teenagers out to the town and the Anderson Institute. Communications were difficult and few returned. Papa Stour and Foula were the two islands which up to 1937 remained without either telegraphic or telephonic communication with the mainland of Shetland. In the case of Papa Stour several dramatic incidents occurred when the doctor and nurse had to be signalled for with a Morse lamp and landed with great difficulty by the Aith lifeboat. The radio telephone link was established in 1938 and a pier built by the Board of Agriculture in 1939. Unfortunately, like Fair Isle's first pier, it was useless except at high water, for at the ebb it was almost completely dry and the war stifled all cries for an extension.

Finally between the County Council and the Council of Social Service, a new pier was built and the island got its first piped water supply. A ferry boat, designed by a Papa Stour man, John Jamieson, and built in Orkney, arrived in the island in 1963. Although these amenities saved the island for the time being, they seemed to have come 50 years too late. The school was closed. The missionary and his wife, the teacher on the island, had moved out to Fair Isle and in 1973 there were only 15 or 16 of the native population left.

Coastguard Willie Tulloch who also runs the island's post office, realised that if the post office went the mail contract would also go, and John Jamieson who ran the mail boat would lose a good part of his living. Several crofts on the island were owned by absentee landlords and Willie, on enquiry found that it was possible for the Crofters' Commission to dispossess them and hand over the crofts to newcomers. He broadcast as widely as he could the fact that immigrants would be welcome and then sat back and waited. In the end after some considerable coming and going four young couples settled on the island.

77   Fishing boats, Scalloway.

At first no one imagined that they would stay. They had few possessions and no idea of crofting life, far less life on an island. Not even
Captain Marryat's young settlers in Canada could have faced a more
unfamiliar or gruelling existence, but unlike the Campbells the
McCarth's, the Colemans' the Tarrants and the Staggs had willing
'native' inhabitants to help. Without their unending hospitality,
generosity and constant advice, few of these young city folk could have
survived. That they have now lived through three summers and two
winters is due partly to their own determination and courage, their
willingness to learn and the truly wonderful help they received from
the islanders.

The Highland and Islands Development Board gave the Colemans
a grant to buy a small lobster boat. The islanders presented the incomers with a flock of 40 sheep, farming tools, and saw them safely
through the lambing season. The newcomers on their side helped in
every way they could even to assisting in the annual dirty job of carrying
up the winter's supply of coal, for there is no peat on the island. Some
of them have begun a market garden and they have now their own
goats. When they arrived they had three children between them and
since coming to live on Papa another four have been added, the last
born on the island, but not, according to one national newspaper, the
first child to be born on Papa Stour for 80 years! Alex Johnson, the
reviver of the Papa Stour Sword Dance was born on the island and
as J.P. he registered several births during his stay on the island. A new
telephone exchange has been installed; there are now nearly 40 people
on the island and the school has been re-opened. From a dying island
new life has sprung into being.

Foula, edge of the world, the most westerly of all the Shetland islands,
is easily the most isolated, the most difficult of access and with the fewest

266

amenities. One hundred miles north-east of the Orkneys, a little further north than Cape Farewell, its 4000 acres tower out of the naked sea, emerging through cloud in summer with the sun strong on its contours like a sculpted monument of rock dominating the skyline. Looking across from St. Ninian's Isle its immense heights swoop upwards from the Atlantic astride the horizon's edge, between it and us a trawler battling back from the Foula Banks, tiny like a child's toy.

In winter, brushed with snow, standing out to sea, bright, glittering like a giant iceberg, it scarcely seems 22 miles across the water. At its southern tip the Noup rises up to 800 feet, dropping down into the long valley of the Daal slicing through the island from east to west. Then the silhouette tilts up magnificently into the shoulder of Hamnafjeld, riddled with sheep gaets and scree, rising 1000 feet in half a mile from the still pool of the Mill Loch, ringed with gold-brown Foula sheep moving just a shade lighter than the surrounding moorland. Beyond Hamnafjeld and westerly the Sneug shoots up to 1369 feet to tumble down and soar again in the green ridge of Soberlie and Logat Head. At the north eastern corner the ground falls again to the rocky promontory of Stremness and on the west side is the second highest sheer cliff in Britain, the Kame, only 25 feet less than St. Kilda.

Above Fughley Isle, Bird Island, the sky is alight with the white flickering shapes of tirricks whirling like grain kernels flung upwards from the flail against a vast ceiling of duck egg blue. And all around

78 Stewart with guillemot exhausted by the storms.

bare land, a land only for sheep and birds. The black scalped moors ring to the wild keening of the Alans: "Keeeelaaaa ... keeeeelaaaaa!" ... with claws outstretched the feathered bellies flash past above you, each individual talon too near for comfort and infinitely more ferocious than their larger unwieldy cousins the Bonxies. Boldly the Alans nest on either side of the one rough, corn-coloured road, now being tarred for the first time in its history, invading the empty crofts all along the flat eastern coastline.

Perhaps one might describe the island and all that it implies as an anachronism in this twentieth century of moonwalks and satellites, of oil spouting from the North Sea, electronics and push-button living. Obstinately however, in spite of all predictions made by historians through the centuries, with irritating repetition and the greatest conviction that the island was on the brink of dissolution, Foula's surviving inhabitants cling tenaciously to their scattered crofts, the majority convinced that some miracle will belie all the gloomy forecasts about their "dying island". So strongly are they attached to Foula, and in spite of the fact that within the last 100 years the population has dwindled from 149 in 1921 to 30 in 1974, with only seven under the age of 50, one is inclined to agree with them. Tudor, reporting in 1883, said that only four women not natives of Foula had married into the island for over 40 years. Even the ravages of the smallpox epidemics at the beginning of the eighteenth century, when Foula was hardest hit of all by "the Muckle Fever" which left a handful of six alive to bury the dead, have not killed Foula.

There are now eight families on the island, their crofts strung out from Hametoun in the south to Ham around the tiny harbour and Burns; the crofts in the north long abandoned—Springs, Freyars, Logat, Soberlie and Wilse. Only the nurse, the minister and perhaps two other dwellings have electricity provided by generators. In summer a group of young people from the Brathay Exploration group in Cumberland arrive to stay at Ristie, the small croft in the north which they have modernised over the years, boys and girls alike known as "The Brathay Boys", infusing for a little time a breath of life and youth into the community. Engaged enthusiastically in bird counts and ecological surveys they have an organised programme of yearly field studies embracing many aspects of biology and geography. Ornithology is a major study and experienced wardens are appointed each year to supervise the work. Quite recently a young English couple have taken over a croft near Ham, the first one hopes of other incomers bringing once again new life to the island.

On the east coast "The Bonnie Isle" of Whalsay is one of the few places in Shetland, along with the Skerries and Burra, where the young

268

men are as devoted to the fishing as they were in the past. The population of the island, five and a half miles long from Symbister Ness to Skaw Taing and rather more than two at its greatest width, has rarely fallen below 900 and within the last 20 years has touched the 1000 mark. Except for Bute, Whalsay is the most densely populated island for its size in Scotland.

Given good weather, fishing is carried on continuously with two trips to Lerwick each week. The greatest emphasis on Whalsay is on white fishing. Only seven of the total fleet of 15 engage in drift netting. In 1822 almost all the men were employed at the haaf fishing, and although Tudor for some obscure reason scathingly remarked that there was nothing to retain the tourist in this island he forecast that the fresh fish trade would develop into "a very profitable business", a prediction more than fulfilled after the Second World War. Today the main fishing is concentrated on haddock and whiting for the fresh fish market in Aberdeen and local processing plants. The practice of sending fish cleaned and packed in ice to Aberdeen and Leith began in the late nineteenth century. Anyone who has not lived on Whalsay and tasted a haddock fresh out of the sea has not tasted fish at all. The finest restaurant in the most sophisticated towns of Europe could not serve a fish as delicate or sweet as a haddock landed that morning.

Most of the Whalsay folks are young and nothing that money can buy is absent from their homes. Nearly all the houses are privately owned except for a row of Council Houses. They are all kept as neat as a new pin. I was scarcely allowed to walk anywhere in the island; my hostess insisted on running me around its few miles by car, but no distraction is allowed to keep the women from the radio at the time their husbands call in from the fishing. Contented, more than comfortably off, there is somehow a clean air that blows over Whalsay, the future assured, no dangers of depopulation. Even the older folk look back, not with nostalgia but with a kind of awe, to the days when the crofter worked through the night, the women baiting lines, children *shilling* yoags for bait, helping to burn kelp to make a livelihood and recount with dry humour tales of the lairds and their schemes to outwit them.

On the Out Skerries, on less than one square mile of rock with thin patches of soil, live 100 people. It has one of the finest sheltered harbours in the islands, a fishing fleet of three large vessels and a number of small lobster boats. In 1970 a highly mechanised fish processing factory was established by private enterprise on the islands. Six miles north east of Whalsay, with three main islands of Housay, Bruray and Grunay, until the erection of the lighthouse in 1852 the Skerries was a continual scene of wrecks, mainly Dutch East Indiamen taking the northabout passage. One of the special attractions of the Skerries must be the hundreds of migrating birds which pass through each year in spring and autumn and it has been suggested more than once that a Bird Observation Station should be erected which would add immensely to the interest of this most easterly group of Shetland islands, far too rarely visited, but likely to benefit from its new airstrip.

Burra Isle is part of a long chain of islands running south from Scalloway, parallel with the west shore and divided from it by the narrow inlet of Clift Sound. When Shetland became part of Scotland, West Burra was known as Kirk Island, called after the early Papil church there, while East Burra was Houss Island where the laird's Haa' stood. David Sinclair, the first laird of Houss, fought at the Battle of Summerdale against the Earl of Caithness in Orkney in 1529.

From Norse times until the early nineteenth century the staple economy was crofting-fishing. As late as the 1790's the islands were self-sufficient in grain for their 300 inhabitants. There was a long-standing dispute between the Burra men and those of Cunningsburgh over pasture rights on the Clift Hills, ending in a pitched battle with several deaths, but about 1786 the rights were sold to the Bruce family of Sumburgh, owners of the Cunningsburgh Estate.

The rise of Burra as one of the premier fishing districts of Shetland was originally due to its position near the rich haaf fishing grounds and its small proportion of arable land. Rather than fish for the merchant-landowners most Burra men went to the Faroe cod fishing in the nineteenth century and were remarkable even then for their skill and endurance. With the decline of the cod fishing Burra pioneered the herring fishing with the first herring sail boat *The Lass o' Gowrie*, several more being added to the fleet before 1879. By 1910 most of the small smacks had been replaced by carvel-built vessels of 60 to 70 feet and Hamnavoe grew up as a fishing village with its own herring stations.

By the late 1930's the fleet attained a peak in its development but like many other stations, due to over-fishing by trawlers, the haddock lines gave way to seine netting and Burra men invested in dual purpose M.F.V.'s some of them new and costing between £20,000 and £30,000. Twelve or thirteen of these boats fish off Burra, many of the bigger boats landing their catches at Aberdeen in winter, otherwise fish was sold to local processors in Scalloway or Lerwick, or shipped in ice to Aberdeen. There was a notable rise in the standard of living with new housing, electricity, water and pier services all completed between 1950 and 1956.

Half of Shetland's fulltime fishermen live on Whalsay and Burra and, like Whalsay, Burra is a flourishing community, the village of Hamnavoe bright with new paint and tidy gardens, communication with the

79   The old and the new: old Ness yoal in foreground and the latest model—the first boat to be built in Bigton for many years, designed and built by Jim Laurenson.

Mainland revolutionised by the erection of the Trondra-Burra bridge. Begun in 1969 at an estimated cost of £500,000 and completed in October 1971, the men dock at Scalloway, discharge their fish, jump into cars and head for home, now only quarter of an hour away.

Each island off Shetland still retains its own distinctive characteristics, its people and its dialect, as different as its shape and size. Even in Whalsay where is a noticeable change in speech between the south end and Skaw, the most northerly point. In Whalsay they speak of "wirhoose" (our house) but in Yell they will talk of going to "wirs" (ours). Unst, according to the Whalsay folk, could be another country and only in the Skerries and Whalsay do you find the soft "s" sound. Although Shetland properly begins at Fair Isle it is probably more familiar to Scots, English and foreign ornithologists than to most Shetlanders. Two and three-quarter miles in length and one and a half miles broad, its highest point is Wart Hill, 712 feet above sea level, but what Fair Isle lacks in height it makes up for by a coastline of rock, geo and stack, each tiny indentation, hole, arch or bank minutely described and so crowded together that the map positively bristles with intriguing and unpronounceable names packed tightly like the teeth of a comb.

Before lighthouses were thought of, Fair Isle, like the Skerries, drew

271

ships towards its reefs like a magnet. Over 100 proved wrecks lie round the island and below geo and skerry, baa and stack the entire coastline is one vast sea graveyard, the waters washing over the broken bones of men and ships. The Fair Isle men are reckoned among the finest seamen in Shetland not only for their skill but for their bravery and fortitude, seldom equalled even in islands where a boat and a pair of oars were the first necessities of life. Many incidents could be quoted but the rescue of 465 people from the emigrant barque the *Lessing*, bound from Bremen to New York in 1868, stands out unique. The barque ran ashore on Clavers Geo and nothing could approach from seaward with great waves crashing on her stern. The canvas helpless, threshed back and forth like thunderclaps and with every second she was pounded deeper and deeper into the rocks. Aboard were a crew of 20 and 445 emigrants including 120 women and children.

Then quite suddenly a small boat appeared below the ship's bow. On the shore side of the Geo is a natural arch just wide enough to admit an island yoal. Only a Fair Isle man would have risked such a passage with the high seas running, but boat after boat, waiting for the right moment, slipped through, loaded up with people and returned again and again until everyone on board was brought to safety. The emigrants eventually reached their destination, and perhaps the story has come down through generations of their rescue by Fair Isle fishermen through the Hole of Shaldicliv.

To most people Fair Isle is synonymous with "Fair Isle Knitting" an art form in itself with an endless variety of complex geometric designs. The introduction of these patterns has invariably been credited to the 300 survivors of the *El Gran Grifon*, an *urca* or transport ship of the Spanish Armada who spent seven weeks on the island after the total wreck of their vessel. Accepted as indigenous to Shetland, knitting, like macramé, was actually an Arabic invention and all Fair Isle knitting patterns are found in one form or another in rugs from the Turkoman basin.

In the early centuries A.D. Balkan nomads made a pilgrimage to Scandinavia carrying the technique of this special form of knitting with them, the patterns derived from the Muslim influence of geometric as opposed to naturalistic designs and both Spanish, by way of the Moors and Scandinavian influences are visible, both deriving from the Arabic root. In the mountains of the Hindu Khush and the Karakoram, even today, the knitted stockings worn by the men under the soft boots of markhor skin, the childrens' socks and Hunza hats are all basically one, geometric designs accepted as Fair Isle, but with a beginning half across the globe.

Both Fair Isle and Foula can lay claim to two creatures of distinctive

272

species, the wren and the field-mouse. The Scottish land area had the northern and western islands separated by submergence before it was possible for any mammals common to Britain, to cross. Somehow the little field-mouse made the crossing, whether by land bridge or carried by man will probably never be known.

On the mainland of Great Britain and islands such as Skye is found *A. sylvaticus*, nevertheless, brought in by settlers possibly from Scandinavia. On Fair Isle, Mainland and Yell the species has a name of its own . . . *A. fridariensis* and the island of Foula has yet another species of field-mouse, smaller than that on the mainland of Shetland and found from sea level up to 1000 feet, *A. fridariensis thules*. The Fair Isle mouse has a bright foxy red coat above and white below with a prominent yellow spot on the chest and weighs twice as much as a mainland field-mouse.

The other tiny creature, the wren, is known delightfully in local Faroese as *musabrooir*—"brother of the mouse"! Shetland has its own distinctive wren too, rather large and dark reddish brown flecked with brown beneath, described and named *Troglodytes t. zetlandicus*, from specimens collected in Dunrossness, only 25 miles from Fair Isle. The Fair Isle wren, however, is very different, "more rufescent on the lower back and rump and suffused with grey on the head and neck in fresh plumage; it is also a little whiter and less heavily marked beneath". It was named by Kenneth Williamson *Troglodytes y. fridariensis*, the ancient Norse name of Fridarey bestowed on Fair Isle in the Orkneyinga Saga, commemorated in two of Shetland's tiniest living creatures.

Papa Stour, Papa ey Storr, the large priests' isle, is memorable too in quite different ways. Sprawled like a giant starfish at the entrance to St. Magnus Bay, it is almost split in two by voes running deep into its heart, Hamna Voe and Culla Voe. Two miles broad from southwest to north-east, half a mile of moorland separates the two, the wide saucer of Garda Water a bright pool between. Its highest hill is Virdie Field, a mere 288 feet high, but the lavas and ashes that went to sculpt the island have been carved and tunnelled into the most outstanding set of caves in Britain with the possible exception of Fingal's Cave itself. Kirstan's Hole, the largest, runs 70 to 80 yards underneath the island to end abruptly in a tiny beach, accessible only in the calmest weather.

Shetlanders have a rare facility for inventing nicknames and the folk of Papa Stour were long known as "Scories", (scorie being the Shetland name for an immature gull), due to their habit of gathering fat young gulls, flaying them and salting them. They collected herring gull eggs from the Stacks o Papa, carrying on a tradition practised also on Foula since man first came to the islands, the only means of making up in spring for the meagre winter diet.

One of the most evocative and best remembered of all Papa's unique distinctions is, oddly enough, the simple scent of flowers carried far out to sea. Like a lodestar the continuing riot of heady perfume faint, yet unmistakable, was as sure a guide to the old haaf fisherman as his own well-known medes. Shetland is known for its 500 species of plants and in Papa red clover, thyme and sea pink, violet and scylla, milkwort, butterwort, tormentil and red campion, marigolds, purple orchis and bluebells sent their message immortalised in "Da Sang o da Papa Men". The Horn of Papa mentioned in the song is a weirdly shaped headland with an arch drilled through the lower part, the summit surmounted by a rhinoceros-like horn. It was swept away in a gale in 1953.

Oot bewast da Horn o Papa
Rowin Foula doon!
Ower a hidden piece o watter
Rowin Foula doon!
Roond da boat da tide-lumps makkin
Sunlicht trowe da clouds is brakkin;
We maan geng whaar fish is takkin,
Rowin Foula doon.

Fishy knots wir boat haes truly
Nae misforen knot.
We hae towes and bowes and cappies,
Ballast i da shott,
Paets fir fire i da kyettle,
Taaties fir da pot.

Laek a lass at's hoidin, lachin,
Coortit be her vooers,
Papa sometimes lies in Simmer
Veiled wi ask an shooers;
Dan upo da wilsom watter
Comes da scent o flooers.

We can bide ashore nae langer—
We maun geng an try.
We'll win back boys, if we soodna
Scrime da moder-dye,
Fir da scent o flooers in Papa
Leds wis aa da wye.

274

Out at the far haaf the boats rowed out "bewast da Horn o Papa" until the cliffs of Foula disappeared on the horizon, known to all haaf men as "Rowin Foula doon". Peats for the kettle had to be cast on the islands of Papa Little and Muckle Roe nine miles away, ferried across the sound and brought home in panniers on ponies, still recalled by the older residents, and few evenings in Papa used to end without the fiddle and "Da Sang o da Papa Men".

The earliest recorded mention of Papa Stour occurs in a legal document of 1299 when allegations were brought against the tax collector of fraudulent practice. Later cleared of suspicion, Lord Thorvald Thoresson, was the agent of a member of the Norwegian royal family. His name is not only perpetuated on the island in the place named Tirval's Skord where the site of his house can barely be traced, but as the Jarl who marooned his daughter on top of one of the highest stacks, the lofty Frau Stack or Maiden's Stack, presumably to preserve her virginity. The sequel has a number of variations but the inevitable happened and one of the girl's suitors, more daring than the rest, scaled the stack and abducted the fair prisoner, more isolated even than Rapunzel who at least was able to let down her hair. However sceptical one may be, the remains of what can only have been a stone hut are there for all to see perched crazily on top of the stack.

There were other prisoners in Papa. The Hon. Edwin Lindsay was confined for 26 years during the early part of the nineteenth century. Refusing to fight a duel, thus bringing disgrace on the family, he was sent off to Papa Stour with a sealed letter to the factor, Gideon Henderson, instructing him to hold him there as he was insane. His eventual escape was engineered by one Catherine Watson, a quaker who discovered his plight while making a preaching tour of the islands. Convinced of his sanity, with the help of another pacifist, and after a complicated series of false starts and warrants for his arrest he was finally declared sane by the Vice Chancellor's Court in London and found entitled to the annuity left by his father. A spring of water at the south end of the island near where Lindsay used to bathe is still known as Lindsay's Well.

The greatest number of Papa's prisoners were not so fortunate. To Papa Stour were sent lepers from Walls, not suffering from true leprosy, which was contagious, but a form of elephantiasis believed later to be hereditary. Their tragedy was implicit in the scant medical knowledge of the times for the poor souls were ostracised, living alone in "failey hooses" built for them and known over the islands as "spilt men's hooses", their food put out for them near the miserable cottages where they lived. Extracts from the Session Books of Walls show the expenses incurred in keeping lepers on Papa from 1736 to 1740. In the Statistical

275

80 The "leper" window in the Old Kirk of Lund, Unst, overlooking Lunda Wick. Built into the wall, it provided a means for the poor untouchables to hear the sermon without contaminating the congregation.

Account the Rev. Dr. Jack of Northmavine refers to leprosy as existing in his parish and the session clerk in Walls mentioned the report of a woman in Papa about the year 1778 who died in the fields before a house could be built for her. In 1798 a Shetland "leper" a patient in the Edinburgh Infirmary was seen by various physicians and his case pronounced as *Elephantiasis Graecorum*, although recent evidence points strongly to the existence of a form of true leprosy.

The diagnosis came too late but no one was able to trace its cause although many attributed it to eating smoked, wind-dried and semi-putrid fish or meats. In the old kirk of Lund on Unst can still be seen what is believed to be a leper window, a tiny hole in the thick wall sloping upwards so that his breath could not contaminate the worshippers inside, and similar "leper windows" exist in many Scottish churches.

Shetland itself is well known for its fiddle music and Shetland reels but its most famous dance comes from Papa Stour—The Papa Stour Sword Dance, described in detail in Scott's *The Pirate*. The island is the last place in Scotland to observe this ancient drama and it was revived by a local man, Alex Johnson, in 1923. The music is traditional and although many subordinate points have changed since Dr. Hibbert and Sir Walter Scott saw the dance the main movements remain the same—a strange and unique performance confined to the island.

Seven young men take part, representing the Seven Champions of Christendom, accompanied by the fiddler. There is St. George of England, St. James of Spain, St. Dennis of France, St. David of Wales, St. Patrick of Ireland, St. Anthony of Italy and St. Andrew of Scotland. Each knight wears a brilliantly coloured sash across his white shirt and carries at his side a sword, made nowadays of a piece of iron hooping, about three feet in length. St. George recites the prologue

"Brave gentles all within this bow'r, if ye delight in any a sport,
Come see me dance upon this floor—you, minstrel man, play me a parte."

The minstrel strikes up: the master bows and dances. After drawing his sword and flourishing it, he returns it to his side.

At the end of the prologue, much more complicated in Hibbert's day, the Master introduces the six knights of Christendom, (seven in the modern version): Stout James of Spain come in our sight and champion Dennis, a French Knight, and David a brave Welshman born and Patrick too who blew the horn; Of Italy brave Anthony the Good, St. George of England and today St. Andrew of Scotland. After the Master addresses each in turn the intricate dance begins, having eight figures, circling underneath uplifted swords, stepping over the swords in a miracle of precision, scarcely a movement repeated and finishing up with all seven swords held aloft forming the solid star of David, then cast on the ground, each man picks up his own sword, raising it aloft with a flourish and St. George delivers the epilogue.

One scarcely associates small islands with any form of export trade but for many years Foula enjoyed a flourishing trade with Orkney, exporting millstones, made from mica schist, called locally "millgrit" and taken from quarries at the Gaads on the east side of the island. The Foula people also exported to Fair Isle, coreloet, or korkeleit, a purple dye obtained from *Lichen tartareus*. Scraped off the rocks, it was ground into powder, steeped in urine for several days, and then made up into one and a half lb. balls ready for use.

Tudor also noted a small peaty hole from which the natives of Foula got the earth for making a black dye. The roots of the plant employed to fix the dye were probably *Tormentilla officianalis* or the *Arbutus uva ursi*. After steeping the article to be dyed, when the liquid was on the boil they threw in the black peat earth impregnated with iron ore. Apparently the roots of the plant were also used medicinally. "After being carefully washed they were chopped up very fine and then boiled

277

with a little Whisky to make it keep." Tudor noted that given in half-teacupful doses "it is said to beat Peruvian bark out of sight as a tonic". Like Fair Isle, natural dyes had to be used for wool and purple was produced by cudbear; yellow or reddish brown from *Lichen saxilitus* or "Old Man" and orange from *Lichen parietinus*—in Shetland "scriota", while *Lichen omhaloides* was occasionally used to give a brownish or blackish purple.

Tonics were unknown as such but both on Foula and in Unst certain waters were believed to have healing powers. On Foula on the steep northerly slopes of the Sneug is hidden away the tiny basin holding the famous "Waters of the Sneug", its story reported first in the *Edinburgh Evening Dispatch* of 1836. In Unst near Watley is the spring of the Yela Brun (the spring of healing) with its legend of an early Christian missionary having been killed near the spot. Pilgrims were accustomed to throw a stone into the burn and drink the waters so that today a substantial mound of stones can be seen.

Perhaps the best tonic appeared to be wholly psychological. Hibbert, famous for his discovery of chromate of iron on the island of Unst, noted that during the church service worshippers were frequently overtaken by some kind of paroxysm. About 50 years before there had been scarcely a Sabbath on which they did not occur. An intelligent and pious minister of the day annoyed by these fits impeding the devotions of his flock assured his parishioners that no treatment was more effectual than immersion in cold water ... "the fear of being carried into the lake acted like a charm and not a single Naiad was made".

Fetlar of the early Viking settlements also has its "chalybeate" springs, the erstwhile "Garden of Shetland", mainly known today as the home of the rare Snowy Owl. In 1967 on a rocky hill in the north of the island one of the ornithological events of the century took place, when for the first time in Britain a pair of Snowy Owls made their nest. The R.S.P.B. in co-operation with the owner of the land and the Secretary of State for Scotland, had the area declared a Statutory Bird Sanctuary. Since then the Society has managed the 1400 acres surrounding the Owl territory as the Fetlar Bird Reserve.

Visitors come from far and near to tramp up the two miles or so of hillside to the "hide", equipped with a powerful telescope focussed on the birds' nesting place. In 1974 five chicks were hatched and devoted watchers kept a constant check on the site. Without a good harbour, Fetlar is far less visited than most and the island seems scarcely to have recovered from the late 1870's when Sir Arthur Nicolson cleared the greater part of his estate of men in order to make room for sheep. The scree slopes and the grassy banks of the East Neap provide a bonus for the Snowy Owls' visitors with one of the largest colonies of Storm

81 Wedding group of the early 1900's. Shetland women might work hard on croft or land but could obviously turn out in the height of fashion for a festive occasion. (The late Mrs. Abernethy's Collection.)

Petrels in Shetland.

In Shetland today only 17 islands are inhabited but nearly all the smaller islands at one time or another in the past had families living on them. The little island of Noss, now famous as a Nature Reserve, consisting of 774 acres, had 24 persons recorded in the 1841 census, and the last family to live permanently on the island were the Jamiesons, the father being shepherd at Maryfield Farm, three of whose four daughters were born on the island. The home farm of the Garth estate Noss has belonged to it for 300 years.

Three miles east of Lerwick, Noss is separated from Bressay by a narrow sound often impassable in rough weather. Sheer cliffs rise on the east side, best seen from the sea, at their highest point at the Noup with an unbroken fall of about 600 feet. The Holm of Noss, a great flat-topped mass of rock with perpendicular walls almost looks part of Noss, so close is it, and the Noup of Noss is marked on the earliest maps of Shetland as a landfall for shipping. One of the great bird islands of Britain, its weathering sandstone cliffs provide ledges for thousands of seabirds, and on the cliff face of the Noup is one of Shetland's two Gannet colonies. The other is at Hermaness in Unst. Their "drums" or nests are shaggy mountains of seaweed and grass added to each year. The "solon goose", as the Gannet is known in Shetland, has great wings tipped with black and pencilled markings on its pale orange yellow head. Several thousand pairs can be seen at most times of the year. They arrive on the breeding ledges during February, breeding in May and June and leaving in October.

The Great Skua, hunted as a rarity for its skins and eggs, was once

279

82 Visitors to Vaila Hall being
seen off to the boat for Burras-
tow by Henry Anderton, the
laird, second row left.

reduced to six or eight pairs. Given protection in Hermaness, Foula
and Noss its territory extends over much of the hill. Guillemots, Razor-
bills Kittiwakes and Fulmars also nest in countless numbers, the
Fulmars given a fairly wide berth by most nesting birds and there is
evidence that even the Raven, Peregrine and Sea Eagle can be driven
from their traditional eyries by the nauseous attentions of the
Fulmar.

The tiny island of Vaila on the west side across the Sound from Bur-
rastoe, owes its preservation to the amazing fortress-like mansion of
Vaila Hall. The island is only roughly a mile each way and the Hall
dominates the entire landscape set up on a hill, its only rival the small
watchtower opposite from where the laird could keep check on his
tenants and make sure that not a fish escaped his eagle eye. The most
beautiful part of Vaila Hall is the old building in which the former
lairds of Melby had their residence. The newer part of the mansion,
imposing and battlemented, was added on in the eighteenth century
with a great panelled dining hall and gallery filled with glass cases of
stuffed birds of rare species, now extinct in Shetland. Vast shallow bowls
from China, teak chests, Jacobean dressers and an enormous dining
table were all brought home from the east by a seafaring Captain and
miraculously ferried over the sound. The walls are hung with sombre
family portraits of rigid stern-visaged, respectable lairds and their
strong-faced, upright women. At the height of its prosperity one girl

280

spent all her day carrying peat to keep the great fires burning, and now four people live in it, the new laird, his wife and daughters. Determined young people, they have restored the house and provide exotic meals, rooms for guests and vast Midsummer's Eve banquets, the Chinese bowls filled with lobster, avocado, chicken, and rice, washed down with glasses of red or white wine, a great turkey carved by the chef, the boatman who ferried you over quickly changing his battledress top for a white jacket. Of Scandinavian ancestry, on his way to occupy land which had been left to him left him in Faroe he stopped in Shetland and never left it.

No mention of the Shetland Islands could be complete without reference to its incredible variety of flora, an entire life story delineated in its growth. At one time in a milder age pine, birch, hazel, rowan, aspen, alder, oak, elm, willow and lime grew wild. Only a few plants of birch, hazel, rowan and aspen remain surviving in remote and inaccessible places. The native birch population was reduced by half between 1954 and 1959 by the admission of sheep to a small island in the loch where it grew. Luckily birch was found on an adjacent island about 10 years ago but if sheep once find their way there—and they can only do so by the thoughtless hand of man—then all we will have to remember are the place names of Birka Ward and Birka Water.

During the Iron Age, Shetland's climate became wetter and colder and today the growing season is short. Not only is the highest concentration of salt found in the Shetlands but it is known as the windiest place in the British Isles, apart from the Butt of Lewis. At 800 feet the annual wind speed is four-fifths of that experienced on the summit of Ben Nevis at 4406 feet. The ubiquitous sheep have been responsible for a complete change in vegetation and only on islands in lochs, ravines and crag sites can the original composition be seen as it was before man, and inevitably sheep, arrived. Peat cutting, especially on Papa Stour, where the island was devoid of true peat, removed the top layer of turf; in Foula scalping probably since before Norse times has almost eroded the natural soil. The Vikings are known to have used dwarf shrubs for cattle bedding, and it is probable that even calluna and willow scrub may have also been gathered for this purpose. Of the 25 or so Arctic flowering plants 15 of them are found on Ronas Hill and it is believed that about six flowering plants have disappeared since about 1800. Incomers have established themselves from far-off lands. The Mimula or Monkey Flower, a native of America, is seen at its best by the stream running into the sandy bay at Mail in Cunningsburgh. The Australian Daisy, a native of Chile and Patagonia, flourishes in its shiny green leaves and nodding clumps of six to eight heads of flowers like enormous daisies. Tussigirse from the Falkland Islands is often encountered

281

around Dunrossness in dense tussocks several feet high while the Slender Speedwell, a native of Asia Minor and the Caucasus, with an amazing growth spread, carpets the ground with its tiny mauve-blue flowers.

Shetland, however, has its own peculiarly native species and one of the plants which helped Edmonston to establish his fame as a botanist was the Arctic Mouse-ear Chickweed, a large plant with handsome white flowers and roundish, purple-coloured leaves. The Unst variety grows nowhere else in the world. A plant hitherto unknown in Britain was discovered by the Shetland botanist Walter Scott in 1962 in limestone pastures and outcrops in the parish of Tingwall. First thought to be Mouse Ear Hawkweed it was sent to Cambridge for identification by experts. Intrigued and completely puzzled, one of them came to see this extraordinary plant in its native setting. Eventually it appeared in the journal of the Botanical Society of the British Isles under the title of *pilosella flagellaris* sub-species *bicapitata*, the Shetland Mouse-ear Hawkweed, and was later discovered in two widely separated and geologically differing areas at West Burrafirth and Ronas Voe.

The total number of plants known to grow in Shetland amounts to about 500 species composed of about 25 rushes, and rush-like plants; 20 sedges, 45 grasses and about 17 ferns, a few stoneworts and several hundred flowering plants. Shetland's flora is as surprising to a botanist as her birds are to an ornithologist. Some plants confined to high areas on Scottish mountains grow right down to sea level in Shetland, one of these the lovely Moss Campion with its pink flowers crowning a cushion of green leaves. Orchids, associated mainly with exotic blooms in hot-houses or in tropical settings, reveal themselves in Shetland in eight miniature native species and one hybrid. Varying from sturdy purple through pink to almost white they grow in abundance in gardens and transplant readily to the rockery. Several of the species only grow in a few areas; in Yell the Bog Orchid and in Unst the Frog Orchid along with the Fragrant Orchid and the Early Purple Orchid. In marshes one can find the Meadow Orchid, the moorland species being the Moorland Spotted Orchid and the Northern Fen Orchid and the Lesser Twayblade.

On Noss alone the total number of species of plant recorded to date is around 140, but all over the islands at certain seasons the roadside, the marshes and the meadows become alight, carpeted and studded with brilliant colours. Red Campion, the short spikes of blue Vernal Squill, wild yellow Iris and fields of Marsh Marigolds with ponies up to their fetlocks in a yellow meadow; tiny yellow stars of Tormentil, Birdsfoot Trefoil; delicate Grass of Parnassus and waving flags of Bog Cotton, the list is endless, and many of the areas have become a pilgrimage for enthusiasts like the botanists who are, unlike many so-called "enthusiasts" content to look, wonder, and photograph the rare *Arenaria norvegica* and *Cerastium edmonstonii*.

Like flowers, Shetland's birds have their own particular breeding places. There are no rivers in the islands as such, but fast-flowing peaty amber burns which are important spawning grounds and access avenues to lochs for Brown Trout, Sea Trout and in two localities at least Salmon. Lochs within agricultural areas like the famous Spiggie Loch in Dunrossness are not only the home of the delicious pink-fleshed "Spiggie Trout" but one of the wintering places of the Whooper Swan, of which five to ten per cent of the British wintering population come to Shetland, suddenly arriving in late September or October, when the loch becomes dappled with white like hundreds of tiny sails, their call as haunting as the loon. In lochs all round the islands in similar locations are Golden Eye, Tufted Duck, Pochard, Widgeon, and Little Grebe while breeding birds include the tiny Red Necked Phalarope, Mallard and Teal.

83   Rows of *dusses* ready to be built into *skroos* or stacks on the long rigs fanning down to Spiggie Loch, one of the most famous of trout lochs in Mainland: beyond a tiny strip of land divides the loch from the Peerie Voe (Dunrossness).

Holms with the least density of sheep are breeding sites for Gulls, Eiders, Terns, Storm Petrels, Oyster Catchers the Black Guillemot, Rock Pipit and Wren, and in winter months they are frequently occupied by geese, particularly Grey Lag, roosting Mallards, the haunt of Otters and breeding sites for the Common Seal. The long voes provide feeding grounds for the Red-Throated Diver, Eider, Merganser, Shag and Black Guillemot which breed on the shore or hill. At the seawards end in winter comes the Little Auk and Long-tailed Duck. In many deeper bays and sounds one might be lucky to see a school of Common Porpoise or White Sided Dolphin, Lesser Rorqual, Pilot Whale and occasionally a Killer Whale. Once we came upon a 30-foot Basking Shark playfully surfacing, uncomfortably for us, between our boat and the shore.

Owing to declining stocks an order banning the hunting of Common Seal was implemented in July 1973. Females produce their pups at four or five years old and it is hoped that this order will allow the stocks to build up again. Of the Atlantic or Grey Seal estimates suggest a total population of 3000, not very many for the long Shetland coastline where once in almost every deep shingly cove one could look down on great numbers hauled out for breeding. Bad weather at the beginning of the breeding season in these very exposed sites can be disastrous and in 1969 almost the entire pup population was lost through severe storms. In 1971 and 1973 aerial surveys were carried out producing an extensive coverage of Grey Seal breeding sites, showing an estimated pup population of around 600.

Perhaps the "Shetland way of life" lies not so much in the ideology of the much vaunted crofter-fisherman clinging to the remnants of his Norse ancestry while making a far better living "at the makkin' machine", on the roads, at the building sites or working for "the oil" than ever he did on croft and land, but in the islands themselves.

Settled, won, lost, the cycle of seasons measured by the meal in the bin; bent backs in a bitter sea—notice how many houses turn their gables to the shore. Islands of contrasts of shadow and sun and cloud, of flower, bird and sea things; endured grumbling through the nights of the long sword of winter, in the bitter wind's embrace, in a day of white sun or blinded by fog—it is only the Shetland way of life.

23. *Shetland and Oil*

A GIANT RIG straddles Brei Wick, the vast platform of its helideck poised above the water. Beneath it miniature tugs, trawlers and cargo vessels float like bright plastic toys. Behind and below crouches Lerwick's skyline, dwarfed into a miniscule backdrop of chimney tops, housing schemes and people hurrying like ants in the absurdity of their Lilliputian relationship. As unreal and incongruous as a science fiction monster, three rust-black legs like outsize tree-trunks support a complex of twentieth-century technology, embodying in its awful proximity all the social, economic and environmental implications of North Sea oil to Shetland.

It may appear to be a far cry from these isolated northern islands to central Africa and the building of the Kariba Dam, but the analogy is there—yet another man-made, deliberate ecological upheaval setting off a chain-reaction impossible to stem. When the inhabitants of the remote Gwembe Valley were told that the Zambesi River would rise up and a giant lake cover the land on which they had been born; that the people of 193 villages would have to leave their homes, their hard-won gardens and the burial grounds of their ancestors, and learn to start life afresh with new methods of agriculture and unfamiliar standards of living, they did not believe it possible.

Opportunities of employment had been held out to men who had not the least desire to earn wages in big cities; a £1,500,000 fishing industry was envisaged in the lake; schools, hospitals, roads were promised. The people of the valley simply wanted to be left alone. In spite of years of warnings and preparation the final stages of Kariba were cataclysmic. The Batonga watched appalled as huge tractors towing lengths of battleship chain ripped through their forests, levelling two million acres of trees. Familiar landmarks disappeared forever. The rains came, and with the rains, floods. Food and shelter were gone. Confrontation ensued and lives were lost. Finally the project became reality and lorry loads of villagers left the valley, clinging to small household effects, taking a last look at their ancient hunting grounds, the water already lapping the roots of trees and tottering shambas. The

84 Exploration rig *Sedco* lying in Brei Wick, Lerwick, with Bressay and the Ward of Bressay lying behind.

valley itself had long been a highway for game, now equally dispossessed. No one foresaw long-drawn-out starvation of animals, cut off on islands, clinging to trees. What rescue work was possible was followed by a wholly unexpected hazard, the monstrous growth of the aquatic weed, *Salvinia auriculata*, covering in dense mats 100 square miles of the new-made lake, the promised harvest of fish dying for want of oxygen. At the end of the day hundreds of animals had been lost; the valley was left with a weed-choked lake and the people with an alien culture and the newly implanted desire for things that money could buy, which successfully destroyed forever the naïve contentment of the simple Batonga.

In an endeavour to emphasise the results that follow any major exploitation of natural resources, a symposium on the Kariba Dam was held in Glasgow's Royal College of Science and Technology for postgraduate engineers, combining the entire spectrum of geophysical, ecological, moral and spiritual consequences, but unfortunately its lesson is one which man has yet to learn. The Shetlander, too, due merely to the unfortunate accident of his place on the map of Britain, has been equally exploited, swept along in the heedless national drive for "oil at all costs". The land his family may have worked for generations is also expendable; his life style will certainly change, for incomers enjoying inflated wage scales and unfamiliar with island life may outnumber

286

him ten to one. Shetland's unique and world-famous bird population is already under threat of extinction. One disaster to rig, pipeline, tanker or jetty would be enough to put colonies of seabirds at risk. The effect on marine life of an almost certainly continuing but incalculable pollution of the North Sea basin, could mean the eventual loss of thousands of years of ecology. Increasing developments by oil companies both in the North Sea and the Atlantic Ocean and all the efforts of county councils, planning authorities or governments may be powerless to prevent the wholesale destruction of life as we know it, and the proliferation of oil-related services will eventually affect many more than the present few acres of land or a handful of crofters.

Like Kariba, oil is with us whether we want it or not, but unlike the Batonga we were not informed at the beginning just what it would mean, how infinite its implications. By 1972 the quest for oil in the North Sea had been under way for 10 years and yet successive governments did little to pave the way for the social, industrial and environmental consequences. The results were chaotic, leaving local authorities desperately trying to keep pace with developments, and a situation in which each county involved, tempted by an advance in economic prosperity, was bedevilled by the ramifications and complexities of oil policies, unsure whether what was right for the oil industry was right for the existing community.

Nowhere was this more apparent than in Shetland. With all the modern methods of communication many Shetlanders, while aware of oil finds in the North Sea, were abysmally ignorant of their future total involvement. Oil companies have never readily revealed the extent of their reserves and are under no obligation to do so except at government level, but the pity of it was that no one in Shetland realised that we were literally planted astride the world's biggest undersea oilfields, nor could we envisage the fringe consequences with which Shetland would be faced.

On Shetland's County Council rested the entire future of the islands, together with the amost insuperable task of balancing the national need to exploit the oil reserves, against Shetland's people, its way of life and its unique flora and fauna. The impact of oil with all its implications somehow had to be controlled. At the outset it must be admitted that the County Council has so far succeeded where many have failed. It will be the end of the day before it is known whether every contingency has been covered and whether the battle of wits will be controlled by Shetland or the oil companies. The Council has been publicly acclaimed for being ahead of most local authorities, and however one may criticise certain aspects of planning or decision making the thought of a Shetland without the control it has fought to exercise would be a nightmare world of speculator and oil company, with money to burn, struggling for possession of every deep water voe in the islands, riding rough-shod over all the Shetlander has held precious.

Suddenly faced with a growth of economic activity on a scale unprecedented in Shetland's history the County Council commissioned a report by Transport Research Ltd. providing a navigational appraisal of five areas for the berthing or mooring of crude oil carriers and determining the suitability of each to accommodate vessels of 200,000 tons. The report, completed in July 1972, suggested Sullom Voe as the area having the greatest potential. Shetland had unfortunately been one of the few counties which had not prepared a County Development Plan under the 1947 Town and Country Planning Act, so the first step taken by the Council was to publish an Interim Development Plan, intended to act as a stop-gap measure until a full structural plan could be prepared.

In March 1973 the Plan was submitted to the Secretary of State and the Council had announced its policy of containment. The Plan covered almost every aspect of development and included a map presenting a comprehensive presentation of the various proposals and policies. Private legislation was sought authorising the Council to exercise port and harbour jurisdiction in respect of certain parts of the island's coastal areas, notably Sullom Voe, Swarbacks Minn and Baltasound in Unst, together with powers of compulsory purchase of land. Messrs Livesey and Henderson had been engaged as consultants to produce a master plan of the Sullom Voe—Swarbacks Minn area and additional local plans for Lerwick and Unst were commissioned.

The Council might equally well have announced wholesale eviction. An immediate outcry greeted the "compulsory purchase" clause in the Interim Plan. Some people in areas designated for oil development received notices of 28 days to quit. Bitter letters flooded the Press. Already speculators had acquired options on areas of land vastly in excess of that designed for compulsory purchase by the Council. Nordport alone claimed to have options to purchase some 40,000 acres around Sullom Voe. Landlords could and did sell part of their estates for ready cash. Eventually it became public knowledge that between Nordport and Total Oil Marine option money to the extent of £26,000 a month was being paid out. Personally convinced that the County Council would have to use their powers of compulsory purchase very little, Shetland's Lord Lieutenant, Mr. Robert Bruce, pointed out that Shetlanders prided themselves more than anything else on their independence. Sadly enough, it became obvious that in exercising that right of independence there were more than a few ready to sell their inheritance for a mess of pottage.

288

Fierce controversy raged and the County Council found itself at the receiving end of a torrent of argument, protest and resentment, directed less against the actual compulsory order itself, but motivated mainly by the high-handed manner in which the County Council had acted on behalf of the general public without revealing or reviewing the whole case. The unhappy situation culminated in five councillors, including the convener and vice-convener of the county, being voted out of office. The House of Commons Select Committee sitting in Edinburgh finally passed the Bill, and the new Council, having learned from bitter experience the costs of its predecessors' reticence, took over the control and administration of the entire range of developments to which the islands were now irrevocably and wholly committed. Livesey and Henderson's Plan for Sullom Voe, costing £70,000—of which half was contributed by the Highlands and Islands Development Board—begun in January, 1973, was completed in August of that year and served as the basic structure for all future discussion.

The team had included the Scottish Development Advisory Group for planning advice; the North of Scotland College of Agriculture providing surveys of agriculture and soils: the Economic Intelligence Unit with oil forecasts: the Warren Spring Laboratory dealing with questions of oil pollution; the Orielton Field Centre for biological monitoring and the British Trust for Ornithology. Captain A. T. Young, Harbourmaster of the Clyde and Captain C. J. Wennick were co-opted for advice on navigational and marine aspects, both with tanker experience but not unfortunately in Shetland waters.

Divided into five phases, Livesey and Henderson's remit was broadly to predict as far as possible the nature of the oil industry's requirements; to examine the suitability of the Sullom Voe area from both marine and planning aspects; to assess how all the necessary related industry could be accommodated with the least harm to the environment and to determine what provision should be made for new housing, schools, welfare and all the facilities needed for enlarged communities. The escalating scale of development is emphasised by the fact that when the consultants produced their report it was based on the expectations of 75 million tons of crude oil being landed in Sullom per annum. Nine months later figures of 200 million were being accepted. All potential sites were examined from every conceivable angle and it was confirmed that Sullom Voe could become one of only a handful of ports in the world capable of handling the larger type of tanker up to 720,000 tons (although the average tonnage is expected to be in the region of 300,000 tons), and that the transhipment of oil from the Persian Gulf to Northern Europe via Shetland would at least appear to be a viable if exotic concept.

289

By Autumn 1973, before the Shetland County Council Bill became law, Shell proposed a £20 million super tanker oil terminal in Sullom. Shetland's ensuing Master Plan for Sullom Voe was explained in leaflets, exhibitions and meetings in the areas involved resulting in a measure of re-orientation and the Council's District Plan was finalised in May 1974. A joint plan for Sullom evolved between Shetland and the oil companies to be eventually ratified in April 1975 as the unique Sullom Voe Association Ltd., involving Shell U.K. Exploration and Production Ltd, British Petroleum Ltd and Shetland County Council. A non-profit making company, the SVA has been formed to administer the construction and operation of the oil terminal complex at Sullom Voe. Four major issues are concerned: industrial development; land use; conservation: the consequences on island life and the effect on indigenous industries of economic pressures and activities unknown in the history of Shetland, with a population growth forecast from 18,000 to around 30,000 at the beginning of next century.

In February 1974 Shell announced its intention of laying a 36-inch pipeline from the Cormorant production platform to Sullom, probably coming ashore at Firth's Voe, then underground the five kilometres to Calback Ness. By the end of July definite proposals to pipe oil to Shetland during 1976–77 had been made by Shell/Esso with an estimated 450,000 barrels a day from the Brent field and 150,000 a day from its Cormorant field. Shell/Esso-Conoco proposed bringing 200,000 barrels a day from the Dunlin field by pipeline via Cormorant: Burmah and BP Ranger's estimate was 400,000 barrels a day from their Ninian field due east of Unst, also by pipeline to Sullom, obviously justifying a separate pipeline altogether: further south Mobil's Beryl field, lying due east of Fair Isle, is nearer to Sullom than any other terminal but with an estimated production of 150,000 barrels a day at the moment, proposed to bring oil ashore initially by tanker by 1975: Signal-Conoco's Thistle field with a throughput of 200,000 barrels a day will also use tankers in the initial stages.

In September, 1974, the giant Brent system was announced by Shell/Esso. Five oilfields will be linked in a £200 million joint production system designed to deliver 50 million tons of oil a year at Sullom Voe by 1980. The fields, due to produce almost half of Britain's current annual consumption of oil, are Brent, Cormorant, Dunlin, and Thistle. There will be a platform on Cormorant to serve that field and also to act as a pumping and storage platform for oil coming from the four other fields by feeder pipelines. The system will be jointly owned, half by Shell/Esso and half by the other companies. Shetland County Council will be associated with the oil companies in a management partnership for the terminal which will also handle future pipelines

290

coming ashore in Shetland.

Burmah Oil and BP also proposed a pipeline to Sullom from the Ninian field. They intend laying the largest diameter pipeline practicable which experts still consider as 36 inches in North Sea conditions, and surplus capacity will be available to other operators. These latest revelations imply that by the early 1980's the East Shetland basin alone could be capable of supplying oil equivalent to the whole of Britain's current requirements and possibly more. Sullom Voe terminal will become the biggest installation of its kind in Europe and three or possibly four pipelines to Sullom will be needed. Tankers will also be loaded at sea, at least until the pipelines have been laid. Some Norwegian oil will probably also be brought to Shetland because of the difficulty of bridging the Trench.

Out of seven potential terminal sites examined, it was obvious that Sullom Voe met most requirements. A deep ice-hewn valley, the North Sea probes far into the land until it stops 400 yards short of the Atlantic at Mavis Grind. A flying boat base during the Second World War, Sullom Voe was the bastion of our northern defences. Three thousand men were stationed there, leaving behind them a scene of utter desolation, a maze of crumbling buildings and foundations where sheep forage for what they can find in an area where even grazing is poor and where after nearly 30 years nature has not yet succeeded in reclaiming the scarred earth.

Of the 2884 acres earmarked for the oil complex only a tiny proportion is arable land. In all there are 16 holdings involved to a greater or lesser extent, seven registered crofts and three extensive farms: Garth Farm (2822 acres): Scatsta Farm (2020 acres) and Voxter Farm (1156 acres). In planning the layout of the site higher-grade land was avoided wherever possible and in selecting development areas the disruption of holdings minimised. Several crofters, however, had already entered into agreements with Nordport and compulsory orders were served in July 1974 on the firm itself.

The tides and currents of Yell Sound were studied in great detail by Livesey and Henderson and the safest approach for tankers was decided to be the western channel between the Mainland shore and the islands of Muckle Holm, Little Holm and Lamba. The pilot would come aboard just north of Ramna Stacks, the jagged group of skerries north of Fedeland, the old haaf station at the point of North Roe, and from abreast of Muckle Holm an approaching tanker would have its escort of tugs whose help would be required once it was abeam of Lamba. In Sullom Voe there is deep water close to the shore line eminently suitable for jetties, although entrance in a northerly gale would be a dangerous undertaking.

The manœuvrability of tankers is notoriously poor and a 230,000-ton tanker would require at least four tugs, a 500,000-tonner, six. Tugs require a crew of six each; boats with three-man crews will be needed to run lines to the mooring dolphins at the jetties, while a minimum of three crews of five each will be required for pilot services with probably 10 to 12 pilots in all. The study team estimated that the port would be closed on an average five to six days a year due to storms and another nine days owing to fog, a minimal assessment, in the view of most Shetlanders. There will also be inevitable tidal delays to vessels over 500,000 tons and there will certainly be many days when the pilot will be unable to board when strong winds and currents will also play their part.

On shore a crude oil terminal will require storage tanks, water and gas separation plant, stabilisation plant and if methane is present in large quantities a liquefied natural gas plant. It is highly possible that in addition to these a liquified petroleum gas plant may also be added. The Plan, however, emphasised that land has *not* been allocated for either a refinery or an LNG plant; areas have simply been *reserved* against such a contingency, but it is one that appears at the moment to be more than a possibility. Oil loading jetties must be close to the shore, safe, deep and sheltered and an area for a crude oil transhipment terminal will be sited at the northern end of Calback Ness near water deep enough to take vessels up to 720,000 tons. Facilities will be required for ballast water in reception and clearing tanks and for separating and disposing of the sludge. The Port Authority will involve a staff for harbour control, a 24-hour radar watch; a VHF radio link; H.M. Customs, all with crews and launches available round the clock.

One of the main needs of a crude-oil terminal is storage tanks with at least a five-day capacity. After a feasibility study on the Ness at Vats Houllands, Shetland County Council decided that cavern storage would not only be visually more acceptable, safer, requiring only 5 acres as opposed to 250 for tanks above ground, but would also provide a by-product of crushed rock. A deadlock ensued until June 1976 when a compromise was reached between the Council and the oil companies. Conventional tanks are being installed above ground but with bund walls designed to direct any spillage through a piping system to a common impounding basin. Propane and butane gases will be refrigerated and stored before shipment and raw gasolines returned to the stabilised crude oil. Four steel floating roof storage tanks of 100,000 cubic metre gross capacity, with bases 37 metres above sea level to provide suction head to the main loading pumps, will stand 22 metres high with a diameter of 76 metres. As the Port Authority, the Shetland Islands Council is building initially two loading jetties capable of handling

292

tankers up to 300,000 deadweight tons with a loading rate of 30,000 tons of oil per hour. All operations will be constantly monitored and we are assured that no environmental damage will occur.

The first contract for a labour camp at Sullom, worth £3 million, was given to the Edinburgh firm of Millar Construction, Northern Ltd. The camp at Firth houses 1200 workers in single rooms in groups of 12 blocks of 50 rooms with TV, bars, snack bars, cinema—all the amenities of a fairly sophisticated village. A sports complex will remain in perpetuity as a centre for residents in the area. A second camp, costing £8½ million is now required to house an extra 1800 men.

Shetland now faces large numbers of immigrants with no real roots and little understanding of local culture. How can one provide for the newcomers without damaging what the existing inhabitants believe to be a unique way of life, only to be found in Shetland? The over-riding concern to accommodate the demands of the incoming industry appears in many ways to have blinded the planners to the social costs of such an influx in relation to the actual benefits to be derived. The Sullom Voe Plan anticipates the intake of at least 1000 families, all of whom need houses. Various methods of distributing this new population were suggested and after amendments in the light of public comment it had been decided that rather than segregate the incomers in one large new "oil" town, they should be spread over the existing communities of Brae, Voe, Mossbank and Firth.

These small areas are all typical of Shetland's way of life, with relatively scattered housing, 90 per cent of all dwellings privately owned, half of them owner-occupied. Most of these areas have a village shop, small church, school and garage. Recreational activities, as in most country districts, are practically nil, with only a sailing club at Brae and football during the summer months. There was already high employment in the predominant primary industries of fishing and agriculture, together with comparatively small but flourishing weaving and knitwear firms.

Although most residents in the Delting district have backed the County's plans to accommodate the incoming families in four small villages rather than one new town, there is an excellent precedent for the latter. It was pointed out some years ago that a town the size of Lerwick, combining as it does over one-third of the total island population, with a monopoly of supplies and acting as the sole administrative centre, is scarcely a healthy development. In Faroe, in addition to the capital, Torshavn, there is also Klakksvik, a service and industrial centre for the north isles with a population of nearly 4000, three fish processing plants, an ice factory, rope works, a spinning mill, sea school and hospital of its own. A similar development in the Sullom Voe area,

293

while housing its temporary residents, could accommodate all these basic industries which would later be invaluable to Shetland and at the same time create a second town in an under-populated part of the islands.

The largest settlement involved is the village of Brae looking out over Busta Voe, where 275 new houses will be built, 150 in the first five years. It is intended to preserve the existing layout with extensions to the north, round the head of Busta Voe and on the west shore of the voe to form a long curved line of mostly single-storey housing. Voe, at the head of Olnafirth, the longest and one of the most beautiful voes in Shetland, clusters round the jetties of the old whaling station with a few houses climbing the hillside behind it to present a tiny village of great scenic beauty. This attractive setting is to be respected, but the new development on the north side of the firth, consisting of 125 houses, is bound to have an immense visual and environmental impact on the entire scene. Like the other new settlements there will be the same provision of unheard-of amenities; a new shop, public house, public convenience, playing fields next to the school, a sea-fishing and sailing centre, foreshore paths, street lighting and the inevitable waste disposal tip which one fervently hopes will in no way resemble the one in Lerwick.

Mossbank, on the promontory looking north to Yell Sound, was until recently the small ferry terminal for Yell, while Toft, another tiny village with many abandoned crofts, is now the departure site of the *Fivla*, the new roll-on roll-off ferry. At present 250 houses are proposed for Mossbank, a new primary school as at Brae, playing fields, shop, hotel, public house, walkways, street lighting and the waste disposal tip, all of which will most probably engulf Toft. Firth, at the head of Firth Voe south of Mossbank, is intended as a local authority "new town" with 350 houses making it eventually about the size of Scalloway.

It is ironical that Shetland has had to wait for the arrival of oil for so many facilities and amenities accepted as the normal pattern of living in the south, and it is almost impossible to envisage these small communities suddenly burgeoning into modern housing schemes largely inhabited by outsiders. Perhaps it is the right thing to endeavour to integrate the new arrivals with the existing population. Time alone can tell. Shetlanders are among the most hospitable of any community in the world and given the opportunity are no doubt capable of absorbing all the incomers within their shores and perhaps even influencing them sufficiently so that they too will appreciate and become part of the Shetland way of life. But both sides will have to make sacrifices.

In most areas in the world intensive industrial development can be screened by landscaping, utilising trees, shrubs and so forth. It is impossible in Shetland where the few reasonably successful plantations occur only in particularly favourable conditions and even with wind breaks have probably the slowest growth rate in the British Isles.

Even before the advent of oil, private and council housing had mushroomed to a degree only rivalled by eight or nine other counties in relation to population. With improvement grants many older dwellings were modernised, one of the most desirable of concepts and entirely fitted to the environment. In 1971, however, tenders for new houses on Bressay and Whalsay were higher than the County Council could accept and they turned to Norway. The timber house kits were quick to erect and the Scottish Development Department was impressed by the speed with which workers in the expanding industries of knitting and fish processing could be accommodated.

The entire programme escalated with the coming of oil and demand soon exceeded supply, so the County Council turned to the Scottish Special Housing Association. At the beginning of 1972 the S.S.H.A. agreed to build 100 houses in Shetland for incoming workers and by May the Norwegian timber house had been decided upon for Phase I of their Shetland programmes, 30 at Sandwick and 15 at Scatness. From the one-storey dwelling the two-storey Bloc Watne houses soon appeared all over the islands and will stand, one hopes not forever, as the worst example of the right thing in the wrong place. Designed for the wooded fjords of Norway, even the Norwegian suppliers admit that they are totally unsuited to the Shetland landscape. But this was only a beginning. The S.S.H.A. had also a contract with Lerwick Town Council to build 106 of these houses at Sound; nearly 40 in Unst, mostly of the same type and on a large site adjacent to the North Road in Lerwick. The present county building programme includes over 130 houses in all parts of the country from Northmavine to Fetlar, Walls and Sandwick and the local authority will again have to turn to the S.S.H.A. for help, which at long last has produced a modified design.

Many famous views are already ruined. In Weisdale Voe, a focal point in this magnificent seascape was the tiny isthmus between Hellister Loch and the Voe. On this confined area a new two-storey housing scheme has risen almost overnight. Perched on the skyline of Burra Isle near Hamnavoe is a row of yellow wooden two-storey boxes in a district where a feature of the landscape is the neatness of the beautifully-kept low stone cottages with bright paint and surrounded by colourful gardens.

Industry has been contained, precariously for the moment, incomers living in areas planned and schools and amenities allocated but countless problems still remain. Shetland's roads, excellent for such a small group of remote islands and adequate for its population and annual holidaymakers, were never designed to carry trucks weighing as much as 30 tons, using the roads purely because of oil developments. In March, 1973, there was one vehicle for every three islanders. Since then the total has jumped by 480 in a year. Major roads are being damaged daily and some minor roads only need a truck to use them once to break them up. Like the proverbial goats, if two of these giant vehicles meet one must come to a full stop to allow the other to pass.

The siting of Sumburgh Airport and its suitability for the larger type of aeroplane has always been a controversial subject. In the summer of 1973 one in six Viscount flights had to be cancelled and the construction of an entirely new airfield was considered. A new terminal building has had to replace the comparatively recent one. In July, 1974, a giant mechanical digger cut the first turf for British Airways' huge helicopter hanger, built, unfortunately, on the local football ground. Its fleet of Sikorski helicopters rose to 10 by the end of September, 1974. At the same time a shorter-range, lighter aircraft, the S 587 will be in service. A second hangar has been built for the 17 Sumburgh-based Bristow Sikorskis. In 1975 nearly 200,000 passengers and 1000 metric tons of freight were flown by helicopter between the shore and rigs, platforms and pipelaying barges.

A major resurfacing of the main runway costing around £700,000 was undertaken and the extension begun to Sumburgh's east–west runway to bring it up to instrument landing standards, which the Civil Aviation Authority has decided upon in place of a new airfield, involved levelling the ground to a distance of 350 feet on either side, the operations highlighted by the possible loss of one of Shetland's most unique prehistoric sites, another side-effect of oil-related developments. Partially excavated by the Shetland Archaeological and Natural History Society between 1967 and 1971, the site came well within the clearance zone as did several houses overlooking Hayes Bay.

A "beat the bulldozers" dig, directed by Dr. Raymond Lamb of Newcastle University for the Department of the Environment, established the most northerly evidence of prehistoric ploughing. On the original soil level marks have been found which may well have been made by a primitive plough in Neolithic times, another discovery consisted of a stone-lined drain. Some pottery identified by Dr. Lamb as Iron Age, found in the drain, suggested that yet another, and later, site, probably lies underneath or near the present-day Department of Environment buildings, which themselves will have to be moved to make way for airport improvements. The Archaeological Society are planning a systematic watch both at Sumburgh and Sullom so that investigations can be made and finds recorded in any area due for development, while the present site, being temporarily covered and protected, is now being further explored.

The possibility of Shetland becoming another "Anchorage" on the Polar Route for E.E.C. countries plus a N.A.T.O. base in place of Iceland has also been forecast. Meanwhile, pioneer work has been carried out by the Britton-Norman *Islander* and the newly arrived *Trislander*, which puts Shetland firmly in the Bergen–Oslo–Copenhagen–Kristiansund–Aberdeen network, and soon B.A.L.P.A. pilots will become familiar with Unst, Fetlar, Sullom, Baltasound, Out Skerries, Whalsay, Papa Stour, Foula and Fair Isle, with all the outlying islands now having airstrips. Charter flights to Faroe and to Europe will undoubtedly increase and a vastly-improved flight schedule between Shetland and Aberdeen is in operation with the new H5 748's.

Shetland's beaches too are threatened. The massive amount of sand needed for building a few large complexes could absorb the entire combined volumes of the present pits at Quendale, St. Ninian's Isle and most other suitable beaches, and after years of lobbying by naturalists and conservationists limits are being imposed of 6000 tons a year from St. Ninian's beach and the extraction of sand from Gulberwick has been banned. Up till 1973 no planning permission was necessary and from early morning till evening sand lorries came and went from St. Ninian's Isle beaches, endangering the ayre that joins the island to the mainland, one of the most beautiful tombolas in the world. Sand can only re-build itself at a certain rate. If extracted in massive quantities it merely spreads itself more thinly especially if offshore reserves are limited as is the case with most Shetland beaches.

Other sources of supply must be found but the Lang Ayre, one of the most suitable beaches for the extraction of sand, could be used only if the beach is considered in isolation from its surroundings. The open heath vegetation on Ronas Hill through which an access road would have to run is fragile and extremely vulnerable to damage from road building or even high levels of tramping. The beach complex at Burrafirth in Unst is considered to be physiographically unique in Shetland and the strictest conservation policies must be adopted now if future visitors and their children are going to be able to enjoy Shetland's seemingly endless crescents of white sand that scallop coast and inlet.

Fortunately it is now an economic proposition to import building aggregate in bulk. Seven hundred tons of gravel were brought from Fraserburgh to Hudsons' Offshore base at Broonie's Taing, Sandwick and if underground tanks had been a viable proposition at Sullom crushed rock from the underground catacombs could have been used.

People, houses, building programmes, airports, roads and water supplies can only be worthwhile, however, in a healthy environment,

297

and uppermost in all minds, is the growing menace of pollution by oil, a danger that not even the most elaborate planning provisions in the world can prevent or nullify. Pollution can occur wherever there is oil; directly through oil spillage; by the discharge of oily ballast from tankers; the escape or leakage at well-heads far out to sea or accidents to a tanker at the terminal or indirectly by way of effluent discharged from chemical plants.

In an oil progress report, John Heaney, Technical Manager for Shell U.K. Exploration and Production, explained some of the problems in extracting oil about 120 miles north-east of Lerwick, in 460 feet of water with storm waves up to 100 feet high and gusts of wind up to 160 m.p.h. Their technical men will be working at depths of water and under weather conditions never before experienced in the whole oil industry. Oil rigs are having to be constructed twice the size of the largest ever made with platforms 777 feet from seabed to the top of the drilling derrick, with a base 328 feet by 328 feet. Weather conditions in the vicinity of Shetland were described as sometimes the worst in the world, worse at times than those around Cape Horn.

The public has been assured that safeguards against pollution of the sea would consist of automatic devices which close up an oil well as soon as anything goes wrong. But automatic devices are not infallible. Major accidents in the oil industry are comparatively rare but like those involving air travel the results are invariably fatal. One oil slick in the Red Sea stretched 800 miles, the distance between Shetland and the Thames.

In some cases, even from oilfields in shallow waters, severe accidental pollution has already occurred from which there may be irreversible effects. Little is known of the possible consequences of dredging or drilling the deep sea floor which technology is making increasingly accessible. Although developments are taking place in inventing improved booms for containing spillage so that oil can be collected before it spreads no present arrangement is capable of dealing with spills in seas with waves over four to six feet. A statistical study revealed that a wave height in excess of five feet could occur over one period of 35 consecutive days over the Forties Field.

In January, 1974, a prolonged period of gale force winds highlighted the problems facing platforms and their related vessels. The rig stand-by boat *Spearfish*, standing by the rig *Sedco* 702 about 100 miles North-east of Shetland in storm force conditions shipped a heavy sea which broke windows on the bridge and washed a small boat overboard. All electrical equipment was put out of action and water washed down the funnel starting a fire in the engine room. *Shetland Shore* went to the rescue, encountering heavy broadside seas with mountainous waves which stove in the glass in a porthole, forcing it 20 feet across a room where it destroyed a door. All navigation lights were swept away from their positions 60 feet above the working deck and on the deck itself a 17-ton anchor broke loose from its chains in 60- to 70-foot waves.

That same evening the crew of the oil rig *Venture*, North-east of Shetland, were taken off by helicopter and transferred to two other rigs as a precaution because a broken-off leg from the rig *Transocean 3* which sank on New Year's day in the Beryl field was in close vicinity in very stormy weather and was in danger of colliding with the *West Venture*. Shortly before midnight the leg floated northwards only 300 feet away from the *West Venture*. On Monday night it had drifted 130 miles since breaking off and lay to the north of a group of rigs. Plans by the Navy to blow it up were abandoned because of weather conditions. A new threat came to shipping and rigs from the second leg which broke free from *Transocean 3* but it disappeared.

When *Transocean 3* capsized another semi-submersible *Transworld 61* was taken in tow by three tugs bound for Stavanger. Over the weekend two tow lines parted and in gale force winds one tug fought to save the rig with 14 men on board from being driven northwards.

The concrete platforms under construction for North Sea fields will have very large integral crude oil storage tanks, so the loss of one of these platforms could release its entire contents into the sea although new wells use valves controlled from the surface which will shut down all producing wells when storms are forecast. One has only to look back over the long history of the Far Haaf to realise that the North Sea seldom gives much warning, and time and again the fishing fleet was caught at sea even in the middle of summer.

The most recent event was the rescue by helicopter in December, 1975, of 4 technicians from Mobil's *Beryl*, a tanker mooring and loading buoy, drifting 100 m east of Sumburgh in mountainous seas during a Force 11 gale. The Queen's Award for Gallantry went to Bristow Helicopters' chief pilot, Capt. T. Wolfe-Milner.

It is under these conditions that the port at Sullum Voe will be handling up to 20 crude carriers weekly ranging from 18,000 to 300,000 tons, plus about ten smaller gas tankers. Although Phillips' Ekofisk combines an underwater storage of a million barrels (three days' production) with tanker moorings the problems of operating this system in northern parts of the North Sea are considerable and the firm eventually proposes an oil pipeline to Teesside. There are still reservations as to the ability of oil companies to bury oil pipelines in the sea bed at depths exceeding 230 feet and in Shetland waters they could be faced with depths of over 500 feet. It is technically possible to bury them adequately, but as Dr. Derek Flynn pointed out the proposals took no account of the geological difficulties involved. The sea floor around Shetland presents problems never encountered elsewhere. The great depth of water, the craggy and rocky nature of the sea floor and the hardness of the rock mean that a route had to be found nearly straight in both plan and elevation and with a soft bottom in which the pipe can be buried to prevent it being fractured by the tide, heavy weather or fishermen's gear. Such lines are uncommon in Shetland waters and it is not surprising that both fishermen and pipelayers were in competition for·them.

On August 30th, 1974, the Shetland Fishermen's Association received its most devastating blow. Shell's pipeline from its Cormorant platform to the oil terminal at Sullom Voe would have to cut through the prolific Pobie Bank and the Skerries-Fetlar area. The Association was told that alternative routes proposed by them were not practicable and the line will run through the area for 96 miles. The adverse effects on the fishing industry from pipelines and during pipelaying operations has always been a major source of worry but the fishermen were assured that everything possible would be done to minimise disturbance with the additional help of £25,000 handed over on May 2nd, 1975. The pipeline, costing over £80 million, will be buried under the sea bed except for several miles. There is, however, no absolute certainty that a pipeline once buried will remain so. In the laying of the Forties-Cruden Bay pipeline divers found when pipelaying was restarted that the end of the pipe had moved hundreds of yards during the course of the winter.

In 1971 earnings by Shetland boats was a record £2,107,000 and in the last 10 months of 1973 white fishing and herring contributed over £22,000 to the Harbour Trust alone. Practically the whole of Shetland's economy is concentrated on fishing and the County Plan has been criticised for dealing so briefly with the effects of pollution on the industry. It is understood that the dangers of spillage or pollution mainly affect shellfish, discolouring their meat, but that for demersal and pelagic fish there is not apparently so much hazard. With the decline of the herring fishing, however, came an expansion of lobster and crab and in 1962 a processing plant was set up in Scalloway. The richest lobster and crab beds are found on the west side of Mainland and in Yell Sound, with landing places at West Burrafirth, Hillswick, Eshaness, Ronas Voe and Graven, Vidlin and Scalloway. In 1962, due to poor catches of of white fish, some of the larger vessels boosted the value of lobsters to £110,000 for the year. By 1968 crab fishing alone was worth £22,200. If Vidlin Voe were to be polluted £10,000 worth of lobsters might die.

In the narrow confines of Shetland's voes, in addition to crude oil spillages a special danger could occur from chemical effluent from drilling mud discharged from plants of various kinds. With the multiplicity of platforms, tankers, pipes and jetties now converging on the East Shetland basin, and quite possibly further developments in Atlantic waters the long-term effect of small but constant seepages over the whole environment is a terrifying one, as disturbing to ecologists as a major disaster, if not more so.

Today oil platforms are being built twice the size of any hitherto constructed and the capabilities of these vast structures to withstand conditions in the North Sea have yet to be tested. The technological problems of construction and installation of these giant platforms are enormous. Low-temperature high-quality steels are needed; anti-corrosion devices such as cathodic protection and polyurethane coatings; making certain the sea bed can stand the platform's weight; protecting the structure against scouring and prolonged wave and tidal action which can move millions of tons of sand around in sea bed waves at about three knots. Sand alone has a fearsome reputation even in small quantities. Filtering through the valve house and down through the penstocks, sand from the Swat River bed at the big hydro-electric station at Malakand in Pakistan's North West Frontier actually pitted and pockmarked the great steel blades of the turbines. Little is known about the effect of saline fluid on pre-stressed and post-stressed concrete. In the North Sea the uncertainty attending all these risk factors is obviously increased. No one knows or admits by how much, but each margin of error adds to pollution danger.

The human factor, in spite of all the sophisticated and computerised devices yet invented, appears to be one to which little thought has been given. With the exception of Shell and BP, drilling rigs and their crews are owned by drilling companies who are in business to hire out their services to anyone who wants them. Among them will inevitably be divers. The offshore industry is expanding so rapidly that it is now seriously outstripping the supply of experienced men. So much money is invested that operators cannot afford to have work held up for any reason and diving contractors are continually under pressure to produce more men. The new safety regulations under the Mineral Workings Act control offshore installations but once outside territorial waters the Act no longer applies so that there is in effect nothing to control diving operations on the Continental Shelf where men are already working at 1000 feet.

The Managing Director of Comex Diving Ltd., Mr. Farrington-Wharton said: "The North Sea Oil industry is very young and I regret that further accidents and 'bends' are inevitable. Long saturation jobs require keeping the divers living at bottom pressure in a decompression chamber on the surface of the rig or barge. Should by accident a crane hook hit the side of the decompression chamber and fracture a fitting or a high pressure pipe and decompressurise the chamber that one small incident will have killed about four divers."

Another problem is that of a team of divers carrying out long decompression on a rig when the rig sinks or there is a blow-out or fire, as has happened off Peru. The diving equipment was destroyed in a matter of minutes. The possibility of a blow-out involving gas or ignited gas or even oil cannot be ignored and in the unlikely event of all safety devices failing, rescue provisions must be prepared incorporating all emergency services—medical, lifeboat, R.A.F., the Navy, police and coastguards.

Shetland County Council has obviously been impressed by the apparent involvement of oil companies in the Shetland environment, with their comings and goings, the frank desire to see everything for themselves, and not least with the recent spontaneous hand-out of £28 million over the rest of the century. This is intended to ease the burdens cast on the community in general by the arrival of oil. The courtship one suspects is instigated largely by the overwhelming need for a marriage of convenience. The oil companies need Shetland and Shetland's goodwill. Without bases they are helpless and while appreciating the extent to which they are prepared to go in this unprecedented wooing, the dangers of social and environmental problems will never grow less.

The Institute of Terrestrial Ecology was responsible for the most comprehensive study yet undertaken in this country. Commissioned by the Nature Conservancy Council, funds were provided by the oil industry. BP carried out its own environmental assessment of the Forties Field and in June 1976 came the controversial seminar presented by the Sullom Voe Environmentalists' Impact Study. Boycotted by the Shetland Council, bitter complaints ensued that no advance publication of the report had been made available; no time was left for discussion and speakers failed to admit their lack of knowledge in certain areas, notably the question of oil spills from tanker accidents at sea. Bland assurances had little effect on over 200 Shetlanders and the sole positive proposal seems to have come from Professor Taylor of the University of Dundee who stressed the need for a preventive occupational health service.

The *Torrey Canyon* disaster highlighted the difficulties of controlling a major spillage and Finland has been stockpiling peat as an antidote to pollution. A Shetlander, Dr. Robin Sinclair, believes peat may eventually prove to have a place in controlling oil pollution round our shores. In the past, chemical dispersants were highly poisonous and

302

probably did more harm than good. The recently-developed emulsifiers are far less toxic to marine life but their use was described in 1971 as "the deliberate tipping of poisons into the sea". The builders of Clickhimin used peat to bed down their animals; the Vikings also were aware of the absorbent qualities of "*muldekause*" but neither they nor their Shetlandic descendants could have imagined in their wildest dreams the purposes for which it might eventually be used. Peat can absorb between eight and twelve times its own weight of oil. In a series of tests made on possible absorbents described in H.M.S.O. booklet *Oil Pollution of Sea and Shore* 14 different substances were tested and the spreading and absorption characteristics of peat compared favourably with such synthetic materials as polypropylene fibre and polystyrene pellets.

The Finns claim to have already proved the suitability of peat and their State Fuel Board produces oil-absorbent compressed peat in 170-litre packs for sale to port authorities and oil companies. Dr. Sinclair has carried his own studies a stage further and believes that dried peat can be made more efficient by coating it with chemicals. His preliminary tests are encouraging but much work has yet to be done in devising methods of storing, drying and treating the peat and in perfecting techniques for spreading and recovery. At least in Shetland there is an abundance of raw material.

The future of Shetland's indigenous industries is now in the balance, overshadowed, outnumbered and financially uneconomic compared with the multiplicity of on-shore service industries connected with the oil industry, either by oil-related services, or on building, roads and airfield requirements. The knitwear industry cannot compete with oil-related wages and lack of housing could drive key workers away. In 1969 there was a record turnover of almost £1·5 million. With a recession in 1973 due mainly to the loss of interest in the French market and the obvious temptations of higher wages elsewhere it now appears that Shetland knitwear will require subsidising by long-term low-cost loans from a fund created by the interest earned on the capital sums advanced or given by the oil companies.

Workmen in local authorities services see other workmen with construction companies and oil-related employment taking home double the amount which the local authority workmen earn. Serious labour problems are foreseen. Many council workers, rather than wait until negotiations are completed, have already left for better jobs and a wholesale breakdown in public services could result. Agriculture, with an annual value to Shetland of at least £1 million, will almost certainly also be hit.

Fish processing is another important part of Shetland's economy with factories precariously near the key positions of oil-related industries.

303

85 Looking from the Town Hall tower towards Gremista and Greenhead and all the new developments due to the oil boom.

The value of Shetland's fish products in 1970 exceeded £2,500,000 but if the factories are to survive, their growth must not be stunted by the needs of the vast oil complexes now encroaching on pier space in Lerwick and Scalloway.

Oil-related industry is bringing work into Shetland but into a community which already enjoyed almost full employment, with the result that more and more men are leaving their present occupations. For Shetlanders it is a comparatively short-term outlook, but a man with family and children, unless he is utterly dedicated to producing knitwear, fish processing, dust collection or baking, can scarcely be expected to remain loyal to his employer with his neighbour earning twice as much. Who will come back to the old life after experiencing the new? The cost of living in Shetland is already the highest in Britain, and those whose wage packets are not based on oil are bound to suffer, while not everyone can be expected to deal sensibly with this new-found affluence. Although crime figures in Shetland have been almost non-existent, even before the arrival of oil on our doorstep scarcely a week passed without four or five cases involving alcohol as the motivating factor, and for the first time in this century thefts are being reported. In a society where it was rare for anyone to lock a door, even in Lerwick, cars are now seldom left unlocked and policies have for the first time been taken out against burglary. With a large proportion of incomers unattached males, without ties, accustomed to an almost nomadic existence, there will come an undoubted lowering of moral standards and all the consequences that are bound to ensue.

To Shetlanders today the whole prospect seems like some incredible pipe dream. With one cinema situated in Lerwick; only four or five public houses in Lerwick and one in Brae, one in Hillswick; three full-time hairdressers also in Lerwick and vastly overworked; one laundry and one dry-cleaner to serve the entire islands, the advent of all the promised amenities is an enticing one—for those who live in development areas. Supplies from the south are uncertain and sporadic. Freight and passenger service charges continue to spiral. The outlying districts have had their bus services cut. Men can rarely be found ready to drive travelling shops. Country districts, ironically, often have to wait for milk, which is taken to Lerwick, pasteurised and then despatched by the following morning's mail van in plastic bags, which must then be collected that day, rain or shine, a very real hardship for mothers with young children, and the elderly.

We may grumble, we may wish for better things, but to be faced with one of the major developments in European history is both terrifying and perplexing. For a group of islands with some of the most beautiful, unspoiled and remote scenery in Britain, where local industries built up over the years were beginning to show profit, with no smoke, no unsightly agglomeration of factory buildings, the outlook seems, on the face of it, grim.

It may be a case of *plus ça change, plus c'est la même chose*, and although with a few notable exceptions the gathering round the peat fire, the fiddle and the "maakin" so beloved of film makers, had been largely abandoned for the oil-fired central heating, the "telly" and the knitting machine, the very fact that what is left to us may be in jeopardy, the greater may be the endeavour to preserve it. The entire spectrum of leisure activities is bound to undergo a startling change. For young Shetlanders, working full-time in a variety of ways from mink farming, to market gardening, from stone polishing to roadworks or driving lorries, leisure invariably had some profit. An evening's fishing in a boat, perhaps built by himself, certainly lovingly and skilfully maintained, was fun, but it also provided fish for deep-freezing or piltaks for drying. Although a man might not be running a full-time croft the tattie patch and the cabbages supplemented the family diet and gave some creative pleasure.

There are still "reistit mutton" suppers, regattas, country shows. The annual room and caa'in of the sheep is a communal effort. Up Helly Aa is a magnificent wholly Shetlandic spectacle of community enjoyment. Villagers help each other with hay, corn, peats, on a mutual benefit level—you help me tonight, I'll help you tomorrow. Are we going to see the end of this kind of activity? Will the young Shetlander of the future, still in "yokit jumper", drive forth in fast cars for a round of golf on the new course at Dale, constructed with a handsome contribution from the oil companies? In the petty bourgeois society which is to come class distinction will inevitably evolve, something hitherto scarcely noticeable, except of course in the pseudo-sophistication of Lerwick.

From Shetland come innumerable talented young people who have yet remained fundamentally Shetlanders, even though like Aly Bain the fiddler they achieve world fame—he still returned to Shetland for a traditional wedding, fiddler, gunner and all. There are artists like Maxie Bain whose intimate involvement with the Shetland scene is innate in his paintings and drawings; Roy Hughson, a sculptor and painter who is willing to work at any job that comes his way in order to be able to earn enough money to pursue his natural talents. There are countless others and it is perhaps invidious to mention only a few names. There is a dedicated group of ornithologists which has recently formed a Bird Club; exceptionally talented photographers like Dennis Coutts whose photographs of Shetland's bird life, its people and its scenery are obviously necessary and vital to him. There are already incomers who have opted out of the rat race and are re-vitalising island life and exiled Shetlanders are now finding jobs at home.

I believe, after all, that there are yet enough born and bred Shetlanders still sufficiently committed to a Shetland way of life to make their impact felt among the newcomers and possibly benefit from a wider angle of interests shared or learned from others. The actual pressure of oil in every sense has emphasised the belief in that way of life, seemingly so permanent and yet so potentially transitory and fragile that more Shetlanders may now be ready to defend it—from pollution, from desecration and from ultimate decimation, with every fibre of their beings, a people whom all the oil moguls in the world should be unable to suppress.

306

Glossary

aalin: or Scootie-aalin: Arctic Skua: *Stercorarius parasiticus*

abune: above

adze: a cutting tool with an arched blade set at right-angles to the handle

aert: direction, usually concerning wind: "the wind's in a bad aert"

Ala moutie: Shetlandic for the Storm Petrel: *Hydrobates pelagicus*

Althing: the yearly parliament of all the various district *things* or courts and held on the Law Ting Holm in Tingwall Loch; the great assemblage of the freemen of the county and the name by which the Icelandic Parliament is known today

ando: to row the boat gently to the line

anker: keg containing about 8·33 Imperial gallons

ard: prehistoric stone plough still being used by Norse settlers in Shetland in A.D. 800

arles: payment made by fish merchants to "gutters" early in the year, usually of £1, which bound them to gut or pack herring for that merchant throughout the season. Girls normally continued to work each year at the same station

ask: drizzle, half rain, half fog: small particles of snow

åttrings: Norwegian fishing boats similar to but larger than the Shetland sixareen and with eight oars instead of six and spelled auchterings in Shetland

ayre: beach, usually of cobble stones used for spreading fish to dry in the days of haaf fishing: also denoting a strand

Baa: a reef, generally of rocks just underneath the surface of the water

baenk: a wooden bench

baes: beasts

bannock: scone

barbel: the beard-like whisker under the jaw of the cod

baukt: or bught: a length or measure of fishing lines made up into a baukt of around 50 fathoms

Beaner Sunday: the Sunday before Christmas when an ox head was hung in the chimney

beards: the "anns" or whiskers of bere, a type of barley

Beltin Ree: the winds that blow strongly around Whitsuntide (Beltane)

ben: the bedroom end of an old croft house

bere: a type of barley common to Shetland bearing six ears

bewast: to the west

bichters: stone sinkers about 22 lbs in weight attached to every line to keep it steady

biddies: method of marking sheep by a cut in the ear

bismer: (bysmar) a steelyard, the recognised weighing machine

bits: mark on a sheep's ear to denote ownership: a small shallow v taken out either at the front or back of the ear: cross-bitted meaning a small v *both* back and front

blaand: a drink from the final product of the churn the result of putting a hot stone into the churn after the buttermilk

Black Backs: the Great Black Backed Gull: (swaabie in Shetlandic) *Larus marinus*

blaedick: milk left in the churn after the butter. Into the blaedick was put a hot stone which turned the milk into *blaand*

bluid: blood: "to bluid da kye", to bleed the cow

blyed: glad, happy: "I'm blyed tae see dee", I'm happy to see you

boards: on the Shetland clinker-built boat each "board" had a different name

böd: booth or trading place built of stone and used by the German merchants

Bog Cotton: a common plant in marshes and bogs with silky-white heads: Cotton Grass: *Eriophorum angustifolium*

böl: A shelter for a lamb or young calf, a stall in a byre, a resting place: (ON Ból a resting place)

bolta-stones: another name for *bichters* (the latter used in the Dunrossness area) sinking stones for lines

böm: Dutch fishing vessel pre-1900 rigged fore and aft with a jib and small mizzen rather like the Scottish drifter's "dandy"

bondi: originally a "dweller", tiller or husbandman, later coming to mean the entire body of Udal-born freemen in Norse times. In Orkney and Shetland they became an important political class and in Shetland, rising in rebellion they slew St. Olaf, their king, at the battle of Sticklastad

bønhoose: Norse for prayer-house or church

Bonxie: the Great Skua: *Catharacta skua*

bool: the carrying part of a bucket or the brass hoop for hanging up the old type of oil lamp

brandiron: iron plate laid over hot peats on the fire on which a variety of scones or bannocks were made

brak: surf along a beach

brakkin: breaking

bratt: apron: oilskin one worn by gutters

brenna: (in place names) a burned-off piece of land (ON brenna—a burning)

brö: water in which meat or other food has been cooked

brönis: thick oatmeal or bere-meal scones

brunt: burned: *brunt* or burnt stane (stone)

burn: a tiny stream

burstin: bere dried hard in a pan then ground in a hand quern. The original method of drying was by heating a stone and keeping the meal close to it. With this they made burstin brönis or scones

buss: Dutch type of herring boat obsolete by about 1860

but: the living end of an old croft house

bygo: district (ON) in modern Norse *bygd* still meaning a district

caadie: a lamb hand-fed on a bottle either an orphan or one which the ewe is unable to feed

caaing whale: the species *Globiocephala malaena*

caa'in: driving: often used when gathering sheep for shearing, dipping or marking

cairdin': carding wool in preparation for spinning; done on two hand-held wire brushes with wooden backs, the raw wool placed between them and brushed with a teasing movement

casting peat: cutting peat

claith: homespun woollen cloth produced up to the late nineteenth century

cleeps: distinctive marks on sheeps' ears denoting ownership: half a "V"

clibbers: see "klibbers"

coll: a small stook of hay, bere, etc. set up to dry

craig-seats: a place on a rock by the sea: once commonly used by the ordinary folk when fishing from the shore. All had names and each the "chosen" and particular "seat" of one crofter. In one mile between Noss and Spiggie were: *da Scolt: da Sillak Gates: da Gray Bard: da Boga: da Gardie Stane* and *Lowrie Eunson's steps:* from ON *berg* and *saeti*, literally a rock seat. Noted in 1633. The men used an 11-foot bamboo rod (if available) or *waandscarfed* together—sections bound with twine to give it greater elasticity and tapered towards the end. The cast or *tome* of horse-hair was twisted by hand, the mashed mussels or limpets prepared in cup-shaped hollows near the seats

cran: a volume measure of 37·5 gallons or 4 baskets (of fish) usually about 3·5 cwts

crappen: a dish made of fish livers mixed with meal and boiled in a cotton bag

crayers: small fishing boats

creepie: a small wooden stool

creesh: or *kreesh:* oil used on wool when spinning, fish oil, seal oil or in modern days colza oil

crö or **Krö:** a small stone-built enclosure in which to pen sheep (Icelandic Kró—a fold: Gaelic cro—a fold)

croft: a small-holding of less than 50 acres

crook baak: a square log of wood centred over the hearth-stone (when in the middle of the room) and stretching from wall to wall

crooks and links: a chain of round iron links hung above the fire from which kettles and pots could be suspended at different heights

cross-bit: a small shear from one side of the sheep's ear: a mark of ownership

cüddie: a kind of flat basket made of docken-stalks or straw, used for carrying bait, limpets or mussels when fishing off craig seats

cumal: a bondswoman (Irish-Celtic)

da eela: going out to sea in the evenings to fish for *piltaks* (young saithe)

delling: digging particularly in respect of the old Shetland spade: formerly a section of the field that could be dug over in a day by a delling team

dochter: daughter: i.e. Margaret Erasmusdochter, Margaret daughter of Erasmus: used before Shetlanders acquired surnames. In 1577 only 141 out of the 759 udallers who had complained against Bruce of Cultmalindie had surnames, after the Scots fashion. The remaining 618 had surnames ending in "son" or were referred to by their farm: i.e. Ola a Hamar. The "son" names were not family surnames but changed with each generation. John Manson might have a son called Nicol Johnson whose son in turn became John Nicolson. This type of naming lasted until the beginning of the nineteenth century and even a few people in 1910 registering for their first Old Age Pension, found that they had been baptized this way. Norse forenames underwent a quick change with the arrival of the Scots clergy who refused to baptise in "heathen" names. Ola, Nicol and Magnus survived as saints' names but Hakon, for example, was transformed to Hector: Asi to the Biblical Hosea, although still verbally Ossi, originating the surname of Hoseason: in women's names Geirhildr became Grizel or Grace and its diminutive Geirsi replaced all three in speech. Auslag became Ursula, spoken as Osla

dogge: Flemish for cod

309

doggers: new type of herring boat introduced from Boulogne after 1866 and used by the Dutch herring fleet

dorro: a handline weighted with a lead. A length of cord, several fathoms long was used, with a cork float attached. From the cord hung a length of about six feet of line, at the end of which was a hook with a large limpet as bait. The shore end of the line was anchored to a suitable stone on the craig seat and both float and tackle thrown out as far as necessary. When the float began to bob up and down, obviously a fish had taken the bait and the tackle was pulled in. Fish caught on the *dorro* were mainly rock cod, large *piltaks* and small tusk or cod. (From ON *dorg*— a trailing fish line)

Drawn strae: used in thatching—oat straw drawn lengthways from one bundle to another to overlap the previous layer of *tekkin* straw

dropstick: landing net used when fishing to catch "cods for the kettle" presumably to eat on board

du: you: used in both Shetland and Norway in talking to friends, relations or children

dusses: In Dunrossness meaning the second process before building the final stack which stood over the winter and was used for fodder. First, small *stooks* composed of four to six bundles are set up; then they are built into *dusses*, larger stacks twisted and held at the top by binding: then finally the *skroos*, the large stacks netted over against the wind. In Foula the sequence is known as "*bullies*", *stooks*, *skroos* while in the north of Mainland it is *sixes*, *stooks* and *skroos*

Dutch: a corruption of Deutsch: north German—merchants who set up booths or *bods* in which they stored and sold their goods

ekker: an ear of barley ekkered, when the grains have appeared

erd: earth

faeley-daek: a wall built of turf (L.Sc. fail-dyke)

fantin: starving

farlins: wooden trays set in front of the gutters into which the herring for gutting and sorting were poured

far haaf: distant waters up to 40 miles: *hav* in modern Norse means ocean

fastie: old anchor chains or ropes used to tie up and secure a boat in her *noost*, the safe resting place (Icelandic *feste*—a rope)

feid: literally "fee'd": boys who joined a boat's crew for a small payment but who drew no share of the catch until they were old enough to be taken on as "hands"

Fifie: both Fifie's and Scaffie's were Scottish herring boats, Fifie's originating in the Firth of Forth and Scaffie's in the Moray Firth

flaa, flaas: a thin turf used in roofing a croft house

flackie: the straw mat on which the corn was winnowed; flat mat made of straw laid over a pony's back to prevent it being hurt by the saddle or *meshie* (thick rope nets) carrying the *kishies* or baskets full of peats, which hung from the wooden *klibbers* (a wooden contrivance strapped over the *flackie*)

flay: removing the top turf along a peat bank to prepare it for *casting* or cutting

flyte: to scold

floss: the common rush

floss baets: rushes cut and tied into bunches before being used to make simmands

fool wadder: foul weather

fore'room: a division of the sixareen's *rooms* or compartments between the rowing benches: near the bows

310

foude: the chief civil officer deriving authority from the Crown or Norway: Norse—*foged*: In a letter from Sir Nicholas Throgmorton to Queen Elizabeth he refers to the principal man of the isle (Shetland) as the "fogge"

fouraering, foureren: a four-oared boat

foy: some kind of merrymaking, a feast: an impromptu gathering to have some fun

fulls: herring with roe: expression used by gutters

gaets: sheep-paths, particularly on a hillside

ganzie: home-knitted sweater

gauts: pigs

geo: a small, usually steep-sided voe or inlet

glebe: an area of farmland attached to the manse of a Presbyterian minister

gigot: a leg of mutton

girsum: or grassum: the sum paid to a landlord for renewal of a lease at first at two shillings for each merk or merkland: then an annual sum of eight shillings Scots per merk of land.

glöds: glows

gloy: oat straw used for making *simments* or *simmands*—straw ropes

grianan: sun-room (Irish Celtic)

grice: pig

grind: a gate, also used in some districts to describe the wooden neck collar to keep sheep from going through fences: known in various localities as *beogs* or *trees*. (ON grind) a wicket gate in a fence

grillocks: "dancing *grillocks*" people in fancy dress or disguise who often arrive at New Year, Christmas or a party

grun: ground

guizers: people coming to a party in disguise: also *grillocks*

haaf: ocean (modern Norse *hav*)

hairst: harvest time

hale: to haul in the lines: Shetlanders never use the word *haul*, always *hale*

halfvkip: type of Norse boat: a ship of all work: an ocean goer, sometimes known as a merchant vessel (kaupskip)

hap: wrap or shawl

hamefers: hamefarin': homecoming used in the sense of celebrations around Shetlanders coming home from abroad or back to the village after a wedding.

hassins: harsings (Goodlad): the second board on a sixareen from the keel up: the ones with the twist in them: "*hassin traa*" signifies "twisted" and is often applied to a person

helli: a week end

hevil-dafficks: wooden tubs or buckets

henti-leggits: a name used certainly in Unst for scraps of sheep's wool caught on fencing or heather and gathered for cleaning, carding and spinning

herred: a body of mounted men riding to an agreed place—eventually to the Lawting. From *herre*, modern Norse for a gentleman

hertstane: hearth stone

Hitland: Dutch name for Shetland

helliks: "ta helliks" meaning the edging stones on a roof

hlao: headdress of ribbon-like streamers with gold embroidery often worn by Norse men on ceremonial occasions

311

hoe: the dogfish: also known as hå: *Squalus acanthius*

hoga-leave: permission to graze animals or cut peats in someone else's scattald, entailing some form of payment for the liberty; (ON hagi—a pasture)

hoidin: hiding

holm: a small, grassy islet: an offshore islet with a grassy top on which sheep were grazed in small numbers

huggistaff: a long wooden instrument with an iron hook near the end: used to haul in big fish like halibut or skate or to catch hold of the jetty

humlaband: the leather thong passed through a hole in the *ruth* a wooden check on the gunwale of Shetland boats and then looped round the oar making it particularly easy to "ship" the oars and preventing them slipping overboard

hummeling: threshing the bere grain to remove the beards

hunska: a kind of black pudding made with "*burstin*" meal and blood drawn from a vein in the neck of the cow—used during times of privation

inbye: inside, close to

immda: a cubicle in the wheelhouse type of building

japple: to stamp clothes in a tub (with the feet)

Jol E'en: Christmas Eve

jougs: an iron neck ring—the old Scottish pillory

kaib: the pin on the gunwale of a Shetland boat against which the oar is pulled and usually detachable.

kail: cabbages with open, curled leaves

kappies: stone sinkers attached to the lines to keep them on the bottom

karfi: Norse vessel the chief one used for coastal and shallow waters: sometimes used as a warship and often as a pirate vessel being able to approach close in to land and then make a hasty depature

kavill: kavilled: kavilt: kaevilt: to take the fish off the hook especially when a big fish had swallowed both hook and bait: also used when lambs were "*kaevilt*" or *kavilled*—a bone or wood bit being tied into their mouths to prevent them sucking from the ewes and done overnight when they had reached a certain stage of growth; the ewes milked in the morning and the milk given to the children: from ON *kefli* a wooden stick or *kavlin* tree, a stick with a notch in the end used in Norse times for taking the hook out of the fish's mouth as also was the custom of "kavilling" the lambs

Klibbers: the wooden frame on a pony's back from which the peats were slung in *Kishies* (baskets) inside the *meshie* or net

kelp: any large brown seaweed or wrack

kemping: racing one against the other

kilnsluggie: funnel in which the fire was lit to dry the grain in the kiln

kirn: a churn

kirn milk: what was left in the churn after making the butter

kishie: a large basket made from dockens or oat straw; slightly oval shaped it was carried on the back, usually when bringing home the peats. Held by a strap across the chest this left the women's hands free to knit all the way

knowe: a grassy mound or hillock

knockin stane or **kubbi:** a large stone hollowed out and used for pounding grain

knorr: or halfvkip: viking boat of all trades, similar to the Gokstad ship but broader in the beam, deeper in the water and with a higher freeboard

312

kolli: (Scots-cruisie): ᴏɴ *kola* Norwegian *kole*: the old lamp usually made of iron by the local blacksmith. Consisting of two separate shells, the upper one was the oil reservoir into which the wick, made of cotton or yarn, was laid. Each shell had a spout, the lower one designed to catch the dripping oil. The upper one was suspended from a toothed or notched bar which projected forward or slanting from the back bar so that a movement from notch to notch could regulate the supply of oil. The bar to which both vessels were attached was provided with a spike so that it could be inserted into an unplastered stone wall. (From Icelandic *kola* and mentioned in the sagas.) In the old laws of Norway it was laid down that men should be provided with lights, either in lanterns of *kollis* of stone or brass

kontor: a chamber of commerce of the Hansa

kringle-bread: a kind of bread brought from Norway

kröddi-moch: gruel made from crushed fish livers and "*burstin*" meal

kubbi: a hollowed out stone for pounding or crushing corn using a *mell* or knocking stane

küml: a pile or mound of stone or grass

küss: (phonetical koos) a heap: Fine peat called *muld* was used all over the islands wherever there was peat to be had. Scraped off the ground just under the turf it was laid in byres in place of straw. Kept in heaps (the heap called the *kuss*) with a stone foundation and covered over with stones or turf, these mounds were known as *muldie-kusses*: from ᴏɴ *myldekause* and used from very ancient times

£1, Scots: equal to 1s 8d sterling

laangbaands: wooden laths used in roofing the croft house

laager: an extemporised fortfication

lagthing: law-thing (lag-law) in Norway: a court of law, a general assembly

laks: salmon: (*laks*—modern Norse): in Shetland Laxfirth, etc.

lambo-teinde: originally a custom during Norse rule of leaving each daughter either a lamb, or a mare, a foal and 15 ewes, as was done last century in Foula. Today in that island children still receive a lamb when they are "named" or cut their first teeth. Thos. Edmonston (1866) explains it as being the wool collected as teinds by the parish minister "now generally commuted to a money payment"

Lammas: the feast of the first fruits on August 1st

land-down: an expression used at the far haaf when the boats were so far to seaward that the land was no longer visible: approximately 30–40 miles

land-mails: rents payable for lands let by the Stewart Earls to tenants or lands let by a lesser landowner

langskip: the true Viking warship or longship

last: about two tons weight

Lawman: The man who held the office of legal adviser and judge of the assize and generally had the superintendence of the framing and interpretation of the law. Nicol Reid of Aith in the island of Bressay, who was elected as 'Lawman General of all Zetland in the Tinholm of Tingwall' on July 27th, 1532, was probably one of the last if not the last of these officials

Lawrightman: Norse: *Lög-retta-madr* "ane discreit man". A tribune of the people, the position lingered on well into the eighteenth century. As late as 1733 Thomas Gifford states that: "There is also in every parish a law-right-man, that is an honest man appointed judicially by the bailiff, as the Rancelmen are. His business is to weigh and measure the rent-butter and oil, and also to judge of the quality thereof, and if he finds it insufficient, to return it as not receivable. He is sworn to justice and keep just weights and measures.'

313

linns: runners laid on the beach to make it easier to pull up the boat. Often wet seaweed was used or halibut (which was useless as it would not take the salt) but what the men liked best were whale ribs which were slippery but did not float

lispund: in 1603 one lispund (lspd) = 12 Scottish or Dutch pounds
             1800   = 32 Scottish pounds

liver-flaakie: two "*sukit*", half-dried *piltaks*, split, fresh liver placed between them, then placed one against the other and roasted

liver krolls: a beremeal pie with finely crushed liver baked in the ashes without a dish

liver muggies: the stomach of a fish (usually ling) stuffed with liver and boiled

lodberris: a store house at the edge of the sea. built of stone and usually attached to a dwelling; derived from ON *hladberg* meaning a loading rock and a lodberri was generally a courtyard built into the sea with a stout sea wall and a door through which goods could be loaded or unloaded from a boat. In the courtyard there was usually a store and sometimes the store was built into the sea with a courtyard behind it. Usually named after the person who owned it, some are still in existence. At the north end of the building now known as the Queen's Hotel, was Hay's Lodberri and between it and Yates' lodberry was Murray's Hol, a passage from the sea with an arched roof and from which a subterranean passage came out in the garden at the top of Scottshall Court. The Hol was a convenient place for landing contraband and later used for buying and storing whelks. The arched entrance now built up, can be seen from the breakwater

lodge: name given to the stone-built houses in which the haaf fishermen lived during the season and situated as near to the fishing grounds as possible. Remains can still be seen on many of the old haaf stations such as Stenness, Fethaland, etc.

lucky-lines: or luckies' lines: plant growing in deep water near the shore which spreads itself over the surface: *Chorda filum*

lum: chimney or opening on the roof of a croft house to let the smoke escape

maakin: Shetland expression for a piece of hand knitting: a woman visitor might bring along her "maakin" and work at it while chatting

maet: feet or food

Matties: or matjes: small full herring, caught at the beginning of the season

Mediums: medium-sized herring—each variety then packed by the packer into the correct barrel for the size

meith: In Dunrossness *meith*, elsewhere in Shetland *mede*: a method of pinpointing a boat's position at sea over the right fishing ground with a cross-bearing from the land wherever possible. With the use of sextant and compass the old meithes became almost forgotten, but in their day there were hundreds all round the coast, all named, their exact location known like places on a land map

merk: sometimes *mark*: the usual denomination of land measurement in Orkney and Shetland from earliest times and representing rather the value of the ground than its extent: one to three acres (ON mörk: a unit of weight and of money: Faeroese: mörk: a unit of weight: a measure of land)

meshie: a course net made of twisted straw ropes with a wide mesh, used for carrying hay or peats and slung on either side of a pony's back from the wooden *klibbers*, or frame, to hold the *kishies* or baskets into which the peats would be packed

mid'room: one of the divisions of a sixareen's *rooms* or, spaces between the *tafts* (rowing benches); roughly in the centre of the boat

mill-gruel: porridge made with milk

misforen: cast away or lost at sea

314

moder-dai: The old fishermen at the far haaf, long before compasses were used, were able to bring their boats home even in thick fog, by the *moder-dai* a strange, inexplicable ripple-like movement of the water against the boat's boards

moorie: snowstorm

Mugildins: small, headless fish cleaned by making an insertion below the gills but leaving in the stomach. They were then stuffed with livers, closed with breadcrumbs and roasted usually on a brandiron over the hot peat embers

muld: fine peat scraped from below the turf and used in byres in place of straw; *muld* can also mean earth from a grave and in Foula, a handful of fresh *muld*, placed under the pillow of a sick person was believed to take away the pain. The patient however must not know that it had been put there. (Skuddimöld—ON *skota*, to shove or scrape: ON *möld*, mould)

muldie kusses: the heaps of *muld* covered with stones or slabs of turf and often with a stone base (ON *myldekause*)

muldie grups: areas of scalped earth or turf from which the fine peat or *muld* had been removed (called *truck* in Dunrossness)

nang: Persian word meaning personal honour and pride: also in Pushtu spoken by the Pathans of the North West Frontier of Pakistan

noost: (ON naust): a hollowed out, roughly boat-shaped space in which boats are tied up away from the water's edge. The winter noosts are well above high water mark for a stormy sea can lift a boat off the beach and turn her over, even when reasonably well secured. Winter noosts are often lined at the bottom with flat stones and every boulder, rusted anchor or capstan available has a *fastie* bound round it either of chains or stout rope

Norrwey yoal: small, double-ended boats built in Shetland or imported from Norway

okrigarth: (okrigord) a fence surrounding the cultivated home field (ON *akr* a corn field, ON *garthr*, a fence)

ouskerri: or auskerri: (ON *auskjer*) a shovel-like scooped wooden baler for use mainly in reasonably good weather. In heavy weather the *scoop*—a wooden shovel— was used.

outsett: an extension of cultivation: a small farm reclaimed from the scattald during the nineteenth century (Danish *udsaet*, an addition to a room or house)

ootbye: outside

owse'room: baling *room* of the sixareen, next the *shott* where the fish were kept

Papa, papae: The name given by the early Norse to the Christian missionaries they found in Shetland, literally "priests" and commemorated in so many place names: Papa Stour—*Papa ey Stor* meaning "the large Priest Island" In Iceland they were called *Papar*

peck: a fourth of a bushel

peerie: Shetlandic for small

pellack: a porpoise

Petta: the Picts, so-called by the first Norse immigrants: i.e. Pettadale, Pettawater, etc.

piltak: or piltock: a young saithe: *Gadus virens* when from one to three years old

pink: herring fishing vessel from Holland, smaller than the herring *buss*

plank: a division of land, a strip of arable land of a definite area

planti-crubs: small, stone-walled enclosures some distance from the cultivated area,

315

in which cabbage seeds were set, in June covered with ash to restrict growth, then netted over. The following spring the seedlings were transferred to the *rigs*. (strips of cultivated ground) (Norse *Krubba*, a crib, a box for holding fodder)

quern: A word loosely used to describe a variety of grinding stones. A small stone hand mill, developed from the old trough type in which the grinding surface was rubbed down into a trough-like hollow open at one end. Used since Neolithic times, first as the trough quern and then as the *sadle* quern (used with a *mell* or pounder), smoother and bigger than the *kubbi* or earliest type. The handmill used up to the beginning of this century, consisted of two circular stones, the top one having a hole and wooden handle fixed obliquely into it. The grain was fed into the "eye" with one hand, the other quickly revolving the upper stone

quoyack: a young cow

raggie-strae: crushed and tangled straw

raisin: term used during the cycle of peat cutting. After the peats have been cut and in doing so each one is placed on top of the bank, flat, in a kind of lattice work so that the air blows through to some extent, the next step is called "the raisin". This is carried out by the women depending largely on the weather and how quickly the cast peats have dried. They are now taken, layer by layer and placed on the ground, a long peat with two or three others up-ended on it forming a rough pyramid. The dryer the peat the larger the initial pyramid. They can then be "turned" if necessary and when completely dry may sometimes be built into stacks on the hillside to wait the arrival of the tractor and trailer to take them "home", or bagged in hessian or plastic sacks, making easier they long task of loading the trailer by throwing them into it from the bank

ranks: strong, tidal streams

ranksman: going out to the "banks" during the haaf fishing, boats usually went in pairs, the accompanying boat being known as the "ranksman"

ranselman: (modern Norwegian *ransake*, to search) He was indeed an authorised searcher into scandals and misdemeanours in his district ... "having the power of a constable to command the inhabitants to keep the peace and to call for assistance and to enter any house within the parish at all hours of the day or night and search the house for stolen goods, which they call '*ranceling*'". Instructions to ranselmen were drawn up in 1724 and are given by Gifford (1733) and in Shirreff's *General View of the Agriculture of the Shetland Islands* (1814). These instructions also included the responsibility for "good neighbourhood", so that grass belonging to crofters was not injured by others or their beasts; that dykes be kept in good repair; to pursue or inform against vagrants and beggars; to see that dogs are only kept with authority from the (then) Bailie; to inquire "in your quarter anent all persons using any manner of witchcraft, charms or any other abominable and devilish superstitions and faithfully inform against such so that they may be brought to condign punishment". In the last instance they were enjoined to so live their own lives in an exemplary fashion. In 1836 in the parish of Lunnasting at the request of Miss Robina Hunter of Lunna, where apparently petty thefts had increased to an alarming extent a Ranselman was sworn in, and Gilbert Goudie noted that there had been some talk of appointing fresh Ranselmen about 1862 or 1863 but it had been then thought that the system was getting out of date and there were doubts of its legality. However as a consequence of complaints of petty thefts in Fair Isle in 1869 Mr. Bruce of Sumburgh as proprietor swore in two Ranselmen, whose offices were very soon discontinued

316

redd: untangle—used of fishing lines to coil and prepare them for the next day's fishing

ree: storm

reebings: In the clinker-built Ness yoals, each board was named from the keel up: boddam runner, first harsing (or hassin) second harsing (or hassin); first swill (or sool), second swill (or sool) and reebing, giving six boards per side. The sixareen had nine boards

reist: In a croft house the reist was placed above the fire a contrivance of laths, rods and simmands netting where meat or fish to be smoked was either laid or hung. (*reist* from roost referring to a cock or hen)

reistit: smoked above the peat fire, hung or placed on the *reist*: reistit mutton is still a favourite dish

reith: an area of sea bottom

reps: ropes laid across the *reist* (above the peat fire) from which hung nets to hold the fish or meat to be smoked

restin shair: a wooden sofa with an arm at each end, the back closed in to half its height and which usually stood against the wall opposite the hearthstone: literally "resting chair"

rigga-rendel: the ancient system of land use whereby each crofter had his share of good land and bad land, working the long narrow strips or *rigs* in rotation

riggin: the ridge of a thatched house

rit: used in marking a sheep—one straight cut on top of the ear

Rivlins: home-made cowhide or sealskin shoes like moccasins, but with the hair left on, the hides stretched and cured in the houses

Rix dollars: Rd. value between 2/3 and 4/6 sterling

rönis: stones cleared from a field about to be cultivated and built into a *röni*, a neat, rectangular stack: from *röni*, a stoney ridge Da Langaröni: Da Fellrönis: ON *hraun*, meaning a stone heap, stoney ground

roo: to pull off the fleece by hand instead of shearing: used only on pure bred Shetland sheep

rooms: the divisions of a sixareen

röst: a fierce tidal stream like the Sumburgh röst or the röst of Skaw

run rig: the Scottish equivalent of rigga rendel

ruth: a one-inch piece of hardwood on the gunwale of Shetland boats. Inserted in a slot through the *ruth* and gunwale is the *kaib* or pin against which the oar is pulled in place of rowlocks

saet: a fishing place (ON *staor*, place or site)

sadle quern: for grinding grain, it developed from the earlier *kubbi*, the simple hollowed-out stone. Bigger than the kubbi and shaped like a trough or a sink, the name may have come from ON *sal*, saddle-shaped. However in west Shetland where the double LL in Norwegian words came to be pronounced dl as in Hordaland, sadle or saddel could also mean fine meal—*salle*. The word *salle* in former times was well known in North Hordaland: *a fare bade med sadlen or saedna*, to scrape together everything both fine and coarse.

saeter: summer pasture: (ON *saetr*) such as Grimsetter; Williamsetter; Setter: Aithsetter: Ellister, etc.

sayes: washing tubs

Scaffie: Scottish type of sailing lugger of the mid-nineteenth century

scattald: the common grazing in the hills around a township—outside the town dykes

scrime: (ON *skeim*) to peer through half-closed eyes

317

selkie: a seal

sett: the complete cycle of shooting and haling the line

shambas: village huts in Zambia

shear: a "V" shaped mark on a sheep's ears

Shetland spade: of Norse origin, a long-bladed implement with a foot rest

shill (yoags): to take the shells off the horse mussel: *Myrtillus mytillae*

shirk: shark

shooders: shoulders

shitterlings: smaller part of the stomach of an animal: used like spaarls to be dried and filled with oatmeal

shooers: showers

shoormil: the water's edge—the edge of the tide

sillak: small saithe: (*Cadus virens*) until one year old

simments or **simmands:** ropes made of twisted rushes or straw

Simmer Dim: midsummer when there are only a couple of hours of twilight

sixareen or **sixearn** in Dunrossness (ON *sexaering*): a six-oared open boat used at the far haaf fishing

shott: one of the sixareen's rooms or divisions where the fish are kept

Skat: land tax levied for the use of the scattald for grazing and peat cutting rights in Norse times

skeo: a small stone building in which meat or fish were dried unsalted

skerry: a rocky islet

skollas: temporary houses or booths or huts: the skollas erected at Scalloway housed people going to the annual Thing or Althing, the Parliament in Tingwall and gave their name to Scalloway: *skolla vå* (N) *voe* of the *skollas*

skoom: spray

skröf: surface

skroos: the final stack of corn or hay

sloo: lazy (woman)

smack: generic name for a sail-powered fishing vessel: in Shetland it used to denote a vessel larger than a sloop rigged fore and aft with one or two masts.

smoor: to cover: the peat fire is *smoored* at night with fine peat to keep it in until the morning.

snecks: fishing grounds—the "codlin" snecks

snekkyes: Norse vessel with shallow draft

soundings: water in which an ordinary sounding line will reach the bottom

souple: part of the flail for beating out the grain; the actual threshing part attached to the flail with leather thongs to give it greater elasticity

sowans: a dish made from the mealy remains of oats

spaarls: small intestines of an animal hung and filled with oatmeal, or sometimes flour with currants

Spent: herring which had spawned

spilt: once used in reference to those people suffering from so-called leprosy (*Elephantiasis graecorum*) which Brand called a kind of "bastard scurvy" although it is now believed that true leprosy did exist as it did in Faroe. The miserable cottages to which these sufferers were consigned were known as "spilt men's houses". Most of the "lepers" from Walls were banished to Papa Stour where food was put out for them but no one would go near them and when they died the houses were frequently burned. In several churches, the old Kirk of Lund in Unst, as in Scotland—a leper window can still be seen, a tiny hole sloping upwards so that the leper's breath could not contaminate the congregation

318

stack: a high, sheer rock, free-standing in the sea

stammerin: a small crooked timber at both bow and stern of a Shetland boat

stane dykes: walls built of stone without cement

stangkulm: a green mound used in the sense of a burial mound

stap: boiled livers laid on top of boiled fish with all the bones removed, mashed up with a fork and seasoned

station: a herring curing base including the jetty belonging to one merchant

stowth: stealing

strae: straw

straen shair: a tall canopied chair with a wooden frame on which straw was tightly laced

strand-hogg: ON. The old Norse custom whereby men on Viking cruises provided themselves with fresh meat by going ashore wherever they happened to be and killing a man's cattle on the nearest beach. (Modern Norwegian—*strand*)

sun-gaets: with the sun: a boat was never turned round against the sun neither was a croft house built in this way. Everything was built *sun-gaets*

swede: six men and a fiddler—a "set" for a Shetland reel

swills: or *sools*, two of the boards on a clinker-built Shetland boat

taft: seating bench for a rower, thwart

tangles: seaweed of the species *Laminaria digitata* usually thrown up in winter gales from the sea bed to which it normally clings with splayed out and clutching roots

tees: (mutton tees) a leg of mutton salted and smoked

teinds: taxes or tithes payable to the church during Scottish rule

tekkin strae: thatching straw: the first layer on a roof

Thing or **Ting:** Norse court of justice held in various districts such as Delting, Nesting, Lunnasting, Aithsting, etc, with the Althing or yearly parliament held in Tingwall

tide: to wait while the lines are in the water to give the fish a chance to take

tide-lumps: sudden "lumps" of water appearing no matter what direction the wind might be and quite unpredictable

tilfers: bottom boards on the Shetland boat

timmer: timber, wood

Tirrick: Arctic Tern: *Sterna macrura*

toam: the trace on a fishing line

towes: lines

trivle: to finger, to ferret out, perhaps not very successfully

troot: trout

Trow: (Norse *troll*): a supernatural being once believed to inhabit lonely places and hills in Shetland, usually of a mischievous and uncertain disposition. Sometimes they were accused of luring folk away from their homes, hence the expression: "Tae'n by the trows"—taken by the trows

trowe: through

Truck System: the barter system whereby rent was paid in kind by the tenant to the landmaster-trader and the tenant was forced to fish for his landlord, buy all his goods from him, shop, and sell him all his own produce

tushkar: (ON *torf-skeri*): Shetland implement for cutting peat the iron part beginning like a Shetland spade but with a blade jutting out at right angles, fitted to a wooden shaft

twaartbaaks: the tie beams on the roof of a croft house

Tystie: Shetlandic for the Black Guillemot: *Cepphus grylle*

Udal Law: Norse legal system still sometimes regarded as binding

udaller: a freeman or landowner under the Udal system

Umboth Duty: The Bishop's rents in 1733

umiak: an open boat made of skins used by Eskimo women

uncon: unkon: strange

vam: a slightly unpleasant smell

variorem: scroll-like decoration: flowers and curlecues picked out usually in gold: seen on old sewing machines and used in Shetland particularly to describe the elaborate embellishments surrounding the name on the bow of a boat. As an old woman was heard to remark when asked about a certain fishing boat which, perhaps fishing inside the limit had blacked out her number: "I couldna see her number but I knew her by the variorem!"

veevers: At one time it meant almost any kind of tasty food not usually eaten—even shop biscuits might have been so regarded

vivda: meat wind-dried in *skeos* (stone huts) and eaten cut in small slices rather like the African *biltong*

voar: (ON *vår*) the season of spring. There is a strong similarity between the seasons in Norway and Shetland. Shetland has *da voar, da simmer, da hairst, da winter.* In Norse we find *våren; sommeren: hosten: vinteren*

voe: (ON *va*) a long, narrow inlet, in its plural form one of the Norse words which lent itself to distortion by the incoming Scots. The Shetland place name Walls was originally *vas* pronounced *waas* (as indeed Walls is still pronounced). However to a Scot a *waa* was a wall and *waas* were therefore walls so down it went on the Ordnance Map. One of the most meaningless names on the Shetland map, Willamina Hoga, in Yell, began in Norse times as Almenning Haga, meaning the public pasture land where cattle were grazed during the warm months

vooers: wooers

waand: a long, preferably bamboo rod in one piece used at the piltak fishing

wilsom: wilsom watter: a piece of water in which one could lose one's bearings: willing in the mist is to lose one's way: "be careful", someone might say, "or you'll will". Like so many Shetland words it is almost impossible to give an exact translation

windlin strae: (or raggie strae) the crushed and tangled straw which has become separated from the straight tekkin strae: used in thatching and twisted into small bundles called *windlins*

wechtie: weighty

wast ower: The area to the west edge of the Burra Haaf—30 to 40 miles south-west of Fugla Ness

wadmel: coarse homespun cloth in which dues were once paid

wick: (N *vik*, a creek) meaning a bay or inlet, i.e. Gulberwick, Channerwick

wis: US, wirs: ours, our house

Wattle: a tax imposed under Scottish rule

yoags: (N, yag) the horse mussel: *Mytilus modiolus*

yoal: an open boat of Norse design used in the fierce rösts or tides mainly for saithe fishing and still used in the Dunrossness area, known as the Ness Yoal, the boat has a high length to beam ratio, great sheer and flared ends

yogourts: ewes (Foula) (ON, yogurt)

yowe: ewe

320

Zetland: The old name for Shetland which appeared and was accepted for many years after a Scots clerk misinterpreted the old 's' for a 'z'

Zulu: Scottish type of fishing vessel with sail, introduced in the late nineteenth century. One or two boats of the old Zulu class converted to diesel were still in use in recent times

Selected Bibliography

A True and Exact Description of the Island of Shetland 1753. Mercat Press, Reprint.

Acts and Statutes of the Lawting Sheriff and Justice Courts Within Orkney and Zetland, 1602–1604.

ANDERSON, J.: *The Orkneyinga Saga.* Edinburgh, 1873.

ANDERSON, S.: *Seals in Shetland: The Natural Environment of Shetland*, p. 114. The Nature Conservancy Council, 1974.

ARBMAN, H.: *The Vikings* (Tr. Alan Binns). London, 1961.

ASTON UNIVERSITY SUB-AQUA CLUB: *The Wreck of the Kennemerland.* Birmingham, 1974.

BALFOUR, D.: *The Oppressions of the 16th Century in the Islands of Orkney and Shetland.* Edinburgh, 1859.

BEATTIE, A. M.: 'Firth, a Small Shetland Community', *New Shetlander*, 104/105.

BEENHAKKER, A. J.: *Hollanders in Shetland.* Lerwick, 1973.

BERRY, R. J.: *The Shetland Fauna: The Natural Environment of Shetland*, p. 151. The Nature Conservancy Council, 1974.

'History in the Evolution of *Apodimus sylvaticus*', *Journal of Zoology*, Vol. 159, Part 3, 1969.

BIBBY, G.: *The Testimony of the Spade.* Fontana Library, 1956.

BOURNE, W. R. P. and DIXON, T. J.: *The Seabirds of the Shetlands: The Natural Environment of Shetland*, p. 130. The Nature Conservancy Council, 1974.

BRAND, I.: *A Brief Description of Orkney, Zetland, Pightland Firth and Caithness.* Edinburgh, 1701.

BRONDSTED, J.: *The Vikings* (Tr. Kalle Skov). Pelican Books, 1965.

BRØGGER, A. W.: *Ancient Emigrants.* Oxford, 1929.

BRYCE, T.: 'Notice of a short Cist at Fraga, Scatness, Shetland', *P.S.A.S.*, 1935–36.

'The so-called Heel-shaped Cairns of Shetland with remarks on the Chambered Tombs of Orkney and Shetland', *P.S.A.S.*, 1940.

CALDER, C. S. T.: 'Report on the Excavations of a Neolithic Temple at Staneydale in the Parish of Sandsting, Shetland. *P.S.A.S.*, 1949–50.

'Yoxie Report', *P.S.A.S.*, 1955.

CARSON, R. L.: *The Sea Around Us.* London, 1951.

CHAPELHOW, R.: 'On Glaciation in North Roe, Shetland', *Geographical Journal*, Vol. 131, Part 1, 1965.

CHILDE, V. G.: *Scotland Before the Scots.* London, 1946.

Prehistoric Communities of the British Isles. London, 1949.

The Dawn of European Civilisation. Edinburgh, 1950.

The Pre-History of Scotland. London, 1935.

CLUNESS, A. T.: *The Shetland Isles.* London, 1951.

COULL, J. R.: 'A Shetland Crofting Parish', *Scottish Geographical Magazine*, 1964.

COWIE, R.: *Shetland and its Inhabitants*. Aberdeen, 1874.

CRUDEN, S.: *The Brochs of Mousa and Clickhimin*. Edinburgh, 1951.

CUMMING, R. P. and TAYLOR, W. (Eds.): *Aspects of Health and Safety in Oil Developments*. Lerwick, 1973.

DANIEL., G.: *The Megalith Builders of Western Europe*. London.

DAVIES, G. L.: 'Early British Geomorphology (1578–1705)', *Geographical Journal, Vol. 132*, Part 2, 1966.

DE PAOR, MÁIRE and L.: *Early Christian Ireland*. London. 1958.

Description of ye Countrey of Zetland. Edinburgh, 1908. (Printed for private circulation.)

DONALDSON, G. (Ed.): *The Court Book of Shetland 1602–1604*. Edinburgh, 1954.
Shetland Life Under Earl Patrick. Edinburgh, 1958.
Northwards by Sea. Edinburgh, 1966.

EDDISON, E. R.: *Egil's Saga*. Cambridge, 1930.

EDMONSTON, T. A.: *An Etymological Glossary of the Shetland and Orkney Dialect*. Edinburgh. 1866.

EDMONSTON, T. A.: *Flora of Shetland*. Aberdeen, 1845.

FENTON, A.: 'Craig Fishing in the Northern Isles of Scotland and Notes on the Poke Net', *Scottish Studies*, Vol. 17, 1973.
The Various Names of Shetland. Edinburgh, 1973.

FLINN, D.: 'Coastal and Submarine Features Around the Shetland Islands', *Proc. Geol. Assoc.*, Vol. 75, p. 3, London, 1964.

FRANCIS, J. and SWAN, N.: *Scotland in Turmoil*. Edinburgh, 1973.

GIEPEL, J.: *The Viking Legacy*. Newton Abbot, 1971.

GIFFORD, T.: *An Historical Description of the Zetland Islands: in the Year 1733*. Edinburgh, 1786.

GJESSING, G.: 'The Circumpolar Stone Age', *Antiquity*, Vol. XXVII, 1953.

GOODLAD, C. A.: *Shetland Fishing Saga*. Lerwick, 1971.

GOUDIE, G. (Ed.): *Diary of the Revd John Mill*. Edinburgh, 1889.
The Celtic and Scandinavian Antiquities of Shetland. Edinburgh, 1904.

HALCROW, A.: *The Sail Fishermen of Shetland*. Lerwick, 1950.

HALLÉ, L. J.: *The Storm Petrel and the Owl of Athena*. Princeton University Press, 1970.

HAMILTON, J. R. C.: 'The Vikings in the Shetlands', *Illustrated London News*, December 3rd, 1949.
'Iron Age Settlements in the Shetlands', *Arch. News Letter*, Vol. IV, 1951–53.
'From the Stone Age to the Broch Builders in Shetland', *Illustrated London News*, May 25th, 1957.
Excavations at Jarlshof Shetland. Edinburgh, 1956.

HAWKES, J.: *Dawn of the Gods*. London, 1968.

HEINEBERG, H.: *Changes in the Economic-Geographical Structure of the Shetland Islands* (Tr. Anne Menzies). H.I.D.B. Reprint of University Thesis (Bochum, 1969).

HENDERSON, I.: *The Picts*. London, 1967.

HENDERSON, T.: 'The Yoal and the Sixern'. *New Shetlander*. Lerwick.

HIBBERT, S.: *Description of the Shetland Islands*. Edinburgh, 1822.

H.I.D.B. Highlands and Islands Development Board.

HOLBOURN, I. B. S.: *The Isle of Foula*. Lerwick, 1938.

HOWARTH, D.: *The Shetland Bus*. Edinburgh, 1951.

ISBISTER, R. W.: *Tales of Foula*. Lerwick, 1970.

JACKSON, E. E.: 'The Birds of Foula', *Journal of the Scottish Ornithologists' Club*, Vol. 4, Special Supplement. Edinburgh, 1966.

JACKSON, K. H.: 'The St Ninian's Isle Inscription: a Re-Appraisal', *Antiquity*, Vol. XXXIV, 1960.

JAKOBSEN, J.: *The Dialect and Place Names of Shetland*. Lerwick, 1897.
  An Etymological Dictionary of the Norn Language in Shetland. London and Copenhagen, 2 vols., 1928–32.

JAMIESON, H. 'Whalsay Boats in the '87 Gale', *New Shetlander*, No. 88.

JAMIESON, P.: 'The Press Gang in Shetland', *Shetland Folk Book*, Vol. V, 1971.

JOHNSON, L. G.: *Laurence Williamson of Mid Yell*. Lerwick, 1971.

JOHNSTON, J. L.: *Shetland Habitats: an outline ecological framework: The Natural Environment of Shetland*, p. 33. The Nature Conservancy Council, Edinburgh, 1974.

JONES, G.: *A History of the Vikings*. London, 1968.

KENT, P. E.: 'North Sea Exploration', *Geographical Journal*, Vol. 133, Part 3. London, 1967.

LAING, L.: *Orkney and Shetland*. London, 1974.

LAURENSON, J. J.: 'John Anderson of Klugen', *New Shetlander*.
  'The Sixern Days', *New Shetlander*, No. 68.
  'Notes on Fetlar', *Shetland Folk Book*, Vol. IV, 1964.

Laxdaela Saga (Tr. Magnus Magnusson and Hermann Pálsson). Penguin Classics, 1969.

LIVINGSTONE, W. P.: *Shetland and the Shetlanders*. Edinburgh, 1947.

LOW, G.: *A Tour Through Orkney and Zetland in 1774*. Kirkwall, 1879.

MANSON: *Manson's Shetland Almanac and Directory*.

MANSON, T.: *Lerwick During the Last Half Century*. Lerwick, 1923.

MANSON, T. and J.: *The Amazing Adventures of Betty Mouat*. Lerwick, 1936.

MANSON, T. M. Y.: *Historical Problems of Shetland to the End of the Old Earldom:* The Viking Congress (Ed. W. D. Simpson), 58–53, 1954.

MCKAY, G. C.: 'Celtic Influences in Shetland', *New Shetlander*, No. 82.

MCQUEEN, J.: *St. Nynia* Edinburgh, 1961.

MOAR, P.: 'Newly Discovered Sculptured Stones from Papil, Shetland', *P.S.A.S.*, Vol. LXXVIII (1943/44), 1944.
  'Two Shetland Finds', *P.S.A.S.*, Vol. LXXXVI, 206, 1952.

MOUAT, F.: *West Viking*. London, 1966.

MOWBRAY, C. L.: 'Excavation at the Ness of Burgi, Shetland', *P.S.A.S.*, Vol. LXX, 1936.

MYKURA, W.: *The Geological Basis of the Shetland Environment: The Natural Environment of Shetland*, p. 1. The Nature Conservancy Council, Edinburgh, 1974.

NASH, G.: *The Hansa*. London and New York, 1929.

NELSON, G. M.: *The Story of Tingwall Kirk*. Lerwick, 1965.

New Statistical Account of Scotland—Shetland. Edinburgh, 1841.

NICOLSON, J.: *Arthur Anderson*. Lerwick, 1932.
  'Shetland Folk Tales', *Shetland Folk Book*, Vol. I, 1947.

NICOLSON, J. R.: *Shetland*. London, 1972.

Njal's Saga (Tr. Magnus Magnusson and Hermann Pálsson). Penguin Classics, 1960.

O'DELL, A. C.: *The Historical Geography of the Shetland Islands*. Lerwick, 1939.

O'DELL, A. C. *et al.*: 'The St. Ninian's Isle Silver Hoard', *Antiquity*, Vol. XXXIII, 241–68, 1959.

O'DELL, A. C. and CAIN, A.: *The St. Ninian's Isle Treasure*. Aberdeen, 1960.

ODELL, P. R.: *Oil and World Power*. Pelican Books, 1972.

PALMER, R. S. and SCOTT, W.: *A Check List of the Flowering Plants and Ferns of the Shetland Islands*. Scalloway and Oxford, 1969.

PEACE, W.: *Handbook to the Shetland Islands*. Kirkwall, 1870.

PETERSON, G. P. S.: *Hairst Blinks Ower Papa.* Lerwick, 1965.

Petroleum Times: 'Shell Wants Shetland for North Sea Oil Reception', October 19th, 1973.

PLOYEN, C.: *Reminiscences of a Voyage to Shetland, Orkney and Scotland.* Lerwick, 1894.

PIGGOT, S.: *Neolithic Cultures of the British Isles.* Cambridge, 1954.

POWELL, M.: *200,000 feet on Foula.* London, 1938.

P.S.A.S.: *Proceedings of the Society of Antiquaries of Scotland* (Edinburgh).

RATTER, W. W.: 'Our Shetland Place Names' *Shetland Folk Book* (ed. E. S. Reid Tait), Vol. I, 1947.

REID TAIT, E. S. (Ed.): *The Hjaltland Miscellany*, Vols 1–5. Lerwick.
   'Press Gang Stories', *Shetland Folk Book*, Vol. IV, 1964.
   (Ed.): *A Lerwick Miscellany.* Lerwick, 1955.

REID, J. T.: *Art Rambles in Shetland.* Edinburgh, 1896.

RIVET, A. L. F. (Ed.): *The Iron Age, Northern Britain.* Edinburgh, 1966.

ROBERTSON, T.: 'A list of Words Relating to Land and Agriculture', *Shetland Folk Book*, Vol. V, 1971.

ROBERTSON, T. A.: 'Shetland Dialect', *New Shetlander.*

SANDISON, C.: *Unst, My Island Home and its Story.* Lerwick, 1968.
   The Sixareen and her Racing Descendants. Lerwick, 1954.
   (Ed.): *A Shetland Merchant's Day Book in 1762.* Lerwick.

SCOTLAND AND OIL: Royal Scottish Geog. Society. *Teachers' Bulletin*, No. 5.

SEIM, E.: 'Shetland Food in Former Times', *Shetland Folk Book*, Vol. IV, 1964.

SENIOR, W. H. and SWAN, W. B.: *Survey of Agriculture in Caithness, Orkney and Shetland.* H.I.D.B., Special Report 8. Inverness.

SHEPHERD, S.: *Like a Mantle the Sea.* London, 1971.

SIBBALD, SIR R.: *Description of the Islands of Orkney and Shetland.* Edinburgh, 1711.

SIMPSON, W. D.: *The Celtic Church in Scotland.* Aberdeen, 1935.
   The Broch of Clickhimin. The Viking Congress (Ed. W. D. Simpson), 1954.

SMITH, M.: 'Shetland Croft Houses and their equipment', *Shetland Folk Book*, Vol. IV, 1964.

SPENCE, C. S.: *Memoirs of Arthur Laurenson.* London, 1901.

STEWART, G.: *Shetland Fireside Tales.* Lerwick, 1923.

STEWART, J.: *Norn in Shetland.* Torshavn, 1964.
   Place names of Foula. Torshavn, 1970.

STOUT, M. B.: *The Shetland Cookery Book.* Lerwick, 1965.

TAYLOR, A. D.: *Shetland Place Names in the Sagas.* The Viking Congress (Ed. W. D. Simpson), 112–29, 1954.

TAYLOR, H. P.: *A Shetland Parish Doctor.* Lerwick, 1948.

TUDOR, J. R.: *The Orkneys and Shetlands.* London, 1883.

TULLOCH, B. and HUNTER, F.: *A Guide to Shetland Birds.* Lerwick, 1973.

VENABLES, L. S. V. and U. M.: *Birds and Mammals of Shetland.* Edinburgh, 1955.

WAINWRIGHT, F. T. (Ed.): *The Problem of the Picts.* London, 1955.
   The Northern Isles. London, 1964.

WEST, J. F.: 'A Tourist to Shetland in 1821', *New Shetlander*, No. 68.

Who are the Scots?: B.B.C.

WILLIAMSON, K.: *Fair Isle and Its Birds.* London, 1965.

WILSON, D. et al.: *St. Ninian's Isle and Its Treasure.* 2 vols. University of Aberdeen, London, 1974.

325

Index

Numbers in italics refer to pages on which illustrations occur

327